The traditional
SUSSEX

A historical guide, description, selected texts, bibliography and discography

Richard Coates

Research Professor in the School of English
University of Sussex
and
Professor of Linguistics
University of the West of England, Bristol

POMEGRANATE PRESS

Published by Pomegranate Press,
Dolphin House, 51 St Nicholas Lane, Lewes, Sussex BN7 2JZ
pomegranatepress@aol.com
www.pomegranate-press.co.uk

ISBN: 978–1–907242–09–0

British Library Cataloguing-in-Publication Data.
A catalogue record for this book is available from the British Library

Printed and bound by 4Edge, 7A Eldon Way, Hockley, Essex SS5 4AD

To the memory of Bob Copper (1915–2004)

Image from the University of Sussex Bulletin, 28/01/2000, used with permission

‘Hyt semeþ a gret wondur houg Englysch, þat ys þe burþ tonge of Englyschmen and here oune longage and tonge, ys so dyvers of soun in þis ylond . . . ’

‘It seems amazing how English, the mother tongue of Englishmen and their own language, sounds so varied throughout this island.’

John Trevisa (c.1385), in his translation
of Ranulph Higden’s *Polychronicon*

‘Sadly, the Sussex dialect died out between the two world wars. The only people who speak it now have learned it as an act of homage to a largely forgotten tongue.’

‘Rouser’ (John Eccles), *Sussex Express* (30 December 2009)

List of images

CONTENTS

PREFACE

The genesis of this work

This book began as a bibliographical guide, an excerpt from my earlier work entitled *A classified bibliography on Sussex place-names, 1586–1987*, published by Younsmere Press, Brighton, in 1987. That included references to dialect material on the presumption that dialect may be represented in local place-names and that knowledge of it is therefore a potentially useful tool in interpreting them.

The traditional dialect of Sussex became a fully separate resource which was being constantly updated during the 1990s and 2000s. The compiler intends the bibliography to be exhaustive (some subsections excepted, as noted at the relevant places), and would be grateful to have information about any item he may have missed; information on a very few items, especially from old newspapers, is incomplete. Any information about items wrongly or incompletely cited would be greatly appreciated.

New and completely unsuspected dialect writings, unmentioned by any other authority in the past, were occasionally coming to hand even at a fairly advanced stage in the development of the book. One example is Stewart M. Thorpe's poem on the Long Man of Wilmington, published with no indication of date or publisher (the general feel is just pre-World War II; perhaps the author was the Stewart Thorpe born in Willingdon in 1886); the compiler found a copy lovingly bound in thin card on the open shelves in the Sussex Archaeological Society's library at Barbican House, Lewes, in 1996. Another is the poem by Robert Sellens published at some time in the 1950s in the *East Grinstead Observer*, discovered accidentally and out of context by a friend and collaborator. Nothing else by Mr Thorpe, and only one other poem by Mr Sellens, has been unearthed. Mr Sellens is now the only known living person who has been a practitioner of the written dialect. The most dramatic fluke has been the 'rediscovery', by electronic means, of the nineteenth-century manuscript novel *Dickey Snickle* by 'Rhymeo' in the catalogue of West Sussex Record Office, on the day this book was completed. News of other such gems by these authors or anyone else would be welcome indeed.

The original concept of *The traditional dialect of Sussex* as a bibliography has now developed to include a concise account of the relation through history between standard and dialectal English, a description of the dialect based mainly on evidence collected in the 1950s as part of a national survey, and a survey of the literature written in Sussex dialect, as well as a discography of songs from the classical period of English folk-song collection. Drafts of Part One were used in teaching undergraduate courses on the cultural history of the English language at the University of Sussex during the 1990s and early 2000s. The book was completed – insofar as a work of this kind can ever be complete – in June 2010.

Acknowledgements

My thanks for assistance in the preparation of this book are due to a large number of people, mentioned here in alphabetical order, most of whom will probably have forgotten what they did to help me, so long ago was it: Dr Barbara Allen, of the University of Sussex; David Arscott of Lewes; Professor Joan C. Beal, of NATCECT, University of Sheffield; John Bleach, of the Sussex Archaeological Society at Lewes; Anthony Chamberlaine Brothers of Eastbourne; the late Bob Copper of Peacehaven; Miles G. Costello of Petworth; Peter Cox of Horsham; the late Joyce Crow, formerly Hon. Librarian of the Sussex Archaeological Society at Lewes; Dr Paul Cullen, of the University of Sussex, later Nottingham; the late Stanley Ellis, formerly of the University of Leeds; Esme Evans, Hon. Librarian of the Sussex Archaeological Society at Lewes; Patrick Funnell of Tunbridge Wells; Peter Gooday, of Elixir Enterprises (Horsham); the late Lord Hailsham of St Marylebone; Berry Harper of Seaford, later Friston; Geoff. Hellman of Brighton; Nicholas Hills of London; Vera Hodsoll of Polegate; Dr Tim Hudson, of the West Sussex Record Office, Chichester; the late Dr Arnold Kellett, of the Yorkshire Dialect Society; Michael J. Leppard of East Grinstead; Dr Ken Lodge, of the Unversity of East Anglia; Timothy J. McCann, of the West Sussex Record Office at Chichester; Geoffrey Mead, of the University of Sussex; the late Stephen Medcalf, of the University of Sussex; Dr Brian Murdoch, formerly of the University of Stirling; Miriam Nixey of Shoreham-by-Sea; M.W.D. Norman of Shoreham-by-Sea; Dr David North of Abinger Common, Surrey; David Padgham of St Leonard's; Steve Peak of Hastings; Dr Janet Pennington of Steyning, archivist of Lancing College; the late Joseph Pettitt of Earley, Berkshire; Professor Patricia Poussa, now of the University of Umeå, Sweden; Dr Jonathan Roper, then of NATCECT, University of Sheffield, and now of the University of Tartu, Estonia; Brian Scott, of Hastings Central Library; Robert Sellens of West Hoathly; David Tait of Shoreham-by-Sea; Cllr Ralph Taylor of Seaford; the late David Tittensor of Maplehurst, later Rowhook; Professor Peter Trudgill, of the University of East Anglia and several European universities; the late Tony Wales of Worthing, previously of Horsham; Professor Max W. Wheeler, of the University of Sussex; Christopher Whittick, of the East Sussex Record Office, Lewes; Professor John Widdowson, formerly of CECTAL/ NATCECT, University of Sheffield; John Worsley of Chichester, formerly of the *West Sussex Gazette*; and all those others who answered my first general requests for information in the *Sussex Archaeological Society Newsletter* no. 64 (August 1991), p. 12, and its successor *(Sussex) Past and Present* no. 71 (December 1993), p. 12. Dr North was kind enough to review the entire manuscript in a middle stage of its development, and I benefited from his criticisms. Dr Roper was also in regular contact during the middle stages and again right at the last moment, and I have gratefully drawn on his comments and his researches, especially his identification of informants on some of the county dialect surveys. I should also like to thank Linda Thompson, of the University of Sussex, my 'sackitry' at the time, who prepared various parts of the manuscript using what was the latest of technological wizardry in the mid-1990s.

I must single out four correspondents for special thanks, if one can do that to four: Miles Costello, at the time a bookseller specializing in dialect and having a long-standing interest in the topic, has extracted all kinds of information from the obscurest places, which would certainly have been lost for ever without his intervention; Michael Leppard has supplied a great deal of bibliographical information over a long period, and pursued many matters of relevance in the pages of the *Bulletin of the East Grinstead Society* and the *East Grinstead Museum Compass*, both of which he edits; and the late Tony Wales provided much information of great interest about local music, commercially recorded or otherwise. Finally, the value of my many years of friendship and correspondence with Christopher Whittick has been incalculable.

My thanks are also, as ever, due to the staff of Inter-Library Loans at the University of Sussex and at the British Library, Boston Spa, for their ability to winkle out the obscurest of the many obscure things recorded in this book, and to locate copies when they themselves could not supply them. The libraries I have found it most useful to visit, and which are most frequently mentioned in the bibliography, are that of the Sussex Archaeological Society in Lewes, Brighton Area Library, West and East Sussex Record Offices in Chichester and Lewes respectively, and those of the University of Sussex and the Centre for English Cultural Tradition and Language (now the National Centre for English Cultural Tradition (NATCECT)) at the University of Sheffield. But others, university, public and private, have also supplied information.

The availability from the late 1980s onwards of JANET-OPACS and then the Internet enabled me, from my own office, to conduct time-saving online searches of the catalogues, or parts of the catalogues, of many university libraries; and from the early 1990s the World Wide Web and later the search engine Google™ (including Google Scholar™) have played an invaluable part. But to not much avail. A significant number of 'little' publications seem to have been invisible to the copyright libraries. There may be material in computer-in-accessible special collections at these places, but the experience gained on visits to the vast collections at Cambridge suggests not. Whilst academic works *about* Sussex dialect are available with relatively little trouble, it seems certain that the bulk of material written *in* the dialect exists only in local libraries, apart from what may still be in private hands. However, a (small) wealth of information about unpublished material that lurks in the county record offices has been unearthed at the last minute thanks to the online Access to Archives (A2A) service of The National Archives at Kew.

Permissions

Permission to use the following images is gratefully acknowledged:

Front cover and Image 14: The Copper family
Image on the dedication page: University of Sussex
Image 1: © Professor Clive S. Upton and Professor J.D.A. Widdowson
Image 4: Sussex Archaeological Society
Image 7: John Worsley
Image 13: David Arscott

Permission to reprint the following material in Part Two is also gratefully acknowledged:

Text 0b: © The English Place-Name Society
Text 2: © Brian O. Murdoch and J.A. Tasioulas
Texts 14a, 14b and 15b: by courtesy of the Sussex Archaeological Society for manuscripts in its keeping
Texts 20b and 20c: by courtesy of the late Bob Copper and the Copper family
Texts 23a and 23b: © Macmillan Inc., for titles formerly of Cassells Ltd
Texts 24, 28a and 28b: © T.R. Beckett Ltd
Text 27: © Harper Collins Ltd
Texts 30a and 30b: © *The West Sussex Gazette*, Arundel
Text 31: © *The Sussex Express*, Lewes
Text 32: © West Sussex Record Office, for the representatives of Mr G. Carley and Dr F.W. Steer
Texts 35a and 35b: © the estate of Bob Copper
Text 36: © Miles Costello and Peter Jerrome, and the Petworth Society
Text 37: © Dr Ken Lodge
Text 38: © Robert A. Sellens
Text 39: © the estate of Pam Hughes, by courtesy of Ralph Taylor
Text 40: by courtesy of David Arscott

Thanks are also extended to West Sussex and East Sussex Record Offices in connection with manuscripts in their care, even where formal copyright does not exist.

Certain other works technically in copyright, and one of unknown authorship possibly in copyright, have been reprinted in Part Two. Where the authors have died, or are presumed to have died, since 1935, or where it is possible that they are still living, serious efforts have been made to discover the copyright owners and to obtain permission to reprint, as the law requires. These efforts have not been successful. If anyone's rights have been inadvertently infringed, this will be rectified in any further edition of this book. Any other quoted text and images used are believed to be in the public domain or usable under the appropriate Creative Commons licence.

I owe a special informal debt to the late Bob Copper for the loan of the precious family heirloom from which I print Texts 20b and 20c with his permission, to John Copper for permission to use family images and to dedicate the book to Bob, and also to the University of Sussex for the picture of Bob accompanying the dedication. Other picture credits are given, where required, alongside the image concerned.

Publication has been made possible by a generous grant from the Marc Fitch Fund, and my thanks are due to the Fund's Council of Managers as well as to David Arscott of Pomegranate Press.

Richard Coates
Shirehampton and Frenchay, Bristol
11 June 2010

PART ONE

DIALECT, DIALECT SCHOLARSHIP AND THE PROBLEM OF DIALECT

References

There are many references to scholarly writings in Part One. Those which are asterisked in the text are of general importance, and are listed in the bibliography following Part One (pp. 81–94). Some of these which are particularly relevant for Sussex in context are repeated in Part Three, the main Sussex bibliography, which can therefore be used as a self-contained resource.

*

The works mentioned in Part One which are of most direct local relevance to Sussex are not asterisked, and they appear only at the appropriate place in the bibliography which makes up Part Three. References to them are accompanied by a note in the section of Part Three (pp. 189–300) in which they can be found: so (Daish 1963, C6) means the letter by W.G. Daish listed under the author's name in Section C6 of Part Three, and (Burstow 1911: 107, C8) means p. 107 of Henry Burstow's book listed under his name in Section C8 of Part Three.

For further guidance in finding particular local works, see the headings at the beginning of Part Three (pp. 189–90).

Part One consists of five chapters. Chapter 1 situates dialect, and dialect writing in particular, in relation to the history of the emergence of standard written English. Chapter 2 presents the contribution of academic linguists and philologists to the study of Sussex dialect. Chapter 3 is a discursive presentation of the Sussex material contained in the Survey of English Dialects and in the *Linguistic atlas of England* which derives from the Survey: i.e. essentially a presentation of the most characteristic non-standard features of the county's dialect(s) and accent(s). Material from other sources is also drawn in. Chapter 4 discusses the work of those who have written in Sussex English, whether because they could not help it or because they chose to. The final chapter is about the meaning and significance of the traditional Sussex dialect, mainly at the time when it flourished most vigorously.

Chapter 1

Dialectal and standard English writing

Traditional Sussex dialect is a regional variety, or set of varieties, of non-standard English. In this opening chapter, we explore the changing nature and purpose of regionally-coloured writing when faced with an evolving standard dialect of English. The emerging Standard English acquires special properties and positive attributes which lead to its being regarded as the culturally most important variety of English. Other varieties are accordingly downgraded. This chapter is about what has happened to non-standard varieties in general, and leads to four chapters considering, from different perspectives, how Sussex dialect has fared as the written standard language comes to be increasingly accepted, and required, in literature, administration, education, and society at large. The knock-on effect on the spoken variety will be considered in due course.

In the history of English, a very striking feature is the abrupt growth of a standard written and printed dialect, or, to look at it the other way round, the abrupt decline in the variety of written and printed dialects. The variation in the language, of the spoken or of the written form, was commented on from time to time in the Middle Ages, but no consistent opinion emerged about which forms, if any, were better than others. However, by 1500, writers regularly, if ritually, apologized for their English just in case it was contaminated by traces of their forebears' spoken dialect background, i.e. in case it did not conform to the London norm of the comfortable classes, shared with the upper mercantile classes of a broad swathe across the east-centre of England. For instance, the printer William Caxton in about 1473 famously mentions his 'brode and rude' Kentish home dialect (quoted in full conveniently by Crystal 2004*: 255).

In fact, dialect variety in literary texts from at least southern and midland England is scarcely discernible after around 1450, and apologetic remarks like Caxton's serve two functions: to express either conventional humility or real social insecurity, and to acknowledge that it was desirable to adhere to an already-existing literary language which was perceived to be uniform. A semi-standard legal English also existed, on the basis of chancery (government record office) usage, from the end of the reign of Henry V (1422) onwards (cf. Fisher 1977*, Hughes 1980*, and more critically Rissanen 2000*), and thereafter local legal documents (where written in English at all) tended to be written in this standardized form with at most just a few local words to mark their provenance (e.g. Part 2, Text 3; and the curious episcopal document of

1440, WSRO MS. EpI/1/2, in which a heretic is accused in English though his answers are recorded in Latin). In addition to this essentially legal register, by around 1450 non-legal texts too showed some evidence of conformity even where their dialect was not in every sense the forerunner of what we now recognize as Standard English (Hogg 2006*: 368–9).

The principal body-blow to dialect writing in the mainstream was, however, the invention of printing. Practically all books printed in English in the fifteenth century were printed at Westminster, and the conventions of London writing (cf. Morsbach 1888*, Chambers and Daunt 1931*) became those of printing in general. Print runs were relatively small, of course, and there was obvious economic and other practical pressure against the production of versions in different dialects. Equally obviously, books (even the fattest of incunabula) are portable items, and they were readily available beyond the limits of the dialect area in which they were produced. The manuscript tradition of translating or transposing from dialect to dialect as required by the audience, within the limits set by the abilities of the professional, workshop-based, scribe, was mortally wounded almost overnight in the late fifteenth century, as the potential of the printed word came to be realized in abundance.

Insofar as the industry of manuscript book-production had survived at all, it finally expired when English monastic life disappeared in the Dissolution (1538-42), because the scriptoria (writing-offices) staffed by specialist monks ceased to exist, and the monks' libraries were dispersed into private hands or lost. Manuscripts continued to be produced, of course, but they were not books; handwritten documents after this period tended to be legal and administrative: wills, probate inventories, contracts, bills, financial agreements, and so on: all manner of private business, of which at most a very small number of copies was required. (On the matters covered in this paragraph, see Baugh and Cable (2002*: esp. chs 6 and 7); Crystal (2004*: ch. 11); Nevalainen and Tieken-Boon van Ostade (2006*: 274–87); also the excellent short account in Leith (1983*: 38–44), and the fuller history in the papers in Wright (2000*) such as that by Rissanen.)

By the sixteenth century, virtually everyone in secular life capable of writing English had had a private or school education driven by the curricula of the universities, or a practical and legal training governed by the norms of the chancery. Important documents which were more than mere legal transactions were consigned to print by professionals trained in the printing dialect. Sixteenth-century Sussex men such as Sir Richard Sackville (Withyham) and Andrew Borde (Cuckfield) wrote the general written English of the day in their private correspondence, with no more than a hint of south-easternism. (Sackville wrote *myche* for *much* and *ayenst* for *against*, for instance, as would be historically expected in Sussex.)[1] The religious world was also overtaken by these events; the monodialectal *Book of common prayer* was in principle available to everyone from 1549, and heard in church nationwide. The general currency of the written London standard rose in harness with the prestige and wider availability of the printed word itself. It soon came to influence the speech of upper-class London and to be, in some measure, identified with it. It was not long before the notion of 'the best English' had come to have a geographical basis rather than a purely stylistic one or a demographic one. George Puttenham, in *The arte of English poesie* (1589: bk 3, ch. 4), notoriously declared that, if you want to be looked up to, 'ye shall . . . take the vsuall speach of the Court, and that of London and the shires lying about London within lx. myles, and not much aboue' (Whigham and Rebhorn 2007*). Prominent people who used non-standard English speech, either strictly regional or simply old-fashioned, became the subject of overt comment; Sir Walter Raleigh and John Milton are two often-mentioned examples, as later is the 'prime minister' Robert Walpole (1676-1745). No-one who was anyone in England wrote in non-standard English after 1500, and the pressure was growing on users of non-courtly accents to abandon them; by the end of the eighteenth century there was a veritable industry involved in producing books to aid the aspiring élite, and more especially their children, to eliminate the taint of provinciality from their speech. The best-known of these were perhaps Thomas Sheridan's *Lectures on elocution* (1762*) and John Walker's *Critical pronouncing dictionary* (1791*). A codified standard was something desired by late-seventeenth century Englishmen, and this goal was served by such scholars and grammar-teachers of the next century as Johnson, Lowth and Lindley Murray, as we shall note below.[2]

Mainstream English official, intellectual and literary non-standard dialect writing in England therefore became extinct in the fifteenth century. The only effective alternative printed prose-writing tradition in Britain was that of Scots, which flourished in the sixteenth century but died out in the seventeenth after the union of the Scottish and English crowns. James VI/I was interested in linguistic matters, and in 1585 produced a remarkable guide to Scots writing, but his own writings became more and more anglicized, as a glance at successive editions of his work the *Basilicon doron* will show. It could be argued that this

[1] It is worth remembering that Latin could also be written in a non-standard form. In Sussex we only have to note the fourteenth-century iron graveslab at Burwash inscribed 'Orate p.annema Jhone Coline' ('Pray for the soul of ?Joan Collin' [widely believed to be 'John']; and not all clerks were first-rate latinists.

[2] For a good basic introduction to the question of how accents and dialects are evaluated in present-day English, see Beal (2000*: unit 3).

anglicization was due to his printers rather than to James himself, but it is clear that he was himself effectively bidialectal and an anglophile to boot (see Templeton 1973*: 7-8, Görlach 1991*: 20). Bald (1926*) showed that books printed in Edinburgh in English or anglicized Scots outnumbered books printed in 'pure Scots' by 1590 and that by 1610 Scots printing was virtually dead. Only five books printed in Scots are known to have appeared between 1610 and 1625. The Scottish religious reformers of the seventeenth century, such as John Knox, were linguistically English, so the language of the most vital intellectual concerns of the time was English rather than Scots. It was a prayer-book in English that circulated north of the border, and there were no Bibles in Scots.

The stage was then set for the uniformity of written prose dialect characterizing the British Age of Reason. Swift, in his *Proposal for correcting, improving and ascertaining the English tongue* (1712*), raised the desire for uniformity to an issue of principle. (*Ascertaining* meant 'fixing'.) For him, uniformity was a guarantee of changelessness, and therefore of the permanence of any writings which had value. Edmund Waller had expressed this idea in a poem of 1693: "But who can hope his lines should long/ Last in a daily changing tongue?" but concluded that those who wanted eternal approbation should write in a language fixed for ever by grammarians and rhetoricians: Latin or Greek. With greater confidence in rational activity to get English into a suitable state, the eighteenth century took the alternative view. Johnson's dictionary (1755*) and Priestley's, Lowth's and Lindley Murray's grammars (1761*, 1762* and 1795* respectively) can be seen as representing the intervention of Reason to achieve the uniformity, and hence the future unchangeability, of English. The same desire for uniformity is well and truly alive in many areas in the third millennium, including in government directives for the promotion of both passive and active competence in written standard English in education. The only challenge to this trend in the eighteenth century came from overseas; in the 1780s appeared the first of Noah Webster's zealous attempts to establish an American English distinct from that of the mother country, at least as regards spelling (Webster 1786*). But even Webster did not doubt the wisdom of the pursuit of standardization *within* American usage.

In case anyone should believe that standard usage was achieved over a relatively short time in the eighteenth century, we should note the Ottawa Grammar Resource on Early Variability in English (OGREVE: Poplack, Van Herk and Harvie 2002*), intended to make available the evidence for variability in the prestige dialect, as represented by its most ideologically standardizing works: the grammar-books written between 1577 and 1898.

On the other hand, there was some stirring of interest in dialect, as in non-classical antiquities in general, from the Elizabethan period onwards (cf. Wakelin

1988b*: 131–40, 164–75). The main manifestation of this interest is the composite dialect of the comic stage rustic, a confection based on those non-standard features of the time which were shared by West Country and Kentish speech and commonly nowadays called *Mummerset*, which is richly recorded from the sixteenth century onwards. The stereotypical Scots was also paraded for comic effect by English writers including Shakespeare (the character Jamy in *Henry V*, for instance). These matters are exhaustively discussed by Eckhardt (1910*); virtually all stage dialect at this period is south-western or Scots and northern, and there is almost nothing that even whiffs of the south-east, except perhaps, very doubtfully, in the mouth of Oliver in *Locrine*, a play of the Shakespeare apocrypha dating from 1585/6.

Hanging on the coat-tails of this stage tradition are some early texts, printed and unprinted, entirely in apparently authentic dialect or at least written with the professed intention of being authentic. These include a remarkable poem transmitted in the autobiography of the Somerset musician Thomas Whythorne, using John Hart's system of spelling, assigned to Gloucester but with some gross stereotypical south-western features (c.1576; see Osborn 1961*: 167–70); the less stereotypical *Pleasant dialogue betweene plaine Truth, and blind Ignorance* by Thomas Deloney, once attributed to Somerset but now thought to be from Devon as early as 1587/8; a seventeenth-century Somerset precursor of the Sussex epic *Tom Cladpole's jurney to Lunnun* (on which see below); and there was also a clutch of other seventeenth-century West Country material which in the main remained unprinted for at least another 100 years (cf. Wakelin 1986*: 16; 1988a*: 611–2).

Another very early printed work is the basically serious creation of George Meriton entitled *A York-shire dialogue* (1683). More typical are the pieces which aim to make fun of rustic speech, for instance William Strode's *The wonders of Plymouth* (c.1620) and George Stuart's *Joco-serious discourse with a Scot* (1686), a basically Scots text which provides an incidental taste of the first writing in the modern dialect of Northumberland. Such things belong, in spirit, in the same category as the Mummerset of the playwrights. Since the purpose of many of the writings in this category is to entertain, dialect features may often be emphasized by repetition and by exaggeration of frequency. The effect of this is to put more distance between the standard and non-standard written forms of the language. When the time eventually comes to consider writing seriously in dialect, the writer, faced with a choice between a local form and a standard form both of which are in common local use, may opt regularly for the purely local form on the grounds of 'authenticity' and the local pride which this both generates and manifests. This again may have the effect of widening the gap between the alternative writing-norms, and of exaggerating the differences – a phenomenon familiar enough, for example, among those nationalists desperate to distinguish at any cost between Serbian and Croatian, Catalan and Valencian, or, historically, Norwegian and Danish. We shall note below, in Chapter 3, that the Sussex writer James Richards made a conscious choice about which local variant to use to render /ð/ in words like *the* and *that* – /d/ or /v/ (not to mention the standard form /ð/ itself). His choice of /d/, whilst in line with the usage of his predecessors, ensured that classic written Sussex dialect was partly false as a representation of the Sussex accent as a result of ignoring some of the contemporary variation in speech.

The eighteenth century was a low period in the fortunes of dialect and dialect study, not least because interest in the matter ran counter to the prevailing obsession with politeness – the mores and behaviours of the affluent classes, including their linguistic fancies (Watts 2002*). In the later part of the century, to some extent arguably as a reaction to that obsession, the Romantics propel the ideologization of folk culture onto centre stage. This intellectual movement was stimulated by the linguistic aspects of the thinking of the German philosophers J.G. Herder and J.G. Hamann. It begins to promote the slowly-reawakening idea of serious writing in more local varieties.

The poets of the Scots tradition including William Dunbar, Gavin Douglas, and numerous balladeers, especially as represented by the collection of their work published by Allan Ramsay in 1724, and Ramsay's own Scots poems, may be seen as a model for the vanguard of the verse wing of this new movement. The influence of Scots vernacular poesy (presumably through Ramsay's anthology) seems to have leaked over the border to inspire some writers in the most northerly counties of England even before the birth of the most significant writer of the new Scots movement, Robert Burns (1759–96). John Collier ('Tim Bobbin') in Lancashire is in print as early as 1746. Josiah Relph of Cumberland's first book of verse emerged in 1747 (significantly, printed in Glasgow), and there was a flourishing Cumbrian literature by the first decade of the nineteenth century. David Lewis was writing and publishing Yorkshire verse by 1815, and Ann Coward Wheeler's four Westmorland dialogues were in their third edition by 1821. These are all texts written far from the heartland of the emerging national standard in the English south-east.

The nineteenth century has justly been called 'that golden age of dialect literatures' (Hobsbawm 1990*: 111). As it progressed, many English writers from further south eventually followed the example of Cumberland: at first only poets, the only ones of acknowledged stature being William Barnes in Dorset and Alfred Tennyson in Lincolnshire (who wrote Lincolnshire dialect poems and drama in addition to his more famous standard English works). John Clare's poems also have some light Northamptonshire dialect colour in their vocabulary, but this usage may well not have been self-consciously dialectal: a matter to which we will return.

These earliest literary efforts were contemporary with, and became more frequent in the same measure as, the first relatively systematic attempts at describing local dialects (on the history of which see Ihalainen 1994*). The first known explicit notes directed particularly to Sussex speech are a small set of negligible and barely interpretable remarks about the local yeomen's and gentry's tone of voice and syllabification by the eighteenth-century antiquary John Burton, who paid a visit in 1751, leading to the publication of his *Iter Sussexiense* (Burton 1752*; see Blaauw 1856*). Worse still for the fate of these remarks was the fact that they were published in classical Greek (mainly) and Latin.

Far more important, and groundbreaking, was John Ray's *Collection of words not generally used . . .*, which dates from 1674* (revised edition 1691*) and ranges over the entire country, not just Sussex. This masterly work, the first English dialect dictionary, was almost out on its own for over a century until the publication of Francis Grose's major work *A provincial glossary* in 1787* (see Farrant 1995*: 75; note however Wakelin 1987*: 157ff., esp. 157-8, for discussion of some smaller-scale contributions).

Dictionaries of provincial usage, slang, and local dialect begin to proliferate only from the later eighteenth century onwards (notice especially the much-reprinted Grose (1785*)), and the first explicitly regional glossaries for particular counties start to appear between about 1815 and 1860, with increasing frequency as this period elapses. Eighty-odd rural dialect glossaries and grammars were published by the English Dialect Society between 1873 and 1896, and Joseph Wright's *English dialect dictionary and English dialect grammar* followed in 1898–1905*. Wright's work was widely felt to be the culmination of the work of the English Dialect Society, and the 'butterfly-collecting' period of dialectology came to an end with its publication.

The Society was wound up, but a regional outstation persisted in the form of the Yorkshire Dialect Society, founded in Bradford by Wright's committee in 1897 (and in 2010 the only English regional dialect society to survive from that period). Little serious dialectology was done then till after the second world war, when systematic nationwide investigation was set in motion by Harold Orton, partly on the model of the inter-war *Deutscher Sprachatlas* and associated studies (see Mitzka 1952*). The result was the Survey of English Dialects, published now as a thirteen-volume work, with several other, mainly map-based, studies deriving from it (Orton and collaborators*).

The American linguists Hans Kurath and Guy S. Lowman jr. (the fieldworker) started a survey before the second world war, but its fruits were not published until 1973*, and then in an incomplete form with material from only the southern counties. It was intended as a reference work for the historical interpretation of (mainly phonological) variation in English dialects of the United States. This survey is available in the UK in only a very few libraries. Other more recent work has been in the tradition either of Uriel Weinreich's structural dialectology (1954*; for Sussex, see especially the work of David North, C2, C4, C6, C8; also B2 Kent, B2 Surrey) or of William Labov's urban sociolinguistics (1972*, 2006*; represented in the literature on Sussex only by the project for the award of the BA degree done by Griffith (1990, C2). For a fuller history of the study of the English dialects, see Petyt (1980*), esp. his chapter 3 on traditional English dialectology, chapter 5 on structural dialectology and chapter 7 on urban sociolinguistics; and Francis (1983*), esp. his chapter 7 on traditional, structural and generative dialectology and chapter 8 on urban sociolinguistics.

Both the literary and the linguistic interest we have seen here can be viewed as attempts to legitimate the dialects, in the sense used about the Romantic ideological approaches to the history of English as a whole by Milroy (2002*: 9-10). That is, they were positioned as part of the common linguistic heritage of the English people: an ancient and pure language with an essentially Germanic pedigree which might be found more untrammelled in the (rural) dialects than in the standard, and many were associated with nostalgic and anti-modern attitudes. But as we shall see, the social and political culture associated with the standard English dialect allowed only a restricted legitimacy to its working-class relatives, and in many respects interest in dialect was a middle-class hobby – a fact which is responsible for the predominant comic tone of dialect writing of the period.

The most characteristic form of dialect writing is not the serious endeavour envisaged, and exemplified, by Ramsay, Relph and the masters down to Barnes. Militating against the enterprise of serious writing in dialect was, and is, the widespread prejudice that only the standard language is a worthy vehicle for the expression of ideas which are elevated, i.e. permanently valuable. This idea, graven in granite since the eighteenth century, originated as a reinterpretation and re-evaluation of the fact that the language of printing and the court had achieved a dominant position. It came to be believed – indeed it was a commonplace of medieval and Renaissance thought – that the dialects (along with variation of any kind, not just linguistic) represented mutability and impermanence, being corruptions of other forms of language. The intellectual model for this argument was the biblical Tower of Babel incident in the Book of Genesis (11:1-9). In the light of views like this, the pressure for a codified standard was brought to bear precisely so as to resist change and provide a permanent vehicle for what was excellent in thought and expression.

The practical repercussions of this idea rumbled on in the unquestioned propriety of Standard English in school education, which has a history going back far before the first great broadening of access to education in the 1870s. Only rather recently was there any challenge to this entrenched position; a debate about the use of Standard English in the school classroom began relatively recently under pressure from linguists such as Trudgill (1975*). As a consequence of the entrenched view, the use of non-standard forms was, and to a considerable extent still is, felt to show ignorance and lack of education, especially in professional contexts which still protect Standard English (e.g. book production, the law, and drafting departments of the civil service), and it therefore invited ridicule. Educated men of humble origins, therefore, would naturally write in the standard; even Sussex's early local writers such as William Hersee (1786–1854) the ploughman (Tibble 1989*), and John Dudeney (1782–1852) the shepherd turned schoolmaster (Blencowe 1849*), would not compromise their hard-won educational standing by dabbling in the vernacular.[3]

It is significant that those who did write in dialect often did so under a pseudonym, and that often flippant (e.g. the Lancastrians John Collier as 'Tim Bobbin' and Benjamin Brierley as 'Ab-o'-th'-Yate'; Westmorland's William Hutton as 'William de Worfat'; and the Sussex man James Richards as 'Jim Cladpole' – Richards published his works in standard English under his own name). Also, the use of local linguistic forms pulls in the opposite direction from the commercial requirement of mass circulation and from the desire for the wide diffusion of ideas. Text 18 in Part Two is included as an unusual indication of the relatively untutored writing of a village boy in the era soon after the beginning of universal education.

A direct consequence of these considerations is the fact that the enormous bulk of self-confessed dialect literature is comic in vein, and local and domestic in its subject matter. In that sense, the dialects are languages which have not got beyond the lowest stage, stage 1, in Kloss's *Ausbau* ('elaboration') model of language development (Kloss 1952*: 28). The single systematic exception is in the rendering of material which is likely to be well known to its readers already, and which amounts therefore to retelling that material with the emphasis on the linguistic form rather than the content. The chief examples of this are overwhelmingly Bible stories, a striking recent example in this tradition being a work in Cockney, with special emphasis on rhyming slang, by Mike Coles (2001*).

Dialect writing is writing for insiders, and, from the point of view of the dominant culture, for an out-group. Choosing to write seriously in dialect, i.e. not just representing in writing the local speech of certain characters (as George Eliot, Scott or Hardy did), is therefore an unmistakable sign that the author has chosen local self-identification (or, as it used to be called disparagingly, 'provinciality') to the exclusion of the national. As Wade (1976*) has pointed

[3] On the significance of literacy in general and in rural Sussex in particular, see for example Howard (1993, C3 and Allen (2006, C3) respectively.

out, there are even special dialect genres which are not normally investigated by academic critics: the north-country almanacs, for instance, e.g. those from Yorkshire by authors from Abel Bywater (1830) and Charles Rogers (1840) through to John Hartley (cf. Wakelin 1988b*: 173–4); and the dialect genres tend to go under alternative names which carry somewhat negative connotations as compared with those of their standard counterparts (poetry is typically *verse*, short stories are typically *tales*).

Only a few authors have tried serious dialect prose writing on a grand scale, and few indeed have received anything like general recognition. In fact, only John Galt (now heading for oblivion again?) and Lewis Grassic Gibbon, both writing in Scots, spring readily to mind, and latterly also William Lorimer with his Scots New Testament (1983). It remains to be seen whether Irving Welch's *Trainspotting* (1994), also in Scots, and further promoted by the major film based on it (1996), keeps its sudden nationwide fame in the longer term. The tradition continues, however, especially, but not exclusively, in areas remote from London, and there are signs of special vigour in some places such as Tyneside, Devon and Yorkshire. Those with a specialist interest in dialect writing may rate highly the efforts of Edwin Waugh from Lancashire, John Hartley and Fred Brown from Yorkshire, A.J. Coles ('Jan Stewer') from Devon, and no doubt others, but the audience in question is more limited, by definition.

Some serious poets have had a little more success, for instance C.M. Grieve ('Hugh MacDiarmid'; again in a variety of revived so-called 'synthetic' Scots), and D.H. Lawrence, whose Nottinghamshire verses ride on the back of his fame as a writer of standard English. But far more typical successful specimens than MacDiarmid or Lawrence are Roger McGough (Liverpool) and Pam Ayres (Oxfordshire). Linguistically, their verse – usually comic verse, though sometimes with more serious undertones – is more properly distinguished by the accent in which it is delivered than by the vocabulary or grammar peculiar to Merseyside or the south-midland counties. The older poets writing principally or exclusively in dialect, however good in literary terms, on the whole remain unknown outside their native counties. Josiah Relph (Cumberland), John Collier, Edwin Waugh and Harvey Kershaw (all Lancashire), John Read (Somerset), W.F. Rock (Devon), Benjamin Preston, Dorothy Una Ratcliffe, Fred Brown and Kit Calvert (all Yorkshire) and Edward Campion (Lincolnshire) are hardly household names nationwide; but William Barnes (Dorset) is the striking exception, championed by Thomas Hardy and popularized by Vaughan Williams's settings of such poems as 'My orcha'd in Linden Lea'.

As regards non-literary writings, an event entirely unique in recent decades was the submission of a doctoral dissertation in Scots by Alasdair Allan at Glasgow University; he reports his experiences in Allan (1995*). The submission was accepted by the university authorities, presumably with one eye on the possible damaging fallout of refusing a work written in what could easily be presented as *the* national language of Scotland. It seems unlikely that many scholars will follow suit.

There exist a few academic studies of the dialect writing of the English counties, all in fact dissertations from the German-speaking world dating from around 1920. The most notable of these relate to Dorset (i.e. William Barnes, by Kurt Urlau (Berlin, 1921*)), Essex (i.e. Charles Benham, by Thomas Albrecht (Berlin, 1916*)), Devon (i.e. William Frederick Rock, by Hans Wiegert (Berlin, 1921*)), and Lancashire (where the very well-known anglicist Karl Brunner, no less, crafted one of his first substantial monographs (Vienna, 1920*) and a journal article (1925*)). For general surveys of the problem of, and the significance of, writing in dialect, see Ives (1971*); Wade (1976*); N. Page (1988*: 55–96); Shepherd (1990*: 33–106); Paulin (1990*: xi-xvi); Joyce (1991*); Toolan (1992*); and Görlach (1999*: ch. 2). This is a matter to which we return in Chapter 5.

The folk-song revival starting in the nineteenth century has had a serious impact on creative modern dialect writers only in Scotland, where the songs of John Ord, Maurice Blytheman, Ronald Williamson, Dick Gaughan, Hamish Henderson and others are well known. Discounting the simpler traditionalism exemplified by many local ensembles and bands such as the Coppers (in Sussex) and the Oldham Tinkers, and the many good singers of old local songs such as Norma Waterson, very little novelty has been found south of the border, unless we consider the Cockney music-hall song tradition and the occasional purveyors of dialect caricature in song such as the Wurzels and the Yetties. It would in any case be reasonable to regard these productions as written-down oral literature rather than primarily as written literature.

Sussex does not have a rich heritage of vernacular literature, or even a tradition of dialect writing, to compare with, say, Dorset and Somerset, Yorkshire, Lancashire, London (Cockney) or the Lowlands of Scotland. In fact, the entire county literature (Part Three, Sections D1.1, D1.2) could probably be contained in a couple of middle-sized hardback volumes. The bulk of that literature, as will be seen more fully below, is contained in the verse writings of the Muddles Green schoolmaster Richard Lower, writing under the pseudonym 'Tim Cladpole', published originally in the second quarter of the nineteenth century (*Tom Cladpole's Jurney to Lunnun* and *Jan Cladpole's trip to 'Merricur*; Part 2, Texts 12a-b) and of the photographer and lay preacher James Richards (pseudonym 'Jim Cladpole'), consisting mainly of renditions of certain portions of the Bible and published mainly in the 1930s (Texts 25a-e). The only other really prolific author was the polypseudonymous Lilian Ramsey, not herself a native of the county but a very long-time resident and a shrewd observer, who wrote a column for many years in the weekly *West Sussex*

Gazette (Texts 30a-b). (Biographies of Richards and Ramsey are catalogued in Part Three, Section G below; they are mainly contained in newspaper obituaries.) The only large-scale work I know of that is not in the public domain is the novel *Dickey Snickle*, said to be by Mark Melford ('Rhymeo' 1872, D1.2); I only discovered that the manuscript was still in existence on the day I finished this book, so I have not yet examined its content.[4] All these and the authors of the other pieces known to me, again dating almost exclusively from the first half of the twentieth century, are catalogued in Section D of the bibliography (Part Three of this book). Even the most cursory look at the material will reveal how well it fits into the countrywide pattern of domestic and local subject matter and comic tone, or versions of Bible stories.

It is of interest, as noted above, that both Lower and Richards were men of some (in Richards's case, elementary) education, and were thus also literate in the standard dialect. The only writers who appear to me to have written extensively in dialect without being fully aware that they were doing so were John Burgess (1751-1825; Texts 10a-c) and James Nye (1822–1892; Texts 14a-b), and even then the dialect colour of their work (not published in their lifetimes, not all of it published yet, and some likely to remain unpublished) is, for perfectly understandable reasons, not very strong.

The blacksmith Gaius Carley (1888–after 1964) wrote his memoirs in 1955; the book shows some dialect features, especially as regards the technical terminology of his trade, but, as in the case of Nye's, not many (Text 32). Interestingly, Carley comments on the way the villagers of Kirdford 'talked funny' (1955: 33–4, D1.1) and gives examples of what he means. Farm bailiff James 'Brasser' Copper (1846-1924) also shows little true regionalism in his transcriptions of folk-songs (perhaps unsurprisingly, as these are not necessarily of Sussex origin). Burgess clearly did not write his diary and letters as 'literature' in any conventional sense; they were not intended for publication. The intention behind Nye's outpourings is less clear. Carley wrote up his memoirs with the intention that they should be available to those interested, but was gratified by their typing-up and publication at the behest of the Earl of Cottenham and of Francis Steer, the then West Sussex county archivist. Copper wrote his songbook at his employer's daughter's request.

Almost nothing else is known of untutored Sussex writing. The little diary of Sophia Miles (1850–62; see Standing 1997, D1.1) stands on its own, but we can hope that more works like this may come to light; also known to me is the unpublished diary of George White of Chiddingly (1829; see Hubble 2003,

[4] Was this Mark Melford, author of the play *Kleptomania: a farcical comedy in three acts*. London and New York: T. Henry French (1888)? The pun on *Romeo* in his pseudonym might suggest an actor.

D1.1). Some other small examples of local writing are of borderline interest as representing relatively untutored and therefore regionally marked English include these four early (probably eighteenth-century) specimens: Edward Austin of Burwash's *Approved medicines and receipts* (1701; known of but unlocated) and Timothy Butt of Tillington's book of remedies and assorted other things (1770-1825; WSRO Add. MS. 1593), the seventeenth/ eighteenth-century marginalia in the Sussex Archaeological Society's copy of Leonard Mascall's *The government of cattel* (4th edition, 1662), and the charms in the pocket account book of the farrier John Skinner (fl. 1690–1732; known of but unlocated) from just over the boundary in Strood Green, Betchworth, Surrey. These display some dialect features, and it would probably be justifiable to call the writing of the second and third untutored.

Chapter 2

Linguistic writings on Sussex dialect, spoken and written

It is often held that there is no distinctively Sussex dialect. For instance, E.V. Lucas, a Sussex patriot and a man inclined to make a case for Sussex's uniqueness if there were one to be sustained, asserted (1904*: 408) that, '[r]oughly speaking, Sussex has little or no dialect absolutely its own; for the country speech of the west is practically that of Hampshire, and of the east, that of Kent'. Despite W.G. Daish's protests (1956a: 8, C2, D1.2), this is broadly true, and unsurprisingly so, despite a fair collection of isoglosses running close to the Hampshire/Sussex boundary. Modern writers on dialect subsume present-day Sussex into the Home Counties Dialect Area (Trudgill 1999*: 65), and this is the expected outcome of a persistent trend. At the levels of vocabulary and grammar especially, Sussex was not too far distant from the emerging standard language based on legal and polite usage in London, and the loss of any major local distinctiveness must have proceeded relatively early and relatively painlessly (cf. McIntosh and others (1986*: introduction)). For instance, the loss from the sixteenth century onwards of the phoneme /x/, spelt <gh>, is common to London and all English dialects of England including Sussex.

More recently, at the level of pronunciation, Sussex has felt the tide of metropolitan usage in two waves, firstly through elocutionists' striving to replace local pronunciation with Received Pronunciation, within and outside the schooling system, and secondly through the influence of the non-élite varieties of London English which can be shown to have spread to the big coastal towns such as Hastings, Brighton and Portsmouth down the main corridors of travel, and from the towns into the adjacent rural villages (North 1985, C2). In this connection, it is interesting that that most striking Sussex stereotype used by all the literary writers, the 'extended *-s* inflection' seen in the plural and possessive case forms of the noun *ghostes* and the third-person present-tense verb-form *persistes*, is condemned as the 'first fault of the Londoners' by Walker (1791*).

As long ago as 1940, Arthur Beckett (1940, C2) quoted the lament that the Sussex dialect had been 'half killed by the Council schools, and now the evacuees had come to finish the job'. It is significant that the dialect portrayed in the anonymous verses known as *The Brighton beach loafer* is that of late Victorian London, not of Brighton at all. The Loafer has left his mark, and in the late twentieth century does so very strongly as the influential vernacular of London is copied in some of its features by young people, especially males, in Brighton and most other large towns of the south and east of England (Trudgill 1986*, esp. chapter 2). This trend was accentuated by the development of Crawley, from the 1950s onwards, as a new town drawing in people from a wide area beyond Sussex, and the trend has extended its geographical range strikingly since the first draft of this chapter was written in the early 1990s. What passes for dialect in Crawley now is essentially the non-standard English of the entire south-east, as this material from a literacy wall in a Crawley school demonstrates (Frater 2002*: 42):

Crawley Dialect
Is good for speaking to your family, and with friends in the playground. When you are writing a story, you can also make your characters use it. This helps the reader to get a feel for what they are like.

- I done my homework
- You done
- We done
- She/he was
- They was
- Wicked!
- I writ it
- You writ
- Can you think of any more?

Sussex, then, is not linguistically insulated from its neighbours. Equally, it has long been the custom to point to at least one internal division within Sussex dialect. Cooper (1836, C6) claimed an east-west split, with each area having linguistic similarities to the neighbouring counties. Lower (1861: 217, C6) also accepted an east-west division for pronunciation. Parish (1875: introduction, C6) identified three areas, defined by lines of longitude passing through Shoreham and Hastings. Both writers left the reason for their opinion vague.

The first trained linguist to attack the problem, Ellis (1889*), used pronunciation criteria to establish dialect areas, two of which covered Sussex. At this highest classificatory level, Ellis identified Eastern Mid Southern and East Southern (1889*: 91–110, 130–45; these are his areas D.5 and D.9 respectively). He admitted that his main information about west Sussex was 'meagre', deriving exclusively from data supplied by W.A. Bartlett, the incumbent of Wisborough Green (and for adjacent parts of Surrey, from

T. Burningham, the incumbent of Charlwood), in his own orthography (i.e. an unsystematic adaptation of normal English spelling). He had lesser information also in informants' own orthography from Bolney, Compton, Eartham, Kirdford, Twineham and West Wittering (bolstered by his fieldworker Thomas Hallam's notes also in the case of Bolney). His eastern data was startlingly richer. He rested on Parish for Selmeston, and had a very good informant, Anna M. Darby, from Marklye, in Heathfield. A further rather diverse set of data-sources enabled him to form a view of Cuckfield and Eastbourne (his own transcriptions from informants), Battle, Lewes and Brighton (Hallam's transcriptions from informants), Leasam (offered in what Ellis called 'systematic spelling', i.e. some kind of phonologically transparent transcription, provided by Bessie C. Curteis), and Ashburnham, Etchingham, Possingworth and the Weald 'near Brighton' in some kind of less systematic informant orthography. The major phonological criterion used by Ellis to divide east from west is the use in the east of /d/ for /ð/.

Ellis placed the boundary between the great areas north-south across Sussex, relying at the Shoreham end explicitly on Mark Antony Lower's opinion. This was very similar to what Parish had done. Parish identified an additional Hastings-area subdivision, and his conclusions were echoed by Rubin (1951, C4, C6). In Middle English studies (to which discipline Rubin's study belongs), it has become orthodox to assign eastern Sussex to the Kentish area, and western Sussex to the Southern; the most substantial contribution to this view is that represented by early work of Ekwall (1917: 61, A). Other opinions lump Sussex as a whole in with Kent (Morsbach 1896*; Moore, Meech and Whitehall 1935*), or to a transitional zone between West-Saxon and Kentish (Luick 1914-21*: 42-5), mainly on the basis of (hardly any) surviving literary texts (see footnote 5 below). The dividers tend to form their views on the basis of the considerably more substantial place-name and documentary evidence. Samuels's view (1971*), that the east, including East Sussex, has been influenced by the continental Germanic languages in historic times, also supports the idea of an east-west split.

Not all commentators who divide Sussex by a north-south line draw their dividing lines in exactly the same places (see also Rubin 1951: 7–8, 13–15, 226, C4). But many are prepared to envisage a split approximately dividing the three western from the three eastern rapes (essentially the pre-1974 counties of West and East Sussex respectively), coinciding roughly with a line heading north from east of the mouth of the Adur, proceeding west of Cuckfield to East Grinstead; Ellis conjecturally includes a section of Buttinghill hundred near East Grinstead (formerly in East Sussex) with the western division. Mawer and Stenton (1929*: xiv-xvi, xxiii-xxv) offer a rather reserved view of the relation between some regional linguistic features and early settlement history, believing that the evidence does not support an original racial unity between Kent and eastern Sussex.

It has been suggested at least once, by E.R. Burder to Helena Hall, the augmenter of Parish's *Dictionary*, that one might envisage, in addition to a north-south split, a Downland/Wealden split (Hall 1957: xiv, C6/C8). None of these considerations in any way invalidates the attempt to describe the way(s) in which English was and is spoken in Sussex. In what follows, I discuss the literature about Sussex dialect in a realistic spirit, and do not try to argue for the existence of a distinctive unique regional English in the county.

In Chapter 4 we shall explore in detail the relative absence of documents attributable to genuinely local learned and bureaucratic centres, but for now let us note that given this absence, almost the only hard evidence for local dialect in the earliest times is that which can be inferred from place-names and local personal names (Löfvenberg 1942*; Rubin 1951, C4; Kristensson 2001–2*). Rubin gives a list of efforts prior to his own to characterize the local Middle English dialect (1951: 7–8, C4), pointing out the poverty of the source material used by previous scholars (only poorly-localized literary texts[5]) and the incomplete cover of the phonology provided by the studies existing at the time he was writing. This is why Rubin makes careful use of the name-evidence of truly local legal documents such as the Assize Rolls and Subsidy Rolls with their wealth of place- and personal names in what can be presumed to be authentically local forms, as opposed to interpretations by central government clerks.

A second substantial survey on the same basis, this time of the whole of southern England, also confined to phonology, is that by Kristensson (2001–2*). The introduction to Mawer and Stenton's *The place-names of Sussex* (1929*: xiv-xvi, xxi-xxii, xxvii-xix) points to some possible dialect features from very early in the Anglo-Saxon period. Coates (2007, C2) isolates a number of distinctive highly localized features of vocabulary, name-formation and pronunciation found in Sussex place-names. A very few studies dealing with ancient place-name elements that seem to me characteristic (if not distinctive) of Sussex are included in the section on vocabulary in the main bibliography in Part Three (e.g. Pullein 1926, C6; Ekwall 1944, C6; Markey 1972, C6; Coates 1979, C6 and 1988, C6).

[5] It has been suggested that at least one MS. of *Piers Plowman*, A-text (Bodleian MS. Rawlinson Poetry 137), has Sussex origins (Horobin 2005* and references there). A case has also been made for the single-manuscript *Canticum de creatione* (Oxford, Bodleian Library, formerly Trinity College MS. 57; *LALME* LP 5850), which bears the date 1375, and the MS. may have been written around 1400 (Murdoch and Tasioulas 2002*; Text 2 in Part Two). See also Chapter 4.

No longitudinal survey exists to connect these studies of the (pre-)medieval dialect of Sussex with the modern dialect, though Rubin's and Kristensson's monographs implicitly work in this direction. However, as far as pronunciation is concerned, it can be predicted with reasonable confidence that any such survey will show: (a) the preservation of a basic nucleus of the medieval language, with the retention of some geographically-based variation, but tempered by developments common to the entire south of England such as the lengthening of /a/ before certain consonants and consonant-groups, the lowering and unrounding of /u/, and the chained (so-called 'Great') vowel shift affecting long vowels; and (b) the retreat of some characteristic features before alternatives emanating from the London area, a retreat which accelerates as time passes.

The only striking innovation clearly not due to London influence is the development of /ð/ to /d/ in the east of the county, for which the influence of the Low Countries (Samuels (1971*); and, unconvincingly, of Normandy (B.C.C. [Bessie Curteis] 1874: 179, C2)) has been invoked. As for vocabulary, the recurring theme of the non-specialist writing on dialect is the replacement of local words and expressions by standard ones, or at least by non-regional ones (which may not be quite the same thing). These lexical losses are generally viewed in a nostalgic light. So too is the loss of truly local place-name pronunciations, for example, very early, by Mark Antony Lower (1861: 210–1, C6), who believed that the modern forms obscured something of importance to the county identity: the origin of the place-names affected.

The same nostalgia cannot be said to attend local non-standard patterns of inflection (like *he doed it* reported from Hastings in the nineteenth century), syntactic features such as double negation, and words carrying grammatical meaning such as the special present-tense negative auxiliary *ain't*. These grammatical phenomena are still fairly regularly berated in classroom and newspaper with the intention of educating, beating or humiliating them out of existence. An early reviewer of Parish's county dictionary (see directly below) wrote: 'There can be no reasonable doubt that, before the country is many years older, education will have so reached every corner that no-one will be heard to say anything improperly' (quoted in a *West Sussex Gazette* editorial, 25/04/1957). In the east of the county, Sheila Kaye-Smith (1933*: *passim*; 1953*: 205–19) regarded the influence of London and the wireless as the most significant factors undermining tradition.

The inter-war period's fine blend of nostalgia and the desire for progress has turned out to be a period-piece. We have already noted how Arthur Beckett (1940) quoted the lament that the Sussex dialect had been 'half killed by the Council schools, and now the evacuees had come to finish the job'. Nowadays the mass media and personal and social mobility must be added to the list of dialecticidal influences; but the death of regional dialect has not meant levelling totally in favour of the prestige dialect, just as it did not in 1450 (see Chapter 1, and Text 40 in Part Two).

Modern interest in Sussex dialect as an object of study begins with the little-known, unprepossessing and unpublished notebook containing some 38 words and their meanings, found among the papers of Col. Francis Davies of Fletching (not precisely datable, but c.1845; ESRO MS. ACC 10360; see Whittick and Coates, in preparation). It is not known for certain whether Davies himself was the compiler, but he supplied the information to the antiquary James Orchard Halliwell who drew on it in his well-known book of regionalisms (1847*, 1850, 1852). But for the later dialect, the key text is W.D. Parish's dictionary (1875; C6, and see Text 15a), which in its turn drew on Halliwell. It is a typical dialect dictionary of its period, in that it was compiled by a sympathetic parson who was not a native speaker, and in that it contains a wealth of anecdote as well as lexical information and a small amount of unreliable philological speculation. The anecdotes show obvious signs of having been invented, or at least their linguistic aspects have been constructed (cf. on this Ellman 1912*: 209; and the subtle and full analysis by Roper 2007, C3, of their role in the work of Parish and other dialect lexicographers). Parish's claim to be reporting 'examples of Sussex conversation' in the illustrative material to some of his entries cannot really be taken seriously; Roper notes (2007: 185) that he 'overlards the dialect pudding' by introducing words from adjacent entries, resulting in a ludicrous excess which hardly convinces the reader of its having been drawn from life. It was, however, highly enough regarded by Walter Skeat and his committee to be distributed to members of the English Dialect Society for the subscription year 1874: no doubt *faute de mieux*.

Several copies exist with significant additions and other annotations, e.g. by James Fraser and J.C. Stenning (copies in the Sussex Archaeological Society library, on open shelves), and by J.C. Clough and H.H. Sturmer (copy in the British Library). (See further the bibliography entry for Parish (1875, C6).) The work was republished by Hall (1957, C6/C8), augmented by words and expressions collected over a period of half a century by herself and her brother J.H.S. Hall. These works deal thoroughly only with vocabulary. The notes on pronunciation, for instance, are unsystematic and misleading. Hall also does a disservice to Parish; Parish was aware of the problem of malapropisms (lexical misunderstandings) which he quotes in the humorous backup to some of his entries, and devotes some space to it in his introduction. Hall, on the other hand, seems unable to distinguish between dialect and idiolect, and some malapropisms actually appear as headwords in her additional material, implying that she regarded them as genuine Sussexisms. Parish's original entries were republished by Dick Richardson (2001, C6), who added some varied material by the Sussex patriot E.V. Lucas, and by Lynne Truss (2008, C6).

We find occasional pieces published explicitly as amplifications of Parish's and Hall's lists, and some new contributions of a few words; e.g., all in C6, Stenning (1907), Butterfield (1916), Harrison (1926), Parsons (1931), Gaston (1940), Donne (1949), Godman (1965), Simpson (1973), Wales (1979, 1992), and Wales (1990, C8); and other small pieces are mentioned at the appropriate point in the bibliography (C6). The earlier glossary by William Durrant Cooper (1836, C6, partly relying on untraced work by Thomas 'Clio' Rickman, writing as 'The Reflector' in the *Brighton Herald*; improved edition 1853) is of some interest, being extensively trawled by Parish, but its historical notes are totally unreliable. An extensive survey of dialect features of the East Grinstead area has recently been published in instalments by Leppard (1999-2008, C6). Relevant material on local names of plants may be found sometimes in Britten and Holland (1878–86*), Arnold (1887/1907*), Whitaker (1935*), Wolley-Dod (1937*) and Grigson (1955*), and on those of birds by Knox (1849*), Swainson (1885*) and Lockwood (1984*), as well as on both these categories in articles and notes in local periodicals.

The work of Ellis (1889*, 1890*) already discussed, the *English dialect dictionary* and *Grammar* of Wright (1898–1905*), and the Survey of English Dialects (SED*) cover Sussex, as they cover the whole of England. The results of the Survey of English Dialects, organized by elicited word or form in thematic groups, may be found in Orton and Wakelin (1967–8*), but these are hard for the layperson to use and evaluate. More accessible are the published map-interpretations of the data, e.g. Orton, Sanderson and Widdowson (1978*); Orton and Wright (1974*); Kolb, Glauser, Elmer and Stamm (1979*), Anderson (1987*) and Upton, Sanderson and Widdowson (1987*); but some of these, too, require specialist knowledge of alphabet of the International Phonetic Association to interpret them satisfactorily. The earlier relatively raw findings have now been partially published in dictionary and grammar form by Upton, Parry and Widdowson (1994*).

The SED collected information in Warnham, East Harting, Sutton, Fletching, Horam and Firle (Sussex points 1-6 respectively), the fieldwork being done from May to November 1959 by Michael V. Barry (see Barry's MA dissertation (1960*) and his derived chapter on the definite article (1972*)). By its method of selecting informants, it was intended to give a picture of rural (i.e. supposedly authentic) dialect as it was when being acquired by its native speakers in c.1900-10. Barry was alive to the dangers of collecting dialect information from people on their best linguistic behaviour for the interview situation, and gave due weight to the material collected in free conversation outside the administration of the questionnaire. Further information was collected by David North in 1979-80, along broadly the same lines, in Bolney, Funtington, Poynings, Robertsbridge, Rotherfield, Turners Hill and Washington (North

1982b, C6). A follow-up lexical survey was done in 1976–80 for the *Atlas Linguarum Europeae (ALE)* project; fieldworker David Leslie operated in Fletching, and in Bignor in place of nearby Sutton (*ALE* points 055 and 052 respectively), but it is not easy for people outside universities to get hold of the published material. This long-term project totters on towards completion. The SED fieldwork notebooks (or copies) are held at the University of Leeds and at the Special Collections department of the Western Bank Library, University of Sheffield, as are the materials of the *ALE*. This library also has the original fieldwork audiotapes of both, and is running the comparative project 'The English dialect lexicon: a review of continuity and change, 1950-1990' (for fruits, see Upton and Widdowson 1999*). The project continues to run at the University of Leeds and at the National Centre for English Cultural Tradition (NATCECT), Sheffield. Outside this set of related academic enterprises, the British Drama League collected at least one specimen of Sussex speech, in Battle in 1936 (BDL 7" disc LYN 675; Turner and Fogerty (no date: 18, C4, and Part Four, G1)).

Lexical surveys specific to certain parishes have since been done. Two of these are follow-up studies to the Survey of English Dialects in Firle done by students at the University of Sussex (Wallisch (1980, MS., C6) and Whitfield (1995, MS., C6), both available from the present author and in selected local libraries); and there is also a fairly recent survey in Petworth, consisting of questions about vocabulary based on those of the Survey of English Dialects (but not exclusively), by Costello and Jerrome (1992, C6; survey and questionnaire deposited in West Sussex Record Office, 1999; Text 36). Work by North (1979, C8/G1; 1984, C4) has filled in the wider picture somewhat, though his intentions in the two mentioned articles relate more especially to matters of linguistic theory. All these tend to show the loss of some of the lexical variants found by the SED.

The question of the extent to which dialect vocabulary is truly being eroded, on a national level, is discussed by Upton and Widdowson (1999*). There was one ambitious enterprise between the great surveys of Ellis and the SED: Guy S. Lowman's survey of southern England (Kurath and Lowman 1973*), done in 1937–8 using a single informant at each of 56 locations (three in Sussex), had as its primary goal the establishment of a frame of reference for the interpretation of differences in the pronunciation of regional dialects in the eastern United States. The study does not state which places were visited, amazingly; but the three in Sussex were East Dean (near Eastbourne; informant Richard Alfred Fowler) and Wepham (informant James Brockhurst) in the 1930s, followed in the 1950s by Loxwood (Ernest Barnett, recorded by Henry Collins[6]).

[6] This information was published by Professor Wolfgang Viereck and pointed out to me by Dr Jonathan Roper.

For a descriptive piece on the modern dialect of Peasmarsh, including a detailed phonetic transcription, see Lodge (1984; Text 37). This work stands quite outside any dialectological tradition; in fact it has more in common with the detailed phonetic transcriptions of numerous languages which used to appear in the periodical *Le Maître phonétique*.

Modern dialect phenomena can rarely be shown conclusively to have systematic impact on place-names, but see Coates (1980a, C4) for an analysis of a clear modern dialect trend affecting where stress falls, apparently exclusively in place-names (also, all in C4, Barraud 1922, Leppard 1992b, 1993a,b, 1994a). An older case is suggested by Coates (1981, C4). For the pronunciation of local names in general, Hope (1882* (second edition 1883)) should be avoided if possible. Better information is buried in Forster (1980*), and the best in Mawer and Stenton (1929/30*). Of some slight interest, in an antiquarian way, are the pieces on distinctive local place-name pronunciations by Lower (1854b, C4), Sawyer (1887, C4) and 'An old-fashioned man' (1920/1933, C4); though there are errors in Sawyer's. 'An old-fashioned man''s piece contains material which I have not seen or heard vouched for elsewhere. Lower's article of 1861 (C6) is also an antiquarian and unsystematic compilation.[7]

There is, of course, a great deal of interest in dialect outside the scholarly and analytic literature, usually taking the form of short commentaries on lexis in books devoted to broader topics, such as the county in general, or the local history of a particular place. It often consists of unsystematic observations, and sometimes draws on published work like Parish's *Dictionary*. Text 19 has been chosen to represent this strand, being a snapshot of the vocabulary used in Burwash around 1900.

[7] Note the good short introduction to the question of Sussex dialect and its relation to local identity by Hare (1995, C2).

Chapter 3

A characterization of traditional spoken Sussex dialect

'. . . the rough, slurring speech of the Sussex man, with great broad vowels like pools in which the consonants drowned.'
(Sheila Kaye-Smith, *The ploughman's progress*, 1933)

This chapter consists of a register of the main features of the traditional spoken dialect of Sussex as recorded by the Survey of English Dialects in 1959 and published in *The linguistic atlas of England* (Orton and others 1978*), the *Atlas of English sounds* (Kolb and others 1979*), and other publications derving from this material. A small amount of information has been gathered from other sources and (more or less) silently added in. Precise information should be sought in the maps in these atlases, and in the basic data volumes of the Survey; the present description is a broad-brush account glossing over minor local variants or the absence of an expected form from some place. Nothing here is meant to suggest that Sussex has a dialect with features unique to itself. There are internal divisions and local and lexical variability, and more importantly there are features shared with adjacent counties.

In most ways, Sussex is a typical south-eastern dialect or set of dialects. Anderwald (2006*: 460) is not even able to point to major grammatical features which are exclusive to the south-east, let alone to Sussex. Accordingly, where nothing is said about some linguistic feature below, it can be inferred with reasonable confidence that dialect-speakers used a form similar to or identical with modern standard English spoken with the characteristic features of Received Pronunciation or another south-eastern type of accent.

The historical phonology of the medieval dialect, tracing the pronunciation as it developed from Old English, is presented systematically by Rubin (1951) and Kristensson (2001–2*), and readers interested in the development of the modern vernacular should compare their accounts with that presented in the publications of the Survey of English Dialects and in this chapter. Some early medieval features are mentioned also in McKinley (1988*: 15–18).

A greater amount of linguistic and phonetic technicality is required in this section than in the rest of Part One, and for the sake of precision it will not be avoided or fudged.

(a) PHONOLOGY (see Part Three, Section C4, for unmarked references)

Note the following conventions in this section about the use of different types of brackets.

- [Square brackets] enclose representations of actual pronunciation, given in the alphabet of the International Phonetic Association.
- /Slashes/ enclose representations of phonemic (phonologically distinctive) units.
- <Angled brackets> enclose spellings, whether of standard dictionary entries or of instances taken from real written texts.

These three notations should not be confused with each other.

In this subsection on phonology alone, I adopt the convention of citing individual lexical words in roman capital letters, but a set of lexical words sharing the feature under discussion is represented by a citation in **BOLDFACE** capitals derived from SED evidence. Compare for instance **CREEP** and SHEEP in the third sub-paragraph below, headed '/eː/'. **CREEP** means, in this context, 'that set of words having the same vowel as CREEP in late Middle English'. SHEEP means simply that word. It is customary in English dialectology to make the Middle English period (c.1100–1485) the reference-point. The words designating sets are linked to the standard designations for Modern English lexical sets introduced by John Wells (1982*: chapter 2), thus: **CREEP (*FLEECE*)**. Readers should note that the Sussex lexical sets are map-derived, and referenced to late Middle English (following SED), and are not in every case congruent with Wells's sets.

It cannot always be determined on the evidence available whether we are dealing with a regular reflex of an earlier pronunciation or an aberration. For instance, in Sussex words having the vowel of **BRUSH (*STRUT*)** are normally pronounced with [ʌ] or [ə], depending on the locality. According to the Survey, however, the word SLUSH is pronounced as if SLOSH at two localities. This could be taken as a separate (though no doubt related) word, relying on the existence of the verb TO SLOSH (AROUND), and not as an aberrant reflex of SLUSH. However, some other words in the **BRUSH** set also have pronunciations which rhyme with COSH, but not systematically, and not always the same words at the same sets of localities. The phenomenon is most noticeable, and most nearly systematic, at Goudhurst (Kent). We cannot always reach reasonably secure conclusions. Some words, such as CHEW, HICCUPING and PALM show remarkable and unexplained diversity over such a small area.

Readers are reminded that the following villages are treated in the Survey: Warnham (survey point 1), Harting (2), Sutton (3), Fletching (4), Horam (5) and Firle (6). North (1982b) surveyed additionally in Turners Hill (11), Rotherfield

(12), Robertsbridge (13), Bolney (14), Poynings (15), Washington (16) and Funtington (17).

As is usual in English dialectology, the vowels which the relevant lexical sets had in the Middle English period are taken as the points of reference. These are used as the paragraph headings in the following sections.

Middle English long vowels and diphthongs

/a:/ and potential homophones deriving from /ɛ:/

The vowel of **MAKE** ***(FACE)*** is usually as in south-eastern English generally, with some hints of London (or rather Crawley) [æi] at Turners Hill. There is almost no sign of the [**ɛə**] of Sussex literary dialect (if that is what is meant by <äa> or Cooper's <e'a> or Parish's <ea>), except at Horam and, varying with the monophthong [**ɛ**:], at Fletching, Rotherfield and Robertsbridge. [**ɛə**] was clearly a recessive phenomenon of eastern Sussex by the time of the Survey. The various ways in which the reflexes of /a:/ and /ai/ are maintained distinct from those of /i:/ are detailed in North (1984). Note however that Text 13c in Part Two suggests that these sets may not always have been kept apart.

/ɛ: + r/

In south Kent and east Sussex, SHEARS has developed in such a way as to rhyme with SHARES. In confirmation of this, the West Sussex writer Gaius Carley inversely writes <shears> for SHARES.

/e:/

Occasionally, a short vowel /i/ may be heard in **CREEP**, and this is general, though recessive, in SHEEP, WEEK and other words. In this small group of words, the feature is also general in the literary texts, which of course will tend to emphasize non-standard features perceived as typical of the dialect irrespective of their true frequency in everyday usage.

/i:/ and homophones deriving from other sources

The vowel of **LIGHT** ***(PRICE)*** is generally [ɔi] in the west of the county and [əi] in the east. This is broadly true also for **ICE**, **WHITE** and numerous other words with Middle English /i:/ also in the modern ***PRICE*** set; though Harting sometimes goes along with the eastern variant. The east of the county, represented by Horam, goes along with Appledore (Kent) in having /i:/ in MICE, regularly deriving from Old Kentish /y:/ through [e:].

/ai/ (and the /ei/ which merged with it)

This, the vowel of **FAINT** and **WEIGH** ***(FACE)***, falls together with /a:/ (see above), as is general in most of England.

/oi/

An older pronunciation of **BOIL (*CHOICE*)** with [ai] or the like, well recorded in early writings in and on the dialect, is virtually lost.

/ɛ:/, /ou/, and /ou + r/

The vowel of **LOAF, GROW (*GOAT*)** is usually [əu], but occasionally recessive [ɛu]. A variant [æu] is found variably at Firle. The literary spelling <oa> or <oä> for this phoneme (used also by Parish in the introduction to his Dictionary; Cooper generally uses <o'a>), if this means [oə], is not found reflected in the Survey; indeed, such a pronunciation is typical of e.g. Yorkshire and the East Midland counties, such as Lincolnshire (as [uə]), but Wright has it in the south and south-west in his day (1905*: 89). Cooper (under *staën* 'stone') also uses <aë>. The implications of this are not clear. It might be a misprint for <stoën> (but it is in the right alphabetical place) or he might have been thinking of the historically problematic pronunciation of the name of the Roman road *Stane Street* (/stein/) or the various Sussex place-names of the type *Steyne* (/sti:n/ in Brighton). FOUR has the diphthong normal in **LOAF, GROW** (again occasionally with [æu]), but with a retroflex-coloured offglide.

/o:/

The vowel of **MOON *(GOOSE)*** is generally slightly diphthongal in the west of the county, but short /u/ may be found in ROOF in the west and widespreadly in ROOTS.

/o: + r/, and other long back vowels before /r/

The vowels of FLOOR and DOOR are normally kept distinct, in a variety of different local renderings (LAE maps Ph145 and 146). Those of **YOUR *(FORCE)*** and **SURE *(CURE)*** collapse with each other, as in much of the South Country and increasingly in modern Received Pronunciation.

/u:/

The vowel of **MOUSE, PLOUGH *(MOUTH)***, is usually [ɛu], though [əu] may be heard especially at Firle. New monophthongal forms ([æ:]) are spreading outwards from London with the large towns as intermediate foci for their spread into the countryside (North 1985); thus, for instance, these forms are well in evidence at Harting and Poynings despite their being rather far from London; we may assume that the new forms have radiated secondarily from Portsmouth and Brighton respectively.

/eu/

The word EWE is pronounced with the vowel of **GO *(GOAT)*** through much of the county.

/au/

The vowel of **STRAW** ***(THOUGHT)*** is recessively diphthongal (with a schwa offglide) in a corridor from the Wash to the Sussex coast and the Isle of Wight.

Middle English short vowels

/a/

The vowel of **APPLE, BAG** etc. (***TRAP***) is variably [æ], especially in the west of Sussex and adjacent parts of Surrey, and universal in CATCH. Early-modern documents show spellings in <e> quite regularly, e.g. in the Rottingdean court books in the early 1600s one finds *thetche* 'thatch' and *errable* 'arable', and we still find *theching* in George White's diary of 1829 (16 November; Hubble 2003, D1.1, transcribes as *thecking*).

The vowel of **GRASS** ***(BATH)*** may be [æ:], especially in the south of the county. This is probably what is intended by Cooper's spelling of *can't*, namely <caunt>, a visual and actual rhyme for *aunt*.

The vowel of HALF is usually short /æ/, as also in much of Kent, with the <l> silent as in most other accents.

/e/

The vowel of KETTLE is regularly [ɛ] in the Survey, but in early inventories and the literary texts it was often /i/, which was widespread in southern England. This feature is found recessively for HEAD throughout Sussex, for READY at Sutton and Horam and in Surrey, for BREAD in mid-county, and it is noted in DEAD at Firle, CRESS at Sutton and THREAD at Warnham. In each case, the raised vowel is before an alveolar consonant. The lowering of /e/ before velar consonants, again well attested in the spelling <a> in early texts, e.g. in LEG, RECKON, is not found; such a lowering is also found in Texts 30b and 35b in YELLOW, presumably due to the back resonance of either the /l/ or of the historic backness of the vowel of the following syllable.

The vowel of HERRINGS is centralized to [ə] in Sussex, Kent and most of Surrey; in a poem (Text 33), W.G. Daish writes <purrish> for PERISH, presumably meaning ['pəriʃ]. The old couplet "To love and to cherish/ From Battle to Berrish" (i.e. Burwash) needs to be interpreted in the light of this. The Middle English sequence /er/ frequently merges with /ar/ in RP, yielding /ɑ:/, as the unadjusted spellings of *clerk* and *sergeant* indicate; this extends to other words in dialect, such as *sartin* in Texts 12a and 26, and *sarved* in Texts 13a and 15b.

An unusual /u/ is found for Middle English /e/ in BURIED in Firle and Sutton, and in BRISTLES in Firle and in mid-Kent.

/o/

The vowel of **CROSS, BROTH, COUGHING** ***(CLOTH)*** and QUARRY is normally long. The lengthening before a voiceless fricative shown by the first three of these is fairly widespread in the south-east, whilst the last, with lengthening before /r/, is a markedly characteristic of Sussex. The unrounding of /ɒ/ to [a], frequently met in the literary dialect and in early descriptions which may particularize it to the west of the county, was not recorded in the Survey, perhaps surprisingly when we consider all the authors with the pseudonym *Cladpole*, i.e. *clodpoll*. But the front phoneme /æ/ was noted in the semi-stressed second syllable of (SHEEP-)DOG at Fletching.

/u/

The stressed vowel of ONION is aberrantly /i/ in mid-county, but recessive even there. That of OVEN is found as [ɒ] in the east of the county in some words, but strikingly frequently at Goudhurst in Kent, just across the county boundary.

Other vowel phenomena

The county divides west/east in the pronunciation of the pronoun ONE as /wun/ or /wʌn/. The adjective is normally /wun/, with /wʌn/ often found in variation with it. ONCE is almost always /wuns/.

Roper (2007: 190, C3) draws attention to the frequent elision of unstressed vowels in the second syllable of initially-stressed trisyllables such as *regular* and *terrible*.

Post-Middle English consonantal phenomena

/r/

Words of the type **FURROW (subsumed into *LETTER*)**, i.e. with final /ə(r)/ for /əu/ after /r/, are generally monosyllabic, as is also the case with CARRY in much early writing from Sussex.

Preconsonantal and prepausal /r/ is regularly pronounced, usually as retroflex coloration of the preceding vowel (postalveolar pronunciations are found in the north of the region, adjoining Kent and Surrey). In realizations of the vowels of **HARE** ***(SQUARE)*****, CORN (*****NORTH)***, a schwa is sometimes present as the carrier of the retroflexion ([ɚ]). /r/ in other positions is normally postalveolar.

Few parts of England preserve the /r/ before voiceless fricatives, as in CURSING; Sussex, with Kent, is one of them. However, at Horam and Fletching /r/ is lost in FIRST, which is confirmed in a monumental inscription at not far distant Lindfield (Text 5f).

As in much of the south-west, the long retroflex-coloured schwa-vowel of **BIRD** ***(NURSE)*** [ɚ] is heard in GREAT. In unstressed position, an unetymological short version may be heard in **WINDOW (subsumed into *LETTER*)**, and also in CHILDREN: cf. also *Jan Cladpole's trip to* ***'Merricur***.

/l/

/l/ is generally dark (velarized) and vocalized in the rhyme of syllables (most generally in the west of the county), especially syllable-finally after a back vowel, and also where /l/ is syllabic. Where this is the case after a front vowel, the resultant diphthong may end in a dark offglide, as with /iu/ in **MEAL** ***(FLEECE)***. This diphthong may occur even where /l/ is retained. /l/ may be dark intervocalically. These features are shared with parts of Surrey, Kent and Essex; there is considerable lexical and geographical variability. In some circumstances, the loss of final /l/ may lead to the emergence of a new diphthongal phoneme, distinguishing HOLE from HOE (North 1988–90: 148).

/w/

Initial /w/ was rendered by /v/ in Hastings in the mid-nineteenth century, if Rock (1862) is to be credited. He believes that the passage he quotes may have been created as mockery of a stereotyped older way of speaking. No academic work of dialectology records this in Sussex. But there is evidence for sporadic rendering of /v/ by /w/, also found elsewhere in south-east England and East Anglia (Poussa 1995). /w/ and /v/ are occasionally exchanged in place-names (Mawer and Stenton 1929*: xxviii).

/j/

Postconsonantal /j/ is variably lost in **DEW** ***(GOOSE)***, especially after a fricative, as in SUIT; this loss appears most prevalent in the north of the county.

/h/

The north of the county is at the southern tip of a corridor in which initial /h/ may be retained, but even there /h/ is variably absent.

Initial fricative voicing and intervocalic development of /ð/

Recessive [v] for [f] is recorded in FURROW, and in words derived from it such as the technical term of ploughing VEERING OUT (North 1984–5: 52), principally in the south of the county (cf. the late-medieval Texts 3 and 4). Judging by Sussex place-name evidence it was once far more widespread (Mawer and Stenton 1929*: xxviii); it is still to be found in west Hampshire and westwards. The phonemic status of the change is unclear; vernacular OE in this area may have had no /f/ until this arrived in borrowed words. Other words with a modern standard initial voiceless fricative appear to retain that, except for some antiques in THREE at Harting (/ð/) and Fletching (/d/). This phenomenon is not to be confused with intervocalic lenition, as in *my* [v]*ather*, recorded as a systematic phenomenon in Peasmarsh by Lodge (1984: 72–3; Text 37).

Initial fricative voicing entered the standard language in 'grammatical' words such as THE, THIS, THAT, (AL)THOUGH. In eastern Sussex, this [ð] in its turn became [d], though it was recessive in Rottingdean by the early years of the twentieth century to the extent that one local shepherd could be referred to as *Disndat* because he stood out through using it (Bob Copper, in conversation). If the change had been completed in all positions in the word, it would have resulted in the phonemic collapse of /d/ and /ð/, though in fact it seems only to have resulted in the variable realization of /ð/. The feature is sometimes taken stereotypically as a pan-Sussex feature, probably because the most significant and widely-read dialect literature, that of Tim and Jim Cladpole, was created in the eastern area. A hint of its former wider spread may be gleaned from the anecdote told to Bob Copper by 'Jim' Swain of Angmering (Copper 1973*: 93), where the generation gap between two characters is shown by the systematic use or non-use of /d/ in *the*, etc. But perhaps the connotations of this are of old age alone, and are not intended to be faithful to place of origin.

Interestingly, James Richards (letter to Capt. Fuller, 18/04/1939), notes a different intervocalic development for [ð]; he says: 'a lot of my old acquaintances would say "farver" and "muvver" and "bruvver" . . . But D was more common among the sounds I heard.' On the face of it, this appears to be a local phenomenon independent of the recent spread into the south-eastern counties of the analogous Cockney phenomenon.

Intervocalic /t/

In **BUTTER**, /t/ is regularly [t], but an early indication of the modern spread of the glottal stop is found at Fletching. The Survey does not record any [d] in this word. This is perhaps surprising, in view of the universal *liddle* for *little* in the literary dialect, and the nickname of the musician *Rabbidy* Baxter. These are examples of the systematic lenition noted from Peasmarsh by Lodge (1984).

Clusters of /s + C/

Metathesis of /sp/ is widespread in **WASP**, and that of /sk/ is notably found in ASK in some texts; but note that the both of these can be found even in Old English.

(b) MORPHOLOGY (see Part Three, Section C5, for unmarked references)

The verb and auxiliary TO BE is characteristically inflected in the present tense by forms such as *(I/you (singular)/she/they) be*, both in affirmative and contradictory uses. *She be*, perhaps contrary to the popular stereotype, is quite restricted, being often found otherwise only on the Isle of Wight and in a patch of the south Midlands with a tongue out to Dorset. These forms persist also where other dialects have contracted forms such as *I'm, she's*, and in question-forms (*be I?* etc.). The negative form *ben't/bain't* is characteristic of the east of the county, whilst the more widespread *ain't/en't* is found in the west. There are some signs that the forms in *b-* were once more widespread. In similar fashion, the inverted form is usually *ben't* (*I* etc.), with *en't* (*I* etc.) featuring in the far west, especially in tag-questions; in alternative-questions, the *b-* forms are general. The first-person past-tense form of TO BE is *(I) were* in the west of the county, and *(she) were* is found sporadically; in the plural, for all persons, *was* is practically universal.

As for the auxiliary TO DO, the third-person singular present tense form without *-s*, *(he) do*, is restricted to western Sussex, and is variable, whilst the inverted *do he?* is apparently stable in the same area. This bare-stem form is also general in the negative *he don't.*

The auxiliary TO HAVE has certain forms which are almost unique to Sussex (there are outliers in the south Midlands and Wiltshire). We find the present-tense negative form *(I/he) hen't*, but under pressure from a range of other non-standard forms. HAVE is usually absent, as over most of the South Country, in *(have) got*, in contexts eliciting a response anaphoric to the lexical verb TO HAVE.

There are non-standard distributions of past-tense forms; TO COME generally – and increasingly – has *come* (occasionally also *comed* in the Texts in Part Two), whilst TO CATCH and TO GROW are widely conjugated weak, as *catched* and *growed.* -EN participles may be absent, with the past-tense form doing duty for the participle, as in *took* for *taken*. Whilst it does not feature in the SED's results, we should note here the unofficial county motto of Sussex, and its most recognizable dialect stereotype: 'We wunt be druv', i.e. 'drove', for 'driven', which is often quoted in writings about Sussex, and which I have seen inscribed on a piggy-bank (cf. Image 13 below). The forms of LAY and LIE are merged in literary material, with forms historically appropriate to LAY frequently appearing for those of LIE.

A narrative first-person present-tense form, or habitual-aspect form, in *-s* is sometimes found in literary material or dictionary example-material (*'I likes to have . . .'*).

The pronoun system is practically standard, though the extreme east of the range of *en* as the third-person object form (Ihalainen 1985*), at least when masculine, enters the west of the county. *We* as direct-object form is practically obsolete. The possessive case of the third-person masculine personal pronoun is *he's* in the south of the county in the Survey (and to some extent in Surrey), and generally in the literary dialect. The second-person singular predicative possessive pronoun may be *yourn*, the third feminine *hern*, and the third plural *theirn*, with signs of instability in all these three. The third-person reflexive is widely *hissel(f)*. The distal demonstrative determiner, standardly *those*, is *they* in the west of the county, as is the case widely but recessively in the South Country, and *them* also occurs in this function (e.g. Parish 1875: 6, C6). Cliticization of *it*, mainly before forms of BE, is found in the literary material and also the Survey (Upton, Parry, and Widdowson 1994*: 487) in the response to question IX.9.2 *(whose 't is)*.

George White's diary (1829, D1.1) has frequent lack of the genitive *-(')s* in preposed noun phrases, e.g. *Mr. Russell Mill, with uncle poney*, but it is not clear whether this is just idiosyncratic.

(c) SYNTAX (see Part Three, Section C5, for unmarked references)

The syntax of the dialect is identical to that of the standard in most respects; they are both typical south-eastern English varieties. Most of the county, as also recessively further west, may omit the subject relative pronoun to form 'contact clauses' (*There was a woman lived in this cottage.*). Unique to Sussex and the adjacent village of Appledore in Kent is the use of postpositional pied-piping in *who to* in the object complement of TO WONDER (*I wonder who to I shall give it*), instead of the more widely-used alternatives: strict pied-piping or preposition-stranding (see also Poussa 1996). (*Pied-piping* is a facetious linguistic technical term for the phenomenon of moving the preposition to the front of its clause in pursuit of a *wh*-word, as in *With whom should I be having this discussion?*, as compared with *Who(m) should I be having this discussion with?*, where the preposition is left or stranded at the end of the clause. In the Sussex case, unusually, the 'pied-piped' preposition finishes up after the pronoun.) Sussex participates in the extreme southern South-Country use of the complementizer FOR TO, recessive everywhere east of the Atlantic under pressure from TO. The direct object pronoun precedes the indirect object pronoun, as in *give it me*, in Kent and Sussex.

Pleonastic (periphrastic) DO is found unaccented in declarative clauses in some dialect material, as are such other widespread regional syntactic features as multiple negation and the use of as as a personal relative pronoun. Some texts (e.g. George White's diary of 1829) have the expression *to go to X-ing* 'to do some X-ing' ('I went to picken up tatres'), but where a prepositional phrase with to intervenes, we find *the a-X-ing* form of the participle ('Father went down to Mr. Aylwin a hog ringen').

The word *jonnick*, reported by Hall (1957, C6/C8) as meaning (1) 'fortunate, pleasant', (2) 'staunch', appears to be used rather like a negative polarity item, i.e. one which always co-occurs with a negative element (like *a clue* in *I haven't got a clue*), in the phrase *not jonnick*, meaning something like 'wrong or unpleasant in either nature or consequences' (cf. Wright 1898–1905*, under *jannick*).

(d) LEXIS (see Part Three, Section C6)

We can identify from the Survey some relatively local words; by which I mean words not shared with all immediately adjacent areas, even if they are additionally found further afield. In farming vocabulary, we note TROUGH for 'crib' (under pressure from MANGER), POUND for 'pigsty' (shared with mid-Kent), COO and COVE for 'dovecote' (restricted to Sussex and adjacent parts of Kent and Surrey; see North (1988)), ROD for 'cart-shaft', TO SHELVE in the east of the county and mid-Kent for 'to tip up' (of a cart).

There is an interesting relation between the distribution of words for parts of the plough and the distribution of the Kent or turnwrest plough, which was known in eastern parts of Sussex as far west as Bolney (North 1984–5). The swingletree was known as the BILLET in Rotherfield and Robertsbridge, as almost universally in Kent. Hedges are generally LAID, but occasionally PLASHED. KINDLING is so called in the west; FAGGOTS is the term more widely used in the east. HENS are normally so called in the east, as in Kent, but tend to be called CHICKENS by preference in the west. A snack is generally BAIT in the east and Romney Marsh. In the construction industry, thatch-pegs are called SPARS.

'Bindweed' is BEAR-BIND in the east and in much of Kent, and 'goose-grass' is CLIVER(S). Peas are found in SHUCKS, as in Hampshire and Surrey. 'Ants' are generally EMMETS, with signs of this term being in retreat. In the house, you WET tea, as in the South Country generally, though TO BREW is known; you are left with the GROUTS in the pot. SOMEWHAT for 'something' is under pressure in most of the South and Midlands, but was noted at Harting, Fletching and Horam. The centre of the county is one of the few zones in England where a bogey-man is called a BLACK-MAN.[8] You are probably AFRAID of him; there is no trace of the FROUGHTENED/

[8] Whether this has anything to do with the local prevalence of the surname *Blackman* is a matter for speculation.

FROUDEN found occasionally in Sussex dictionaries and reminiscences. The use of the historically transitive verb TO LAY for intransitive TO LIE (i.e. DOWN) is general.

These are findings principally derived from the Survey of English Dialects and its cartographical incarnation the *Linguistic atlas of England*, and are only intended as a sample. For many other lexical localisms, dialect dictionaries should be consulted (see Part Three, Section C, the main Sussex bibliography).

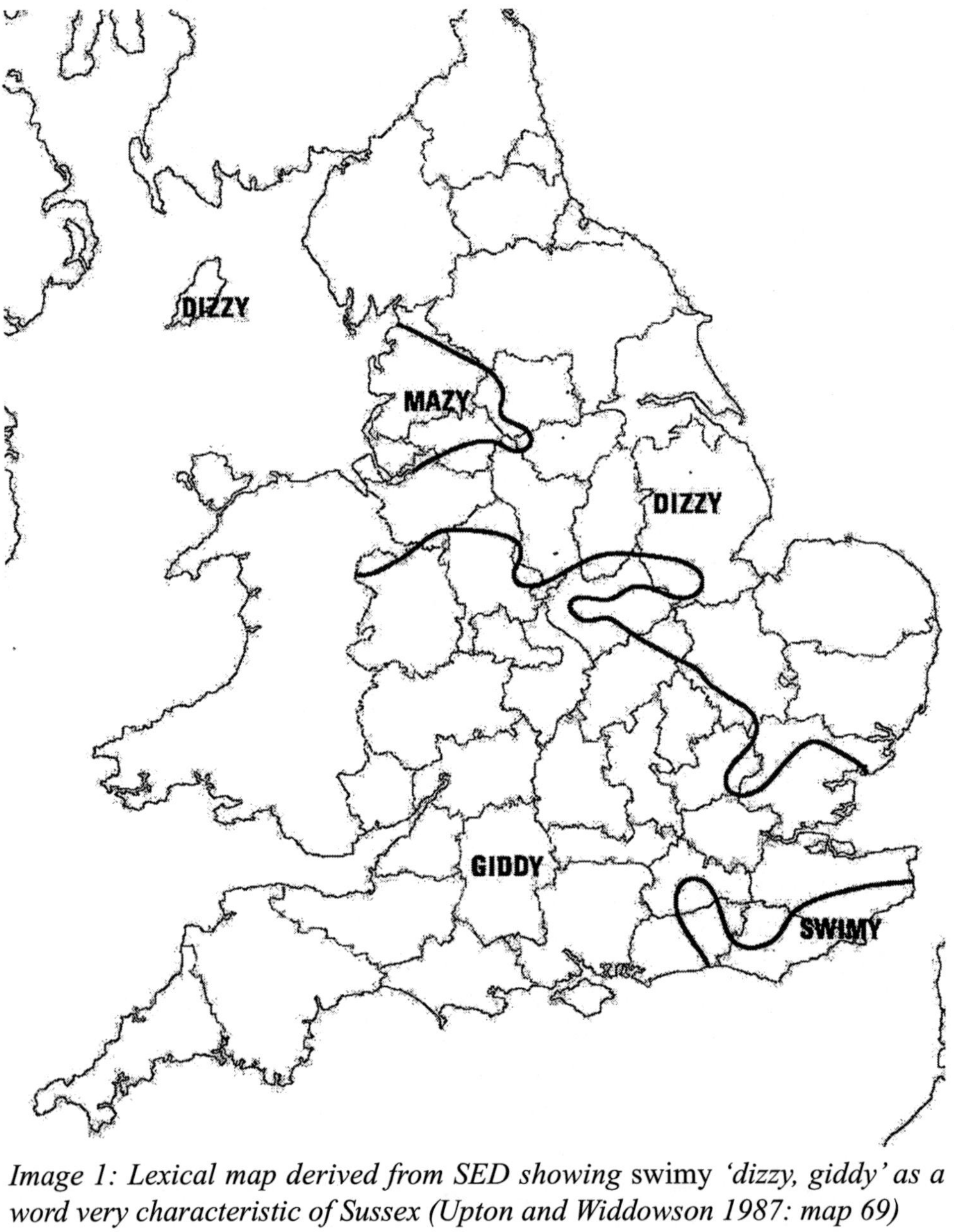

Image 1: Lexical map derived from SED showing swimy *'dizzy, giddy' as a word very characteristic of Sussex (Upton and Widdowson 1987: map 69)*

(e) SUMMING-UP

A commentator who declares a particular dialect or accent to be dead invites a certain sort of critical rejoinder, namely that this is to falsely regard an accent or dialect as an all-or-nothing package and that, really, the regional speech has evolved, and taken colours from other accents and dialects. Nevertheless, it is appropriate, with due caution (because one can still hear some older speakers who pronounce preconsonantal and prepausal /r/, or certain /r/-coloured vowels – perhaps the single most distinctive non-standard phonological survival), to say that the collection of features representing spoken Sussex dialect in the catalogue above has practically died out and is no longer being transmitted by native speakers to their children; or that if it is, the children are no longer sustaining it except for features which coincide with those of other influential southern accents such as [ɔi] in **LIGHT** and velarized or vocalized [l].[9]

A major factor in this is demographic discontinuity. It is not just a matter of the local accent evolving by a kind of linguistic natural selection; a very significant proportion of the population of Sussex was born elsewhere and has in-migrated, bringing a wide range of other varieties with it. This has helped to marginalize further a variety which was already on the way to shedding its most distinctive characteristics through the familiar pressures of education and proximity to London. Already in census year 1851 in Brighton, just ten years after the opening of the railway from London, only 39.7 per cent of railway workers (admittedly a more than usually mobile group) were born in Sussex, let alone in Brighton (Sheppard 2001*: 195), and the 20th-century county-wide trend of in-migration, especially for retirement, is too well known to need further comment. These newcomers have not adapted their own usage to the speech that they found in place. We shall return to this matter in Chapter 5.

[9] For what it is worth, five or six of the nine people on the streets of Brighton interviewed by Richard Gurner of the *Argus* (12/01/2010) deny or doubt the existence of a specifically Sussex accent.

Chapter 4

Sussex writing and the county's dialect literature

Kent is rather well represented by texts surviving from the Old English period (before 1100–25 or so), especially from the ninth century, and there is a good deal of academic literature about them (see Part Three, Bibliography, Section B: Kent). The supply of local texts tails off noticeably during the Middle English period (1100–1485 or so). But unlike Kent, Sussex had no vigorous literate archiepiscopal court; and, unlike Wessex, for much of Anglo-Saxon times, no independent royal court. Anglo-Saxon charters relating to Sussex cannot therefore be relied upon to furnish examples of truly Sussex usage (hence the rather reticent numbering of Text 0a in Part Two) – and few in any case have boundary clauses in English, the only place where English is likely to be found in such documents. Those that were known by the mid-twentieth century were collected and analysed by Barker (1947–9*).

The charter-boundaries of some of these Sussex documents are, however, potential sources of genuinely local linguistic information, because they are derived from actual surveys taken locally, though such documents cannot be guaranteed to represent local dialect since they may have been copied in other areas or in central royal scriptoria, soon after drafting or even centuries later. When eventually published, the study by Peter R. Kitson on the language of such charter-boundaries is likely to improve very substantially the precision of our knowledge of the grammar and vocabulary of the Old English of Sussex, especially as regards the detailed geographical distribution of structures and words.

To the best of my knowledge, only one extant Anglo-Saxon document has been explicitly proposed as a product of Sussex: a contemporary land-grant by Oslac, dux of the South Saxons dated 780 C.E. 'in a curiously "provincial" script', WSRO MS. Cap. I/17/2, no. 1334 in Birch's *Cartularium saxonicum* and Selsey charter no. 11 (Sawyer no. 1184; the quote is taken from the 'Electronic Sawyer', now on the 'Kemble' web-site, www.trin.cam.ac.uk/kemble/; Kelly 1998*: no. 11). The proposal was made by Chadwick (1924*: 62), but he may have been resting on Birch (1892*), which I have not seen. Oslac's land-grant contains names in Old English but no connected text; the <io> in *Siolesaei* 'Selsey' is dialectally Kentish, which might include Sussex, and that is all we have to go on. Certain Selsey charters do contain boundary clauses written in Old English (Kelly 1998*: nos 4, 17, 20 and 21). It might have seemed more appropriate to include one of these in place of Text 0a in Part

Two. However, the MS. written before the Conquest, no. 4, is a forgery written in West Saxon dialect, and the other three are medieval copies; none of them carries any linguistic suggestion of a distinctively local original drafting, and they have unclarities within their brief spans.

The rarity of such documents is compensated for to some extent by the wealth of place-names coined in English during the Anglo-Saxon period, and the introduction to Mawer and Stenton's *The place-names of Sussex* (1929*: xiv-xvi, xxi-xxii, xxvii-xix) points to some possible phonological and lexical features from very early in that period, and one of these is exemplified in Text 0b, which is not truly a 'text' like all the others.

As noted in Chapter 1, the absence of an early large class of documents attributable to local learned and bureaucratic centres means that the bulk of the hard evidence for medieval Sussex English phonology is buried in what can be inferred from place-names and local personal names recorded for the most part in the Middle Ages (Löfvenberg 1942*; Rubin 1951, C4; Kristensson 2001–2*). Rubin gives a list of efforts prior to his own to characterize the local Middle English dialect (1951: 7-8, C4), pointing out that previous scholars had used only poorly-localized literary texts[10]). This is why he makes careful use of the evidence in legal and administrative documents produced locally, such as the Assize Rolls and Subsidy Rolls, with their wealth of place- and personal names in what can be presumed to be authentically local forms, as opposed to interpretations by central government clerks. A second substantial phonological survey on the same basis, this time covering the whole of southern England, is that by Kristensson (2001-2*).

The name-lists provided by these types of document are all very well, but we find that practically no connected text in English which can be confidently ascribed to medieval Sussex has survived. The best candidate is the letter written from besieged Pevensey Castle by John Pelham to the Duke of Northumberland in 1399 (Walker 1991*: 75–9). The original is lost; the text that has come down to us is an eighteenth-century transcript, but this looks faithful, and on that basis it is included in Part Two as Text 1. A handful of unpublished Ancient Petitions of the fifteenth century probably originating in Sussex are written in English (e.g. TNA SC 8/1260/1280 (Arundel, 1433)), but these have not been systematically investigated; the Arundel document is written in the London chancery standard language of the period and shows no

[10] Cf. footnote 5, repeated here. It has been suggested that at least one MS. of *Piers Plowman*, A-text (Bodleian MS. Rawlinson Poetry 137), has Sussex origins (Horobin 2005* and references there). A case has also been made for the single-manuscript *Canticum de creatione* (Oxford, Bodleian Library, formerly Trinity College MS. 57; *LALME* LP 5850), which bears the date 1375, and the MS. may have been written around 1400 (Murdoch and Tasioulas 2002*; Text 2 in Part Two).

clear imprint of Sussex. A few local documents begin to appear in the record from about 1450 onwards, for example the Cowfold churchwardens' accounts (Text 4), and Sir John Scott's comments on the account rolls of the manor of Mote, in Iden near Rye (in Gardiner and Whittick, forthcoming*).

Other documents are mentioned in the only extensive source of analysed information about the later Middle English period (defined for the purpose of the work as c.1350–1460/1): the justly celebrated *Linguistic atlas of late Middle English* (*LALME*; McIntosh and others 1986*; and cf. also Samuels 1971*: 11-12 and fn. 52). In this are analysed, for three-hundred-odd dialect-sensitive features, a small number of texts known to be from Sussex, and some assigned to Sussex on the methodological grounds explained in volume 1 (the method of 'best fit'). These texts include both literary ones (in the broadest sense) and legal or administrative ones (also in the broadest sense), and also some personal letters. A detailed dialect profile of each text is presented in *LALME* (vol. 3), and the data for sixty-two of the features are also mapped (vol. 2). On the basis of the profile, or from external knowledge, the following are assigned to Sussex:

- *Canticum de Creatione* (Text 2 in this book; see footnote 5)
- William Langland, *Piers Plowman*, the A-version (see footnote 5: Oxford: Bodleian Library MS. Rawl. poet. 137)
- *Dialogue between Saint Bernard and the Virgin (2)* (about 1400?; Oxford, Bodleian Library, MS. Trinity College 57)
- *South English Legendary: St. Brendan* (about 1400?; Oxford, Bodleian Library, MS. Trinity College 57)
- *Life of Saint Alexis (2)* (about 1400?; Oxford, Bodleian Library, MS. Trinity College 57)
- Will of William Finch (1443)
- The churchwardens' accounts for the parish of Cowfold, Sussex (Text 4 in this book) mentioned above
- Letters of John Dycons and Richard Cely (1472-88; some of Cely's correspondents are said to display London features but has 'various forms to be associated rather with Kent, Sussex, and Surrey')

Dating from just outside the Middle English period as usually understood are:

- The incipit of 'Wite thou wel . . .' (about 1500?; Oxford, Bodleian Library, MS. Douce 84)
- Translation of William of Wadington's *Manuel de Pechiez* (about 1500?; Cambridge, St John's College MS. G.30 (197))

Inclusion in this list means that at least one extant MS. of the work in question has been identified in *LALME* as (probably) originating in Sussex. Notice that three of the literary texts are derived from a single manuscript in the Bodleian Library. Full bibliographical details of published editions of these works are given in *LALME*, and also in the Hyperbibliography of the online *Middle English dictionary*.[11] The *LALME* list also includes the four published volumes of Sussex wills mentioned in Part Three, Section D2b below.

From the Early Modern English period, i.e. after that which is covered by *LALME*, small numbers of dialect phenomena may be noted in local texts, e.g. churchwardens' presentments, tradesmen's accounts, probate inventories, sale catalogues and monumental inscriptions. No systematic study of the language of these in Sussex has ever been done, however, though glossaries of inventories in other counties have been published. A brief indicative list of published inventories and some indications about inscriptions are given in Section D of the bibliography in Part Three of this book; Texts 4, 5a-f, 6 and 8a-b in Part Two illustrate the categories in question. As we noted in Chapter One, literary evidence from the Early Modern period is minimal, being confined to a few lexical peculiarities in the writings of such local authors as Sackville and Borde.

Before about 1785, our view of what Sussex dialect was like is constrained by a distinct paucity of direct evidence in the form of connected texts, by the fact that much of the information available takes the form of word-lists and name-evidence rather than connected texts, and by the fact that such evidence as exists is filtered, to a frustrating degree, through other varieties of English. Of the literature of the very earliest times, only the Old English *Proverbs of Alfred* have been attributed to Sussex with any confidence (Arngart 1942*), but this attribution may be misleading because the work only exists in copies made outside the county, which therefore give, at best, seven-veiled hints about what the county's pre-Conquest dialect was like.

As we have seen, a case has been made that a few Middle English literary texts (or at least certain manuscripts of them) can be attributed to Sussex, including one manuscript of Langland's poem *Piers Plowman* and an anonymous translation of the *Canticum de creatione* or life of Adam and Eve (see footnotes 5 and 10 above). Whilst some late medieval Sussex documents, literary and administrative, are analysed for their dialect features in *LALME*, quite a few such works of the period can already be properly described as in standard legal (chancery) English with at best a few concessions to local usage.

The distance between chancery English and the non-Kentish south-eastern dialects in general was relatively small, and the linguistic symbolization of administrative centralization must have proceeded without much pain. One of

[11] quod.lib.umich.edu/cgi/m/mec/hyp-idx?type=lalme&size=First+100&q1=Sussex

the administrative texts analysed is the churchwardens' accounts and parish inventory book of Cowfold (Otter 1849; Text 4), which squeezes into *LALME* by virtue of the date of its first entry (1460). It is written in a rare old amalgam of English and desperate Latin, of the type analysed and explained by Wright (1995*). The English shows marked dialect features. ('It[em]. pro faciende de cleper de campanis . . . Water Dunstall yowthe to my master . . . It[em]. for a loke at ostiam de ecclesie . . .') This document stands out for dialect-hunters, because later inventories (see Part 3, Section D) show a diminishing regional colour except in the words used for domestic objects.

A faint glimpse of the dialect of the sixteenth century can be obtained from a look at the works of the grammarian and spelling reformer William Bullokar, now known to have been a Sussex man (Danielsson and Alston 1966*: x ff.). Dobson (1957*) originally thought the linguistic evidence of his vocabulary and rhymes pointed to East Anglian origin, and there is undeniably a case for this to be made on linguistic as opposed to biographical criteria. But in the second edition of his *English pronunciation, 1500–1700* (1968*), Dobson concedes the accuracy of Danielsson and Alston's demonstration, and notes that Bullokar does use dialectal words known to be or have been in use in Sussex, though few if any which are unique to Sussex: e.g. *unfitty* 'unfit', *heal* 'to cover'; and shows evidence of a disyllabic pronunciation of such words as *down, brown*, which is known also from documents emanating from Billingshurst. This last feature was noted by Hilda Hulme in her review of the first edition of Dobson's book (*Essays in Criticism* 8 (1958*), 422–8, esp. 426–7); regrettably, and so far as I know, Hulme never published these observations more systematically. Interestingly, a disyllabic pronunciation of the diphthongs in *wine* and *boy* is suggested in Bob Copper's anecdotes of George Attrill from Fittleworth, six miles from Billingshurst (Copper 1973*: 75–82).

The textual evidence for the modern dialect begins to be available in significant quantities from about 1785 onwards. The key authors are now presented chronologically.

John Burgess (D1.1, F)

Of the modern printed literature, nothing specific to Sussex appears in Alston's *Bibliography of the English language from the invention of printing to the year 1800*, vol. 9, the volume devoted to dialect writings (Alston 1971*). In fact, it is only relatively recently that the complete writings of John Burgess of Ditchling, General Baptist republican leatherdresser and glover, have become available to a wider audience. Their importance for local and family history has long been recognized, but until now their linguistic value has not been properly understood.

Burgess kept a diary during 1785–90 until the illness that pushed an already poor man to the verge of ruin (see Text 10a), and after emigrating to America in 1794 he sent letters home, some of which have been preserved (1794–1819; see Texts 10b-c). Both have now been conveniently published by his descendant Donald F. Burgess (1989, D1.1). In both the diary and the letters, his grasp of the principles of spelling – such as consistency – is precarious; one of the more constant features is his use of *whright* for *write*. But, when this is allowed for, there is an interesting residue of genuine dialect features which are in line with characteristics noted by later writers.

There is clear evidence of local pronunciation (e.g. *arn* 'earn', *kittle* 'kettle', *wick* 'week', *spile* 'spoil', *sence* 'since'), of local grammar (e.g. *beleft* 'believed', *we was*, *I are not spaking, no danger of been* [i.e. *being*] *pressed*), and of local vocabulary (e.g. *spray wood* 'brushwood', *flaw* 'flay', *rigrels* 'sand-eels'). It should be added that some of his non-standard grammar and diction are biblical rather than dialectal, e.g. his occasional use of third-person singular present-tense forms in *-eth*, which by this time was stone dead in the casual speech of the south.

Burgess is of the greatest interest as an untutored writer who wrote dialect naturally; he applied his knowledge of the principles of writing to English as he spoke it, and not to the rising Standard English of the schoolroom and of polite society. He did not write in dialect because he chose to do so, but because it was all that came naturally. (For the schoolroom attitude to English at this period in Lewes, see Brent 1993*: 97–8.) Burgess's written dialect is closer to the vernacular than that of James Nye (see below), the only other writer known to me of comparable background, education and achievement. It is provoking, but fully understandable in the historical context, that some of these earliest and the most authentic writings in Sussex dialect emanated from New York State. One wonders how many other diaries and letters of this period written by people of John Burgess's condition remain in archives and in personal collections, their potential significance for the history of the language not grasped. A recent appeal by Barbara Allen has produced some further material which may in time be published.

Richard Lower and Mark Antony Lower (D1.2, F)

The earliest author to write connected prose in Sussex dialect intentionally (i.e. consciously choosing not to write in Standard English) began to do so in the 1830s, and thereby became the 'father' of Sussex dialect literature. Writing as 'Tim Cladpole', he was Richard Lower (1782–1865), a schoolmaster at Muddles Green, Chiddingly, son of a barge-owner. His two sixpenny Cladpole pamphlets, *Tom Cladpole's jurney to Lunnun* and *Jan Cladpole's trip to*

Image 2: The cover of a twentieth-century Farncombe reprint of the Trip to 'Merricur

'Merricur, are repeatedly said to have sold 20,000 or more copies (see e.g. Evans 1933*: 182). Lower's own note in his book *Stray leaves from an old tree* (1862) states that he had 18,000 copies of the *Jurney to Lunnun* printed, all told, and that some thousands more bootleg copies were in circulation (see Text 12a). I wonder what became of them all, for even some of the later, posthumous, reprints produced by Farncombe's of Lewes are expensive today, and I have never seen a first edition of the *Jurney to Lunnun*. His success may have carried a cost, for according to his obituary notice in the *Gentleman's Magazine* (1865, vol. 2: 792) his satirical tone about working-class life did not always go down too well with his readership, who were largely of that stock.

These verses were the first, and remain the most extended, original writing in Sussex dialect. Tales about journeys made by rustics to far-flung places, especially London, fit into an established genre which, as far as English dialects are concerned, can be traced back as far as the anonymous seventeenth-century verses commonly known as the *Visit of a Zummerzet man to London*

Image 3: Henry Burstow, in the frontispiece of his book (1911)

(printed by J.O. Halliwell in 1843* from MS. Bodley Ashmole 36, ff. 112–3). I do not know whether Lower would have been aware of the existence of this manuscript; I doubt it. A more immediate inspiration may have been John White Masters' Kentish epic *Dick and Sal at Canterbury Fair* (B, Kent (b)), which dates from the early nineteenth century. Lower's verses were the staple of the Sussex dialect 'industry' for a century.

A major claim to fame of the bellringer and folk-singer Henry Burstow of Horsham, and of James Richards (of whom more below), was their being able to recite large portions of the Cladpole epics from memory. Burstow was especially proud of his achievement; they were the longest items in his repertoire of over 400 (Burstow 1911: 107, C8).

Richard Lower's son Mark Antony (1813–76) was a prominent gentleman-scholar and antiquary, who wrote a Sussex dialect version of the Song of Solomon (see Text 13b) for Prince Louis-Lucien Bonaparte's national dialect survey. It is not known whether he consulted his father about the project. (Frederick Sawyer, in 1884b, C2, called Richard the *uncle* of Mark Antony; the original *Dictionary of national biography*, vol. 12, 204, has it right, as Richard's dedication of *Stray leaves from an old tree* to his son makes clear.)

In his version of the Song of Solomon, the younger Lower was rather anxious to preserve features of local speech already obsolescent or dead in his own day, whilst Bonaparte – being a linguist rather than an

Image 4: Mark Antony Lower, by H. Weir (by kind permission of the Sussex Archaeological Society, Barbican House Museum, Lewes)

antiquary – was concerned to record the dialect as it really was, warts and all, in 1859. Godman (1961, C3) also noted this strategic difference. The correspondence between them reveals the effect that Bonaparte's restraining hand has had on the final version of Lower's text. Lower also put into print, in his *Contributions to literature* . . . , some passages with a greater or lesser dialect colour told to him by others, and the true author is not always discoverable (see Texts 13a, 13c).

*John Mason Neal*e (D1.2, F)

John Mason Neale (1818–66), Anglican priest and hymn-writer, a leading light in the Oxford Movement, was a man of wide linguistic abilities and interests. He took an active interest in Sussex dialect on his appointment as warden of Sackville College, East Grinstead, and became, as recently shown by Michael J. Leppard, 'the first writer of [prose] fiction consciously to employ Sussex dialect' (but see James Hewlett in 'Writers of standard English' below).

He wrote two short stories with sparse dialect features, and left other traces of his interest in published and unpublished work (Leppard (MS.); Text 11).

Image 5: Dr John Mason Neale (public domain image)

James Nye and Michael Blann (D1.1, F)

The working man James Nye (1822–92) of Ashcombe near Lewes compiled a chronicle of his life, entitled 'A small account of my travels through the willderness', in about 1860, and continued it with occasional entries in diary form till 1888. This sometimes harrowing personal and spiritual autobiography of a poor man with a small amount of hard-won education is written in regionally-coloured English with totally idiosyncratic spelling and punctuation and no concession to any rules of paragraphing. It was edited for publication by Vic Gammon in c.1981 in a normalized form, regrettably reducing the usefulness of his booklet for those interested in dialect; Text 14a reproduces part of the original.

In the present connection, its main interest is that it is the only extensive work (bar that of Burgess) written in something close to Sussex vernacular by a person not knowing in detail that that was what he was doing; i.e. he did not choose to write a text coloured in this way, though he was clearly aware in a general sense of the lack of education that his writing demonstrated, since he asks his readers' pity for it. The other writers, Richard Lower, Mark Antony Lower, even James Richards, G.D. Martineau, Amy Sawyer, and so on, were all more thoroughly educated and wrote dialect in addition to works in standard English. They were writing in dialect consciously when they did so, therefore, and with some specific purpose in mind, unlike Nye, who bares his soul in the most natural means of expression available to him. Nye also wrote fifty-odd simple poems with no striking local colour (see Text 14b), and some biblical pieces set to music. Most of these remain unpublished; the MSS. are held by the Sussex Archaeological Society.

The songs of the shepherd Michael Blann (1843–1933), collected and published by Colin Andrews (1979), are, like Nye's work, unconscious in their use of a small amount of dialect. (Blann's manuscript notebook is in Worthing public library; one song is reproduced as Text 20a.) The same is true of James 'Brasser' Copper's transcriptions (Texts 20b, 20c, from a manuscript in private hands, some published in a normalized form by the Copper family (1995, D1.1)).

James Richards (D1.2, F)

The later Victorian years and the first quarter of the twentieth century were a fallow period before the last crop of dialect writings sprouted on Sussex's thin soils. The most significant author of the subsequent period, James Richards (1866–1949), was born of working-class parents in Hailsham, and, after a brief stay in Australia, lived most of his life in other furrin' parts, viz. Tunbridge

Wells, where he worked, in spite of his chronic tendency to bronchitis, as a photographer, preacher and Labour Party activist.

After Burgess and Nye, he has the best claim to authenticity of any Sussex dialect author, as well as supplying the bulk (computed by number of items) of the county's published literature. He wrote his first, and now lost, dialect work for the newsletter of the Tunbridge Wells Labour Party in the late 1920s, already aged 60, and contributed a piece in 'Kentish' dialect about the Town Hall to Dick Baker's *Guide to Tunbridge Wells* in around 1934, as well as printing and publishing the whole *Guide*. (I suspect, but cannot prove, that 'Dick Baker' was one of Richards's several pseudonyms.)

He used the name by which he is widely known, 'Jim Cladpole', as a tribute to the earlier work of Richard Lower, who wrote as 'Tim Cladpole'. His talent had come to light through his ability to recite large chunks of Lower's verses by heart (letter to Capt. A.W.F. Fuller, 07/04/1939; this MS. letter and the others referred to in the main bibliography are in the care of Sussex Archaeological Society ('Cladpole' box)).

He was a Methodist lay preacher ('evangelist', as it says on his marriage certificate, revealing that he regarded this as his main occupation). After publishing a few attempts at secular verse in his early sixties (1927–30), he wrote a now-forgotten tract in standard English called *The carpenter. Glimpses at the lives of Joseph of Nazareth and of Jesus,* and then harnessed his dialect talent to his religious convictions.

Image 6: James Richards in about 1938 in Sussex persona; image in the Sussex Express, *26/11/1999 (ultimate source unknown)*

By far the greater part of his work from 1934 onwards consists of translations of familiar passages of the Bible; his rendering of Psalm 23 (Text 25c) is now well known. Much other dialect literature is of this biblical kind. The extent of Biblical literature in dialectal English may be gauged from entries 345–67 in Eugene A. Nida's edited collection (second edition 1972*); well-known writers in this genre include the Devonian Henry Baird and the Yorkshireman Kit Calvert. In addition to his strictly biblical material, Richards composed a brief homespun sermon on *De lilies of de fills* (1935).

Richards printed and published his own work, the most productive period being 1934–8, until failing health and eyesight, and the effort of producing his large anthology, *Bits from de Old Book* (see Text 25e), dried up his flow in 1938–9. The labour he undertook in pursuit of his hobby and in the face of his infirmities may be grasped by comparing the various 'editions' or printings in which some of his works appeared. There are differences, for instance, between the two editions of *De sermons of Amos* (January 1935 and March 1936), the second containing errors which are absent from the first. On a hand-press which could have coped with double the amount, the seventy-year-old Richards had to typeset and print a single page at a time because of his infirmity, often working by candlelight. There is a photo of him doing this in the *Methodist Times* of 19/12/1935 (see Image 7 below). Then, for lack of type, he had to dismantle each page after printing the first modest run of (usually) 100; none could be kept on one side set up for re-use. Naturally, any second printing had to be typeset, page by page, all over again from scratch – hence the rarity of his work in secondhand bookshops today.

In this laborious way he printed two runs of the following booklets: *'Bout me: or my ottybograffy, De good news according to Mark, De sermons of Amos, De lilies of de fills, De Song of Songs* and *De letter of James*. In fact *'Bout me* and *Mark* were each fully set three times over. He partly reset some of the Bible renderings yet again in his anthology of *Bits from de Old Book*. No single print-run of a work in dialect ever amounted to more than 150 copies, though his standard English guide to High Brooms (see below) ran to 250.

The dialect colour, or the attempt to render dialect features, appears to get weaker in his later works, where indications of nonstandard pronunciation are restricted to only the most noticeable ones, mainly the consonantal peculiarities. Some of his more curious spellings, e.g. *fadir* and *modir*, he says he took from the biblical translation of John Wycliffe (letter to Capt. Fuller, 18/04/1939) to represent the current local pronunciation; his learning has led him to acknowledge his 14th-century predecessor rather than to decide on a truly suitable phonetically- or phonemically-based system. He does not say exactly why he thought Wycliffe relevant to modern Sussex, but the <d> (as if a true Sussex representative of the /ð/ in modern *father, mother*, but in fact etymological, not dialectal, in Middle English) probably caught his attention and the <i> of Wycliffe's form must have followed ("In the hous of my fadir ben many dwellyngis …." (John 14:2)). The local features which he does register are pretty thinly marked, and variable, in his last religious work in dialect, *De A.B.C. Psalms* (1938; unpublished in his lifetime), and his own declining strength must have been an important contributory factor in this. Nonetheless it is interesting that he regarded vocabulary, syntax and idiom as the essence of dialect, rather than pronunciation, much as modern sociolinguists do. In 'De wicket gäate', the preface to *De good news according to Mark* (1934), he says 'A dialect bëant maade up so much by de shäape of words as how dey be put togedder.' More perspicuously, he notes in the interview with the *Methodist Times* accompanying the photo mentioned above that '[t]he dialect consists of rearrangements of words, an especially of simple words'. In his letter to Capt. Fuller dated 18/04/1939, he reiterates his view that he has 'been more concerned with the phraseology than the mere form of the words'.

Richards was well aware of the social class implications of dialect, noting in the preface to *De sermons of Amos* that 'De reasons for choosing Amos be dese – like me, he was a working chep, and as fur as I can see, more like some of de old dialecters I used to know, dan any oder writer in de Bible.' But he was encouraged to write in dialect to 'show some of my brodir local preachers dat de Good News could be put into simple language, and dat dat was how de Master preched' ('Bout dis book', the preface to *Bits from de Old Book* (1938)). He was also aware of the historical dimension, observing in the 'Note' serving as a preface to *De letter of James* (1935) that his work had found favour with people 'acos it be jess as dere faders used to talk', and in 'De wicket gäate' to *De good news according to Mark* (1934) that Sussex was 'a dialect dat be dying out'.

Image 7: James Richards in 1935; image from Methodist Times, *19/12/1935 (supplied by courtesy of John Worsley)*

Richards has been hailed as 'the greatest of our Sussex dialect authors' (Costello 1991b, F), but the competition is not stiff. His prose at its best is direct and clear, and is possibly seen at its best in *De story of Ruth* (1936; Text 25c); his humorous verse is doggerel and deliberately so (Text 25b), and his more serious verse is fairly hackneyed and short of resources for handling the metre (Text 25a). Some of *De A.B.C. Psalms* do not rise above the turgidity of some of the originals; for some are turgid even in the Authorized Version. No longer being at the height of his powers when he wrote them, he was in no way a master of the strict form he imposed on himself for the 'prayers, praises and professions of obedience' of Psalm 119. The syntax is often convoluted, and very far from embodying the simplicity of diction which he felt was the essence of dialect writing for ordinary folk. As a dialect writer, Richards was no Burns or Barnes, John Hartley or John Read. He was a modest man who set himself limited goals, worked hard at them, gave much pleasure in doing so, and occupies a justifiably honoured place in Sussex lore.

James Richards's writings in standard English are less well known. Under yet another pseudonym, 'Old Jim', he wrote in 1937 a guide to High Brooms near Tunbridge Wells (chapter 4, 24–31 of which is about dialect), the proceeds from which went to his local chapel. He also wrote a couple of religious tracts under his own name: *The carpenter. Glimpses at the lives of Joseph of Nazareth and of Jesus* (mentioned above) and *Joseph, the husband of Mary* (February 1932 and 1946 respectively), publishing the first himself and entrusting the second, which appeared when he was 80, to C. Baldwin of Tunbridge Wells. (I have never seen a copy of the latter.) His interest in the carpenter of Nazareth testifies to the same sympathy with ordinary working people which caused him to light on the Book of Amos, the 'cowman and local preacher from Tekoa' (1935), and the Book of Ruth, 'a gell from de country' (1936), to put into dialect. He also wrote occasional pieces for local newspapers.

¶ All these Cladpoles (i.e. *clodpoll* 'country bumpkin, yokel') may cause bibliographical headaches. They should be distinguished clearly: 'TIM Cladpole' is the pseudonym of Richard Lower, who wrote about characters called TOM Cladpole (ostensibly Tim's nephew) and JAN Cladpole (ostensibly Tim's son). James Richards wrote as 'JIM Cladpole'. A further anonymous writer, actually John Coker Egerton (see below), played on these names by calling himself 'Paul Claypuddle'. Another arrogated the name of the famous TOM to himself, but I have not established who this was.

William Douglas Parish (C6, F)

The compiler of the *Dictionary of the Sussex dialect*, William Douglas Parish (1833–1904), vicar of Selmeston and chancellor of Chichester Cathedral, was the author of a few short pieces in letter form printed in local newspapers under pseudonyms in the 1870s. (The originals are not, however, among Parish's autograph manuscripts held by the Sussex Archaeological Society.) As is usual for such writings, they are humorous pieces written as if by uneducated locals – and the present writer finds them funnier than most efforts in this genre. One of the letters is based on the well-worn idea of a rustic's visit to London (of which Richard Lower's *Tom Cladpole's jurney to Lunnun* is a further specimen), though there is an unusual twist to it; the other is a rustic's view of a local society wedding (Text 15b).

Parish is identified as John Hogpound in Henry Wace's (third) edition of Egerton's *Sussex folk and Sussex ways*, where the two Hogpound letters are reprinted. There is no reason to doubt Wace's information since Egerton is known to have provided Parish with material for his dictionary, acknowledged in his preface. There are also a couple of pseudonymous pieces from the same period, by 'Paul Claypuddle' and 'Tom Cladpole', mentioned above, the first of these being from the pen of Egerton. It is in some ways a response to one of the Hogpound letters (and 'I be a little aken to Master Hogpound'; the *Dictionary* duly notes *ken* as a 'corruption' of *kin*). The 'Tom Cladpole' piece has features that do not seem to me to be Sussex dialect as Parish understood and recorded it, and its authorship remains a complete mystery.

Image 8: William Douglas Parish. From a photograph lent to Sussex County Magazine *in 1956 by Mr H.W. Parish (copyright status unknown)*

It has to be said that many of the later Sussex voices are the stepchildren of the 'vicar of Simpson'. His *Dictionary* is rich in anecdotes and in curiosities (which tend to undermine his own claim that they represent authentic conversational Sussex dialect). So many of these crop up regularly in the dialect writings of others that it is tempting, and a little depressing, to conclude that they wrote with Parish at their elbow to help them out when they found that their own inauthentic voices were not up to their self-imposed task. This has been noticed before. W.G. Daish related an excellent quip about Sussex dialect authors, that '[s]ome writers get pretty good characterization . . . but they are so *parochial*' (Daish 1956: 12, C2).

Other writers (D1.2, F)

The rector of Burwash from 1857–88, John Coker Egerton (1829–88), recorded a few words and anecdotes in dialect in his diary, which he drew on (amongst other things) when writing his book *Sussex folk and Sussex ways* (1884); he also wrote at least one published dialect piece – ostensibly a letter (1878; see above) – and contributed around a hundred words to Parish's *Dictionary*.

Amy Sawyer wrote, over an unascertained period of time, a collection of plays for her village dramatic society in Ditchling, many of which are all or mainly in dialect (see for instance Text 26). She published them with the assistance of Arthur Beckett, founder and editor of the *Sussex County Magazine*, in 1934. (Beckett had already given her good publicity in an earlier article in *Sussex County Magazine* (1927*).) I do not know whether she was related by blood or marriage to F.E. Sawyer, an active student of dialect and local customs in the 1880s, based in Brighton. She was not a native speaker, but relied on the services of the Ditchlingites Fred Wood and George Davey to keep her on the strait and narrow dialect path. Fred Wood was an author in his own right and incorporated convincing snippets of dialect into his books on local sporting pastimes (1925 and 1928, D1.2).

(While we are on the subject of *Sussex County Magazine*: during the thirty years of its existence, this periodical provided the only regular forum for small writings in and on Sussex dialect, volumes 3 (1929), 5 (1931), 16 (1942) and 30 (1956) containing especially significant amounts. These pieces are listed in Section C of the main bibliography under *Sussex County Magazine*.)

Lilian Ramsey contributed a column to the *West Sussex Gazette* over a period from 1930 till her death in 1974 at the age of about 97. It centred on a gentlewoman-charwoman relationship presented in dialogue form, with the charwoman, Mrs Paddick, speaking a rich vernacular such as Miss Ramsey had closely observed, but of which she, again, was not a native speaker. Actually, she was not even a Sussex woman by birth, but coolly published her column over the pseudonym 'A Sussex woman'. She was concerned to conceal her identity at almost any price, in case the source of anecdote dried up.

The original columns have been reprinted several times since her death (e.g. Text 30b in 1991) – that is a curious thing to do, because this time around relatively few readers will have heard the Sussex speech which served as the basis for the pieces when they first appeared; so for them, the columns will read as merely quaint rather than passably authentic. Some of the pieces were collected and published in book form (see Text 30a), as detailed below in the main bibliography (Part 3, Section D). Typically for the genre, the dialect of her charwoman character was supplemented by malapropisms and by indications of the character's general ignorance of the larger world.

Much the same might be said for the less endearing Sussex character Ol' Jarge created by E. Walford Lloyd, who appeared in a column in the *Hampshire Telegraph and Post* in the 1930s and in (now very rare) book form in 1946 (from which Text 31 is reproduced).

Stanley Godman, a Lewes man with an interest in the history of music (including folk-dance), is said to have been an authority on the dialect but was not himself a writer of it, so far as I can ascertain. He wrote in 1957 that in his opinion the only (living) writers of convincing dialect were Mr [W.G.] Daish and Mrs Paddick. Certainly the bulk of the very small literature that we have petered out in the late 1930s except for the 'Mrs Paddick' pieces, and even they began pre-War, as already noted. I have found very little written in dialect by Daish, though he wrote with some authority about it (e.g. Daish 1956a, C2). His creative abilities may be judged by Text 33.

The actor and museum curator Anthony Chamberlaine Brothers has put Lewis Carroll's *Alice in Wonderland* into a dialect based on that of north-central Sussex. This was done as part of the celebrations for the 125th anniversary of its publication, but the organization promoting these celebrations, the Carroll Foundation, disappeared with the Melbourne fraud squad in hot pursuit (*Eastbourne Gazette*, 13/05/1992, p. 13) and did not therefore publish the 125 various renderings of Alice that it commissioned. Brothers has, however, recorded his version (see Part 3, Section G). His written text is thoroughgoingly destandardized, i.e. it contains eye-dialect, spellings chosen to suggest greater 'dialectness' than the text warrants. Though I am not wholly persuaded of its accuracy as a dialect rendering, it is certainly a good continuation of the written dialect tradition established by earlier writers. The spelling system deviates in various ways from that earlier tradition, and sometimes does a better job of conveying Sussex phonology than its predecessors.

Brothers is, like Lilian Ramsey, not a Sussexer by birth. He is a Yorkshireman, but a long-time Sussex resident and, as an actor, has a good mimic's ear. (See also *[Brighton] Evening Argus*, 05/09/1992, p. 13; Coates, in prep., D1.2, under Brothers.)

Writing in Sussex dialect had sputtered to a halt in the 1950s, it seemed, at about the time of the demise of *Sussex County Magazine*, by which time it was already an artificial activity, and one dependent to a large extent on recycling the material in the efforts of predecessors. But revivalism, represented by aspects of the heritage industry, historical re-enactment, and breathing fitful new life into dying languages, is one of the great cultural movements of the early third millennium. In 2004 we witnessed the unusual spectacle of a new work in the dialect: a poem by Pam Hughes of Seaford, called 'Jawbation' ('Scolding', 'Rebuke'), which won second prize in the Poetry London competition of that year. It is a strange exercise, though one with many prestigious antecedents, to write literature in a dead language, but even more curious is that this late flourish might be seen as the finest work, in literary terms, ever written in the dialect; let readers make up their own minds, especially in view of what is said about the text in the notes below (i.e. on Text 39).[12]

In a sense, perhaps this 'Other writers' section is the one in which to note the existence of the copious Sussex folk-song tradition. But the anonymous writers of the songs collected by the founders of the movement, the Broadwoods, Butterworth, Lee, and so on, left practically nothing with a strong dialect flavour (though see Part Two, Texts 20a-c), and it is not at all clear to what extent the Sussex folk-songs should be regarded as county property. Readers' attention is drawn to the warnings by Percy Grainger and Dick Leith on this issue printed at the head of Part Four, Section G2. The many song recordings listed in Part Four are essentially performances in which the accent is that of Sussex, which does not make the songs themselves Sussex songs. It is almost exclusively for the accent that the discography is included.

Writers of standard English (E)

Some authors of books in standard English include conversations with local characters showing dialect traits of varying degrees of depth, specificity and authenticity. Among those using, or purporting to use, Sussex speech during the last 120 years have been Hilaire Belloc, R.D. Blackmore, Mavis Budd, Bob Copper, E. Tickner Edwardes, 'Michael Fairless', 'John Halsham', James Hewlett, Louis J. Jennings, Sheila Kaye-Smith, Rudyard Kipling, Kate Wiggins and Barclay Wills (Text 21), and most recently 'Dirk Bogarde'.

Only a few of these carry much conviction as having true insight into local linguistic forms and patterns. Unsurprisingly, the natives like Kaye-Smith ('the

[12] The lexis of the poem is undoubtedly Sussex. Some of the grammar is questionably Sussex; the author was born in Devon.

novelist of Sussex'; Texts 23a-b; also F), Budd and Copper (Texts 35a-b) perform better than the 'blow-ins' like Belloc and Blackmore; and we can grade Budd and Copper, the true insiders of the vernacular culture, as superior to Kaye-Smith. But Kipling has a pretty good stab, and, commendably, does not stoop to using dialect for a cheap smear on or a cheap laugh at his characters. These 'quotative' writings are catalogued in brief in Part 3, Section E. James Hewlett's trilogy *The parish clerk* (1841) is of some interest because the author actually draws attention to Sussex dialect (vol. 1, page 77): a character's children were picking up 'sundry slang phrases and vulgar expressions . . . in the broad Sussex dialect'. Hewlett's actual representations of dialect are stereotypical and to some extent inaccurate for our county, but he does get [r]-deletion before a fricative, which is at least known in Sussex: 'by James the *fust*, king, etc. etc., the mayor wanted to know if their *wosships* had any orders for him' (part 3, page 104)[13].

The once widely-read author W.H. Hudson (an Argentine-born American who settled in Sussex) was dismissive about the contribution of Sussex-bred writers about Sussex to literature (1923*: 13). His words are quoted a little inappropriately as the epigraph to Part 3, Section D; I am sure Hudson was totally unaware of any writing in dialect, but was actually referring to the likes of William Collins, William Hay, William Hayley and James Hurdis, who all used standard English. He allows that the Wiltshire-born Richard Jefferies might have made a great Sussex author had he lived longer. The occasional local word is found in some of Jefferies's works such as the book *The gamekeeper at home* and the essays 'Clematis Lane', originally printed in *The Standard* (September 1883) and reprinted in the collection *The life of the fields*, and 'The pine wood', also originally printed in *The Standard* (September 1885), and reprinted in a further collection called *The open air*. More recently, the same may be said of 'Dirk Bogarde''s *Great Meadow*, recorded and read in instalments by Bogarde himself on BBC Radio 4 in 1993; this is a book of reminiscence which recalls the dialect of the inter-war years.

The vast majority of other dialect pieces are short conversations, notes or letters, often seemingly the sole production of the writer in question, and often contained within pieces of wider scope. Little generalization is possible about them except that they usually represent reported monologues of rustics, or conversations with or between rustics (compare what is said in the previous

[13] I am grateful to Jonathan Roper for introducing me to Hewlett. Let readers make what they will of Hewlett's gamekeeper when he says: 'You mought be right, and you mought be wrong, measter . . . but Oi have a notion what, while Oi gowes to West Wood, the poarchers meyans to gwo to East Wood. Howvever, I'll gwo to bwoth, and then I'se sure to be roight.' (vol. 3, p. 91)

section, 'Other writers'), and are usually local in import and comic in tone, just as the larger works already discussed are. Sussex practitioners of this art, which is essentially that of Mrs Paddick writ small (or at least less bulkily), include E. Hatchett Jackson, M. Fletcher Jones, G. Herbert White, I.P.M., Harriet Ansell and Florence Aylward. This genre is represented by Texts 17 and 24 in Part Two.

Educated writers of Standard English also tried their hand at incorporating Sussexisms into their verses. The result rarely rises above a mediocre pudding with the most obvious Sussex plums in. Martineau (Text 22) does this, as do Arthur Beckett, W.V. Cook and A.S. Cooke. We often find such dialect talismans in the service of a mysticism or local Merrie-Englandism, much as the supposed Sussex 'national' sport of stoolball was used at the same period (Lowerson 1995*). The *Pharisees* or fairies, usefully combining the local and the preternatural, were particularly prone to find themselves used in this way; see for instance the Standard English poem 'Invitation to the dance' by Joyce Sambrook in *Sussex County Magazine* 4 (1930), p. 42 and the representative of the letter P in Eleanor Farjeon's *A Sussex alphabet* (Bognor: Pear Tree Press (1924)) – two among many, following Mark Antony Lower (see Text 13a). Unpublished verse of somewhat mysterious origin in this genteel tradition of Beckett (though without his usual facility or flippancy) can be found as Text 34; it can be attributed to Salome Bridger of Alciston.

Dialect writing in Sussex is now effectively dead, as noted in the previous section, and the traditional form of the spoken dialect itself will soon follow it, with a few localized words and expressions no doubt hanging on as ghostly reminders of the past (at different periods of increasing deregionalization, Texts 3, 36 and 37). It appears not to be handed down across the generations any more in the form represented by what is found in the Survey of English Dialects, but there are phonetic and lexical echoes in the current regional English which has few very local variants. The chronicler of Mrs Paddick believed that Sussex folk could be told by their intonation even when they had given up everything else of their linguistic heritage (*West Sussex Gazette*, 15/11/1945), but that view was impossible to sustain in the last years of the second millennium. In any event, no adequate description exists of any distinctive Sussex intonation. This is a pity, in view of the hints of a rise-fall nucleus as the norm for declarative sentences that I have sometimes heard myself but not investigated systematically, and especially in view of the 'unaccountable Welsh intonation' discerned by Marshall (1978, C6) in Hailsham and the Downland, which may allude to the same thing.

The speech most typically heard in urban Sussex at present has much in common with the urban accents of London and other large southern towns. There is almost no specifically local colour in grammar or vocabulary, as we have noted several times; a south-eastern English *koiné* or broader regional dialect is in the process of emerging (cf. Trudgill 1986*: 46–57, 107–8; Kerswill and Williams 1994* and 2000*; Kerswill 1994* and 2003*; and implicitly in Kortmann *et al.* 2005*). A closely-related London-based accent has emerged which has earned the journalistic label 'Estuary English' (Rosewarne 1984*; Przedlacka 2002*), and in popular accounts this is often treated as the same thing as the *koiné*.

Writing in English is generally now standard, except where it has a clear cultural or political outgroup to serve as a base for it, as in the case of Scots or of London Jamaican. A relatively few older people maintain some more traditional features, and some local musicians, such as The Coppers, keep alive some of the local songs (though not always showing much local linguistic colour). The literature – and certainly the authentic literature – is now a collection that can be finalized, and I hope to have tabulated it all in the bibliography which follows in Part Three. If readers notice errors and omissions, the compiler would be most grateful for the information to be sent to him at the following address:

Richard Coates
Department of English, Linguistics and Communication
University of the West of England
Bristol BS16 1QY
Email: richard.coates@uwe.ac.uk

Chapter 5

What was Sussex dialect?

'In the south-east, Kent, Essex and East and West Sussex are all losing ther distinctive accents while the capital's own Cockney is under threat.'
(Professor Paul Kerswill, January 2010)

What can we say about the dialect and accent of Sussex as it has been transmitted to us by those who wrote English in the county (Chapter 2), by those who recorded what they heard and saw written in the county (Chapter 3), and by those who were creative in using what they took to be the English of the county (Chapter 4)?

English as spoken in the county is a matter of continuity: from a traditional local English with subtle ever more local variation to a type of English which represents a broader and more diverse geographical area, including London (Trudgill 1999*; Altendorf and Watt 2006*; Anderwald 2006*; and cf. the negative evidence of the absence of mentions of Sussex from Kortmann and others 2005*).[14] The newcomer is now, in a real sense, the dialect of Sussex, but this English is not only of Sussex, and the variety that people took as identifying and symbolizing the county has very largely gone. Probably there never was a set of linguistic elements or usages which were unique to the county, or perhaps no more than a couple of minor grammatical and lexical features, such as post-positional pied-piping or FROUGHTENED 'frightened' (see Chapter 3: sections on Grammar and Lexis). Even those might not be found everywhere in the county, or used on all possible occasions.

Arguably there was a collection of features found over areas of the south-east whose spatial overlap at any one time amounted to a unique Sussex profile, though that profile clearly varied across the county, especially from east to west. Its most important attribute was being different from the emerging national standard language. While no such thing existed, the differences between county or regional dialects were of little importance; these dialects simply constituted English, and their differences amounted to inconveniences of communication more than to markers of local identity. That is what they became as standard English grew and spread into some important domains of

[14] For a modern linguistic view of what distinguishes Standard from non-Standard English, see Milroy and Milroy (1993*) and Kerswill (2007*).

usage and into the mouths of the socially and economically important; traditional English was non-standard by definition, and that became its raison d'être. Local traditional English was non-standard in different ways, and those different ways assumed the newly important role of markers associated with and symbolizing different places, as town and country competed for human resources in the Industrial Revolution and as different places competed for influence.

It fell to traditional English in Sussex, as in some other counties, to be a marker of the rurality that was retreating before the tide of industrial urban development, holidaymaking and retirement in-migration. There was no specifically local emerging urban Sussex dialect to fulfil the same role as the distinctive dialects of, say, Liverpool and Bristol in their respective hinterlands; the new Sussex urban dialect had much in common with that of the south-east in general.

Enough of the traditional collection of features has been in full retreat during the twentieth century for us to say that traditional Sussex dialect is dead. The retreat has been quite abrupt: since about 1840, Sussex has been open to outside influences and pressures, including the linguistic ones that went with those of economics and fashion, in a way that would have been unimaginable in what was still a remote and isolated county with lousy roads as late as 1760. The nineteenth century understood well that a rural way of life was passing, and those with historical or nostalgic inclinations – are they the same thing? – understood that the dialect could be a focus for those feelings.

Image 9: W.H. Hudson (public domain image)

They fell into three broad groups. The first took up the challenge of describing what they understood to be the old language in the spirit of rescue archaeology, in case the threatened dialect offered features that might one day be academically useful, for example in understanding the way the Germanic languages collectively had developed over their 1500-year history, and how the South Saxons had colonized this stretch of countryside. Those distinctive old words and place-names might be just such evidence. Romantic scholars and poets took a profound interest in what was oldest, confounding the notion of age with authenticity (see also Milroy 2002*: 16–19); that is why a verse of what became the Swedish national anthem refers to part of the country as 'Thou ancient, thou fresh, thou fell-crowned north': the supposedly unchanging and therefore 'ancient' north was the heart of authentic Swedishness.

The second group, those addressing a wider audience, took the opportunity to collect and preserve these nuggets, and to entertain at the same time, sometimes with warmth, sometimes with satire, but almost always with condescension towards the working people who were the cultural Other (the out-group) and had become, in the eyes of this opinion-forming class, the bearers of the burden of tradition.[15] Parish is ambivalent: he wishes to instruct and entertain his readers at the same time, but emphasizes that 'many of the words and expressions which raise the laugh are purer specimens of the English language than the words which are used to tell the story in which they are introduced' (1875: 1, C6).

The condescension of the educated was often expressed affectionately, but the patrician view endemic in it is hard to hide. Sometimes the satire seems vicious to third-millennium eyes, but anti-working-class sentiment is nothing new. A particularly striking example of the gentry's supercilious incomprehension of the 'peasantry' is offered by W.H. Hudson (1900*: chapter 15). Walking the Downs above Bepton, he accosts a youth and asked him the name of the hill over which he had just walked. He is exasperated by the lad, who declares that the hill has no name, to his knowledge, but adds: 'We call it Bepton Hill.' On another occasion he askes a man the name of the inn to which he has been directed. 'We call it the Oak,' he said, 'but if it has a name I never heard it . . . ' It does not seem to have occurred to him that the locals understood *name* primarily as a word for what was bestowed at the font: just look at the prominence of the word in the baptismal service in the Book of Common Prayer

[15] The Yokel (understood as the Dialect-Speaker) shares much with the Eccentric: he is natural and intuitive, and enshrines non-mainstream values and mores in a way tolerated condescendingly by the normgiving society at large; the character appears in the early-modern period, but crystallizes in the Victorian era. See Hemming (2008*, esp. his chapter 5).

which all would have known. The personal name is the name *par excellence*. Hudson's victims must have wondered at the stranger's implication that a hill might be called *Alice* or a pub *Robert*; he on the other hand sees only a 'streak or vein of stupidity'.

Other writers are more ambivalent. In Parish's dictionary, for instance, we can find examples of gentle mockery of working people and their talk (under e.g. ADONE, CONCERNED IN LIQUOR, FROUDEN, HALF-BAPTIZED[1], HOB-UP, JOHNNY, PARLY, PECK[2], ROUND-FROCK, TIGHT), but these may have a sting in the tail whereby the 'peasant' gets the better of a gentleman inquisitor, gets in a knowing dig, or shows good common sense (e.g. BEAT THE DEVIL ROUND THE GOOSEBERRY-BUSH, UNACCOUNTABLE, and often in the county literature; cf. also Roper 2007: 189, C3).

The third group did what might seem remarkable. They created Sussex dialect. There was no Sussex dialect to speak of until the revolution of the late eighteenth century and early nineteenth centuries. We have seen that there was indeed a regionally coloured English, which occasionally showed itself in written texts, such as Burgess's *Jernal*. It had no significance, in the sense that its writers did not use it to make a point about belonging to Sussex. They just did what came naturally, armed only with their own speech and some hard-won rules for transposing speech into written form. The outcome was writing which anybody with sufficient linguistic knowledge could identify as hailing from Sussex. To the writers themselves it was presumably just writing, though some of them may have been aware that other folk, the social leaders, did it differently, and in a way which they took to be superior and could not aspire to; sometimes they apologized for their own perceived literacy shortcomings. But Sussex dialect as we now know it came into existence only when educated people started to use the traditional features of their county's speech as a conscious alternative to standard English in the main mode of standard English: writing.

Sussex dialect was a creation. It was of course *based* on the local regionally coloured English, but it rapidly acquired features which became stereotypical, whether they were accurate representations of the contemporary Sussex regional speech or not, as James Richards admitted; remember that his quest for authenticity led him to exaggerate the incidence of certain features on the grounds that they were more different or distinctive than their competitors, and therefore more representative of the assumed body of 'de old dialecters'.

It is appropriate to say that Richard Lower invented Sussex dialect, an essentially literary phenomenon, as an alternative to the literature of high culture, with a partly different audience in mind: the sort that would buy cheap pamphlets rather than grand books (Texts 12a-b). Since the educated classes of this period were also busy inventing the county as a focus of their own loyalty

– a Romantic loyalty to the native soil within agreed boundaries[16] – they could play at being 'locals' by supporting the new alternative literature (encouraging the authors and buying the pamphlets), or by being one of the other two types of historico-nostalgic, both of whose projects were to some degree academic in intent: the local historian and the genealogist. It was a useful linguistic complement to a county identity which embraced the genealogy of 'county' families, county-based regiments, county-based administration and implementation of justice, and organized competitive county-level sport (e.g. cricket; not to mention the within-county 'national' sport, stoolball[17]).

The educated could know, read, and take an interest in their county Englishes without being required to be insiders in the culture which generated the ancient regional varieties. They could manipulate it by using stereotyped tokens of dialect in their non-dialect speech or writing (e.g. 'Wunt be druv') to indicate a desired identity without full commitment to the culture which those linguistic tokens symbolized. An important aspect of that culture in Sussex is symbolized also by the figure of the shepherd, which is the reason for the choice of the grainy and hackneyed image on the front cover of this book; John Dudeney of Ovingdean, snapped in 1927, can stand for the soil in which Sussex dialect grew, at the point in history at which that soil became barren of native life.

There has been an interesting modern reincarnation of the notion of 'dialect' as it has just been described. Since the 1980s, much of Europe has seen tourist authorities use local languages, or aspects of them, as talismans, pieces of cultural capital, touristic commodities. Shandler (2006*) calls these uses 'postvernacular cultural practices', implying that in many cases the local languages which are being used to represent, set apart, or even create, local cultures no longer have full local currency, or, to put it more bluntly, are dying. There is a pertinent study, for example, of Low German or Plattdeutsch (Reershemius 2009*). Others have viewed the situation from an English-speaking tourist's perspective (Jaworski, Thurlow, Lawson and Ylänne-McEwen 2003*).

The ideas involved apply as much to dialects as to languages, and the appearance of characteristic Bristolian phrases on T-shirts sold locally as a good illustration of what is involved. As for Sussex: it has a ghostly existence. We find occasional hints of the kind of thing Shandler is getting at: uses of the unofficial county motto 'Wunt be druv' in otherwise Standard English prose (perhaps the one Sussex phrase which is widely known); occasional specifically

[16] 'Our old land, it likes our old ploughs.' (Said to be a local proverb, referring specifically to farmland not national land.)

[17] For other 'local' sports, see the brief popular article by Gibbons (1992*).

local pronunciations of place-names (e.g. Coates 1980); the persistence of polished traditional performances of local songs, for instance by The Coppers; and public discourse about the dialect or accent, seen for example in newspaper debate about whether it still survives in any guise. But that's about all, except Walter, the Talking Shepherd, whom you may meet at the Beachy Head Countryside Centre, reminiscing about life on the Downs long ago.

Such is the Sussex dialect and its literature which are left to us. In truth, a large proportion of the literature is recycled from the work of the main nineteenth century authors Richard Lower and W.D. Parish, with the creditable exception of the major twentieth-century figure of James Richards. They created what we now think of as the vernacular literature of Sussex, and to a large extent they are it. As we noted earlier, this literature is essentially complete. Nothing truly new is emerging, because the cultural (and physical) landscape out of which it grew has changed for ever.

Traditional regional speech is a different concept from Sussex dialect in the sense proposed for the term here; this is what inspires the division between Sections D1.1 and D1.2 in the bibliography below (Part Three), although readers will have noted that I made concessions to ordinary usage in the previous chapters and used *Sussex dialect* as a cover term for both where nothing hinges on the distinction. Now traditional regional speech and the writing it sometimes gave rise to, just like Sussex dialect narrowly defined, has no basis in human geography any more. The Downs have been towned and recently also National Parked; the Weald has been intensive-farmed and commutered; the sea has been marinaed.

Sussex people will continue to speak English and it will be a Sussex English, by trivial definition. But it is time to write the epitaph for both the varieties which grew out of and were supported by the old ways, both the traditional regional English and Sussex dialect as I have defined it. Let this book be that epitaph, to complement David Arscott's celebration (2006, C2/C8).

Envoi

It seems appropriate to end Part One with a real epitaph, one which expresses a mystical relation between a person and their place in a way suitable for the thoughtways of the era in which the modern concept of Sussex dialect was forged: the thoughtways famously expressed by Kipling in 'Sussex' (1902):

> GOD gave all men all earth to love,
> But since our hearts are small,
> Ordained for each one spot should prove
> Belovèd over all . . .

The chosen epitaph, that of the poet Blunt, even contains a local Sussex word.

> That name [i.e. Sussex] is thine. How often I have fled
> To thy deep hedgerows and embraced each field,
> Each lag, each pasture – fields which gave me birth,
> And saw my youth, and which must hold me dead.
>
> Wilfred Scawen Blunt (1840–1922), 'Chanclebury Ring';
> inscribed on his tomb at Newbuildings Place, Southwater

References to scholarly works mentioned in Part One, which are asterisked in the text

Sussex items not asterisked in the text can be found at the appropriate place in the main bibliography, i.e. Part Three, indicated by a Section-reference, e.g. A or C6

Works mentioned in Part One written in dialects other than those of Sussex do not appear in these lists

Albrecht, Thomas (1916) *Der Sprachgebrauch des Dialektdichters Charles E. Benham zu Colchester in Essex*. Doctoral dissertation, University of Berlin. Published Berlin: Mayer and Müller (special issue 111 in the series *Palaestra*).

Allan, Alasdair (1995) Scots spellin – Ettlin efter the quantum lowp. *English World-Wide* 16.1, 61–103.

Alston, Robin C. (compiler) (1971) *A bibliography of the English language from the invention of printing to the year 1800*, vol. IX: *English dialects, Scottish dialects, cant and vulgar English*. London: private.

Anderson, Peter M. (1987) *A structural atlas of the English dialects*. London: Croom Helm.

Altendorf, Ulrike, and Dominic Watt (2006) The dialects in the south of England: phonology. In Bernd Kortmann and Clive Upton, eds, *Varieties of English, vol. 1: The British Isles*. Berlin and New York: Mouton de Gruyter, 194–222.

Anderwald, Lieselotte (2006) The varieties of English spoken in the south-east of England: morphology and syntax. In Bernd Kortmann and Clive Upton, eds, *Varieties of English, vol. 1: The British Isles*. Berlin and New York: Mouton de Gruyter, 440-62.

Arngart, O.S. (1942) *The proverbs of Alfred*. Lund: Gleerup.

Arnold, F.H. (1887) *Sussex flora*. London: Simpkin; Arundel & Horsham: Mitchell.

Bald, M.A. (1926) The anglicisation of Scottish printing. *Scottish Historical Review* 23, 107–15.

Barker, Eric E. (1947-9) Sussex Anglo-Saxon charters. *Sussex Archaeological Collections* 86, 42-101; 87, 112–63; 88, 51–113.

Barry, Michael V. (1960) Studies in the linguistic geography of Kent, Sussex and Surrey, 2 vols. Dissertation for the degree of Master of Arts, University of Leeds.

Barry, Michael V. (1972) The morphemic distribution of the definite article in contemporary regional English. In Martyn Wakelin, ed., *Patterns of folk speech in the British Isles*. London: Athlone Press, chapter 8, 164–81.

Baugh, Albert C., and Thomas Cable (2002) *A history of the English language* (5th edn). London: Routledge.

Beal, Joan C. (2006) *Language and region*. London: Routledge.

Beckett, Arthur (1927b) Village drama in Sussex and the Ditchling Players. *Sussex County Magazine* 1, 114–7.

Birch, W. de Gray, ed. (1885-93) *Cartularium saxonicum: a collection of charters relating to Anglo-Saxon history*, 3 vols. London: Whiting & Company, 1885-1887 (vols 1 and 2); London: Chas. J. Clark, 1893 (vol. 3).

Birch, W. de Gray (1892) *The Anglo-Saxon charter of Oslac, Duke of the South-Saxons, A.D. 780*. London.

Blaauw, William (1856) Extracts from the 'Iter Sussexiense' of Dr John Burton. *Sussex Archaeological Collections* 8, 250–65.

Blencowe, R.W. (1849) South-Down shepherds. *Sussex Archaeological Collections* 2, 247–56 [especially 253–6, quoted verbatim from a once-lost autograph MS. of John Dudeney's, in the care of the Sussex Archaeological Society, now edited and published in full by Richard Coates in *Locus focus: forum of the Sussex Place-Names Net* 5.1 (2001), 13–18].

Blunt, Wilfred Scawen (1885) 'Chanclebury Ring.' In *The love sonnets of Proteus*. London: Kegan Paul Trench.

Brent, Colin (1993) *Georgian Lewes, 1714–1830: the heyday of a county town.* Lewes: Colin Brent Publications.

Britten, James, and Robert Holland (1878–86) *A dictionary of English plant-names*, 3 vols. London: Trübner, for the English Dialect Society (vols. 22, 26, 45).

Brunner, Karl (1920) Die Dialektliteratur von Lancashire. Doctoral dissertation, University of Vienna.

Brunner, Karl (1925) Die Schreibtradition der Dialekt-Schriftsteller von Lancashire. *Englische Studien* 60.1, 158–79.

Burton, John (1752) *Hodoiporuntos meletēmata sive Iter Surriense et Sussexiense*. London and Oxford. [Selections are printed by Blaauw (1856).]

Chadwick, Henry Munro (1924) *The origin of the English nation*. Cambridge: Cambridge University Press.

Chambers, R.W., and Marjorie Daunt, eds (1931) *A book of London English* 1384-1425. Oxford: Clarendon Press.

Coles, Mike (2001, 2002) *The Bible in Cockney* and *More Bible in Cockney.* London: Bible Reading Fellowship.

Copper, Bob (1976) *Early to rise: a Sussex boyhood*. London: Heinemann. [Further printing: Javelin (1988).]

Crystal, David (2004) *The stories of English*. London: Allen Lane.

Danielsson, Bror, and Robin C. Alston, eds (1966) *The works of William Bullokar*, vol. I. Leeds: University of Leeds School of English.

Dobson, E.J. (1968) *English pronunciation, 1500–1700*, 2 vols, 2nd edn. Oxford: Oxford University Press.

Eckhardt, Eduard (1910) *Die Dialekt- und Ausländertypen des älteren englischen Dramas.* Teil I. Louvain: A. Uystpruyst [etc.] (Materialien zur Kunde des älteren englischen Dramas).

Ellis, Alexander J. (1889) *On early English pronunciation, part V: the existing pronunciation of English dialects*. London: Trübner (Early English Text Society, ES 53).

Ellis, Alexander J. (1890) *English dialects, their sounds and homes*. London: Kegan Paul, for the English Dialect Society (vol. 60). [Abridged version of the previous item.]

Ellman, John Boys (1912) *Recollections of a Sussex parson*. London: Skeffington and sons (especially chapter 52).

Evans, A.A. (1933) *On foot in Sussex: a loiterer's notebook.* London: Methuen.

Farrant, John H. (1995) The travels and travails of Francis Grose, F.S.A. *Antiquaries Journal* 75, 365–80.

Fisher, John H. (1977) Chancery and the emergence of standard written English in the fifteenth century. *Speculum* 52, 870–99.

Forster, Klaus (1980) *A pronouncing dictionary of English place-names*. London: Routledge and Kegan Paul.

Francis, W. Nelson (1983) *Dialectology: an introduction*. London: Longman.

Frater, Graham (2002) *Effective practice in writing at key stage 2: essential extras.* London: Basic Skills Agency and Cardiff: National Assembly for Wales.

Gardiner, Mark F., and Christopher H.C. Whittick, eds (2010, forthcoming) *Accounts and records of the manor of Mote in Iden, 1442–1551, 1673*. Lewes: Sussex Record Society (vol. 92).

Gibbons, Fiachra (1992) We're not just here for the beer! *[Brighton] Evening Argus* 02/06/1992, 12–13.

Görlach, Manfred (1991) *Introduction to Early Modern English*. Cambridge: Cambridge University Press.

Görlach, Manfred (1999) *English in nineteenth-century England: an introduction*. Cambridge: Cambridge University Press.

Grigson, Geoffrey (1955) *The Englishman's flora*. London: Phoenix House. [Reprinted London: Michael Joseph (1959); London: Hart-Davis (1975).]

Grose, Francis (1785) *A classical dictionary of the vulgar tongue*. London. [Actually published anonymously; second edition, also anonymous (1788); third by Pierce Egan (1823); new edition by E.H. Partridge, London: Scholaris Press (1931).]

Grose, Francis (1787) *A provincial glossary, with a collection of local proverbs and superstitions*. London. [Later printings (1811, 1839). Facsimile reprint Menston: Scolar Press (English Linguistics 1500–1800) (1968).]

Halliwell, James Orchard, ed. (1843) *A collection of pieces in the dialect of Zummerzet*. London: John Russell Smith.

Halliwell, James Orchard (1847) *A dictionary of archaic and provincial words, obsolete phrases, proverbs, and ancient customs, from the fourteenth century*. London: J. Russell Smith. [Second edition (1850); a further private printing of 112 copies, Brixton Hill (1852). Facsimile of second edition (1989).]

Hart, John (1569) *An orthographie*. London. [Reprinted Menston: Scolar Press (1969).]

Hemming, Henry (2008) *In search of the English eccentric*. London: John Murray.

Hobsbawm, Eric (1990) *Nations and nationalism since 1780*. Cambridge: Cambridge University Press.

Hogg, Richard (2006) English in Britain. In Richard Hogg and David Denison, eds, *A history of the English language*. Cambridge: Cambridge University Press, 352–83.

Hope, R.C. (1882) *A glossary of dialectal place-nomenclature*. London: Simpkin, Marshall. [Second edition (1883), of which Sussex entries are on 124–8. Reprinted Detroit: Gale (1968).]

Horobin, Simon (2005) The scribe of Rawlinson Poetry 137 and the copying and circulation of Piers Plowman. *Yearbook of Langland Studies* 19, 3–26.

Hudson, W.H. (1900) *Nature in downland.* London: Longmans, Green. [New edition Dent (1923).]

Hughes, Susan (1980) Guildhall and Chancery English. *Guildhall Studies in London History* 4, 53–622.

Hulme, Hilda (1958) Review of E.J. Dobson, *English pronunciation, 1500–1700. Essays in Criticism* 8, 422–8.

Ihalainen, Ossi (1985) 'He took the bottle and put 'n in his pocket.' The object pronoun it in present-day Somerset. In Wolfgang Viereck, ed., *Focus on: England and Wales*. Amsterdam: John Benjamins, 153–61.

Ihalainen, Ossi (1994) The dialects of English since 1776. In R.W. Burchfield, ed., *Cambridge history of the English language*, vol. V. Cambridge: Cambridge University Press, chapter 5.

Ives, Sumner (1971) A theory of literary dialects. In J.V. Williamson and V.M. Burke, eds, *A various language – perspectives on American dialects.* New York: Holt, Rinehart and Winston, 147–77.

Jaworski, Adam, Crispin Thurlow, Sarah Lawson, and Virpi Ylänne-McEwen (2003) The uses and representations of local languages in tourist destinations. A view from British TV holiday programmes. *Language Awareness* 12.1, 5–29.

Johnson, Samuel (1755) *Dictionary of the English language*. [Numerous reprintings and new editions.]

Joyce, Patrick (1991) *Visions of the people: industrial England and the question of class, 1848–1914*. Cambridge: Cambridge University Press. [See esp. chapters 11 and 12 on dialect literature in general.]

Kaye-Smith, Sheila (1933) *The ploughman's progress*. London: Cassell and New York: Harper & Brothers. [Published in North America as *Gipsy waggon. The story of a ploughman's progress.*]

Kaye-Smith, Sheila (1953) *The Weald of Kent and Sussex*. London: Hale. [Part 2, chapter 5, 211–9, has material on dialects, as do 205–10 of the previous chapter.]

Kelly, Susan E., ed. (1998) *The charters of Selsey*. Oxford: Oxford University Press (Anglo-Saxon Charters 6).

"Kemble". See Sawyer (1968).

Kerswill, Paul (1994) Babel in Buckinghamshire? Pre-school children acquiring accent features in the new town of Milton Keynes. In Gunnel Melchers, ed., *Nonstandard varieties of language*. Stockholm: Almqvist and Wiksell (Acta Universitatis Stockholmiensis), 64–84.

Kerswill, Paul (2003) Dialect levelling and geographical diffusion in British English. In David Britain and Jenny Cheshire, eds, *Social dialectology. In honour of Peter Trudgill*. Amsterdam: Benjamins, 223–43.

Kerswill, Paul (2007) Standard English and non-standard English. In David Britain, ed., *Language in the British Isles*. Cambridge: Cambridge University Press, 34–51.

Kerswill, Paul, and Ann Williams (1994) A new dialect in a new city: children's and adults' speech in Milton Keynes. Economic and Social Research Council award no. R000237366, final report. [Developed as: Paul Kerswill and Ann Williams (2000) Creating a new town koiné: children and language change in Milton Keynes. *Language in Society* 29, 65–115.]

Kipling, Rudyard (1903) 'Sussex'. In *The five nations*. London: Methuen. [Written 1902.]

Kloss, Heinz (1952) *Die Entwicklung neuer germanischer Kultursprachen, 1870-1950*. Munich: Pohl.

Knox, A.E. (1849) *Ornithological rambles in Sussex. With a systematic catalogue of the birds of that county*. London.

Kolb, Eduard, Beat Glauser, Willi Elmer, and Renate Stamm (1979) *Atlas of English sounds*. Bern: Francke.

Kortmann, Bernd, Tanja Herrmann, Lukas Pietsch and Susanne Wagner (2005) *A comparative grammar of British English dialects: agreement, gender, relative clauses.* Berlin and New York: Mouton de Gruyter. [Based on the Freiburg English Dialect Project and Corpus (FRED).]

Kristensson, Gillis (2001-2) *A survey of Middle English dialects 1290–1350: the southern counties.* Vol. 1: *Vowels (except diphthongs)*. Vol. 2: *Diphthongs and consonants*. Lund: Lund University Press (Publications of the New Society of Letters at Lund 93 and 94).

Kurath, Hans, and Guy S. Lowman, jr. (1973 for 1970) *The dialectal structure of southern England: phonological evidence.* University (Ala.): University of Alabama Press (Publication of the American Dialect Society 54).

Labov, William (1972) *Sociolinguistic patterns*. Philadelphia: University of Pennsylvania Press.

Labov, William (2006) *The social stratification of English in New York City*, second edn. Cambridge: Cambridge University Press.

Leith, Dick (1983) *A social history of English*. London: Routledge and Kegan Paul. [Second edn (1997).]

Lockwood, William B. (1984) *The Oxford book of British bird names*. Oxford: Oxford University Press.

Löfvenberg, Matthias T. (1942) *Studies in Middle English local surnames*. Lund: Gleerup.

Lowerson, John (1995) Stoolball: conflicting values in the revivals of a ‘traditional Sussex game’. *Sussex Archaeological Collections* 133, 263–74.

Lowth, Robert (1761) *A short introduction to English grammar*. [Reprinted Menston: Scolar Press (1967).]

Lucas, E.V. (1904) *Highways and byways in Sussex*. London: Macmillan.

Luick, Karl (1914-21) *Historische Grammatik der englischen Sprache*, volume I, part I [volume 2 never appeared]. Stuttgart: Tauchnitz. [Reprinted Oxford: Blackwell (1964).]

McIntosh, Angus, Michael L. Samuels and Michael Benskin, with the assistance of M. Laing and K. Williamson (1986) *A linguistic atlas of late Middle English*, vols 1–4. Aberdeen: Aberdeen University Press.

McKinley, Richard (1988) *The surnames of Sussex*. Oxford: Leopard's Head Press (English Surnames series volume 5).

Mawer, Allen H., and Frank M. Stenton; with the assistance of J.E.B. Gover (1929/30) *The place-names of Sussex*, two vols. Cambridge: CUP (EPNS vols 6/7).

Milroy, James (1992) Middle English dialectology. In Norman Blake, ed., *The Cambridge history of the English language*, vol. 2. Cambridge: Cambridge University Press, 156–206.

Milroy, James, and Lesley Milroy, eds (1993) *Real English: the grammar of English dialects in the British Isles*. Harlow: Longmans.

Milroy, James (2002) The legitimate language: giving a history to English. In Watts and Trudgill, 7–25.

Mitzka, Walther (1952) *Handbuch zum Deutschen Sprachatlas*. Marburg: Elwertsche Universitätsbuchhandlung.

Moore, S., S.B. Meech and H. Whitehall (1935) *Middle English dialect characteristics and dialect boundaries*. Ann Arbor: University of Michigan (Essays and Studies in English and Comparative Literature 13, 1–60).

Morsbach, Lorenz (1888) *Über den Ursprung der neuenglischen Schriftsprache*. Heilbronn: Henninger.

Morsbach, Lorenz (1896) *Mittelenglische Grammatik*. Halle an der Saale: Niemeyer.

Murdoch, Brian, and J[acqueline] A. Tasioulas, eds (2002) *The apocryphal lives of Adam and Eve*. Exeter: Exeter: University of Exeter Press (Exeter Medieval English Texts and Studies). [The second *Life, Canticum de creatione* (1375), is claimed to have been written in Sussex. See Part Two, Text 2.]

Murray, Lindley (1795) *English grammar*. [Reprinted Menston: Scolar Press (1968).]

Nevalainen, Terttu, and Ingrid Tieken-Boon van Ostade (2006) Standardisation. Chapter 5 of Richard Hogg and David Denison, eds, *A history of the English language*. Cambridge: Cambridge University Press, 271–311.

Nida, Eugene A., ed. (1972) *The book of a thousand tongues*, 2nd edn. London: United Bible Societies.

Orton, Harold, Stuart F. Sanderson, and J[ohn] D.A. Widdowson (1978) *The linguistic atlas of England*. London: Croom Helm/Humanities Press.

Orton, Harold, and Martyn Wakelin (1967/8) *The Survey of English Dialects: basic materials. The southern area,* parts 1–3. Leeds: Edward Arnold for the University of Leeds.

Orton, Harold, and Nathalia Wright (1974) *A word geography of England.* London: Seminar Press.

Osborn, James M., ed. (1961) *The autobiography of Thomas Whythorne.* Oxford: Clarendon Press.

Page, Norman (1988) *Speech in the English novel* [second edition]. Basingstoke: Macmillan. [Esp. chapter 3 'Speech and dialect: character', 55–96. First edition (1973).]

Paulin, Tom (1990) Introduction. In Tom Paulin, ed., *The Faber book of vernacular verse.* London: Faber and Faber, ix-xxii.

Petyt, Keith M. (1980) *The study of dialect. An introduction to dialectology.* London: André Deutsch. [Note especially chapter 3, 68–100, on traditional English dialectology.]

Poplack, Shana, Gerard Van Herk and Dawn Harvie (2002) "Deformed in the dialects": an alternative history of non-standard English. In Watts and Trudgill, 87–110.

Poussa, Patricia (1995) Ellis's 'Land of wee'. *Neuphilologische Mitteilungen* 96, 295–307.

Przedlacka, Joanna (2002) *Estuary English?* Frankfurt am Main [etc.]: Peter Lang (Polish Studies in English Language and Literature 4).

Priestley, Joseph (1761) *The rudiments of English grammar*. London. [Reprinted Menston: Scolar Press (1969).]

Ray, John (1674) *A collection of English words, not generally used, with their signification and original* [etc.]. [Second edn 1691.]

Reershemius, Gertrud (2009) Post-vernacular language use in a Low German linguistic community. *Journal of Germanic Linguistics* 21.2, 131–47.

Rissanen, Matti (2000) Standardisation and the language of early statutes. In Laura Wright, ed., *The development of Standard English, 1300–1800*. Cambridge: Cambridge University Press.

Samuels, Michael L. (1971) Kent and the Low Countries: some linguistic evidence. In Adam J. Aitken, Angus McIntosh and Hermann Pálsson, eds, *Edinburgh studies in English and Scots*. London: Longman, 3–19.

Sawyer, P[eter] H. (1968) *Anglo-Saxon charters: an annotated list and bibliography.* London: Royal Historical Society. [Now being updated; electronic version available on Simon Keynes's web-site 'Kemble', www.trin.cam.ac.uk/kemble.]

Shandler, Jeffrey (2006) *Adventures in Yiddishland: post-vernacular language and culture*. Berkeley, CA: University of California.

Shepherd, Valerie (1990) *Language variety and the art of the everyday.* London: Pinter. [Esp. chapter 2 'The language of men, poets and linguists', 33–72, and chapter 3 'A poetry of their own?', 73–106.]

Sheppard, June (2001) Brighton's railway workers in the 1850s. *Sussex Archaeological Collections* 139, 191–201.

Sheridan, Thomas (1762) *A course of lectures on elocution*. London. [Reprinted Menston: Scolar Press (1968).]

Swainson, Charles (1885) *Provincial words and folk lore of British birds*. London: Trübner, for the English Dialect Society (vol. 47)/Folk-Lore Society.

Swift, Jonathan (1712) *A proposal for correcting, improving and ascertaining the English tongue*. London. [Reprinted Menston: Scolar Press (1968).]

Templeton, Janet M. (1973) Scots: an outline history. In A.J. Aitken, ed., *Lowland Scots: papers presented to an Edinburgh conference*. Edinburgh: Association for Scottish Literary Studies (Occasional Paper 2), 4–19.

Tibble, Ronald (1989) William Hersee, 1786–1854. *West Sussex History* 42 (January), 11–15.

Toolan, Michael (1992) The significations of representing dialect in writing. *Language and Literature* 1, 29–46.

Trudgill, Peter (1975) *Accent, dialect and the school*. London: Edward Arnold.

Trudgill, Peter (1986) *Dialects in contact*. Oxford: Blackwell.

Trudgill, Peter (1990) *The dialects of England* (2nd edn 1999). Oxford: Blackwell.

Upton, Clive S., David Parry, and J.D.A. Widdowson (1994) *Survey of English Dialects: the dictionary and grammar*. London: Routledge.

Upton, Clive S., Stuart F. Sanderson, and J.D.A. Widdowson (1987) *Word maps: an atlas of English dialects*. London: Croom Helm. [See also Upton and Widdowson (2006).]

Upton, Clive S., and J.D.A. Widdowson (1999) *Lexical erosion in English regional dialects*. Sheffield: NATCECT (occasional publication 7).

Upton, Clive S., and J.D.A. Widdowson (2006) *Atlas of English dialects*, 2nd edn. London: Routledge.

Urlau, Kurt (1921) Die Sprache des Dialektdichters William Barnes. Inaugural dissertation, University of Berlin.

Wade, Stephen (1976) Dialect literature: true and false. *Transactions of the Yorkshire Dialect Society* 14, 30–4.

Wakelin, Martyn (1986) *The southwest of England*. Amsterdam: John Benjamins (Varieties of English Around the World T5).

Wakelin, Martyn (1987) The treatment of dialect in English dictionaries. Chapter 9 in Robert Burchfield, ed., *Studies in lexicography*. Oxford: Clarendon Press, 56–77.

Wakelin, Martyn (1988a) The phonology of South-Western English, 1500–1700. In Jacek Fisiak, ed., *Historical dialectology: regional and social*. Berlin: Mouton de Gruyter, 609–44.

Wakelin, Martyn (1988b) *The archaeology of English*. London: Batsford.

Walker, John (1791) *A critical pronouncing dictionary*. London. [Reprinted Menston: Scolar Press (1968).]

Walker, Simon (1991) Letters to the Dukes of Lancaster in 1381 and 1399. *English Historical Review* 106, 68–79.

Watts, Richard (2002) From polite language to educated language: the re-emergence of an ideology. In Watts and Trudgill, 155–72.

Watts, Richard, and Peter Trudgill, eds (2002) *Alternative histories of English*. London: Routledge.

Webster, Noah (1786) *The American spelling book*. Privately published. [384 subsequent editions in the author's lifetime.]

Weinreich, Uriel (1954) Is a structural dialectology possible? *Word* 10, 388–40.

Wells, John C. (1982) *Accents of English*, 3 vols. Cambridge: Cambridge University Press.

Whigham, Frank, and Wayne A. Rebhorn, eds (2007) *The art of English poesy, by George Puttenham*. Ithaca, N.Y., and London: Cornell University Press.

Whitaker, F.O. (1935) The popular names of Sussex plants. In "Sussex nature notes", *Sussex County Magazine* 9, 387–8, 519–20.

Wiegert, Hans (1921) *'Jim an' Nell' von W.F. Rock: eine Studie zum Dialekt von Devonshire*. Doctoral dissertation, University of Berlin. Berlin: Mayer and Müller (special issue 137 in the series *Palaestra*).

Wolley-Dod, A.H. (1937) *The flora of Sussex*. Hastings: Saville. [New edition 1970.]

Wright, Joseph (1898–1905) *The English dialect dictionary*, vols 1–6. London: Oxford University Press. [The last vol. was also published separately as *The English dialect grammar.*]

Wright, Laura (1995) *Sources of London English: medieval Thames vocabulary.* Oxford: Oxford University Press.

Wright, Laura, ed. (2000) *The development of Standard English, 1300–1800.* Cambridge: Cambridge University Press.

PART TWO

SUSSEX DIALECT TEXTS and WORD-LISTS

CONTENTS

The commentary on each text is not intended to be exhaustive, but to give a linguistically accurate account of some of the most prominent non-standard features, many of which are mentioned in the description of the dialect given in Part One, Chapter 3.

Some of the items are not strictly texts, but the term is used for convenience throughout.

TEXT 0a

The Old English bounds of South Stoke (975)

> Ærest óf þám more on mærce cumb 7 swa to mærc hamme 7 swa to héan hammæ . 7 swa to ulan hyrste . 7 swa to þam west hliþe norð 7 lang to hogebura mearce . 7 swa útt to crawan ersce 7 swá to hean lea 7 swá bé norðan dyrnan hammæ nyþær innan þá ea.
>
> Þys sinð ða ðen into Stoce siblingc hyrst 7 trowing sceaddas 7 rocisfald .

First of all, a translation element by element. Some of the baroque hyphenated expressions represent an effort to do justice to the subtlety of the Saxons' topographical vocabulary. I have equipped what seem to be proper names, judging by their lack of an article and other syntactic criteria, with an initial capital letter.

> First from the marshland to/at Boundary-valley and so to Boundary-land-hemmed-in-on-at-least-two-sides-by-some-natural-obstacle and so to High-land-hemmed-in-[etc.] and so to Owl's-wood-on-an-eminence and so to the west steep-slope north along to Heel-peasants' boundary and so out to Crow's-stubblefield and so to High-wood/clearing and so north of Hidden-land-hemmed-in-[etc.] down within the sizeable-river.
>
> These [literally 'this'] are the swinepastures belonging to Dependent-farm: Kinsman-wood-on-an-eminence and [???] Log-sheds and Hroc's- (or Rook's-) fold.

Now a translation into idiomatic modern English, substituting for all expressions serving as place-names a form such as might have developed from the Old English expression without interference from non-phonological factors (these are marked with an asterisk).

> First from the marsh to/at *Markcomb, then to *Markham, then to *High(n)am, then to *Owlhurst, then to the west slope north along to the boundary of the peasants dwelling at *Hough/Hoe ((The) Heel), then out to *Crow(n)arsh, then to *Henley/*Highley, then north of *Durnham down on the hither side of the river.

These are the swinepastures belonging to *Stoke:
*Siblinghurst /Sullinghurst, *Trow(en)sheds, *Rooksfold.

In the twelfth-century manuscript B.L. Add. MS. 15350 (fo. 69r), printed in Rune Forsberg (1950) *Contribution to a dictionary of Old English place-names*. Uppsala: Lundequist (Nomina Germanica 9), 214-5.

The manuscript contains a copy of a grant of four hides (by local estimation) of land by king Edgar to his *propinquus* 'kinsman' Osward, dated A.D. 975. It is written in Latin, but the bounds of the territory involved are given in Old English. The grant was drawn up at the king's command, according to the preamble, to replace an earlier one destroyed by fire. It relates to a place called (*saxonice*) Æt Stoce. Forsberg was the first to associate it with South Stoke near Arundel.

Despite the date of the copy, the grant is in reasonably normal West Saxon dialect of the later period of Old English, though it may not represent anything linguistically specific to Sussex. It is offered here simply as a token text from the first millennium in the absence of any Anglo-Saxon document that has been identified as definitely originating in Sussex (but see comments on this matter in Part One, Chapter Two). Indications of vowel length are inconsistent; the accented letters sometimes indicate unstressed monosyllables (*be, of*). There are two erroneous uses of the letter <ð> instead of <d>, in *sinð* and *ðen*, in the sentence containing the list of swinepastures at the end. These might suggest that the medieval copyist took the obsolescent letter <ð> 'eth' as an ornamental variant of <d> as he neared the end of the text he was transcribing.

The use of the word *fald* in the swinepasture name *rocisfald* is characteristic of western Sussex; swinepastures are often named with OE *fal(o)d* 'fold' in western Sussex as opposed to *denn* in eastern Sussex. But note that it is actually described as a *denn* in this text.

TEXT 0b

A striking Old English regional feature: *nīge* 'new' in the western rapes of Sussex (5th century onwards)

> In *Nyewoods*, in two examples of *Nyetimber*, and in the early forms of *Newtimber*, just over the eastern border of the Rape of Bramber, we have OE *nige* in place of the common OE *niwe*. This is a peculiarity so far noticed only in south-east Hampshire and in the Isle of Wight. One gets it in *Niton* and in some of the early forms of *Newchurch* in the Isle of Wight and in the early forms of *Newtimber* in Warblington in south-east Hampshire. Cf. also the frequent *Niman* or *Nyman* as a pers[onal] name in the Sussex Rolls in place of the more usual *Niweman, Nyweman*, but confined to the four western Rapes . . . It corresponds to O[ld] Fris[ian] *ny, ni*, O[ld] Sax[on] *nigi* in contrast to the OE *niwe*, OSax *niwi*, O[ld] H[igh] G[erman] *niuwi*.

From the introductory material in A.H. Mawer and Frank Stenton, eds (1929) *The place-names of Sussex*, vol. 1. Cambridge: Cambridge University Press (Survey of English Place-Names 6), xxix.

TEXT 1

Sir John Pelham's letter to the Duke of Northumberland from besieged Pevensey castle (1399)

> My dere Lord, I recommande me to yowr hie Lordeschipp wyth hert and body and all my pore myght, and wyth all this I think zow, as my dere Lorde, derest and best yloved off all erthlyche Lordes; I say for me, and thanke yhow my dere Lord, with all thys that I say before, off your comfortable lettre, that ze send me from Pownefraite [Pontefract] that com to me on Mary Magdaleyn day; ffor by my trowth I was never so gladd as when I herd by your lettre, that ye warr stronge ynogh wyth the grace off God, for to kepe yow fro the malyce of your ennemys. And dere Lord iff it lyk to your hyee Lordeschippthat als son als ye mycht, that I myght her off your gracious spede, whyche God Allmyghty

contynue and encresse. And my dere Lord iff it lyk zow for
to know off my ffare, I am here by layd in manner off a
sege, with the countes of Sussex, Sudray, and a great parcyll
off Kentte; so that I ne may noght out, nor none vitayles
gette ine, bot w[t] myche hard. Wharfore my dere iff it lyk
zow, by the awyse off zowr wyse counsell, for to sett
remedye off the salvation off yhower castell, and wt stand
the malyce of ther schires foresayde. And also that ye be
fullyche enformed off there grett malyce wyrkers in these
schyres, whyche y[t] haffes so dispytfful y wrogth to zow, and
to zowr castell, to yhowr men, and to zour tenaunts ffore
this cuntree, have yai wastede for a gret whyle. Fare wele
my dere Lorde, the Holy Trinyte zow kepe fro zowr
ennemys, and son send me gud tythyngs off yhow. Ywryten
at Pevensay in the castell, on Saynt Jacobe day last past.

By yhowr awnn pore,
J. Pelham

The text is based on that printed by Simon Walker (1991) Letters to the Dukes of Lancaster in 1381 and 1399. *English Historical Review* 106, 68–79 [at 76–9]. Walker debunks the claim that this was written by 'Joan Pelham' to her husband John. As it stands, it is an 18th-century transcription of the original, which is lost. The underlined words are emended by Christopher Whittick and the present author. This is one of the earliest surviving private letters written in English.

There is little to attribute the letter to Sussex, but Pelham was born to two Sussex parents. *Haffes* 'has' is peculiar, since it seems to be a northern verb-form; a form ending in *-eth* would be expected in Sussex. *Warr* 'were' might also be interpreted as northern, with a Scandinavian source, but could represent more general earlier Middle English past tense plural *wǣron. Wharfore* 'wherefore' respects the word's etymology. The degree of variation between <y> and <z> (representing the letter yogh) at this date is remarkable.

TEXT 2

The Middle English Canticum de creatione*, Oxford, Bodleian Library, MS. Trinity College 57 (c.1400)*

[Lines 31-6: The Devil tempts Eve]

[The Devil] seyde: ‘eteþ an appel tyth,
And beþ as wyse as God almyth.’
Þus he tarede hem þere,
And dude furst Eue, and suþþe þe man,
Taken an appel and byten þeran.
Anon boþe naked þeȝ were.

[The Devil] said: ‘Eat an apple at once, and be as wise as God Almighty.’ Thus he provoked them there, and made first Eve, and then the man, take an apple and bite into it. Straight away they were both naked.

[Lines 61-72: Ejected from Paradise, Eve gets hungry]

And eyȝte days soȝten aboute,
Bote mete founde þeȝ non, saun doute,
Such as hy hadden byfore.
Anon to Adam Eue gan seye:
‘Sire, for honger y neȝ deye!
Wolde God ded y wore!

Al þat God is wroþ wiþ þe,
Wel y wot it is for me.’
Adam answered þere:
‘His creature is gret and ay shel be,
Whaþer it be for þe or me,
Sertis y wot neuere.’

. . . and [they] sought about for eight days, but they doubtlessly found no food such as they had before. At once Eve began to say to Adam: ‘Sire, I am nearly dying of hunger! Would to God I were dead! Even though God is angry with you, I know well that it is for me [i.e. it is my fault].’ Adam answered: ‘His creation is great and always shall be; whether it is for you or me I certainly never [shall] know.’

[Lines 559-70: Adam is about to die, and is reviewing his life for his son Seth]

Whanne God made ȝoure moder and me,
And putte vs in paradys for to be,
And bad vs wiþ word and þoȝt,
Of alle þe frutes taken oure fille,
Of þe tre of wit of guod and ille
He bad vs taken riȝt noȝt,

Þat in myddes of paradys stod.
Þus he bad vs for oure guod,
Ȝif we hadden had gras,
And ȝaf me myȝt of norþ and est,
And ȝoure moder wiþ south and west,
To don what oure wille was.

'. . . When God made your mother and me and put us in Paradise, and told us with word and thought to take our fill of all the fruits, he told us to take absolutely nothing from the tree of knowledge of good and evil that stood in the middle of Paradise. That's what he told us for our [own] good, if we had had grace, and gave me power over north and east, and your mother over south and west, to do what[ever] we wished . . . '

[Lines 899-914: The events following Adam's death]

Þo sixe days were gon
Eue to Seth þus gan seye:
'Tak and make tables tweye
Of al oure lyf anon,

Tweye of erthe and tweye of ston,
writ þeron oure lyf anon,
Þat we haue had here;
For longe er domesday falle
Þis worlde shel be fordon alle
By water or by fere.

Ȝif it be by water fordon,
Þane shollen þe tables of ston
Lasten withouten lye;

ȝif it þorghe fer be broȝt to nouȝt,
Þane sholle þe tables of erthe wroȝt
Lasten sikerlye.'

When sixty days were gone, Eve began saying this to Seth: 'Take and straight away make two tablets of all our life, two of earth and two of stone, straight away write [on them] our life that we have had here; for long before Doomsday happens, this world shall all be destroyed by water or by fire. If it be destroyed by water, then the tablets of stone will truly last; if it be brought to nothing by fire, then the tablets made of earth will surely last.'

Published by Brian Murdoch and J.A. Tasioulas, eds, in *The apocryphal lives of Adam and Eve edited from the Auchinleck Manuscript and from Trinity College, Oxford, MS 57.* Exeter: University of Exeter Press (2002).

On page 6 of their introduction, the editors describe the features which permit the *Linguistic atlas of Later Medieval English* to allocate the poem to Sussex, and the verses printed here are chosen to illustrate these rather than to give a coherent chunk of narrative. The editors' expanded scribal contractions have been silently adopted. The punctuation is modern.

There are some lexemes common to the whole south of England, such as *tweye* 'two' (901), the descendant of the Old English masculine nominative form, and *ble* 'bly, appearance' (79, not in the selected text, but antedating by over 200 years the records in OED). The third-person plural pronouns in <h-> (33 *(hem)* and 63); and the plural imperative ending in <-þ> (31, 32) are also southern. Murdoch and Tasioulas call the form *suthen* (in the text *suþþe* 'since' (34)) 'very southern', by contrast with *sitthen* and the like. *Whaþer* for 'whether' (71) is found most frequently south of London, and *fer(e)* 'fire' (908, 912) indicates the eastern part of the south, as does the spelling *guod* for 'good' (563, 566). These features permit us to infer that the text may represent Sussex dialect.

Note the maintenance of the Old English distinction between the vowels of singular and plural forms of the verb *shulen* 'shall', here *shel* (70, 907) and *sholle(n)* (910, 913). *Wore* 'were' (66) is believed to be an originally Scandinavian form of the verb, which migrated southwards during the Old and Middle English periods along with the words *both* (36) and *take* (901), and was taken into the standard language. Note also the inconsistent representation of the present-tense plural verb inflection *-n* (910, 913), and the inconsistent spelling of /θ/ as either <th> or <þ> (throughout).

If this poem, or its manuscript, is genuinely of Sussex, it may be found surprising that there are no instances of initial <v> as in Texts 4 and 6, except in French loanwords such as *vanschede* 'vanished' (685) and *voys* 'voice' (1011), neither in the selected text.

TEXT 3

Indenture, Arundel Castle Muniments MD 413 (1476)

> This indentur' made atte Arundell the Furst day of Marche the xve yere of the Rengne of Kyng Edward the / iiijthe wittenessith that Edward Ponyngges mayster of the College of the holy Trinite of Arundell and the chapleyns of / the same place havyn yeve and grauntyd unto John Dudley squyar a Tombe of marbyll stondyng in the chauncell / of the chirche of Arundell callyd the Vicaryyschauncell The whyche Tombe afore tyme was made and ordeynyd / for on Richard Dalyngrygg' squyar The seid John to have the seid tombe to hym and his assign' so that at / no season the seid Tombe be had nor in no maner wyse takyn ner removyd from the place hit now stondyth yn / In Wittenesse here of to the on party of these indentur' remaynyng with the seyd maystr' and chapleynys / The seid John Dudley squyar hath putte hys seal To the othir party of these indentur' remaynyng with the / seid John Dudley The seid mayster and chapellayns havyn putte here comyn seal yevyn at Arundell / aforesaid in oure chapitour hous the day and yere Aboveseid.

Published by Nigel Saul in *Sussex Archaeological Collections* 147 (2009), 126.

This legal document is written in chancery-inspired very late Middle English with precious few regional features. Note the *-n* inflection of the third person plural of the verb in *havyn* (twice) and the optionality of the *-n* of the past participle of the verb GIVE (*yeve* vs. *yevyn*), which retains its original initial <y>. <o> before a nasal consonant, as in *stondyng,* is originally typical of the West Midland dialect, but late in the ME period (as here) it also shows up in south-eastern texts (Milroy 1992*: 175 – see bibliography of Part One).

TEXT 4

Cowfold churchwardens' accounts (late fifteenth century, extracts)

1460
It. pro lavare de festment and awter clothes v d.
A remembrans that we Jon Waterman, of the parishe of Asheyngton, brother of Wylliam Waterman and Jon Waterman, of the parishe of Wormyngherst, haf recd. a stok . . .

1470
It. eodem Jon Dowsse hav deliferid the same stok unto the wardeynis agen.

1471
. . . collectores of owr sofferyn lord the kyng . . .

before 1476?
It. pro costagies et faciende de cere et costagies de vetel xij d.

1481–2
It. pro lavare de festments and sorpliss ij d.
It. for setyng to a stapyl for the fys dor j d.

Published in *Sussex Archaeological Collections* 2 (1849), 316–25.

The extracts are chosen to illustrate the variation in the usage of the letters <f> and <v>, which suggests that the distinction between /f/ and /v/ was not maintained rigidly, and in particular that the old south-western feature admitting only /v/ in initial position still held good at this time. *Vetel* is modern non-standard English *fettle* 'arrangement'; *fys* is *vis* 'spiral staircase'. Both initial <f> and <v> very probably mean /v/, even medially (*deliferid, sofferyn*) and finally (*haf/hav*). *Costagies* means 'expenses', and is not a dialect word.

TEXTS 5a-f

Epitaphs (sixteenth to eighteenth centuries)

(a) St Michael's church, Lewes: epitaph of Sir Nicholas Pelham, 1559 (extract)

> What time the French sought to have sack't Sea-foord,
> This Pelham did Repellthem back aboord.

This epitaph has been much quoted in support of the authenticity of a pronunciation of *Seaford* with stress on the second syllable, because of the requirements of the rhyme.

(b) East Grinstead: epitaph of Francis Haselden, 1616

> HERE . LYETH . BVRYED . FRANCIS . HASELDEN . LATE . WIFE / VNTO . IOHN . HASELDEN . OF . HALY . DAFTER . VNTO . HUMFRY / [CO]VERT . ESQVYRE . WHO . DYED . AVGVST . 26 . ANNO . 16[16]

(c) Wadhurst: epitaph of Hellen Dunmoll, 1651

> HEER . LYETH. THE / BODY . OF . HELL= / EN . THE . WIFE . OF / JOSEPH . DVNMOLL / GENT. WHO . WAS / DAFTAR . OF . DAV= / ID . BARHAM . GENT / WHICH . DIED / THE . SIXTH . DAY / OF . FEBRUARY . 1651

Spellings like *daftar* are found in many places at this period. Note, for instance, *doffter* and *dafter* in the Bishop's Transcripts of the parish registers (1584) for West Thorney at the extreme western margin of the county; similarly in the Hove parish registers (1632 onwards).

(d) Hartfield: epitaph of John Mills, 1702

> Heere lyethe body of / Muster John Mills / of Cotchford in Hartfield

Muster underlies the formerly general Sussex use of *Mus'* for the title *mister*.

(e) Poling: epitaph of Alice Wooldridge, 1740 (extract)

> The World is a round thing
> And full of crooked streets.
> Death is a market place
> Where all Men meets; ....

The non-standard verb agreement in the fourth line is guaranteed by the rhyme.

(f) Lindfield: epitaph of Richard Turner, died aged 21, 1768

> Long was my Pain, great was my Grief,
> Surgeons I'd many, but no Relief
> I trust through Christ to rise with the just
> My Leg and Thigh was buried fust.

This famous inscription was recut in the 1950s by John Skelton at the instance of Helena Hall. It shows the general Sussex loss of /r/ before /s/ within the same morpheme, guaranteed by the rhyme.

Image 10: Richard Turner's gravestone at Lindfield (1768), recut by John Skelton; 'was buried fust' is just about legible bottom right of the pale band

TEXT 6

Daniell Seymor: Bill for repairs to Chichester cathedral weathercock (1638)

A noate of the materialles used and emplied and for the makinge of the Weather Cocke.

	£. s. d.
Imprimis in Copper 32lb. at 8d. the pound comes to	2 8 0
Item in Brasse 24lb. at 15d. the pound come to	1 10 0
Item in silver soder	0 5 0
Item in Tin to soder the Cock 4lb. at 1s. the pound	0 4 0
Item in leafe gold to gild the Cocke twise over with it beinge 16 bookes at2s. 6d. a booke comes to	2 0 0
Item for makinge and gilding the Cocke	3 10 0
	9 17 0

Item allowed backe for 20lb. of shrufe that was Cut and viled of
in the m[a]kinge of the coke which yelded 9d. the pound and
Came to 0 15 0
Soe that take 15s. out of £9 17s. then doth Remayne the some of 9 2 0
The materiales in grosse about the Cocke unmade wayed 60lb.
The Cocke beinge made wayed 32lb.
The pipe beinge wayed 2
The Shrufe Cut of and allowed for above wayed 20
The wast in making Cutting and viling was 6

Item being all Cast up make the Just 60lb.

Receved in full of This bill of Mr. Lawrence Pay Doctor in Devinetie the sume of £9 2s. and for 20lb. of Shruffe 15s. that I sold it being both the full deamand of this bill I say Receaved in full by me Daniell Seymor the sum of £9 17s. paid and entred.

Published by C.E. Welch in *Sussex Notes and Queries* 15 (1961), 273–4.

Note the retention of initial <v> for /f/ in *viled, viling* 'filed, filing'. Perhaps this feature remained in technical (and therefore vernacular) parlance only; for in the non-technical but contractual (and therefore official) parts of the bill we find *full* three times, not *vull*. The form *emplied* 'employed' suggests [ai] for

/oi/, or perhaps rather that /oi/ and /ai/ had merged and could be spelt either way. *Wayed* indicates that /x/, spelt <gh>, has been completely lost by the date of the text. The spelling *soder* for *solder* is the formerly normal one; spellings with <l> begin to be found only from the 17th century onwards. *Shruff* is a now-obsolete term for the surplus metal clipped or filed off from the edge of a rough casting.

TEXT 7

William Peachey: sword inscriptions (1643/4)

Peachey's 40 known sword inscriptions in English show several instances of local vernacular usage. This may be of East Hampshire or of West Sussex, but we treat these here as a single area relevant to the theme of this book. They are presented below, analysed by grammatical feature.

(i) The use of *be* for the present tense of the copula, in all persons recorded:

first person:

I John Cooke bee
Thee dye bye mee
– sword of John Cooke of Westburton [in Bury, Sussex]

Cross be mee
Cross I bee
– sword of Johnathon Cross of Blendworth [Hampshire]

I, Joe Eyles
Bee full o' wiles
– sword of Joseph Eyles of Hambledon [Hampshire]

I be fitt
– sword of William Fitt of Purbrooke [Hampshire]

Mann bee mee
Man I bee
– sword of Nehemiah Mann of Colhook [in North Chapel, Sussex]

When I be wraught on
Thee migt'st have naught on!
– sword of Richard Norton (i.e. Col. Dick Norton)
[Norton was a magnate living at Old Alresford and Southwick, Hampshire]

second person:

Ware thy head . . . John Benstead
Splits they [sic] head . . . thee be dead
– sword of John Benstead of Hambledon

third person, either number:

If Carisbrooke shee must be tooke,
Ye waye aloan be knowne to Cooke
– sword of Robert Cooke of Carisbrooke

Cross be mee
Cross I bee
– sword of Johnathon Cross of Blendworth

My n[a]ym be mayd from grat Crusade
Soe toe just cause I give mye aide
– sword of William Dacre [construed as d'Acre] of Benefoulde [in Petworth (or Lurgashall?), Sussex]

Mann bee mee
Man I bee
– sword of Nehemiah Mann of Colhook

Few foes wyl bee founde
When Pellatt bee a'rounde
– sword of John Pellatt of Burie [Sussex] (punning on *pellet* in the sense of 'round metal shot' and, heraldically, 'roundel sable')

What coloure bee lockes on thy hed
Matters nott ... I stayn 'em red
– sword of John Silverlock of Farlington [Hampshire]

(ii) the use of thee as the second person singular subject form, with a bare-stem form of the verb in most, but not all, instances:

Ware thy head ... John Benstead
Splits they head ... thee be dead
– sword of John Benstead of Hambledon

I John Cooke bee
Thee dye bye mee
– sword of John Cooke of Westburton

Royalist, fie! Bye mee thee dye
Unless thee flye from mee John Frye!
– sword of John Frye of Battylhyrst [in Kirdford, Sussex]

When I be wraught on
Thee migt'st have naught on!
– sword of Richard Norton (i.e. Col. Dick Norton)

Inscriptions published by Richard Coates (1999), in *Neophilologus* 83, 617–21, with fuller description and analysis. William Peachey (1622–88), blacksmith, lived and worked at East Dean, near Chichester. Among his commissions were broadswords for the Hambledon Boys of the Parliamentarian army's cavalry, under Col. Dick Norton, in 1643/4.

Although the swords themselves have disappeared, the mottoes engraved on them were written down. The whereabouts of the document preserving them are not known. But a transcript was in the hands of one of Peachey's descendants, Mr R. J. Mullens Harrison, who made it available to the Rev. John H. Bishop, former rector of Singleton. The mottoes are reproduced just as they appear in Bishop's booklet *A Sussex pot-pourri*, privately published, no date [?1987].

Data-sets (i) and (ii), and especially the Benstead inscription which illustrates both of them, are of great interest in the light of the fact that the *Linguistic atlas of England* (map M6) shows nearby Hambledon (Hampshire survey point no. 5) to be (as of c.1960) the only survey point for some considerable distance in any direction which shows both of these features. Feature (i) is characteristic of Sussex and east Hampshire, whilst feature (ii) can generally be found markedly further west than east Hampshire.

Notice also the pun *naught on* ~ *Norton*, which demonstrates the loss of /r/ before a consonant.

TEXT 8a

Inventory of the Lord Admiral Thomas Seymour's brewhouse at Cheseworth (1549)

A grete copper in the fornase
iij. grete fatts
a grete covyll of ffyr
smale kelers xix.
stykmands viij.
hop mands j.
a long trough from the wall
a peyer of slyngs
ij. towells
copper kettylls ij.
stykforks ij.
rothers iiij.
shovylls ij.
skopatts ij.
coole bak j.
an ax j.
kymells ij.
ffyer prongs ij.
baralls xxxvj.
a carte wt whelys
a payer wooddyn tonggs

Published by Sir Henry Ellis in *Sussex Archaeological Collections* 13 (1861), 123–4.

Notice the spellings suggesting a two-syllable pronunciation of *pair* and *fire*. *Fatts* illustrates the word which is now commonly used in its originally West Country form *vats*. *Keelers, kimmels* and *kivers* are various kinds of tub; a *scoppet* is a malt-shovel. A *mand* is a maund, a type of wicker basket with handles. A good illustration of the use in a local document of local terminology for household items, though some of the terms are found wider afield than Sussex.

TEXT 8b

Inventory of William Strudwick of Hills Green, Kirdford (1678, extracts)

In the kicthen.

-- pond of pewter, £4. 14s. 8d., thre brass fore iron potts 3 iron kittels three brass pootts 4 brass kitteles to brass panes 3 brass skillets three iron driping panes 8 spitts one pare of andirons firepan and tongs three pare of pootthangers and jacks one tapele dreser & form and other things, £3. 17s.

In the hall.

a table and to ioned forms and a ston taple one copord & a still, £2.

In the beakehouse.

2 cheesprees a beaking trow a sillting trow a kneall tub & flouer tub & kiver hopes & valles 3 sershes to spining whilles & other lumber, £2. 10s.

In the chamber over the parlor.

one bed & bedstedel curtains & wallins one coverlett to blancets one table to chears & a stoll 2 boolsters & one under beed to pellows, £6.

Published by G.H. Kenyon in *Sussex Archaeological Collections* 93 (1955), 116–8.

The spelling of this is less standard than that of most published Kirdford inventories of the period – 'unusually wayward', as Kenyon puts it, and not merely indicating the dialect of the writer (probably one Henry Penfold). There is a marked tendency to write short vowels with a double letter, as in *-prees* 'press', *poott-* 'pot'. *Ioned* is 'joined', i.e. made by joinery not carpentry. *Valles* may be vallors or wooden dishes; *wallins* are presumably valances. The Sussex (i.e. 'Kentish') treatment of Old English /y/ is seen in the regular *pellows*, and *kitteles* shows a not unfamiliar raising of Middle English /e/ before an alveolar consonant, still found in this word in many places by the time of the Survey of English Dialects.

TEXT 9

West Thorney churchwardens' accounts (1725–6; extract)

> Robert Lane choase Church warden [attempted erasure of these two words; the insert is illegible] of the paresh of west thorney thes day the 1 day of aprell 1725 and Robert Lane has in hand 4 shellings to penss three farthings.
>
> Robard Lane Chosen Chorch wordden for the paresh of west thornay this yere 1726 he hath in hand siex shillines and won hapny.

From 1744 onwards, the operative word is regularly written *church wordings*.

From West Sussex Record Office document Par 196/12.

These pieces are remarkable for the persistence of <e> for <i> (especially 1725), and the evidence for it offered by the inverse spelling in *wordings*. Other irregular spellings dictated by general (not just Sussex) pronunciation can be seen, e.g. *yere, won. Hath* in 1726 is already archaic, perhaps evidence of a deliberate attempt at cultivated written style; witness also the emerging Standard English normal form *chosen* (1726) instead of the local form of the passive participle without *-en* visible in the previous entry.

TEXT 10a

John Burgess, Jernal *(1785–90, extracts)*

> Monday 11 April 1785
>
> Work in ye shop in ye forenoon and in ye afternoon went to Franklins to see Mas Burne because he was going to Billingshurst to live that nix Day ...
>
> Saturday 30 April 1785
>
> Went to Newwick Fayer

Sunday 1 May 1785

. . . This evening about 1/4 past 8 oclock my son Jesse Died he was atween Something upwards of a year old never was well from the day of its Birth to the day of its Death &c

Monday 19 September 1785

... Mr Baldy is to have the old fince in the hedge . . . But Mr Baldy is to find curbe Bucket & rope &c & alow what Water is wanting to soply the yard for a sertain tarm of years . . . the post aluded to in the garn is the first post of the pale fenc southward.

Tuesday 29 August 1786

Was asisting in opening a Steen Grave in order to inlarge it for to put Mr Chatfield in it was his Fathers Grave & he had Been Buried 50 years the Coffin was very much Decayed but not so much but that we Could see the date &c

Wednesday 30 August 1786

12 men to Car Each a Silk Hatban I had one . . .

Friday 22 September 1786

this Morning went to the Rookery took my mony for Reeping one acre & half weat in the Brooms Croat at 8/ acre Mas Geering & I Reeped it betwen us we had no bait nor Beer all the time

Monday 4 December 1786

. . . Went to ye Crown Lewes to See a Very remarkable Ox that was their for a Show it was Like other oxen in every respect except its Head and that had only one Horne Growed Strait out of its poul of a bout 3 feet 8 inches or near 4 feet round & was so Long as to prevent his grasing So that he Cant Get his mouth to ye Ground So that he is oblidge to be fed with bran &c in a diffirant manner he is about 5 years old breiad in Scotland Gave 2d to see him – his Horne Spreed So wide that it Nearly Covered one of his eyes - he is a very Large well mad ox of a ridish Caller &c ------

Wednesday 20 June 1787

Went to Brighthelmstone after a letpass to Car 2 packs Wool to Lewes to mr Chatfield &c I Bot 7 Mackril for 6d & Quart of Rigrels for 2d went packing wool after I Came home has mas Geering to help me &c

Tuesday 1 January 1788

Work in ye Shop &c Flawing Mr Linfields Horse that died Last Night gave 3/ Hide

Friday 14 March 1788

Went to Fryers Oake to a Bull Bait to Sell My Dog I Sold him for 1 Guineay upon Condition he was Hurt but as he recvd no Hurt I took him again at the same price I Had all my Expences paid Because I had a dog there was 5 or 6 dogs but mine was Calld the best we had a good dinner a round of Beef Boild A good piece roasted a Lag of mutten & Ham of pork & plum pudden plenty of wine & punch all the after Noon there was a great many people

Monday 26 May 1788

Was Caring mould out of ye Garden mas Geering & I began to dig a Draw Well in ye garden for ye use of ye yard &c we got only about 6 feet deep to day &c

Friday 30 May 1788

We was Well diging & mound [mould?] Caring &c

Wednesday 19 August 1789

Went to Brighthelmstone to See many devertions on account of the Rial Family that is the Duke of Yorks Birth day Cricketing Stool Ball Foot Ball Dancing &c fire works &c 2 Large Beast Rosted upon the Hill a large Quantity of Bread & Strong Beer Given With the Beef Some said there was 20000 people

East Sussex Record Office MS. AMS 5853/1. Privately published by Leonard Maguire (1982) *The journal and correspondence of John Burgess*, 1785–1819; and republished privately by Donald F. Burgess (1989) in *No continuing city. The diary and letters of John Burgess, a craftsman from Sussex, from 1785–1819.*

Notice the striking evidence for a one-syllable pronunciation of *carry* and (variably) *garden*, and the evidence for a two-syllable pronunciation of *fair*. There is also much evidence for non-standard vowel-height in such words as *next, fence, reddish* (raising of /e/ before an alveolar consonant), *leg* and *term* (lowering of /e/ before a velar consonant and before /r/), and also a non-standard diphthong /ai/ in *royal*. *Croat* is a widespread and common enough alternative to *croft* 'house-plot'. Non-standard inflection can be seen in *growed.* The neuter possessive pronoun is used to refer to Burgess's sickly child. Regional words include *bait* 'afternoon snack', *rigrels* 'sand-eels' and *flaw* 'strip the hide from'.

TEXT 10b

John Burgess, letter to his son John Burgess (18 September 1794, extract)

[Advice to his son in case he should decide to join his father in Mount Pleasant, Westchester County, New York State.]

> . . . if you Boord your self I would advise you to take plenty
> good flour dry & fit for Sea Some Bread we had 3 half
> hundread wait But dont think we used them half take plenty
> Chees & Butter Suger & plumbs potatoes peas Ginger
> Bread tea Coffe Chocolot &c pepper Salt Bacon Eggs these
> are all useful things I found flour & Butter Suger & plumbs
> the most useful Because of making puddings you will want
> tin pudding pan to Bake in tea kittle & tea pot &c tin or
> coper saus pan Wood Bould or Something large enuff to
> wett a pudding in gallon Bottle will be Very useful to take
> your lowance of water every Morning if the Captain finds
> Water which you had better agree for him to do that you will
> Most likely want a Chamber pot or tin kittle or sume shuch
> thing as you may be sick strung Chest with Several partings
> in it would be Very handy for most likely you will be very
> Crouded we was that we was not able to find were to set our
> Chest if you dont Boord your self you will Suffer much if

> you dont take Some of these things with you without you Can eat Salt beef & pork Better than I can So porter will be very handy But take Care to have Boxes or Chests Enuff to Lock up your Close & provicions & look sharp to your Neethbours pudden Cloth will be wanted Nothing to ly upon Except you find it but any thing will do in the Summer time any old Close the very worst you have will be good enuff on Ship Boord for it spiles Cloth very much indeed

East Sussex Record Office MS. AMS 5853/3. Privately published by Leonard Maguire (1982) *The journal and correspondence of John Burgess, 1785–1819*; and republished privately by Donald F. Burgess (1989) in *No continuing city. The diary and letters of John Burgess, a craftsman from Sussex, from 1785–1819.*

Further regional pronunciations are indicated by *kittle* (cf. *kitteles* in Text 8b) and *spiles*. Notice the absence of an unstressed initial syllable in *lowance*. *Bould* appears to be for *bowl* and *strung* for *strong*, and these may be idiosyncrasies among other more obvious ones such as *Neethbours*.

TEXT 10c

John Burgess, letter to his son John Burgess (14 May 1815, extract)

[A further letter from New York State.]

> . . . I formerly beleft in the doctrin of Endless mesery but I find that has no foundation in scripture nor Reason or Justice so I have given that up the doctrine of original sin of atonement of personal Election & reprobation are to me doctrins absurd in the Extreem ---------------
>
> I am very glad to hear that the doctrin of the unity of god prevails so much I wish it Could be planted hear for we hear nothing but rank Calvanism Except the methodist I very sildum go to meeting now I am So deaf & when I Could hear I did not believe one half what I heard So that I injoy myself much better in reading & I have the use of a very large Library belonging to a gentleman who Came from London long Since I Came --------------

East Sussex Record Office MS. AMS 5853/3. Privately published by Leonard Maguire (1982) *The journal and correspondence of John Burgess, 1785–1819*; and republished privately by Donald F. Burgess (1989) in *No continuing city. The diary and letters of John Burgess, a craftsman from Sussex, from 1785–1819.*

Regional pronunciations may be indicated by *mesery* and *sildum*, but they may represent a response to the difficulty offered to spellers by the varying pronunciation of words like *kettle/kittle*. Non-standard inflection can be seen in *beleft*, the past tense of *believe*.

TEXT 11

Regional vocabulary hangs on in 1846

Rubbish brought in by birds.

> 10. If jackdaws (or caddows) are allowed to come often be up there to scrape the bells, to which otherwise they do a great deal of harm, and to carry away the stacks of rubbish which they bring in, and leave about. I have sometimes seen the Tower stairs so choked up with this rubbish, that I could hardly make my way up them. I knew one church where the Clerk was allowed by the Churchwarden to have for his own use all that the caddows had brought into the Tower: and he took home, at one time, two cart-loads of good firewood, besides a great quantity of rubbish which he threw away. Birds also often leave sticks under the eaves of a church, and behind the cornice. This you should watch your time and take away as you can.

John Mason Neale (1846) *A few word to parish clerks and sextons of country parishes.* London: Joseph Masters (The Ecclesiological late Cambridge Camden Society).

Even writers fully conversant with the literary standard language used local vocabulary with no more than a nod in the direction of alternatives. Neale seems to have preferred the local word *caddow* (interestingly not in Parish 1875 or Hall 1957, but described as dialectal in the *Oxford English dictionary*, which quotes from the above passage), because that is the one he uses to achieve lexical cohesion in the passage.

TEXT 12a

'Tim Cladpole' (Richard Lower), Jurney to Lunnun *(1832: extracts)*

[Tom Cladpole decides to seek his fortune in London.]

Well so next morning up scratch'd I,
And mother up scratch'd she,
She cry'd and 'lowd tud braak ur hert,
In parten thus wud me!

"Now, Tom," says she, "besure [sic] Tom do,
'Have well were ya be gwyn,
Whatever others do to you,
An never turn agin."

"Yes, very purty fancy dat?
No blow ma jacket tight,
If dey begin der rigs wud me
I'll dewced soon show fight!

"So good-bye, mother." Off I goos,
As fast as I could brish;
But thought, as I went by our shaa,
I'd cut a *liddle swish.*

'Twas ashen butt, both tuff and strong,
De gurt en' had a nub;
An spose we say 'bout three fut long,
And taper'd loike a club.

Now whislin up de grove I goos,
Close by ol' Grinder's Mill,
Birds sung and seem'd to cheer me up,
As I went down de hill.

Many long miles I shuffled on,
As fast as I coud goo;
At last I gun to feel, ya see,
De haboot ring ma toe.

•••••••••••••

[Tom has seen some sights and got himself into trouble.]

Dey sen, an puffen out ov breath,
Along come *Squyer Brown*;
He sed I ment no hort, and was
A simple country clown.

So arter dun-a-much more glib,
Dey did agree at lass,
Dat I shud pay *ten shillings* down,
Fer braaking ov de glass.

I paid de brads, an turnen roun,
I thaut to come away,
"No no," dey sed, "ya luckless lad,
Ya've *twenty more to pay*!"

"Fer what?" I ax'd; dey sed, "Fer cost,"
(Dat I cud never know,)
So I dubb'd down de stuff, ya see,
An *den dey let ma goo*.

I growl'd, but not a single word
Ov all that I could say,
Would dey attend, -- so fierd crass,
At lass I cum away.

If dis be Lunnun, now thinks I,
I'll soon be bodgen home,
I told our Sal and Squyer too,
I wish'd I'd never cum.

She sed uf I'd goo back wud ur,
She'd ge me a new hat, --
But dash ma wig I'd no more peace
In Lunnun arter dat.

An so nex mornen up I scratch'd
We buss'd an sed gud-bye,
I cum away ternation crass,
But Sally pip'd ur eye.

Ma bag was gran nigh empty too,
An dat ya know is bad,
Fer *ninepence* now, to tell de truth,
Was all de brass I had.

•••••••••••••

So I got home dat self-same nite,
Which mother star'd to see,
I told ur how it wos ud Sal,
An how it wos ud me.

I sed I'd been to Lunnun wonce,
But I goo dere no more;
Fer I cum back a bigger fool
Dan I had been afore!

But Mother never simd to mind,
Tho' all my brads wos gone,
Yet arter all 'tis very true
I ha'nt bin dere fer naun.

Fer I have larn't a thing or two,
From what I now have sin;
An wise anuf I'm sartin sure,
Never to goo agin!

'Tim Cladpole' (Richard Lower), *Tom Cladpole's jurney to Lunnun* (1842), verses 18–24, 118–26 and 149–52. The spelling and punctuation are that of the Farncombe edition (1928).

TEXT 12b

'Tim Cladpole' (Richard Lower), Jan Cladpole's Trip to 'Merricur in search of dollar trees *(1844: extract).*

[Jan Cladpole has been deluded into going to America to seek his fortune, and is trying to get back to Sussex.]

I told the Captain wot I'd sin,
He sed 'twas badish luck,

An uf I longed fer home agen
I might goo back a *Duck.**

"A Duck! wot goo a paddle quack
"Acrass that gurt wide sea?
Why, I can't swim a bit," says I.
"Not sich a Duck!" says he.

"But work yer way, as ya have done,
"Fer me to England's shore."
Says I, "I woll goo back a duck,
"I've bin a *Goose* afore.

"Or else I never shud a left
"*Ma Dad* an good *ol' Mum*;
"Who woll ma' goo to 'Merricur,
"Uf I can once get home!"

Thinks I dere's no more trouble now
(As I have had sich luck),
But soon I foun deres nothen else
Fer them as cums *Jim Duck.*

De Capten was a swellen blade,
Sailors as bad an wus,
Jim here – Jim dere – Jim everywhere –
And dey did swear and cuss.

"Ya lubber, goo an swab de deck –
"Now goo an feed de hogs" –
Dey give me stinking beef to eat,
Not fit to fling to dogs.

Dey made me pump de water up,
And ge me meny a swack
Wud a tarnashun gurt ol' rup
Upon ma poor sore back.

* Sich Cheps wot work dere way home de sailors call um Jimmy Ducks.

An as fer bed, deres none ov dat,
However went de weather,
Jim Duck an hogs upon de deck
Turn'd in an slept together!

De ol' black Cook did favour me
Wud otherwile a bite;
Or I shud never liv'd to tell,
But starv'd an died outright.

At last we got to Liverpool,
An when I went ashore,
Dey told me I had got to goo
Two hundred miles an more.

A purty mess – ma clothes is gone –
No brass at all have I,
An wether I can beg or no,
I don't know – but I'll try!

So I set up a *Beggar Man*,
An matches I did sell;
Jim Duck's was much a wosser job,
Nor liv'd nor lodg'd so well!

After a fortnit's beggaren,
Ma home at las I found;
Mother she cry'd and father laff'd –
But all wos safe and soun.

[Jan confronts ol' Wax, his persuader.]

"Ah, never mind, ol' gal, says I –
An den to Father sed,
"I'll ge *ol' Wax a blowen up*
"*Afore I goo to bed.*"

I went, and dere I see un stan,
A readen ov de news;
"Ya lying rip," says I, "git in,
"An sole and mend yer shoes!

“Ya sed ya’d maak *a Man* ov me,
“Deny it uf ya can,
“Dese rags wud dat do well agree,
“But ’tis a *Beggar man!* . . . ”

‘Tim Cladpole’ (Richard Lower), *Jan Cladpole’s trip to ’Merricur in search of dollar trees* (c.1844), verses 133–49. The spelling and punctuation are that of the Farncombe edition (undated, ‘new edition’).

The first consciously dialectal writings from Sussex, and two of the classic texts. The author hailed from Chiddingly, and the type is eastern, as illustrated by consistent /d/ for initial /ð/. The retention of <l> in *ol’* may also suggest the east or centre of the county (*LAE* map Ph133), but that may be an over-interpretation. The spelling indicates that word-final /nd/ is almost regularly simplified to /n/, and final /st/ is variably reduced to /s/. *Ud* is phonologically regular for *with*. *Go* appears as *goo* in these and practically every other Sussex text. [ɒ] is unrounded in *(a)crass*. Eye-dialect is in evidence, e.g. *tuff*, *fut*, *ment*, *nite*, *wos*, *wether*, *cry’d*. In both texts *ge me* is for *gave (gev) me*.

In Text 12a, *haboot* is presumably ‘half-boot’. *Rigs* is a cant word for ‘swindle’ as in *thimble-rigs*, *shaa* is for *shaw* ‘strip of woodland’, *glib* could be rendered ‘yakking’, *dub down* (not in the *Oxford English dictionary* in this exact form) is ‘pay up’, usually now *dib up*, *brads* is ‘cash’. *Naun* is ‘nothing’, as widely in the south of England.

In Text 12b, a *swack* is a blow; *otherwhile* means ‘sometimes’. *Rip* is a widespread colloquial term of mild abuse in the 19th century. The rhyme *home* = *Mum* requires /um/ in both words, but this is not really supported by the data in Wright (1905: 487–9) nor by the *LAE* maps Ph129a-d. Note the resumptive pronoun for the topicalized direct object in the footnote, *wot* as the personal relative pronoun in the same place, and the double morphological comparative *wosser* ‘worse’ in the main text. *A readen ov* (from a Middle English construction amounting to *on reading of*) shows the use of a verbal noun where a participle construction would now be used (*reading the news*).

The author provides a glossary to his poems in his book *Stray leaves from an old tree* (1862; Part Three, Section D1.2).

TEXT 13a

Mark Antony Lower: Chols Packham's experiences with fairies (1854)

"When I was a liddle boy and lived with my gurt uncle, old Jan Duly at —, dere was a old place dey used to call Burlow Castle. It wa'nt much ov a castle onny a fow old walls like -- but it had been a famous place in de time when dere was a king in every county.[1] Well, whatever it had been afore, at the time I speak an, it was de very hem of a place for Pharisees, and nobody didn't like to goo by it ahter dark for fear an um. One dee as Chols Packham, uncle's grandfather (I've heerd uncle tell de story a dunnamany times), was at plough up dere, jest about *cojer*[2] time, he heerd a queer sort of a noise right down under de groun dat frightened him uncommonly sure-lie. 'Hullow,' says Chols to his mate, 'did you hear dat, Harry?' 'Yahs,' says Harry, 'what was it?' 'I reckon 'twas a Pharisee,' says uncle's grandfather. 'No 'twa'nt,' says Harry, 'dere a'nt no Pharisees now. Dere *was once* -- at Jerusalem; but dey was full-growed people, and has been dead hunderds o' years.' Well, while dey was a talkin', Chols heerd de noise agin. 'Help! help! help!' Chols was terribly afeard, but he plucked up heart enough to ax what was wanted. 'I've been a bakin,' said de liddle voice, 'and have broke my peel,' (dat's a sort o' thing dat's used to put loaves into de oven wud) 'and I dunnow what upon de airth to do.' *Under* de airth, Chols thought she ought to a said, but howsonever he didn't say so. And being a tender-hearted kind of a chap dat didn't like any body to be in trouble, he made answer without any peramble, 'Put it up, and I'll try and mend it.' No soonder said dan done; dere was a chink in de groun', for de season was dryish, and sure enough, through dat chink dere come up a liddle peel not bigger dan a bren-cheese knife. Chols couldn't hardly help laughin', it was such a monstus liddle peel, not big enough to hold a gingey-bread nut hardly; but howsonever he thought 'twas too seerous a thing to laugh at, for he knowed of old how dahngerous 'twas to offend any of dem liddle customers. So he outs wud a tin-tack or two as he happened to have in his weskit pocket, and wud de help ov his cojer knife for a hammer, and his knee for a bench, he soon mended de peel and put it down de chink again. Harry was back-turned while dis was a gooin on, and when he come back Chols up and told him all about it; but Harry said ’twas all stuff, and he didn’t believe a word consarnin’ ant, for Master Pettit, de parish clerk, had told him ’twas all a galusion, and dere wa’nt no Pharisees now-adays.

“But howsonever he proved to be wrong more ways dan one; for de nixt dee at cojer time when Harry was back-turned agin, Chols Packham heerd de voice as afore a comin’ up out ov de chink and a sayin’, ‘Look here!’ Well Chols turned roun’, not quite so much frightened dis time, and what should he see standin’ close agin de chink but a liddle bowl full of summut dat smelt a hem-an-all better dan small beer. ‘Hullow!’ thinks Chols to his-self, ‘dis is worth havin’, he thinks. So he tasted it, and at last drunk it all up; and he ’llowed, dat of all de stuff *he* ever tasted dat was de very best. He was a gooin to save de liddle bowl to show Harry that dere certainly was fairies, but whelst he was a thinking, about it, all of a sudden de bowl slipped out of his hands and deshed itself into a hunderd pieces; so dat Harry onny laughed at him, and said ’twas naun but a cracked basin. But howsonever Harry got sarved out for bein’ so unbelievin’, for he fell into a poor way, and coudn’t goo to work as usual, and he got so tedious bad, dat he fell away to mere skin and boän, and no doctors couldn’t do him no good, and dat very day twelmont he died, at de very same hour dat de Pharisees was fust heerd, and dat he spoke agin ’em.

“An ol’ brother of my wife’s gurt gran’mother see some Pharisees once, and ’twould a been a power better if so be he hadn’t never seen ’em, or leastways never offended ’em. I’ll tell ye how it happened. Jeems Meppom -- dat was his naüm -- Jeems was a liddle farmer, and used to thresh his own corn. His barn stood in a very *elenge* lonesome place, a goodish bit from de house, and de Pharisees used to come dere a nights and thresh out some wheat and wuts for him, so dat de hep o’ threshed corn was ginnerly bigger in de mornin dan what he left it overnight. Well, ye see, Mas’ Meppom thought dis a liddle odd, and didn’t know rightly what to make ant. So bein’ an out-and-out bold chep, dat didn’t fear man nor devil, as de sayin is, he made up his mind dat he'd goo over some night to see how 'twas managed. Well accordingly he went out rather airly in de evenin', and laid up behind de mow, for a long while, till he got rather tired and sleepy, and thought 'twaunt no use a watchin' no longer. It was gittin' pretty handy to midnight, and he thought how he'd goo home to bed. But jest as he was upon de move he heerd a odd sort of a soun' comin' tóe-ards the barn, and so he stopped to see what it was. He looked out of de strah, and what should he catch sight an but a couple of liddle cheps about eighteen inches high or dereaway come into de barn without uppening the doores. Dey pulled off dere jackets and begun to thresh wud two liddle frails as dey had brung wud em at de hem of a rate. Mas' Meppom would a been froughten if dey had been bigger, but as dey was such tedious liddle fellers he couldn't hardly help bustin right out a laffin'. Howsonever he pushed a hanful of strah into his mouth an so managed to kip quiet a few minutes a lookin' at um -- thump, thump, as riglar as a clock."

Lower's notes:

[1] It is a common notion in the South that every county once had its king.

[2] A Sussexism for luncheon taken about eleven o'clock.

Extract from his book *Contributions to literature* [etc.] (1854), 158–63.

Mark Antony Lower was Richard Lower's son (see Texts 12a-b). Readers may judge what he learnt from his father, and what he learned through listening for himself.

The regional features are those of eastern Sussex, and include, strikingly, the largely-vanished unrounding of <o> seen in *ant* 'on it'. The exact implications of the <ah> in *dahngerous* and *strah* are unclear; the latter may indicate unrounding of the long vowel corresponding to <o>.

This passage contains the first published allusion to the Sussexism for 'fairies', which is rendered here as *Pharisees*. Practically every writer on Sussex since has been amused by this, especially in times when knowledge of who the biblical Pharisees (Jewish zealots of 2000 years ago) were could have been taken for granted. Widespread knowledge of this phenomenon, with its once-appealing apparent mixture of true dialectalism and rustic ignorance, was guaranteed by the above passage and the entry in Parish's *Dictionary.*

This double plural, 'fairies-es', seems to have been completely general only after final consonant clusters, as illustrated in the Sussex stereotype verse:

> I saw the ghostesses,
> Sitting on their postesses,
> Eating of their toastesses,
> And fighting with their fistesses.
>
> (Quoted by Miles Costello, *West Sussex Gazette*, 14/02/1991.)

TEXT 13b

Mark Antony Lower: The Song of Songs *(1860)*

Written at the request of Prince Louis-Lucien Bonaparte for a national dialectological project

Chapter V

1 I be come into my garn, my sister, my spouse: I've gethered my myrrh wud my spice. I have ait my honeycomb wud my honey: I've drunk my wine wud my melk. Ait, O friens; drink, yâhs, drink a gurt plenty, O beloved.

2 I sleep, but my heart is awake. 'Tis de voice of my beloved dat is a-knockin, an he a-sayin: Ubben to me, my sister, my love, my dove, my clain un; for my head is felled wud deäw, an my locks wud de draps of de night.

3 I have pulled off my cooät; how shall I put it aön? I have washed my fit; how shull I make em dirty?

4 My beloved put in his han by de hoäl of de dooär an my bowels was moved for him.

5 I got up to ubben to my beloved, an my hans drapped wud myrrh, an my fingers wud sweet-smellin myrrh upon de handles of de lock.

6 I ubbened to my beloved; but my beloved had took hisself off, an was gone: my soul failed when he spoke. I sarched âhter him, but I couldn't find him; I called him, but he maüd me no answer.

7 De watchmen dat went about de city foun me; dey hit me, dey wownded me; de kippers of de walls took away my veil fram me.

8 I charge ye, O dâhters of Jerusalem, if ye find my beloved, dat ye tell him dat I be sick wud love.

9 What is yooär beloved more dan another beloved, O purtiest among women? what is yooär beloved more dan another beloved, dat ye charge us like dat?

10 My beloved is white an fresh-coloured, de best among ten thousan.

11 His head is lik de finest gold, his locks be bushy an black as a raövn.

12 His eyes be lik de eyes of doves by de rivers of waters, washed wud melk, an fitly set.

13 His chakes be lik a bed of spices, lik sweet flowers; his lips lik lilies drappin sweet-smellin myrrh.

14 His hans be lik golden rings set wud de beryl; his belly is lik bright ivory kivered over wud sapphires.

15 His ligs be lik poästés of marble set upon sockuts of fine gold; his faüs is lik Lebanon, axcellent as de cedars.

16 His mouth is uncommon sweet; yâhs, he is altogether lovely. Dis is my beloved, an dis is my frien, O dâhters of Jerusalem.

Lower was asked to write the piece in the way that he thought native speakers might do it. The artificiality of this exercise is apparent. We have here a reinterpretation of a translation (of a translation) of a piece of sophisticated erotic poetry about 2100 years old – hardly folksy material. It contains a relatively few salient features of the eastern variety, such as the use of *lik* for *like* and /d/ in the words beginning with /ð/. James Richards ('Jim Cladpole') also wrote a version (Text 25d), with which this should be compared.

Stimulated by the needs of this exercise to produce a phonetically precise rendering, Lower seems to have been the first writer to use the diaeresis (umlaut) to notate the Sussex centring diphthongs, as in *hole* and *face*, but the usage is not systematic in this piece, and it is drafted in for other purposes (what is intended by *aön* for *on*?)

TEXT 13c

Anonymous 'kind of proverbial dialogue' reported by Mark Antony Lower (1861)

'What's yer naüm?'

'Pudden and taüm;
Ax me agin, and I'll tell ye de saüm.'

The sense of *tame* (if that is what is meant) is obscure; perhaps 'thyme'? Variants of the rhyme found elsewhere in England are discussed in *Notes and Queries*, 6th series, nos 2 and 3 (1880-1). Many of the variants are obscure in content and intent. If *thyme* is meant, it may suggest that /ei/ and /ai/ were not always kept apart in Sussex, though there is no convincing evidence to support the idea that that was generally the case. The phonemes may each often be inconsistently represented, which is a complication; note for example *time (= thyme)* and *noice (= nice)*, both from the PRICE set, in Text 25b.

TEXT 14a

James Nye: A small account of my travels in the willderness *(1862, extracts)*

> o this is a sad Place for a Poor soul to be in i have felt so rached in these fits of unbelief that I should like to have lain dow [sic] and died in desperate sorrow. but when the diar lord brakes the hart with a sence of his goodness it is all right in a moment. bless the lord o my soul for all his goodness but to return i had got the Place at ashcombe but there was no house for me to live in. so i was aforst to go to lewes to live. this my wife kickd hard against. but i was determond to have my own way. now i was a gardner ofcorse i must have a respectable house. so i hiered one ranted at four shilings Per week and taxes. and my wages was saven^teen^ Per week so of i went to lewes to live with six Chirlden and my wife and myself nade [sic] eight in famley. but the oldes boy ernt three shillings Per week which made up a Pound a week alltogather well thought i shourly i can do Pretty well with that. but when i got theire i lernt a Pretty good lesson for theare was so many expences

> that i never thought of for with the rent and taxses and firing and baking and Chrldens schooting [sic] alltogather Came to seven shlings [sic] and five Pence Per week this left twelve shillings and seven Pence Per week for eight of us to live on this drove my wife nearly to her wits ^end^ for things was very dear at that time and she kept saying she wished she had never seen lewes and so did i but i did not like to own to it at this time i was as dark and as dead to the things of god as any Poor soul Could be and this was a grate disapointment for i thought if i livd in lewes i should go to Chapple every time the doors was open and be as happey as anybods [sic] Could be but insted of that i had no heart to go at all and when i did go i dragd their as heavey as posable and when i was at home my wife was allways baiting me about the old house or else the taxes untill i got as hard and rebelous as the daviel Could make me. and thats for religon i sometimes made up my mind to give up alltogather but this i Could not do. try what ^i^ would not alltogather. then soon after i got to lewes my wife faided ill and one Child. both togather and i was a stranger in the Place so i had no friends. and i was onley just hand to mouth so i raley was in deep destress. . . . one sunday morning i had a Pretty good dose of old house for brakefast i most times had i[t] for supper but sunday mornings i had it for brakefast. And i see my Chirlden i[n] such a destressed state and my wife had no desier to go to Chappel puting all these things togather i was rached in deed. now i determoned to go to Chappel no more. and have no more to do with regleon. So after brakefast i made up my mind to go on the hills for the day. whare no eye Could se me . . .

From Sussex Archaeological Society manuscript B/NYE.

Note on spelling and punctuation: Nye regularly writes a large <C> and <P> at the beginning of words, and therefore makes no true distinction between small and capital letters at all. (A curious exception is in <Barns> in the poem printed as the next text.) He writes a small cross on the line which I have transcribed as a full stop; this is his only punctuation mark, and he does not paragraph. Later corrections in Nye's own hand I have placed between raised carets (so: ^xxx^).

There are two features that are consistent indicators of dialect: the representation of the vowel /e/ by <a> as in *ranted* and *rached* for *rented* and *wretched* (though *(all)togather* might be evidence of analogical pressure from *gather*), and the use of the form was with a plural subject. *Aforst* 'forced' is a striking instance of the former general use of the prefixed passive participle. Note the slang expression *a dose of old house* 'a load of trouble; an earful'.

TEXT 14b

James Nye: 'Lines on the bountiful harvest of 1863' *(1863)*

Come all ye faithfull husbandmen
That Culavate [sic] the land
and bless the god of Provadence
who opend wide his hand

----

and made the seed to multiply
thats Cast into the ground
and Crownd our labours with sucsess
all the Cuntry round

Come bless and Prayse his holy nam
who Caused the sun to shine
to nuresh up the tender Plant
and Chear our gloomy minds

----

hes faithfull to his Promises
up to this Presant day
that seedtime and harvest should
never Past away

----

what Can us render to his nam
for blessings grate as these
our Barns are filld with Pleny [sic] and thers
fruit upon the trees

----

and now hes sent the latter rain
to Chear our winter crops
Pasturer [sic] for the ox and cow
and also for the flocks

----

now we have Peace and Plenty in
this favored Cuntry
and may the same be realissd
fir beyond the sea

----

and may the fearfull ravages
of war Come to an end
and once mor Peace and unity
amongst aur fellow men

J Nye September 14th

From Sussex Archaeological Society manuscript B/NYE.

There is little, if anything, of a truly dialectal character in this text, unless *fir* for 'far' indicates an unusual vowel-quality. But, with Text 10a, it is a striking example of the unmonitored practice of literacy by an adult after small education.

TEXT 15a

W.D. Parish: A dictionary of the Sussex dialect *(1875, extracts)*

BEACH, mid-Sussex. Shingle brought from the sea-coast is always called beach, as opposed to the inland gravel.

BOUGH-HOUSE, mid-Sussex. A private house allowed to be open at fairs for the sale of liquor.

> An old person describing the glories of Selmeston fair, which has now been discontinued many years, said "There was all manner of booths and bough-houses."
>
> In former times putting up boughs upon anything was an indication that it was to be sold, and a bush at the end of a pole was the badge of a country ale house; which gives rise to the proverb, "Good wine needs no bush," i.e., nothing to point out where it is sold.

DUBERSOME, mid-Sussex. Doubtful. This Anglo-Saxon form of termination is not uncommon in Sussex; we find it in timersome for timid, wearisome, and other words.

FITTY. Subject to fits.

The following extract from the Selmeston parochial account-book shows how afflicted persons were dealt with in former times,--

"Ladiday, 1790. This is an agreement which is between the Churchwardens and Overseers and Parishioners of the Parish of Selmeston, in the County of Sussex.

"The said parishioners do agree that R. Hillman should take Jas. Norman at two shillings and sixpence per week so long as he continues in the fitty state, but when Mt=r. Hillman shall give it that he can work well, and equal with other boys, he, the said Hillman, will do and keep him, the said boy, for as little and little money as any parishioner shall think proper."

HEEN, mid-Sussex. [Hæn, Ang.Sax.] A hen.

"I throwed a stone at a liddle hedge-pick* a settin' on the heave-geat**, and killed Mrs. Pankurstes' gurt old packled*** heen."

* [HEDGE-PICK, or HEDGE-MIKE, mid-Sussex. The hedge sparrow.]

** [HEAVE-GATE, mid-Sussex. [Hefan and geat, Ang.Sax.] A low gate, so constructed as to lift out from the posts, instead of opening with hinges.]

*** [PACKLED, mid-Sussex. Speckled.]

HOGPOUND, mid-Sussex. The pigstye; a favourite rendezvous on Sundays.

"Ah! many's the time as we've stood over the hog-pound together, and looked 'em over, and rackoned 'em up, whiles people was in church; little did he think as he'd be putt in before that hog was killed! and he always allowed she'd weigh sixty stun."*

* [STONE. A weight of eight pounds.]

HOX, west Sussex. To cut the hamstrings; to cut the sinew of a rabbit's leg and put the other foot through, in order to hang it up.

KIME, mid-Sussex. A weazel.

> A lady who had been giving a lesson to a Sunday school class upon Pharoah's dreams, was startled to find that all the boys supposed that the fat and lean kine were weazels.

LAWYER, east Sussex. A long bramble full of thorns, so called because, "When once they gets a holt an ye, ye doant easy get shut of 'em."

MIDDLING. This word has many different meanings which are expressed by the tone of voice in which it is said.

> It may mean very much, as "He lashed out middlin', I can tell ye!"
>
> Or it may mean tolerably well, as "I doant know but what she made out purty middlin'."
>
> Or it may mean very bad, as, "How did the wedding go off?" "Middling, thank you, sir." "What, only middling! wasn't it all right?" "Why, no sir, not quite, for you see the parson he entirely forgot all about it, and he'd gone away, so we was forced to wait in church two hours."

MOTHERY. Mouldy; generally applied to liquor which has become thick and incrusted.

ROBBUT. [Corruption of Rabbit.] Sometimes pronounced as broadly as robert.

> "Robbuts! Ah, I lay you never see such a plääce for robbuts as what ourn is! I never should have beleft, without I'd seen 'em in my garden, that there was so many robbuts in the wurreld. Why they be ready to eat us up alive!"

SAUCE, mid-Sussex. (Pronounced Sass.) Vegetables; but generally used of cabbages. The Americans speak of garden-sass.

> "I reckon I shaant have no sass at all this year, all through along on account of the drythe."*
>
> * {DRYTHE. [Drugath, Ang.Sax.] Drought.}

SHOD. [Perfect of Shed.] Spilt. This word is correct, the Anglo-Saxon past tense being sceód.

> "I sent him up to fetch a little beer, but he shod half of it bringing of it home."

STOLT, east Sussex. Stout; strong; generally said of fowls.

> "The chickens are quite stolt."

SUSSEX-PUDDING. A compound of flour and water made up in an oblong shape and boiled. There is a moment when it is first taken out of the saucepan, when it can be eaten with impunity; but it is usually eaten cold, and in that form I believe that it becomes the foundation of all the ills that Sussex spirit and flesh are heir to. It promotes a dyspeptic form of dissent which is unknown elsewhere. It aggravates every natural infirmity of temper by the promotion of chronic indigestion, and finally undermines the constitution; for the first symptom of the decay of nature which a Sussex man describes is invariably that he can't get his pudding to set.

THROW[1] [Through.] A thorough-fare: a public way. The four-throws is a point where four roads meet.

TOT[1], mid-Sussex. A bush; a tuft of grass.

> "There warn't any grass at all when we fust come here; naum but a passel o' gurt old tots and tussicks. You see there was one of these here new-fashioned men had had the farm, and he'd properly starved the land and the labourers, and the cattle and everything, without it was hisself."

The extracts are chosen to illustrate a variety of things. Parish often illuminates his definitions with invented snippets or dialogues in dialect; these often allude to adjacent entries in the dictionary (as most of the starred examples do). He allows himself a few jokes and a few sardonic remarks about social conditions, makes the odd sly dig at his parishioners, and offers other amusing observations which have nothing to do with definition.

He includes entries that one suspects of being nonce-forms, spur-of-the-moment witticisms (as with LAWYER). The last sentence under SUSSEX-PUDDING is probably an arch allusion to the Victorian slang *pudding* 'penis'. Parish was a man of his age; his scholarship is historically oriented. He gives etymological notes, not always reliable; the note on SHOD is both inaccurate and misleading, because the OE form he cites should be *sceād*, which, as it happens, really is a possible ancestor of *shod*. STOLT is included as representing, apparently unbeknown to him, a genuine English relative, not recorded in Anglo-Saxon times, of Low German *stolt*, High German *stolz* 'magnificent, proud'; the word *stout* is of the same stock filtered through Norman French.

He attends to word-structure and to the grammatical forms of words in a historical way, and notes special local pronunciations (sometimes noting them as 'corruptions' where they do not correspond to Old English regional forms). He also uses evidence from primary written sources as if they constituted examples of current dialect usage (FITTY); he regards dialect (like others of his age) as representing a survival of older usage, and therefore readily points to usages agreeing with those of the great Tudor authors and with proverbs. Occasionally, as with BEACH, we find a word which is still current – this is used in the building trade in Sussex for '(small) rounded stones' (also PEA-BEACH). Other terms may retain currency in place-names, as with (FOUR) THROWS.

Parish's technique of lexicography is analysed by Roper (2007), along with that of other Sussex glossarists.

TEXT 15b

W.D. Parish: the first John Hogpound story (early 1870s)

ACCOUNT OF THE WEDDING
OF _______ AT _______, SUSSEX

By a Labourer of the Parish

Hond. Sir, –

I takes the libbaty to write these few lines hopping they will leave you quite well as they finds me at present, to tell you all 'bout dis here gurt weddin and todo up at Furrel, for I thort as you'd like to have a pertickler and kract account ont all, to put into de peaper a Saddaday.

'Twas one of my lord's grandarters as was to be married, but I can't spell her name nohows in de wurreld.

Dey do say as she be a gurt favrite of my lord's and no wonder nother, for she's a honaccountable plessan peart young laddy surelye, and tarks to any one jes as free, and as for the rheumatticks!! Lar bless ye! 'Twould make ye forgit ye'ed ever had 'em to hear her larf.

Wall, dere was to be over three hunderd people had in to dinner up at the ridin' school; 'twas de cheldern, and de laybrers, and all as was 'bove sixty yeeres of age.

So 'twas over a wick agoo, de passon he comed down our house, and ast me whedder I was 'bove sixty yeeres of age.

"Wall, sir," I sez, "I doan't jesly know how old I be, but I noos I be 'bove sixty yeeres of age, for ye see I went to work when I was somewheres 'bout nine yeeres old (dat was in old Mus Ridge's time) and I kep on till I was sumwheres 'bout fower and twenty, and den a young woman got me into trouble, and I was force to goo away to sea, but I diddun hold to that not much 'bove six or seven yeeres, and den I come home and got drawed for de meleshia and sarved ten yeeres, and den volunteered for a sodger and sarved my time fefteen yeeres, and den I come back to de farm, and dere I've worked for fower and forty yeer, till I got quite entirely eat up wid de rheumatticks, and now I ain't done naun for dese las' ten yeeres, and sometimes dey be better dan what dey be othersome. So I noos I be 'bove sixty yeeres of age."

But, howsomever, I must be gittin on, for de womenfolk 'ul be wantin to read all 'bout dis weddin.

And, fuss of all, I mus tell you dat I've had a very gurt misfortin, all through along on account of losin a hog: and she jes wos a purty hog tew. I bought her when she warn't but seven wicks old, off Old Master Chawbery, time he lived down de street, up agin de church.

Supprisin gurt hog she growed tew be sure!

Dere was a man come from Uckful one day and looked at her; and dere was a man from Lunnun, he see her, and dey both allowed as dey'd never seed sich a hog all dere lives. And she hadn't had naun but three bushels of pollard nother.

Ah, you'd have been pleased to see her, I know. Dere was a many used to come down of a Sunday and looked at her; and Old Master Chawbery and me, we'ev stood over de poun whiles people was in church, and rackoned her up and looked her over for hours together; and we both guv it in as she wouldn'd weigh no less than seventy stun.

And she hadn'd had naun but three bushels of pollard nother.

Wall, one marnin, 'bout three wicks agoo ('twas of a Saddaday) I was gwine ra-ound by de pa-ound, and I looks over, and dere was de hog, seemingly 'bout as common, and pensley I looks round agun, and dere she was all stratched out and gaspin for breath.

So I goos indoors and ses, "Mestress," I ses, "de hog be countable ornary."

"Wall," ses she, "dere aint no call for yew to come spannelin' 'bout my clean ketchen naun de moor for dat," she ses.

"Ah," ses I, "but she be countable bad, mestress," I ses, "and I dunno but what she be gwine to die."

"Massy pon me," ses she, "gwine to die! Never! Surelye."

"Yew come ra'ound and look at her, den," I ses.

Soon as ever she seen her, she ses to me, she ses, "Why doant ye give her somethin," she ses, "standin here!"

So I got down a gurt bottle of stuff what I had from de doctor time my leg was so bad, and took and mixed it in with some skim-milk and a liddle pollard and give it her, jes lew warm.

But it didn't seem as she was anyways de better for it, and all nex day she kep on getting wus, and she died de Monday night as she was took de Saddaday. And it seemed jus a thought 'twas to be, for naun as we could give her didn't do her no good whatsumdever.

Dere was a dunnamany people come and looked at her. And we had her opened, and Master Chawbery he allowed as she was took wid de information.

No more at present; but I though I'd write and tell ye all 'bout our gurt doins, for de women folks moast always likes to read 'bout a wedding.

Yours spackfully,

JOHN HOGPOUND.

Poscrip. – Come to think ont and rackont up, I dunno as she did have three bushels pollard, not by pert nigh half a gallon.

Published by [Rev.] William Douglas Parish (writing as 'John Hogpound') (c.1870) Account of the wedding of _____ at _____, Sussex, by a labourer of the parish. Unascertained local newspaper, perhaps the *Sussex Agricultural Express*.

A typical kind of dialect text of the period: humorous prose fathered on a country bumpkin by a parson who had intimate knowledge of the vernacular but was not a native speaker, and where the humour is used against the bumpkin as a class. The authorship of Parish will not be disputed after a comparison of this text with the entry for HOGPOUND in the *Dictionary of the Sussex dialect*, quoted in Text 15a.

The most conspicuous genuine regional features are those of eastern Sussex noted elsewhere in this book. But there are also instances of eye-dialect (e.g. <r> to indicate vowel-length in *tarks* and *larf*) and instances of general uneducated usage. *Pollard* is 'The refuse siftings of flour, finer than bran and coarser than sharps,' according to Parish's *Dictionary* (cf. *sharps and middlins* in Text 26).

TEXT 16

John Coker Egerton: Extracts from his diary (kept 1857–88)

[1859] 26 Mar . . . 2 Sisters Relf signed their name in 3 diff[erent] ways Relf Relph Ralph . . .

[1870] Sun. 13 Feb. Most bitterly cold. . . . Luck told me that he never did know pigs ears to be freezed afore but their pigs' ears had freezed in the night! . . .

[1871] 17 Mar. . . . Spoke to Js. Russell about ye fees for Steeped [?] grave, head-stone & body-stone for his wife.

[1878] 25 Feb . . . A Burwash man explained to me his view of political honesty the following apologue. "I've got a sow in my yard with twelve little 'uns. They can't all suck at once because there aren't tits enough. So I shut six of 'em outside while t'other six be feeding. And the six be shut out jus to make a hem of a noise till they be let in again, & when they be let in, they be just as quiet as the rest; that my idea about politics".

[1878] Sun. 3 Nov . . . A disturbance in ye belfry before aft: serv: Master Tom Hyland holding that Belfry means Bell-free, & that it is free to all! was very "akkard" & troublesome.

[1880] 10 Nov . . . Mr Gillham told me that in parishes in Kent near ye Sussex border forty or fifty years ago bad vulgar language was called "Burwash Grammar" . . .

[1885] 2 June .... [Egerton meets Tom and chides him for having been drunk. Tom replies that it did him good.] "Well Sir," he replied, "it worked me uppards & downwards at such a rate that it was better than goin' to any doctor, & that shows I wasn't used to it" . . .

Egerton was Rector of Burwash, and extracts from his diary were published by Roger Wells, ed. (1992) *Victorian village: the diaries of the Reverend John Coker Egerton.* Stroud: Alan Sutton. The entries above are quoted from Wells's edition.

These entries relate to incomplete literacy among local people and folk-etymological understanding, interspersed with quotations of striking utterances containing non-standard forms, usually presented also for their perceived quaintness or their homespun insights. Occasional local words are used comfortably by Egerton – I suspect *steeped* is really *steened* 'stone-lined', whilst others are placed in "scare-quotes" to distance the writer from them.

TEXT 17

E. Hatchett Jackson: A bang on the head (1894)

An so ye loike us Sussex folk! Well so be as ya do laff 'tis rite anuff, but sum on us do otherwile meet wud a ruff hedge to scratch thro an denit ge us naun fer laffin. An now I remember dis follerin: A vine upstandin. downsittin fellur was Joe Grits, an he had made out rite bravely fer dunna-many yere ov he's life. But tis awves de best as is tuk, an Joe he wur bothered awile all-along-on-account-of an exceldent as cauled un out ov de cart an cauled un wud a hem ov a clatter rite on top ov his hed, wot bring pore Joe a gurt denial fer it deared un summat.

So wick followed wick an Joe gun ter doddle roun a bit -- but a dezzick! No, he had na dun a dezzick for more dan nine wicks. So wen brass an brads wos gone Joe he went a beggaren fer wurk an fur brencheese, quyrin fust at won an den at anuder till he cum to Ol' Bill's doar gran nigh beazled an axed un fer a bit ov bred.

But ol' Bill he wur midlin chuff ower it I rackon an cheeked at Joe fer cadgin: fer he was awves up-a-top-ov-de-house drackly-minute, wos Bill.

"Ya gurt crummy chep," ses he, "ya be misagaft an ef ya think as I wol ge ya brencheese and beer fer naun. A valiant fellur loike yerself shud git a trade an work at he's busness loike I does. Nub'dy ud kip me, I bluv!"

Published as the second of a series of five 'pages of Sussex dialect' in *Southward Ho!* 1 (1894), 250-1.

This is one of those notorious pieces, familiar in all regions, that strives to cram in every dialect feature contained in the existing literature. This one trawls Parish's *Dictionary* with a net that would have an illegally small mesh nowadays; the author elsewhere raids M.A. Lower's *Contributions to literature*.

The main features are eastern. The <v> in *awves* 'always' for /w/ is remarkable in Sussex, and suggests the kind of dialectal feature used by Dickens to characterize Sam Weller. It is probably therefore not genuinely local. The initial <v> for /f/ in *fine* recessive or obsolete even in 1895. *Denial* is 'hindrance', *deared* 'deafened', *beazled* 'tired out'. Note *misagaft* 'mistaken'; Parish actually has *misagift*, and the form used is first picked up in Hall's new edition of Parish (1957). There is eye-dialect (*ov*, *tuk*).

TEXT 18

The vocabulary list of Daniel White, aged 10 (1890s)

Place of abode not known; probably west of county

Almtrees	Hyican	Soldiersbuttons	Lilly	Whiteleaftrees
Delyards	Johnquil	Hoxslips	Orger	Forgetmo
Stertions	Geraniam	Succle-dead-man	Turningiron	Trouses
Britches slops	Swaller	Pole	Vains	Daffidills
Withytrees	Micomas	Birdeyes	Pinplers	Everlastingpee
Pairtrees	Maregulls	Pencis	Lave	Hads
Tolips	Batchlerbuttons	Canimiles	Shimese	Girnseys
Winepipe	Entrels	Musell	Thivybone	Recklus
Hapstrees	Audertrees	Holleyock	Wilentoniatrees	
Minenett	Shovel	Bloodcups	Nots	Woodflowers
Anbil	Fag-hook	Sawl	Cotal	Magontuses
Nostrils	Crown	Collour-bone	Shin-bone	Calf
Wash-stan	Boils	Parseley	Mars	Guinefowl
Diswasher	Plaices	Mourins	Dumberdore	
Dinerngroom	Macroo	Cafincher	Ruebob	Milkmaids
Jajuary	Nettle-creeper	Hingis	Oisters	Guinepigs
Instups	Musculs	Lyrebird	Brocklow	Brucks
Feasent	Ceil	Quid-worm	Scutty	Tailorbird
Turbots	Squeakers	Parsenips	Squirrels	Appers
Window-bline	Emets	Landrill	Ostrich	Sicclemontrees
Paridisebird	Scullips	Willowtrees	Addocks	Tommyhock

Excerpts printed by Robert Barrett (1894) How large is the vocabulary of Hodge? (part I). *Southward Ho!* 1, 18–19. The full list of 500 words was in the hands of the magazine's editor, and has since disappeared. The list was elicited from Daniel as a free recall exercise, in an attempt to test the claim that country folk had very limited vocabulary.

A few of these 103 words are enigmatic; is a *Landrill* a *land-drill* or a *land-rail*? Others I cannot interpret at all; could a *Macroo* be a mushroom? But Daniel obviously knew a lot of trees, flowering plants, animals, body-parts and household objects and tools by name.

The use of <h> word-initially is variable and subject to hypercorrection; teaching its use to small boys and girls was the principal and least rewarding task of teachers after the introduction of mass education in the 1870s.

The words *cafincher* 'chaffinch' and *dumberdore* 'bumble-bee' are said by Parish to be specific to the western dialect. *Quid-worm* 'centipede' may also be western, as it is known through the notes of James Fraser of Chichester.

TEXT 19

Margaretta Bell-Irving: Words overheard in Mayfield (1903)

> A stranger may find, if he exchanges a few words with people returning from the day's work, that they use words quite unfamiliar to him. An old man with bowed shoulders will say that his "bat" is a great help in getting along, meaning the hedge-stake on which he leans. A strong young labourer will inform him he was "terrified" about something or other, not meaning it at all in the sense of being alarmed, merely that he was vexed. A girl will say her "trug" – a wooden basket – is full of "chucks" for lighting fires; a cheery old woman with her may tell how she does not feel the cold in winter so much as some do, for she has such good "healing" (coverings) to her bed. "Yes! the girl is her granddaughter, as anyone might tell, as she has quite the 'bly' (look or likeness) of her family." If he asks where some particular house in the village is situated, he will be directed "up-town" or "down-town", as the case may be. If he inquires after some person, he may be told he or she is "ornary" or "adle"; both mean "not quite well".
>
> When as children we cried, we were told by our nurse not to "grizzle". When troublesome we were "contrairy". When we fretted, we were "grievous". Did our hair get untidy, it was "as rough as a badger." Did we crumple our frocks, we had made them "sleezy." Once we were called up to see the "shay" (glow) of a burning rick in the distance. The youngest was the "sock" or pet. She sometimes announced she was "chuffy" (short-tempered), if she was put out about anything.

From chapter 2 of E. Margaretta Bell-Irving (1903) *Mayfield – the story of an old Wealden village*. London: William Clowes.

This text is self-explanatory. *Trug* is now a general English word because the object it denotes has spread beyond Sussex, and other words may be felt to be general and colloquial now rather than dialectal, such as *grizzle* and *contrary*, whilst *sleezy*, now spelt *sleazy*, has shifted ground from a concrete sense to an abstract one. *Bat* and *ornary* are met frequently in the county's dialect texts, and *terrified* in this local sense is widely made fun of.

TEXT 20a

Michael Blann: version of the song 'Dame Durden' (written down around 1901)

Dame derden keept five servants
To carry the milking pail
She also keept five laberman
To use the spade and frail

Chorous

Twas Moly & Betty & Doly & ketty
And Doltry Draggull tail
Twas John & Dick & Joe & Jack
& Humprey with his frail,
And ketty she was the charing girl
To carrey the milking Pail.

Chorous

Twas John kiss Moly & Dick kiss Betty
& Joe Kiss Dolly & Jack Kiss Ketty
& Humphery with his frail
& Ketty she was the charming gril
To carry the milking Pail.

2

Dame darden in morn so soon
She did begin to call
To rose her servants maids & men
She did begin to ball.

3

Twas on the morn of valetine
The birds begin to Prate
Dame dardens servants maids & men
They all begin to mate.

M Blann

On a loose and damaged sheet of paper in Michael Blann's manuscript songbook, Worthing Museum. Conjectural reconstructions of the damaged text by Colin Andrews (1979) have been silently added in.

Dialect is evident in the word *frail* for 'flail', showing dissimilation of resonants, and in the use of <e> in the name *Kitty*; and perhaps also in the regularized past-tense form *keept*. For the first of these words, 'Brasser' Copper (author of Texts 20b and 20c as they stand) has *thrail* in his version of this song.

TEXT 20b

'Brasser' Copper's version of the song 'Adieu sweet lovely Nancy' (1922)

Hears a Dew sweet loveley Nancy ten thousands times a Dew
I am goeing round the Ocan to seek for something new
Come chaing your ring with me Dear Girl come change your ring with me
for it mite be a token off true love wile I am on the sea

When I am far upon the seas you know not wher I am
Kind letters I will rite to you from every forreind land
The scecrets of your mind Dear Girl is the best of my good will
So let your body be wher it mite my Hart shall be with you still

Ther is a heavey storm arisen see how it gathers round
While whe poor sailors are on the sea are all fighting for the crown
Ther is nothing to defend us love Nor to keep us from the cold
On the Ocan wide wher whe must bide like Jolley Seamen Bold

Ther is tinkers taylors shoemakers lye snoreing fast asleep
Wile whe poor solds on the Ocan wide are all Ploughing through the deep
Our Officers comanded us and them whe must obey
Expecten every moment all too get cast away

And when the wars are all over ther will be peice on every shore
Whe will drink to our wifes and children and the girls wich whe adore
Whe will call for lickore mirrle whe will spend our money free
And when our money his all gone whe will boldly go to sea

In a manuscript book formerly in the possession of Bob Copper, the writer's grandson.

Copper uses a script where capital and small letters are not in the main distinguished, and I may have misread his intention at some points here and in Text 20c.

Notice *expecten* with *-en* for *-ing* (repeated in other songs in the book); the two-syllable pronunciation indicated by *mirrle* 'merrily'; and the clear evidence of the loss of the *w-/wh-* distinction in the inverse spellings such as *whe*.

TEXT 20c

'Brasser' Copper's version of the song 'The echoin' horn' (1922)

The echoin horn sounds well in the morn
to call the brave sportsman away
When the cry of the Hounds make A music el sound
So greatley enlighten the day

Whe will away to some shaw to hear some brave noise
Our Hounds they do open ther throats
When the fox he breaks cover Harkforward I over
Whe will follow ther musicel Notes

Wile our Hounds are at fals whe hold on our Horse
till the sent of the fox whe have gaind
With an I teleo and away whe will goe
Whe will gallop him over the plain

Hedges gates and stiles call us no denile
Our Horses they leap them so well
with the crying Harkforward I over Harkforward
What pleasure can Hunting exsell

Over mountings he fly then afterwards dies
he has led us an exlant chase
Whe will take of his brush and then home whe will push
In order our spirits to rase

With A bottle and freind the evening whe will spend
Whe will crown the brave sports of the day
Our wifes shal at Nite gave us grate delight
And sow all our sorrow away

Mr Stenning Beard faveret song

In a manuscript book formerly in the possession of Bob Copper, the writer's grandson.

Here we find *mountings* showing the inverse of *expecten* in Text 20b, and *denile* 'hindrance' as evidence of a two-syllable pronunciation. Steyning Beard was the last 'squire' of Rottingdean, who died in 1909 having run up large debts.

TEXT 21

Barclay Wills reports a shepherd's practical joke (1938)

> A shepherd amused me with an account of some blackberry pickers. "They berry-pickers be a noosance, times," he said. "I mind one day there was some as comed too near t' sheep fur my likin', all rampagin' 'bout an' shoutin'. So I crep' up behin' t' thick booshes, an' med a noise like a bull. Then I shouts: 'Look out, Jim! – head 'un off if 'e breaks thro' thet side,' an' I rustles t' booshes wi' t' crook-stick. Diddun they jes run! Lord! they went like flies, an' I wur soon quiet agen!"

From Barclay Wills, *Shepherds of Sussex* (1938), 198.

Wills wrote about the downland at the eastern end of the western area. His use of *t'* for *the* is remarkable, because this is generally a feature of northern dialects, in particular Yorkshire, but it agrees with the usage of Fred Woods from Ditchling, who was writing at roughly the same time. In the Survey of English Dialects material, though, *t'* appears only before *other*. In the work of Bob Copper (see Text 35a), we sometimes find *th'* before a word beginning with a vowel (e.g. *'ill* 'hill'), whilst in Copper's work *t'* is exclusively for *to*.

TEXT 22

G.D. Martineau: 'The Midnight Bells. A legend of Selsey' (1925)

> There's surelye folks nigh Selsey Bill
> 'Z go to church at night,
> Fur, though I've never seed 'em, still
> I rackon as I'm right.

’Tis midnight, just about, they ring
A gurt big chimin’ bell,
An’ fur away they starts to sing,
All mixin’ wud the swell.

Folk say Mus’ Wilfrid used to preach
(Uz church’s sunk below)
To seals an’ such like on the beach
A purty time ago.

An’, whatsumdever’s wrong or right,
One thing’z cert’n true:
There’s folk ’z go to church at night,
Fur Tom ’z ’urd ’em too.

Published in *The way of the south wind*. Steyning: The Vine Press (1925).

The Sussex features consist only of a collection of the most stereotypical ones drawn from the county literature (e.g. *surelye, rackon, gurt big, whatsumdever*). Martineau defamiliarizes the text further by using <z> instead of <s> (inconsistently) for final /z/.

TEXT 23a

Sheila Kaye-Smith: The child born at the Plough *(1926, extracts)*

In her nativity play *The child born at the Plough*, Kaye-Smith has three Romney Marsh shepherds (‘lookers’) with finely-graded standardization of their dialect according to decreasing age. These are most of the contributions to Scene I of the oldest looker, Mr Stuppeny, the ‘looker at Slinches’, the character with the most deeply vernacular English:

“Never have I met such a tedious nonsensical notion, and I’ve bin looker man and boy in all parts of the marsh. Twenty-seven year was I wud old Mus’ Vidler over at Honeychild, and nigh on fifteen wud Mus’ Godden at the Loose – but never a lamb before April – no such thing heard of on the marsh. It wants a furriner lik the new Squire to come along from the Shires and buy up the old pläace and teach us our business.”

“It’s all them Shires. Setting themselves up for wisdom all over the country. Christmas lambing ain’t the only bad thing that’s come to us from the Shires.

There's an outlandish heathen tune that Parson's brought to sing to-morrow instead of Spiffkins."

"My voice is a tedious fine voice, young feller, and you've no call to speak so to your elders. Year after year I've sung 'O Lord, the only begotten son.' and there ain't naun the matter wud the tune, nor wud my voice neither."

"You ain't naun but an ill-conditioned brat. All the school-larnin' you've had ain't taught you to respect your elders."

"Christ was born at an inn in an old pläace called Bethlehem a dunnamany years ago. Reckon it ud be middling fine if he cud be born at the Plough up at Udimore for all us folk to see."

"I dreamed I saw an angel wunst. He wur dressed lik Parson, but had wings sticking out of his back."

"Surelye, surelye. We've got to go and greet the babe, wheresumdever he's born."

The expression of dialect is restrained, presumably for the benefit of readers with an education only in Standard English. A number of stereotypical features appear (sometimes inconsistently), e.g. *surelye, wheresumdever, tedious* 'very', *naun* 'nothing' (also in Texts 12a, 13a, 17, 22, 23b), but the normal eastern rendering of /ð/ by <d> is avoided except in unstressed wud 'with'.

TEXT 23b

Sheila Kaye-Smith: Looking for Bob (1920)

Clem was glad to leave Bob with his wife. He would be too busy that morning to keep an eye on him, and he could trust Polly to see that his brother did not make a fool of himself in any way. If only Bob would behave himself and keep quiet, things might take a turn for the better now. Anyhow he was happy and rational again – more rational than he had ever been since his conversion. If only he would go on like this, perhaps in time, when she saw what an improved man her husband was, Mabel might think of coming back . . .

Thus Clem's imagination painted some glowing pictures that morning at his work, and during a tramp he had to make into the village, to see Pepper about a horse – pictures which were one and all darkened when he came back to the farm, and found Polly waiting for him there. "She's come after Mus'

Robert," said Pickdick. "I said as you'd a-gone into the town, and maybe he wur wud you."

Clem groaned.

"I haven't seen the chap. Why cudn't you have kipt a better eye on him, missus?"

"I did but run out to see after the eggs whilst the water wur boiling, and he wur picking over the liddle green gooseberries – then when I come back, he wur a-gone, having got through wud the picking; so I thought maybe he'd be up at the pläace."

"He aun't bin aräound here this marnun," said Pickdick.

"Then I can't think where's he's a-got to."

"I can, surelye," said Clem with another groan.

He had remembered that to-day was Salehurst market.

"Whur, then?"

"He's a-gone to Salehurst, lik the hem fool as he is. He'll be telling them all about this new conversion of his'n. Bless my soul, missus – why cudn't you have looked after him?"

"I did but go out five minnut – and I never thought as mortal man cud have picked over them gooseberries so quick."

"Well, I mun go after him, anyways; föalkes wöan't stand his preaching at 'em after all that's happened – maybe they'll do him some harm."

"Wait and have your dinner, mäaster."

" No – I'll go now, and mäake him behave sensible if I can. He's lik a child some ways, is Bob, and I'm afeard he'll git himself into trouble."

He started off at once. The day was hot, but he walked fast, and had soon reached the cross-roads outside Salehurst. It was only one of the smaller markets, and so far he had not met anyone, but at the Throws he saw a trap coming towards him. The driver hailed him from the distance:

"That you, Mus' Fuller?"

"Surelye, Mus' Cox."

"I wur driving out to fetch you – your brother's started his preaching agäun, and I'm afeard as there'll be trouble."

"I wur just a-coming after him myself."

"Then jump in and I'll drive you."

Clem put his foot on the wheel and sprang up. Cox turned the horse's head towards Salehurst.

"I knew as you wur the only chap as cud stop him, so I thought as I'd go fur you at wunst. I did my best, but he wur set on gitting up and telling 'em all some wonderful new thing as had happened to him; he never seemed to think that föalkses wöan't stand that sort of thing from the likes of him – begging your pardon."

"Bob's a valiant chap," said Clem, "but he äun't got all the sense that he might."

"Seemingly he's got religion agäun," said Cox. "I'd bin töald as he'd a-done wud all that sort of thing, having a notion as he wur lost. But now he wur saying as God's showed Himself to him agäun as the God of love and I know not wot else beside. Foalkses wöan't stand it."

"Had they begun to play up rough?"

"Oh, only a few that wur hollering at him . . . But them Egyptians are about agäun; I cud see Darius Ripley there listening, and you know as Darius said as he'd git even wud Bob Fuller for gitting him seven months in quod?"

"I never heard it; and anyways Bob didn't git him locked up – it wur fur dog-stealing."

"Yes, but if Bob hadn't mäade all that row and brung in the police, Ripley ud never have bin caught. It wur Bob's trouble wot showed the police where he wur. Reckon if there's any skylarking, Darius ull mäake it wuss – and there's other Egyptians about too."

Clem looked scared.

"D'you think they'll – they'd never do him any harm?"

"Oh, döan't you vrother – all they'd do at the wust ud be to give him a ducking."

"I döan't want Bob to git a ducking."

"Maybe we'll be in time to stop it – not as we can do anything if the trouble's begun, but if they're only jeering and hollering, and you git Bob to give over . . . "

"He wöan't give over fur me . . . Wot's that?"

"Where?"

"Down on the Marsh – yonder – it's lik a lot of folkses running."

"That's it – that's them. Reckon we're too late, and they've got your brother."

He pulled the horse up violently, and they both jumped out of the trap. They had just reached the bridge at the foot of the station hill, where the Rother runs under the road and turns northward towards the River Dudwell. Two or three furlongs away a little eddying group of people was moving over the marsh. The centre was very close, a dense dark mass, but the edges sprayed and scattered, contracted and expanded, changing its shape from a circle to a long ellipse.

Clem had never run so fast in his life -- he left Cox, who was a trifle unwieldy, far behind. He caught up with the crowd while it was still some way from the spot where the Rother spreads and deepens for Bugshull Mill. They were evidently bound for the mill-pond; Clem could hear no cries, but a confused murmur, and a heavy, running sound . . . as when the Salehurst

United charge up the field at a football match and the Etchingham goal goes down before them . . . At first he experienced a certain relief to find that they were so few; after all, the respectable farmers of Salehurst market would not take part in such an orgie, even though they might allow it – but as he drew even with them he realized that it would be about as hopeless for him to tackle twenty men as two hundred. Their numbers were made up of the rougher elements of the market -- gipsies (among whom, however, he did not see Darius), young rowdy labourers and farm-boys, and one or two of the smaller farmers' sons.

"Stop," cried Clem." Stop!"

No one took any notice, and he could only run beside the others, panting and imploring. The centre was just a closely knotted mass – there was no struggle; evidently Robert was submitting to his fate, either as a matter of policy, or, more likely, of conscience.

"Stop!" gasped Clem. "Let him go. He äun't done you no harm. You're a hem set of bullies."

"You höald your jaw," said Stan Shovell, running near, "or maybe we'll chuck you in after him."

"Adone-do, Mus' Clem," broke in Cox, who had now reached them." You can't meddle. They wöan't do your brother any harm if he goes quiet."

"They'll drownd him."

"No, they wöan't – they'll only give him a bit of a ducking, as ull do him all the good in the warld, between ourselves."

"Oh, Lard!" panted Clem. "Oh, Lard!"

They had reached the pool at last – the sheet of water that holds the reflection of Bugshull Mill and its Lombardy poplars. The wheel was not working, so there was no danger of Robert being sucked under and drowned, but Clem was frantic at the thought of what was to happen. He suddenly caught sight of his brother, a stumbling dishevelled figure . . . and then, to his horror, Robert began to struggle. The sight of the stretch of cold water of unknown depth filled him with mortal fear.

"Lemme go!" he shrieked. "Lemme go!"

Clem made a plunge towards him, but was seized and held by Cox of Haiselman's and Stan Shovell. He fought them both, friend and foe, with the same fury. Then suddenly there was a big splash, and he became still. Silence hung for an instant. Everyone was staring at the place where Robert had vanished. The water spread in ever wider eddies . . .

"He's drownded!" cried Clem.

But the next moment Robert appeared, standing up to his waist in water, a ludicrous figure with his hair dripping in his eyes, and the water pouring off him as he choked and gasped.

There was a loud burst of laughter from the men on the bank.
"Now, Robert Fuller – preach to us about the goodness of God."
"Are you Säaved?"
"He's washed, anyway."
"Pull him out and chuck him in agäun."
"No – he's had enough."
"Three times is the dose."
"Git höald of him wud your stick, he can't run away."
"No, let him stay thur and preach to us."
"He says God's in everything. Have you found Him in the water, Bob?"
Robert opened his mouth.
"He's going to begin."
A torrent of blood suddenly poured from Robert's mouth.
"Lard, you've hurt him!"
"Help him to shore – we mun't kill him."
"It's naun – it's only his nose bleeding."
"No – it's coming from inside. He shudn't ought to have fought so."
Robert struggled slowly through the water towards the bank, seized two tufts of grass to pull himself up, and then fell forward unconscious, still half in the water.

From *Green apple harvest* (1920), 310–5.

As with Text 23a, a somewhat sanitized literary Sussex for the consumption of outsiders. The county diphthongs are marked using letters with a diaeresis (umlaut), though inconsistently (*aunt/äunt* for *ain't*). *Morning* and *Lord* appear with unrounding of [ɒ] or [ɔ] (*marnun, Lard*), and general southern [ɚː] appears as <ar> in *world*. *Little* exhibits voicing of [t] to [d]. The last of these is the only concession to the medial voicing observed in natural speech from the not far distant village of Peasmarsh (Text 37; see also *Saddaday* in Text 13a).

The 'double plural' appears in *foalkses* (spelt in three different ways); the past tense form *kept* appears as *kipt*, and we find *brung* for *brought*. As in most Sussex texts, the past tense of BE is expressed by the single form *wur*, whether singular or plural. Some well-known lexical talismans appear such as *adone-do* 'stop it!', the euphemistic expletive *hem*, and the inevitable *surelye*. *Vrother* 'to fuss' is more unusual; this seems to be the same root as Parish's *vlothered* 'agitated'. There are other non-standard forms not specific to Sussex.

TEXT 24

M. Fletcher Jones, 'Dr. Blackett' (1931, extract)

These 'talks' are actual reports of conversations with an old woodman who lives in a West Sussex village.

> Old Cherry Boxall an' Zeb Trussler an' me was a-rining up Istead 'oods. CherryBoxall was pulling a strip of rine off a tree, an' it broke – he were pulling wi' 'is 'and-bill – an' the bill caught 'im whack agin 'is ribs. Gor! it were a whack. 'E caught cold in it, besides, an' were rare bad. Ol' doc. didn't like climming up Istead 'ill, an' left some days afore 'e went to un, an' then 'e were baad. I went to see 'ow 'e were gettin' on an' found ol' gentleman there. 'E 'ad a big tray an' a gurt big bowl an' was just a-cupping 'im. The gurt big basin were full o' black blood. 'E got well arter that. One day at Farnhurst Fair I clim up Maypole an' cum down too fast and scrapped my shins. I went to Doctor an' 'e sez, "What you been up to, lad?" I sez, "Clim up Maypole, sir, an' cum down too fast." 'E laffed and sez, "You be all right. You be gurt strong lad," and gives me a bottle o' lotion stuff to bathe un. 'E were the club doctor, you understand.

Published in *Sussex County Magazine* 5 (1931), 431.

Rine and *rining* are 'rind' and 'rinding' – the men were removing bark from trees. The Sussex features of this text are the expected ones, but note the short vowel in *scrapped* and *clim(ming)*. It is not clear whether the long vowel marked in *baad* is just for emphasis. The absence of a definite article before *ol' gentleman* and *Maypole* and an indefinite one before *gurt strong lad* are hard to explain.

TEXT 25a

'Jim Cladpole': 'Firle Beacon' (1927)

On Furrel Beacon, han in han,
My woife an I togedir stand
An look across de weald.
We git a purty middlin view
Ov things to us both ol and new,
Wid up above de sky so blue,
An down below a field.

At ol Caburn we taak a look;
He tells us better dan a book
Ov never ending change.
He tells us how dat long agoo
Millions ov things under sea blue
Lived dere, and died, dat I, an you,
Now over him may range.

We turn roun, an look out to sea,
Where waves roll on unceasingly,
An ev'rything sims free.
In ev'ry quarter ov de earth
Be friens ov whom we know de worth,
Dat in dis county had dere birth,
In Sussex by de sea.

Our fit away wid us wunt run,
Fer we be over sixty-one,
An so we beant too spry.
But hearts aint bliged to tell de yeers,
Nor taak too gurt a stock ov tears,
Nor give house-room to doubts and fears,
An never shud say die.

Now up here ev'rything 'pears gurt,
An nothing sims as ef twud hurt
Aldo we be so small.
So in our mellur days, we two
Wull often think about dis view,
An offer up our praises to
Our God, who maad it all.

Aug. 1927

TEXT 25b

'Jim Cladpole': Summat 'bout Sussex an sum Sussexers *(1930, extracts)*

Twos dunameny yeers agoo
Dat Sussex cum to light.
De hills wos wunce under de sea,
And packed dere purty tight.

De hills, ya kno, be maad ov chalk,
And dat wos wunce alive;
As live as be de busy bees
Inside a ol skip hive.

Millyuns ov critters, liddle uns,
Lived, died and skellington'd;
An now dey be foundations fer
Meny a ol dewpond.

I dunno how it happened, kwite,
Twos long afore my day,
De hills cum up abuv de ses,
An sim as ef dey'll stay.

De hills be noice to doddle on,
An smell de time an sea.
De air be alwis noice an fresh,
As fresh as it can be.

De grass is scrumptious under foot
On top ov Beachy Head.
From dere Sem Sisters you may see,
Dat "wunt be druv" nor led.

****

Atimes dere's not so much concarn
Wid wot folk say an do,
As dere be wid de 'ticklar way
Dey puts der pints of view.

Sum knabble on, an on, an on,
An den dere's nothing in it.
Wile others maak ye think fer wicks,
Ef dey talk but a minnit.

An now I have jes a few "dunts"
Fer furriners to read.
It wunt hurt much to read em all,
Afore dey goo to bed.

Dunt think bout Sussex you kno all,
Jes cos you've bin to Brighton.
Dat does sum ov de other parts
Put jes a liddle slight on.

Dey call it Lunnun-by-de-Sea.
But taint loike Liddle Lunnun,
Ware de grass grows in ev'ry road
Dat folk be free to run on.

The extract consists of verses 1–6 and 87–91.

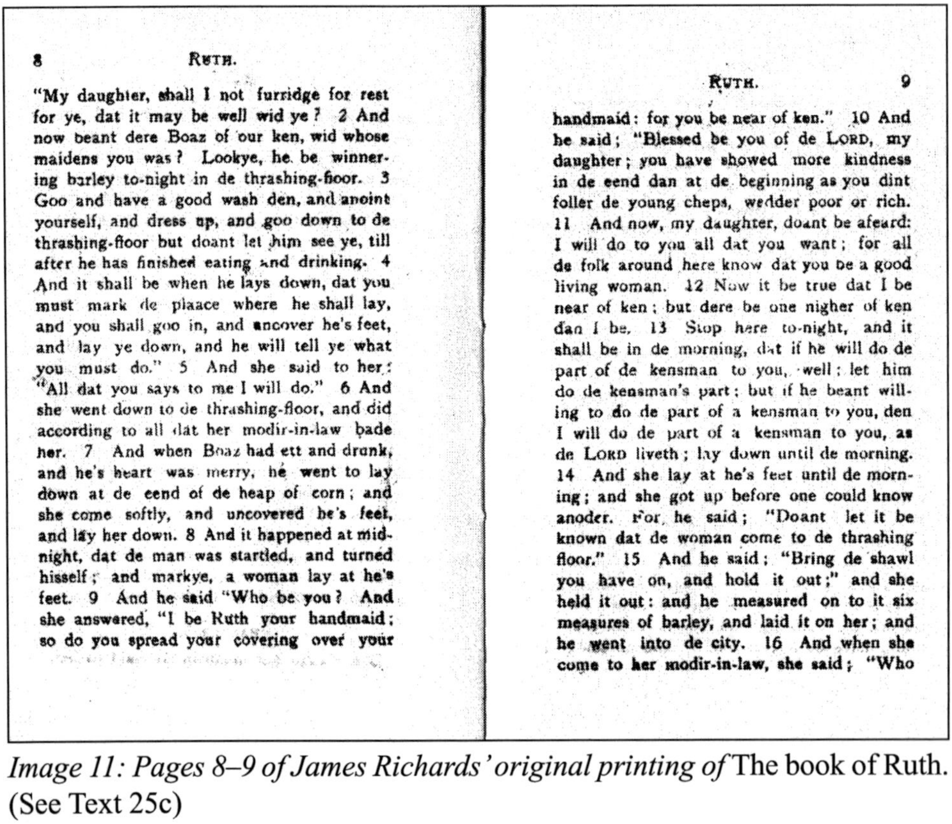

8 RUTH.

"My daughter, shall I not furridge for rest
for ye, dat it may be well wid ye? 2 And
now beant dere Boaz of our ken, wid whose
maidens you was? Lookye, he be winner-
ing barley to-night in de thrashing-floor. 3
Goo and have a good wash den, and anoint
yourself, and dress up, and goo down to de
thrashing-floor but doant let him see ye, till
after he has finished eating and drinking. 4
And it shall be when he lays down, dat you
must mark de plaace where he shall lay,
and you shall goo in, and uncover he's feet,
and lay ye down, and he will tell ye what
you must do." 5 And she said to her:
"All dat you says to me I will do." 6 And
she went down to de thrashing-floor, and did
according to all dat her modir-in-law bade
her. 7 And when Boaz had ett and drunk,
and he's heart was merry, he went to lay
down at de eend of de heap of corn; and
she come softly, and uncovered he's feet,
and lay her down. 8 And it happened at mid-
night, dat de man was startled, and turned
hisself; and markye, a woman lay at he's
feet. 9 And he said "Who be you? And
she answered, "I be Ruth your handmaid;
so do you spread your covering over your

RUTH. 9

handmaid: for you be near of ken." 10 And
he said; "Blessed be you of de LORD, my
daughter; you have showed more kindness
in de eend dan at de beginning as you dint
foller de young cheps, wedder poor or rich.
11 And now, my daughter, doant be afeard:
I will do to you all dat you want; for all
de folk around here know dat you be a good
living woman. 12 Now it be true dat I be
near of ken; but dere be one nigher of ken
dan I be. 13 Stop here to-night, and it
shall be in de morning, dat if he will do de
part of de kensman to you, well; let him
do de kensman's part; but if he beant will-
ing to do de part of a kensman to you, den
I will do de part of a kensman to you, as
de LORD liveth; lay down until de morning.
14 And she lay at he's feet until de morn-
ing; and she got up before one could know
anoder. For, he said; "Doant let it be
known dat de woman come to de thrashing
floor." 15 And he said; "Bring de shawl
you have on, and hold it out;" and she
held it out: and he measured on to it six
measures of barley, and laid it on her; and
he went into de city. 16 And when she
come to her modir-in-law, she said; "Who

Image 11: Pages 8–9 of James Richards' original printing of The book of Ruth. (See Text 25c)

TEXT 25c

'Jim Cladpole': The Book of Ruth *(1936, chapter 3)*

1 Den Naomi her modir-in-law said to her, "My daughter, shall I not furridge
for rest for ye, dat it may be well wid ye? 2 And now beant dere Boaz of our
ken, wid whose maidens you was? Lookye, he be winnering barley to-night
in de thrashing-floor. 3 Goo and have a good wash den, and anoint yourself,
and dress up, and goo down to de thrashing-floor but doant let him see ye, till
after he has finished eating and drinking. 4 And it shall be when he lays
down, dat you must mark de plaace where he shall lay, and you shall goo in,
and uncover he's feet, and lay ye down, and he will tell ye what you must
do." 5 And she said to her: "All dat you says to me I will do." 6 And she
went down to de thrashing-floor, and did according to all dat her modir-in-
law bade her. 7 And when Boaz had ett and drunk, and he's heart was merry,
he went to lay down at de eend of de heap of corn; and she come softly, and
uncovered he's feet, and lay her down. 8 And it happened at midnight, dat de
man was startled, and turned hisself; and markye, a woman lay at he's feet. 9
And he said "Who be you? And she answered, "I be Ruth your handmaid; so
do you spread your covering over your handmaid: for you be near of ken."
10 And he said; "Blessed be you of de LORD, my daughter; you have
showed more kindness in de eend dan at de beginning as you dint foller de
young cheps, wedder poor or rich. 11 And now, my daughter, doant be
afeard: I will do to you all dat you want; for all de folk around here know dat
you be a good living woman. 12 Now it be true dat I be near of ken; but dere
be one nigher of ken dan I be. 13 Stop here to-night, and it shall be in de
morning, dat if he will do de part of de kensman to you, well; let him do de
kensman's part; but if he beant willing to do de part of a kensman to you, den
I will do de part of a kensman to you, as de LORD liveth; lay down until de
morning. 14 And she lay at he's feet until de morning; and she got up before
one could know anoder. For he said; "Doant let it be known dat de woman
come to de thrashing floor." 15 And he said; "Bring de shawl you have on,
and hold it out;" and she held it out: and he measured on to it six measures of
barley, and laid it on her; and he went into de city. 16 And when she come to
her modir-in-law, she said; "Who be you my daughter?" And she told her all
dat de man had done to her. 17 And she said "Dese six measures of barley he
guv to me; for he said: 'Doant goo empty handed to your modir-in-law.' 18
Den she said, "Set still, my daughter, till you know how de matter will fall;
for de man wunt rest, till he has finished de thing dis day.

TEXT 25d

'Jim Cladpole': De shepherd psalm (1937)

De Lord my shepherd be
Surelye I shall not lack.
He leads me into fresh green grass
(Along de daily track).

And where de waters sweet
Flow gently, gently on
He leads me; (and He maaks me feel
Dat I be He's own son.)

My soul He does restore
And in right paths does guide
For He's naame's sake; (and so dat I
Doant wander from He's side.)

Yea, though I walk 'tween hills
De shaades of death all through,
Of evil I wunt be afeardt
Acos I walk wid you.

Your kind of Sussex bat,
Your kind of Pyecombe crook,
Dey comfort me; (and 'sure me I
To You for help can look.)

A table You've prepared
Dere I may set and feast
Where enemies be all around:
(You'll see dey doant molest.)

You've poured iol on my head
(As ef I was a king:)
My cup of jy runs over loike
A ever bubbling spring.

Goodness and marcy too,
Shall surelye follow me,
All through de days of earthly life
Wherever I may be.

And surelye after dat
In de house of de Lord
I'll live for ever. (For dat be
According to He's word.)

Privately printed (1937), and reprinted and anthologized several times since. This version is precisely as originally printed except for the positioning of the lines on the page. It should be compared with the anonymous rendering published by Kathleen Lee (Text 29).

TEXT 25e

'Jim Cladpole': The Gospel of Mark *(1938, extract)*

> Once when He was gwine through de cornfills on de Rest-day wid He's prentices as dey was doddling along, broke off some ears of corn. "Look ye," said de Priders to him "How dey be doing what beant allowed?" And He said to hem. "Aint you ever read what David did when he was needy and hungry, he and de folk wid him? How he went into de house of God, in de days of Abiathar, who was a High Priest, and ett de shew-bread which onny priestes was allowed to eat, and he guv some as well to hem dat was wid him? And He said to hem, "De Restday be maad for man, and not man for de Rest-day. So de Son of Man be Master also of de Rest-Day."

This version was published in *Bits from de Old Book* (1938), and consists of the Gospel according to Mark, chapter 2, verses 23–8.

He's prentices are of course Jesus' disciples and *the Priders* are the Pharisees. Elsewhere in Richards' work, Jesus is regularly called *Saver*.

James Richards was born in Hailsham, and spent most of his later life in Tunbridge Wells, maintaining his Sussex contacts. Texts 25a-e are among the Sussex classics, Richards being the most prolific twentieth-century author writing in 'grand dialect', i.e. whole texts in dialect as opposed to just the speech of selected characters. The religious texts sometimes show dialect and biblical diction in an uneasy coexistence. Where free of the latter, the texts read quite naturally, within the constraints imposed by the doggerel verse-forms which Richards chose.

Vowel features to note include some short vowels where the standard dialect has long (*sims, wicks*) ; an apparent exchange of short front vowels (*git* vs. *ef, set*) which is clearly not due to the nature of the following consonant; the universalized <d> for [ð]. Over the five texts as a whole, the Sussex 'inverted' diphthongs are apparent. The 'exchange' of /ai/ and /oi/ commented on by Parish can be seen in *jy* and *iol* (where the <o> represents the influence of the following dark [l]) vs. *woife*, for example. The once widespread change of ME <er> to <ar>, as in the British (RP) pronunciation of *clerk*, is apparent non-standardly here in *concerned* (25b) and *mercy* (25d). Reduction of ME unstressed /ow/ to schwa, which then either is rhoticized and/or gains a sandhi-[r], is seen in *foller, mellur* and *winnering. Eend* for *end* in 25c, Verse 7, is interesting, as it shows the late preservation of the Late Old English lengthened etymological short vowel in this word, not otherwise noted in Sussex but known to Wright (1905: 422-3) in north and east Kent.

The present tense of BE shows forms in <b> (she *be*, we *beant*). Non-standard past tense is seen in *guv* for *gave.* There are other widely-recorded non-standard forms such as *gwine* and *afeardt* (though the spelling of the latter is unusual).

The usual range of eye-dialect can be seen: *time* in Text 25b is of course *thyme*.

TEXT 26

Amy Sawyer: The black tea-party *(1931, extract)*

UNCLE JAMES: He wur my feyther's half-brother's son, hees mother wur a furriner from the sheers, so I doän't rackon he be a proper Pennifather at all; but Marthy, she be set on makin' a party an it and it saves a lot o' trouble to give a woman 'er 'ead. She'll git 'er own way afore she'll leave 'ee in peace as you'll find out some day, John.

TOBIAS: That's right. 'E'll find out when hees time comes. There ain't no gittin' away from that.

UNCLE JAMES: Yes, 'e'll git took in, same as the rest an us, though 'im bein' a laawyer makes the odds more even. Well any'ow 'tworn't no use keepin' that 'og no longer. 'E wur puttin' on flesh, gittin' fat as a maggit, an' you doänt want to be payin' for sharps an' middlins, the price they be a gallon, to be makin' lard at eightpence a pound.

TOBIAS: Be this the paper? Ah, here it be, surelye. Plain as print. You read it, John, wool 'ee? I ain't got my sparticles.

••••••••

UNCLE JAMES: Seein' as 'ow 'e didn't never know naun 'bout Jonas it be very mannerly o' John payin' hees respexes.

TOBIAS: Alice said as how he'd sartinly be 'ere.

UNCLE JAMES: 'Ow'd she know?

TOBIAS: 'Ow'd I know? Like sassidges women be – bags o' mystery.

UNCLE JAMES: They disagrees wid 'ee often nuff. I knows that.

From Amy Sawyer, *Sussex village plays* (1934, opening scene, extracts).

Amy Sawyer wrote plays for the local dramatic society in Ditchling. Since this is a play, the actors were presumably relied upon to produce pronunciation features which might be expected but which do not appear in the script.

Of phonological interest is *sassidges* for *sausages*, with unrounding of [ɒ]. We see *-s* marking the first person singular present tense in *knows* (narrator-subject), and third plural in *disagrees*. BE is in use uninflected, by contrast, in the third person singular present declarative and interrogative (*she be set, Be this . . ?*) *Sharps and middlins* are grades of refuse flour (cf. *pollard* in Text 15b). Other frequent and stereotypical features represented in these Texts can be found here.

TEXT 27

W. Ruskin Butterfield: Some terms used by Hastings fishermen (1933)

The bushel baskets used to contain mackerel, herrings, and sprats, but not for trawl fish, are called "prickles"; half bushel baskets are "pads," and quarter-bushel baskets "no-resters," the last being obviously a corrupted word. Lobster-pots, crab-pots, and whelk-pots are all called "stalkers." A long line used in fishing is called a "trott," a short line, a "micket"; "nuzzles" are lengths of twisted cords of about eleven inches. The fish-room in a boat is called the "plarum" or "pladam"; the net-room the "chey," and the afterpart the "pat." Lofts where herrings are cured are called "deezes," and a herring that has deposited its roe is a "shotner." When the deck of a boat has been rendered slippery with fish-mucus, it is said to be “glincey.” “Barbalee” fish are those just on the point of decomposing. “Gloit” is the term applied to oily patches on the sea, caused when fish entrails are thrown overboard.

A selection of weather terms used by the fishermen may be given. When there is a dead calm, with the air hot and moist, the weather is said to be “planety.” If it is oppressively sultry, with a heavy sky and oily sea, it is “swallocky,” and presages a storm which often breaks suddenly with a roaring squall. Uncertain and changeable weather is said to be “shucky”; when there is everv prospect of bad weather it is “truggy”; foul weather is described as “coarse.” Blown-out streamers of white clouds are “win-dogs,” the same name being applied to a solar halo; large wool pack-like clouds are “messengers”, small widely-scattered clouds floating in an otherwise clear sky are “postboys.” Occasionally when the sun is setting, a mock sun is seen on each side of the solar disc, a phenomenon which goes by the name of “smither-diddles.”

From “The Hastings fishermen”, in William Gray, ed., *The book of Hastings* (1933), 73–6.

In traditional fishing communities around Britain there was, and maybe is, often special vocabulary for use while out at sea. It can be regarded as a taboo system, where certain objects and processes may not be called by their regular names for fear of adverse consequences. What Butterfield reports here may be regarded as a vocabulary of that sort. It can also be viewed as a professional vocabulary which those joining the trade as apprentices need to learn and use to symbolize their bond with the older generation in a dangerous occupation.

TEXTS 28a-b

Sussex sheep-counting scores (traditional, date unknown)

Saddlescombe (for counting one at a time)

Wintherum
Wontherum
Twintherum
Twontherum
WAGTAIL

Whitebelly
Coram
Dar
Diddle
DEN

Etherum
Atherum
Shootherum
Cootherum
WINDBAR

Bobtail
Inadik
Dyadik
Bumpit
ECACK-TALLY

Slindon (for counting in pairs)

One the rum
Two the rum
Cocker rum
Quther rum
Shether rum
Shather rum
Wine berry
Wig tail
Tarry diddle
Den

Published by James White, *Sussex County Magazine* 9 (1937), 305–6.

Some sheep-counting scores in other parts of England have been viewed as survivals of British Celtic; some scholars interpret them as having been imported by later Welsh drovers. The versions here seem to have no connection whatever with Celtic, except for *bumpit* in the Saddlescombe score. This numeral in other versions has been taken to derive from Welsh *pymtheg* 'fifteen', which it resembles to some extent. But in Saddlescombe it meant 'nineteen', which creates a problem for any simple philological or contact-linguistic explanation of these scores.

TEXT 29

A shepherd's version of Psalm 23 (1940s)

Thur Lord is me shepherd, I sharn't want fur nothin'.

He goes afore me ower thur green downs, an guides me by thur quiet waters of thur Adur.

He comforts me soul, an leads me along good paarths for his naame's sake.

Yea, tho' I walks thru shadowery ways I aunt afeared, for his Shepherds crook'll guide me.

He'll fin' a quiet plaace fer to eat ower food arter we overcome ower difficulties an us'll be happy.

Shurlye this lovliness 'ul be wi'me aul me days, till I coome to thur home o' me Lord forever.

This version was found in Thakeham church, and was copied out by the discoverer. The version as copied is what appears here. However, it has actually been published; first, I believe, by Kathleen Lee in *The Countryman* (Winter 1971/2), and then reprinted elsewhere. Miss Lee adds: 'Recited by an old shepherd, surrounded by his flock on the Downs overlooking the River Adur.'

This text is interesting as it is not dependent to any significant extent on the spelling-tradition which had evolved for Sussex dialect on the basis of its nineteenth-century 'classical' writings. How convincing it is is another matter, as is the question of its authorship.

It should be compared with the fully versified version written by James Richards ('Jim Cladpole') in 1937 (Text 25d). The two versions appear to me to share an origin in experimentation with dialect writing by a person literate in the standard language. This one can hardly be attributed to the shepherd from whom it was collected, at least not in exactly its present form.

TEXT 30a

'Mrs Paddick': Cheeky kids (1930s or 1940s)

"What's that for, Mrs. Paddick?" I asked.

"It was lodged up on your gate, Mum. Them young scaddles 'uv been at their tricks again."

"Oh, aren't they silly, Mrs. Paddick? They seem to have only one idea. Why can't they find something to do, instead of annoying people?"

Mrs. Paddick prepared to help me wash the contents of the china cupboard.

"Young scaddles!" she repeated. "They all seems to do it. My husband is terrible down on 'em now, but I says to he, 'Put your hand before your face, Charlie. Don't you mind that night you stuck Mr. Wheatcroft's board Funerals in the old doctor's front garden as the policeman come an' caught you at it?' And he says as our Syd ain't gooin' to carry on same as that or he'll know the reason why."

"Do you think it's because the lads aren't wanted at home of an evening, Mrs. Paddick?"

She shook her head.

"Can't be that, Mum, else why is it the bettermost folk do's just the same? It's same as my aunt at Pompey told me as some young scaddles as was learnin' to be officers in the Navy went round an' changed the numbers of the houses and a dockhand on a late shift couldn't fit his latch-key into No. 16 as was changed to 26 an' rang an' rang till No. 16 come downstairs an' hollered at he through the letter-box as my aunt next-door said his language was terrible."

"I suppose they think it's funny," I said.

"It's trippical of lads, Mum. Same as they young gentleman in that place I told you I was in, forever dressin' up an' playin' tricks on folk. As they used to zarnick about, turnin' out the street lamps as was all gas then. One of 'em climbed up an' turned out the lamp just outside the door an' when he slithered down agen, there was a bobby standing there as says to he: 'Climb like a monkey, can't you? Well, up you goo agen an' light that there lamp.' And he went up like a lamb. Not as I ever see a lamb climb a lamp-post," added Mrs. Paddick hastily and we both laughed.

"I learnt the youngest one not to play his tricks on me," went on Mrs. Paddick. "I was expectin' the sweep an' was up at five waitin' for he, when along comes my young gentleman as black as a cotterell. But I reckernised he by his jib for all his soot, so I says to he: 'This way. But where's your brooms?' 'Oh, my mate'll be along with they,' he says. 'Well, while you're waitin' for he, you can clear out the bunny in the backyard. It's all stopped up,' I says. 'That ain't part of a sweep's duties,' he says, as lippy as you please. 'Oh yes it is,' I says. 'I'll give you a flue brush an' you can unstop that drain afore your mate comes along,' I says. I thought he was gooin' to jack up then, but I stood over he an' made him do it. I justabout did enjoy myself. An' when 'twas all flushed an' proper, I says to he: 'Looks as if your mate ain't comin',' I says. 'So maybe you'd better goo an' have a good sloosh in the bathroom afore your ma sees you, an' you'll be down in time for breakfast for once in yer life,' I says. Oh, I was a saucy little faggit in them days."

Mrs. Paddick chuckled. There was no doubt that 'our Syd' would meet his match if he zarnicked about. But I think it is a pity she has only one. She could certainly cope with any number of boys, and girls too, for that matter. I am always interested in the way she copes with children. One day, she arrived and announced that her neighbour's little girl had been taken to hospital to have an appendix operation.

"Always grizzlin' that child is," said Mrs. Paddick. "Now if our Syd starts grizzlin' I knows he ain't well, for he's not one to grizzle, so I knows he's rebellious and I take an' give he a little old liver pill."

"I think it's true of most children that they aren't well if they're always grizzling, Mrs. Paddick."

"Most-in-ginral, Mum. But there's some as is terrible rafty, same as my sister, Sarah. She'd git in sech a stodge if my mother wanted she to do anything she didn't want to, she wouldn't speak for days. Dad give she a good bannickin' now and agen, but it didn't do no good. And she's jest the same now she's married, though her husband's one of the best. Oh, he is a nice still man, Mum, but she do's give he a life of it."

Mrs. Paddick nodded.

"It's same as my husband told me when our Syd was a little chap, he fell down an' bumped his head while I was out and his Dad comforted he and he stopped cryin'. Then, when he heard me comin' home, he started mimperin' and his dad says, 'What's the matter, Syd?' And he says, 'What was it I was cryin' for, Dad? Mum won't know nothing about it if I don't cry.' We had a good laugh about it."

Originally published in the *West Sussex Gazette*, and reprinted in 'Margaret Wyndham', *Mrs Paddick* (1947), 99–100.

TEXT 30b

'Mrs Paddick': Argufying and worriting

"My nephew from London's been down for a holiday along of we," said Mrs Paddick. "I wasn't sorry to see the back of him. Such a sessions we had every night. A middlin' rookery 'twas! But, there, Leonard'ud argue the hind foot off a donkey."

"Politics, Mrs Paddick?" I suggested.

"I s'pose you might call it that, Mum. Unaccountable put out I was, with our Syd an' young Bill drinkin' it all in. He said as 'twan't no use thinkin' as things was ever gooin' to be the same as they was afore the war on account they wasn't gooin' to be. And a good job too, he says!"

"Oh, he's quite content with things as they are then, Mrs Paddick?"

"My husband, he never says much. But he was cuttin' some brenbutter, an' he says: 'I s'pose you likes this chizzly bread then?' An' Leonard gits in a hoe an' says as that ain't nothin' to do with it. I says as 'twas e'en a'most time they give over argufyin', but I was terrible put out. An' then, as I come along here today, I seen the gipsies here again. An' somehow it made me unaccountable pleased to see they."

"They've come for the haying, I suppose, Mrs Paddick?"

"Yes, Mum, an' they'll stay till the harvest's in. An' there they were just the same. Mout'uv been the same as I recollect when I was little, with their yaller caravan an' the lace curtains at the windows an' the boys an' girls all helpin' in the fields while our childern are at school."

"That's always puzzled me, Mrs Paddick. How is it they're not made to go to school?"

Mrs Paddick chuckled. "On account of it ain't easy to make gipsies do what they don't want to. One of 'em said to my husband as they knowed a unaccountable lot more than what we do on account of you can't learn 'em out of books. And you know, Mum, it queers me how 'tis gipsies is out all weathers, but you don't hear tell of 'em bein' ill, do you? Never see doctor gooin' to the caravan."

"I've heard that the only time gipsies are ill is when they are made to sleep under a roof."

Mrs Paddick nodded. "It's what they're used to, I s'pose. But one thing that gipsy said to my husband made me think. He said as gipsies don't never worrit. They don't know what the word means. An' when I seen 'em this mornin' I says to myself, I says: "They gipsies has got more brains in their little fingers than what Leonard's got in his head."

First published in the *West Sussex Gazette*, 25 July 1946, and reprinted 25 July 1996.

The author, like many others writing this kind of story, is not only interested in dialect, but also in the country thoughtways and attitudes that she thinks are typical of dialect-speakers. As in many such texts, the uneducated speaker is expected to use mispronunciations, and here we have *trippical* for *typical.*

Mrs Paddick's speech is intended to represent that of the coastal plain in the far west of the county. The dialect is expressed mainly through vocabulary (*zarnick about* 'mess around', *cotterell* 'pothook', *rafty* 'ill-tempered', *chizzly* 'gritty'), but we also find historic subject personal pronouns used in direct object role (*give he a life of it*) and governed by prepositions (*hollered at he*), and topicalization is often expressed though left dislocation (*Unaccountable put out I was . . .*). There is occasional narrator-subject *-s* (see notes to Texts 26 and 31). The use of *on account of* as a subordinating conjunction ('because') is now more widespread in non-standard English. Much of Mrs Paddick's usage is non-standard over a much wider area than Sussex.

For *yaller* see also Text 35b. *Mout'uv* is 'might have'. Today, *mought* is almost exclusively American.

TEXT 31

E. Walford Lloyd: Paranoia (1930s or 1940s)

[Jarge is telling Tom about an incident on a bus where he believed he was being insulted to his face.]

"Ol' Mother Goster, she took on amazin' an' turned on I like a she-fox, wot she is!

"'Wot ails yeou ol' fule,' she sez, just like that. 'Wot be matter wi' 'ee Jarge? I ain't sed a word agin yeou yet.'

"Why yeou bin a miscallin' me an' scandalizin' me unaccountable bad, Mother Goster, I sez. I'll 'ave the law on yeou for all this 'ere piece of work. Takin' 'way my chalicter-like an' yeou no call to do ut. I'll have the law o'yeou."

"'Law of me,' sez Mother Goster, 'law of me? Ol' Jarge yeou bin gone mad, I allow, or your dotage 'as come on suddent, for I ain't spoken yer name,' sez she.

"'Why,' sez I, 'Yeou bin a miscallin' me 'orrid ever since got in this 'ere bus. I 'eard it wi' me own ears.'

"Maaster Tom, thet ol' she-fox bust out a-larfin, an' doubled up wi' larfin', made a 'orrid nise she did, same as ol' Ben's donkey makes in the medder when 'ee sees Ben come out wi' 'is whip. 'Yeou've no call to larf, Mother Goster,' I sez. 'No more call than nawthin'. Maybe 'ee'll larf at the back of yer faace when yeou stans' in the box afore the beaks fer scandalizin' a pore, innercent ol' man.'

"'Jarge, my man,' sez Mother Goster, 'yeou'm got a mighty bad conscience, an' yeou be a rare ol' eaves-dropper too,' sez she.

"'I woren't talking ef yeou at all but ef ol' Gaffer Smith, wot yeou knows very well. But -- Jarge -- ef the cap fits 'ee -- wear it my man! Never thought yeou wore sich a bad un, Jarge! Still yer conscience must prick 'ee crooel bad ter make yeou rekernise yerself in 'nother man's bad 'abits ! I allus sort ef spicioned 'ee Jarge, as beein' a cunnin' sort ef ol' raskal!'

"Maaster Tom, when I 'eard that wicked ooman a miscallin' I like thet, all afront of t'other folkses in the bus, I jist caught holt ef that there bell-pull good an' pra'per, an' when that there bumblesome bus 'ad stopped I gits outer un pretty smartish, an' I starts to walk 'ome, till I gets to The Stile, where a good wet ef beer (wot I could do wi' now) putts me near-so-matter right -- but I wore thet leer. Still, Maaster Tom, thet she-fox's words stuck in me gizzard, an' there they be to this day, an' ever will be. Fair scandilized I wore by it arl, an' kin't show me faace in that there bus agin'. 'Cos why? 'Cos when they sees I, thet lil' conductor-bloke a-busts wi' larfin', an' I knows very well 'ee bin an' told 'most everyone. Thet's why I 'ates that girt lummickin' bumblesome stinkin' bus!

"Thankin' yeou kindly, Maaster Tom, but talkin' allus made I dry an' feel THET LEER."

The stories of Ol' Jarge were first published in the *Hampshire Telegraph and Post* and rewritten for publication in book form under the title *Ol' Jarge* (1946); this extract is from 66–7 of the book.

The dialect is of a broadly south-western type, to some degree doubtfully Sussex. *Pra'per* 'proper' shows the obsolete unrounding of /ɒ/; *Jarge* and *arl* show the same phenomenon for the corresponding long vowel. *All* was noted with a non-round vowel by Joseph Wright from East Sussex; *nawthing* reflects a pronunciation recorded by Wright from West Sussex. Final /r/ in *meadow* is a genuine local phenomenon (*LAE* map Ph206), though not exclusively so; but <r> in *all* and *laughing* is just an indicator of a long vowel.

Other phonological features might be taken as general southern. Inconsistent *thet* for *that* is hard to interpret; the item is not treated in Sussex in this way according to Wright. *'ee* for *ye* (object form) not recorded in Sussex in Survey of English Dialects materials. *En* for *it* (object), as in *gits outer un* (i.e. the bus), is more typical of dialects further west and halts at the county boundary in the Survey (LAE map M71); however, representing *him* it is found in West Sussex (M70).

The spelling <yeou> for *you* suggests forms proper to the West Country. It is not clear what the implications of the form *yeou'm* 'you have (auxiliary)' are. A doubly-marked plural appears in *folkses*. *Leer* is 'empty, thirsty'. First-person narrator-subject -*s* inflection is seen. There is a token mispronunciation in *chalicter*.

TEXT 32

Gaius Carley: Tools of the farrier's trade (1955)

> All kinds and shapes of these tools were used, sets, mandrells, punches and drifts were used, swedge blocks – large slabs fixed on a stand with all sizes and shapes of holes in this heavy block of iron, fullers, compasses and callipers, squares and various named tools, many of them not used today. Plough shears we made for the old wooden plough. Two anvils were used for this job. One of the anvils was on the slant almost upside down, the under or bottom of the beak horn, the pointed end of the anvil, made a good mould or mandrell for the shaping of the sheare. Some man was clever when he spotted this.

From
Gaius Carley, *Memoirs* (second edition, 1964), 18.

Gaius Carley was born at Upper Dicker, but spent most of his working life as a blacksmith in various places in the west of the county. This passage illustrates the local words for smithing tools.

TEXT 33

W.G. Daish: Poem *(1957)*

Yest'day raglar as a clock,
De o'd Wes Sussex come along;
So down I sets to git a look
En see what news from home she brung.

I looks to Horsham fust, yore sure,
To find out how me clawneys be,
Afore I turns de page for more
O' things dat means so much to me.

I warnt aaf pleased to see yore bit,
Right in de place whur she belongs,
'Bout all de Sussex talk en wit
Of o'd Mus' Richards en he's songs.

Otherwhile, works o' heart en mind
Gits overgrowed be all dat's new;
En, aaf fergot be humandkind,
Hengs jest like hollerds in de lew,

Till some as knows de rare en good,
Pints out de kelm dat restes still
Adin de shadder o' dur 'ood
En time wunt purrish, behowtwil.

I rackon round dey pearly geats,
Whur de o'd young 'uns sets en jaws,
Mark Lower en James Richards weats
To lease sich bits o' Sussex news!

Sent to Stanley Godman (August 1957), and published in the *West Sussex Gazette* of 29 August 1963. *Yore bit* refers to an article by Godman about James Richards, published in the same paper on 1 August 1957.

A good example of literary Sussex by one of the last capable practitioners, Daish – and not a *surelye* in sight. The dialect features are all found in other Texts in this book, and Daish's usage is, not surprisingly, closely similar to that of James Richards.

Clawneys means 'relatives'; *hollerds* is 'dead branches of trees'; *adin* is phonologically regular for 'within'.

TEXT 34

S.B.: the Michelham poem (date unknown; ?late 1940s). Anonymous verses found in a notebook at Michelham Priory

Downland oxen

1

Dere lived a good farmer once on a tyme
He'd fower an twenty oxen fyne
And for yeeres and yeeres he's pride an prime
Were fower an twenty oxen fyne
And over de downland hills and vales
He sang de old familiar chyme
Wid "Cum kup cumalong cum kup cum
Ye fower an twenty oxen fyne."

2

Goliath an Gore goo afore
Spark an Spittle goo in de middle
Duke an Dine good [sic] behind
Dutch and Dane foller 'n lyne
Wid Curtis an Crowner
Lamb an Lion
Turk an Tiger
Winch an Winder
Brown an Berry
Buck an Benbow
March an Merry.

3

Quick an Nimble
Sw[?]aller an Blyde
Stout an Sturdy (ebony hide,)
Wonder an Broad (beautiful kine)
Little boy, Jim boy, foller behind
And over de Downland coombes dey toiled
And moiled in sunshine rigor or ryme
Wid "Cum kup cum along cum kup cum"
Ye fower an twenty oxen fyne".

4

When ploug[h]ing was done dey took dere fill
O' de watercress pond, aside o' de Hill
Den whoam at de Barn dey bellured dere lays
While de rooks an de ringdoves circled dere praise
An de windmill groun de corn
An de bells rang Harvest Home.

And still de watercresses grow
And distant voices call de chyme
Wid "Cum kup cum along, Cum kup cum"
Ye fower an twenty oxen fyne.

S.B.

First published in this book. The author is believed to be Salome Bridger of Alciston.

The dialect is of the eastern type, with regular [d] for [ð]. The spelling *whoam* seems to represent something like [hwuəm] or maybe [huəm]; /ʍ/ from Middle English /hw/ would have been obsolete in Sussex by this time. The disyllabic pronunciation of *four* is usual in Sussex. Eye-dialect abounds, especially with <y> for <i>. *Moiled* is 'troubled, vexed'.

TEXT 35a

Bob Copper: A boyhood in Rottingdean (1976)

But the weekly caller to whom my attention was inclined more fondly was Uncle John who looked in about tea-time on a Monday to pay the Slate and Tontine clubs. These were voluntary savings and sickness benefit schemes, run by the landlords of the local pubs, and Dad would take Uncle John's subscriptions to save him a journey to the pub later in the evening. Coming straight off the downs where he had been all day tending his flocks Uncle John brought into the tiny kitchen not only the smell of Cooper's No. I sheep dip and St Bruno tobacco, but also a breath of the big, open hill country where he spent all his working days and his tales, told in a leisurely way yet with great enthusiasm, smacked of that country where the wind whistles through the bents and the gorse and stunted blackthorn lay their backs to the sea. He would tell how 't'would be two-an'-twenty year ago come May' when they 'dag' lambs from the snowdrifts 'up 'Oneysocks' or how he had once met a colony of rats on the move.

'We wuz comin' 'ome up along Smuggler's Track one evenin' – about October time as I recall – th' ol' sun wuz jes' a-gooin' down an' 'twuz gittin' a li'l dusky-like under th' 'ill, when prensly th' ol' dawg stops sudden-like and stands stock still. Whumperin' an' tremblin' from 'ead t' tail 'e wuz. "What's up then, mairt?" I sez.'

Fosh, who lay on the cornsack that served as a doormat, looked up at his master, as if he remembered the occasion well.

'Then over th' brow o' th' 'ill I sees this big, dark patch, like a damn grut pool o' treacle, slowly pourin' down th' steep side 'ill. It 'ad me guessin' fer a bit, I can tell ye, but as it got a li'l closer I could see 'twas thousands 'pon thousands o' rats, movin' along like an army an' leavin' a swathe o' trodden grass behin' 'em as they went.

'I've never sin th' ol' dawg s' upset afore. 'E kinda cowered down at m' fit with 'is back arched, tail tucked tight up between 'is legs an' 'is eyes stickin' out of 'is 'ead like organ stops -- an' I 'ad the wind up a notch or two, I dun't mind tellin' ye.

'But they went past us about five an' twenty yards away t' th' east'ard an' there was so many an 'em that took th' best part o' twenny minutes for 'em t' pass. I should think they was makin' f' 'Arvey's Crawss, be th' way they wuz 'eadin' an', thinks I t' meself, ol' 'steady Pettit's in f' a load o' trouble if they are. Never sin anythin' like it afore nor since, 'ave we, mairt?' he said to Fosh.

TEXT 35b

Bob Copper: A boyhood in Rottingdean (1976)

[Dad] had the knack of driving home a point with a practical demonstration which ensured that it was never forgotten. 'What d'you think that is, then?' he asked one day as we passed a clump of 'keck'-like flowers on the bankside.

'Looks loike yaller keow-paarsley, t'me,' I said, for this was before the spanner of necessity had tightened up my vowels for job-hunting in London in the '30's.

'Pull a plant up an' bring it 'ere t'me.' He took his knife, topped and tailed the root, scraped it clean and passed it back. 'Taste that an' then you'll know what it is.'

'Tastes loike paarsnip,' I said.

'Yeah, would do – that's what it is, wild parsnip, an' don't let me 'ear y' call it "yaller keow-paarsley" n'more.'

He taught me that the corn-bunting was a 'cloddy-bird' and the kestrel was a 'wind-hover' – to rhyme with plover – . . .

Both passages from *Early to rise: a Sussex boyhood* (1976), 19–20, 97–8.

These two texts display many of the features also found in those presented above. Of phonological note is the rounding of a front vowel after [w] implied in *whumpering*. The shortening of the long vowel in *sin* and the converse lengthenings in *dawg* and *Crawss* are widespread in older non-standard usage. The lowering of the stressed vowel in *yaller* is seen also in Text 30b, and the raising-cum-fronting of the first element of the diphthong in *keow* ('cow') is noted in the Survey of English Dialects materials for Sussex as [ɛu] (LAE map Ph154). Notice *mairt* for 'mate', where the <air> is to be read as the diphthong [ɛə], as in standard *air*, and does not indicate the presence of [r].

Kecks is a fairly widespread word for a range of plants of the family Umbelliferae.

TEXT 36

Memory for dialect (1992)

Some results of Costello and Jerrome's dialect survey in Petworth, 1992

8. *What do you call the beards of barley?*
OILS (various spellings) 11: AWNS 9: AWLES.

9. *What is your word for putting sheaves together in the harvest field for drying?*
STOOKING 29: SHOCKING 22: some gave both answers.

10. *What do you call the bottom-end of a sheaf?*
BUTT 33: HEEL.

11. *What tool was used for threshing before machines came in?*
FLAIL 36: also the older spelling FRAIL or FRAL.

12. *What do you call a mixture of oats and barley sown together?*
DREDGE (CORN) 23: MIXED CORN, TARES.

13. *What do you call the grass of a meadow after haying?*
AFTERMATH 11: LEY 6: SWARD.

14. *What do you call the grass or partly dried hay, raked into rows for fully drying?*
WINDROWS 19: SWATHES, SWARVES, RIDGES, RUING.

15. *What do you call the straw of peas, beans, tares, etc?*
HAULM (various spellings) 33: there were no alternatives given.

16. *What do you call the strips of land at the sides of a field, left until last before ploughing in?*
HEADLANDS 41: SIDELANDS 2.

17. *What do you call the raised parts in a ploughed field?*
RIDGES 10: FURROWS 7: VOORS, OPENINGS, WHIPS, BACK-UPS, LANDS, SEAMS, VEERINGS.

*18. *What do you call the type of plough used for turf-cutting?*
SCIMMER 2: DENSHIRE-PLOUGH, TURF IRON, DIGGER, SPINNER, LEY PLOUGH.

From *The Petworth Society Magazine* 69 (1992), 33–7.

These responses give some idea of the extent of lexical variation in the Petworth area around 1990, and comparison with Survey of English Dialect materials indicates the extent of lexical change. Note though that because of changes in farming techniques some of the concepts asked about must only be remembered, not in current usage.

TEXT 37

The pronunciation of an 87-year-old woman from Peasmarsh (1980s)

(iii) *The transcription of speaker W*

1 ʔɛ́ɪwɔɹdn̩ ǽɷs ɪʔ wəz̥ kɔ́ːɫd | jɨ́ɹz əgʌɷ | bʌt ɑɪ θɪ́ŋg̊ ɪʔs
2 kɔ́ːɫd̥ sʌ́mθɪ̥ŋ ɛ́ɫs næɷ

Hawarden House it was called / years ago / but I think it's called something else now.

3 ðɪ ʌ́ɷɫd fǽʃn̩n nɛɪm wəz̥ ɛ́ɪwɔɹdn̩ | ðæt̚ kɒ́tɪdʒ

The old-fashioned name was Hawarden / that cottage.

4 ʃɪi njɪ́ɷ wɛn ɪʔ wəz̥ gɷ́ɪnə ɹɛ́ɪn | wɛ́n̠ ʃɪ wəz dɷ́uɪŋ kɔ́ɹsɪts |
5 ɐn̠ ʃɪ jɪ́ɷst'ə lɛ́ɪ əɹ kɔ́ɹsɪts dǽɷn pɷ́d̥ əɹ ǽ·n^{d}z ɑ̈n̪ ðə tɛ́ɪbɫ
6 n̩ gʌ́ɷ ɔ·f tə slɪ́ip

She knew when it was going to rain / when she was doing corsets / and she used to lay her corsets down put her hands on the table and go off to sleep.

7 wɛ́n̠ ʃɪ wəz mǽɹɪd ʃɪ wəz wəɹkɪŋ fə mɪ́stəɹ fɪ̠́ɫməɹ | ðə
8 glʌ́vɹɪ | glʌ́vz̥ ən lɛ́gɪnz̥ ən spǽts əz ðɛɪ jɪ́ɷstə kɔ́ːɫ ɫəm

When she was married she was working for Mister Filmer / the glovery / Gloves and leggings and spats as they used to call them.

9 ðɛɪ stáɹtɪd ɪm wɑ́̈ɪʔtnɑ́̈ɪts | ðə mɪ́dɫ̩ ǽɷs əv ðʌ́ɷs θɹɨ́i

They started in Whiteknights / the middle house of those 3.

10 ʃɪi dɪdn̩ wə́ɹkʔ fəɹ ɛ́nibɑɾɪ

She didn't work for anybody.

11 ɐ spö̥ɷz̥ ɪʔ̰ wɒ́·z̥ | ɑɪ ka·n ɪ́vn̪ ɹɪmɛ́mbɹ̩ ɹ̩ dɷ́uɪŋ əm | ʌɷ́nɪ
12 ðətʔ ʃɪi dɪ́d̚ dɷu əm

I suppose it was / I can't even remember her doing them / only that she did do them.

13 ɹɑ́ɪt ʌp ʔ ðə tɑ́p əv ðə stɹɨ́it̚

Right up at the top of the street.

14 mɑɪ fá·ðəɹ ɪz̥ nɪ́əɹɪs ðə fɛ́n^{t}s | mɑɪ mʌ́ðəɹ ən ɑɪ əɹ ət̪ ðə

15 gɛɪt

My father is nearest the fence / My mother and I are at the gate.

16 ʌ́ɷnɪ dʒʌ́st ə pɛ́ɪvmɨn? nǽɹöɷ pɛ́ɪvmɨn? bɪtwíi̯n n̪ë hǽɷs ən n̪ë

17 | fɛ́ns

Only just a pavement narrow pavement between the house and the fence.

18 dǽɷn ɛgzɔ́ᶷɫ | bádm̩ əv ðə híɫ | ən θɹíi p'ɫíismən äñm pɔ̢́ɪnt˺

19 dɪ́utɪ | ən maɪ vá·ðəɹ sɛd ə | ɪ? wəz əβǽɷ? mɪ́dnaɪt' | sʌ́ɷ

20 áɪ æd t'ə gʌ́ɷ wɪ́ð ɪm ë‿ɛ́ɫp˺ p'ɷ́ʃ ðə g̊aɹt | dʒʌ́ss ə t'ɷ́u

21 wɪ́iɫd tɹʌ́k laɪk | köɹs z̥ə k'áfɪm wəz̥ kʌ́vəɹd ʌ́·p' | əʒ jɷ́uʒɷ

22 | wɛ́m wɪi gát˺ dǽɷn də ðə báɾm̩ əv ɛ́gz̥ʌɷɫ ?ḭ́ɫ ðɛ wəɹ θɹíi

23 p'ɫíismən äñm pɔ̢́ɪnt˺ dɪ́ut'ɪ | ænd maɪ v̥á·ðəɹ sɛ́d˺ t'ɷ əm ɪts

24 ɔ́: ɹáɪ? wɪiv gád̥ ə lǽ·ntəɹn bəd ɪts bǽk ʌp ðə ɹʌ́ɷd

Down Eggshole / bottom of the hill / and three policemen on point duty / and my father said er / it was about midnight / so I had to go with him er help push the cart / Just a two-wheeled truck, like / 'Course the coffin was covered up / as usual / When we got down to the bottom of Eggshole Hill, there were three policemen on point duty / and my father said to them it's all right, we've got a lantern but it's back up the road.

25 ?ǽd tɷ ɪn̪ n̪ə féɹs wéɹɫd wɔ́ɹ kəz ɔ́:ɫ ɪz mɛ́n wə kɔ́:ɫd ʌ́·p |

26 ðɛn aɪ ǽd˺ tə bɪ bɔ́ɪ | gɹáɪn̪n̪ n̪ə wáɪ? lɛ́d n̩d ðə ɹɛ́d lɛ́d fə

27 ðə pɛɪn? | mɪ́ks ʌp ðə pʌ́tɪi ən sʌtʃ laɪk | s·g̊ɹáɪnd ɪt ʌ́p

28 ət ðǽt˺ táɪm ə dɛɪ kəz ɪ? jɷ́us? k'ʌ́m ɪn ə bɪ́g˺ k'ɛ́g | ɪ́n̪ n̪ðə

29 pɛ́ɪnt | jɷ ad̥˺ tə gɹáɪnd ɪd̥ ʌ́p kəz ɪtp wəz láɪk:˺ klágg˺

30 təgɛ́ðəɹ jə sɪ́i

Had to in the First World War 'cos all his men were called up / Then I had to be boy / Grind the white lead and the red lead for the paint / mix up the putty and such like / Used to grind it up at that time of day 'cos it used to come in a big keg / In the paint / you had to grind it up 'cos it was like clogged together, you see.

31 jɷu ad˺ t'ə mɪ́ks ɪt ʃəsɛ́ɫf

You had to mix it yourself.

32 ɪ́i wəz̥ bɔ́ɹn̄ ðɛ ɪɲ ə sɛ̢́ɪm ɹɷum áɪ wəz bɔ́ɹn̄ ɪn

He was born there in the same room I was born in.

33 ðə fə́ɹs lɑɾ ə bǽʃfəɹdz̥̊ lívd ɪn: | wɛ̈ɹ mɑɪ gɹǽŋ̊vəɹ lívv̥ |
34 ɪn̪ n̪ǽʔ kɔ́ɹn̠ɹ æɷs

The first lot of Bashfords lived in / where my granfer (= grandfather) lived / in that corner house.

35 jɷ́u kɧ̂ ɹɪmɛ́mbɹ əm ðə́əɹ

You can remember them there.

36 wɒ́z ɪʔ ʔmɑ́ɪd ə bín

Was it? It might have been.

37 ðɛɪ dɑ́ɪd ɔ̣:f

They died off.

38 ən̪ ðə ʔǽɷs wəz̥ dʒəs lɛ́f tə ɹɷ́uɪnz̥

And the house was just left to ruins.

39 ɟi lívd əd̥ ə sɔ́ɹd̠ əv ə gɛ́ɪt' | ə lɪdɫ̩ bʌ́ŋgɫ̩ʌ́ɷ ɔ̜ɫ ɑn ɪz ʌ́ɷn
40 | fíɫθɪi də́ɹt̠ʻɪi ʌɷɫ mǽ:n

He lived at a sort of a gate / a little bungalow all on his own / filthy dirty old man.

41 ɪ jɷ́us tə wə́ɹç f ɛ́nɪbɒdɪ əd ɪmpʻlɔ̜́ɪ ɉm | bət nʌ́ɷbᵊdɪ ɑ́ɹdlɪ
42 wɷ́d: ɪmpʻlɔ̜́ɪ ɉm

He used to work for anybody who'd employ him / but nobody hardly would employ him.

43 ɪt͡p wɷ́d˺ bɟi

It would be.

44 wɛ̣ᵊ mɑɪ sístɹɪnlɔ́: lívv ðæd ǽɷs ɪz̥ dǽɷn tə ðə gɹǽɷn

Where my sister-in-law lived, that house is down to the ground.

45 wɪ ad ən ɔ́ɹgənɪss fɹəm ɹɑ́ɪ | ən əɹ fɹɛ́nn | ən̪ ðɛ́n̠ ʃɪi wəz̥
46 t'ɷk íɫ wɪð ə nə́ɹvəs bɹɛ́ɪkd̆æɷn

We had an organist from Rye / and her friend / and then she was took ill with a nervous breakdown.

47 ðə víkəɹ | wʌ́ndəɹz if jɷu kɷd ɛ́ɫp ǽɷʔ wɪð ðə | fə́ɹs lɑ́ɪn
48 əv ɛ́vɹɪ ím

The vicar / wonders if you could help out with the / first line of every hymn.

49 ɑɪv nɛ́vəɹ tʌ́tʃt ə ɔ́ɹgən ɪn mɪ lɑ́ɪf | ɑɪ dʌnɷ ˀɛ́nɪθɪn əbæɷd

50 ən ɔ́ɹgən | ən ɑɪ dʌ́ɷnˀ θɪ́ŋkˀ ˀǽtˀ nʌ́ɷz̥ ɛ́nɪθɪŋ əbæɷˀ mɪ̯́i

I've never touched a organ in my life / I don't know anything about an organ / and I don't think that knows anything about me.

51 ɪi sɛd w jɷ́u tɔ́:g ɪd ʌ́ɷvə wɪð ǽɹɪi wɛn ɪi kʌ́mz̥ ɪn tə lʌ́ntʃ

He said, Well, you talk it over with Harry when he comes in to lunch.

52 ɪi stɑ́ɹtɪd ɔ:f bǽk̚ t'ə wə́ɹk | əm bǽk ɪi kʌ́m | ɪi sɛ́d wɛ́ɫ |

53 pɹǽpʃ jɷud̚ gɛt θɹɷ́u ðǽ·t̚ | sʌɷ ɔ́:f ʌp ðə vɪ́kəɹz̥ ɑɪ wɛ́nˀ | ɪ:

54 wəz̥ | ʌ́p̚ tɑ́ps kəz̥ ɑɪd̚ gɔ́:n ʌp ˀ sɪ́i ɪm | ən ɑɪ ǽt ˀ gɷ ...

55 ˀɔɫ θɹɷu ðɪi ɪ́mz̥ ɑn ə blɷ́umɪn πɪǽnʌɷ

He started off back to work / and back he come / He said, Well / perhaps you'd get through that / So off up the vicar's I went / He was / up tops 'cos I'd gone up to see him / and I had to go ... all through the hymns on a blooming piano.

Published in K.R. Lodge, *Studies in the phonology of colloquial English.* London: Routledge (1984), chapter 3. The transcription is basically in the alphabet of the International Phonetic Association, with some further conventions explained on pp. 26–7 of Lodge's book.

Apart from the expected southern features such as preserved preconsonantal /r/, and general non-standard features such as the frequent absence of /h/, the text shows a fairly frequent intervocalic lenition of voiceless consonants after a word-boundary resulting in either a lenis or a fully voiced sound, and the preservation of a non-rounded variant of /ɒ/ in several words (e.g. *top, bottom, clogged, coffin, on*). Final voiceless plosives may be glottalized, whilst /t/ may appear as a glottal stop (< ˀ > in this Text).

Note the lack of liaison-/n/ in *a organ* (line 49).

TEXT 38

Robert Sellens: 'Turnin' up rough' (about 1956)

'Ave you bin up t' the gardens
The 'lotments* atop o' the 'ill
And stood in a good north-easter?
It blows fit t' turn a mill
It cuts middlin' sharp right through y'
Dun git sweaty an' then stand still!

The ol' wind over from Grinstead
Do dry up the clods do y' see
They stand up all steely like brick-'eads
Cus ther ent no shelter ne lee.
Dun't you be tempted to kick em
T'ud break yer leg off at the knee

I've 'eard say 'ow years agoo
When that place was unny a fill,
T'was jest as bad, if not wusser
An' turned up all puggy an' chill.
An' the clods set 'ard like concrate
Jest as unny Sussex clay will.

It sims as one chep who worked there
Was good with 'is 'ands when e'd try
And med hisself an ash cudgel
Nigh as thick as a wench's thigh
And said "I'll break it up drackly,
As sure as the sow's in the sty!"

Next day 'e brought this 'ere basher
Long the 'Oller from Chapel Row
An' while 'is mates stood lookin'
'E set about showin' 'em 'ow.
'E spet on is 'ands and rubbed 'em
And struck out with a smartish blow.

* The allotment gardens were near the Vinols Cross in West Hoathly, in what is now known as Finche Field (R.S.)

’E swung agin middlin’ spiteful
An’ brought ’er down hemnition ’ard
But the clods wadn’t even dented
They druv down like skewers in lard
Ther’ tops fair shown where ’e clouted
’E druv ’em down pret near a yard!

This is all true – so they tell me!
An’ now I’ve told it agin
Though I’ve bin all round Will’s mother’s
I ’up the moral be plain
If you’re gwin to do rough diggin’
Leave the work to the frawst and the rain.

Published in *East Grinstead Museum Compass* 8 (2002), 4, and reprinted with the author’s permission from a word-processed script.

Although the poem shows some of the stereotypical lexical features of the literary dialect (*middlin’, drackly*), it reads convincingly, with original imagery and the unforced effect of speech. *Hemnition* is an adverb, a derivative of *hem*, the Sussex euphemism for *hell*, used for ‘very’.

Note the lowered vowels in *concrate, drackly* and *spet* (also in Text 39) and the raised vowel in *chep* and *git*; the shortened vowels implied by *med, druv, dun/dun’t* and *’up* and the vowel in *frawst* lengthened before the cluster /st/. *LAE* does not record a short vowel in *make/made* or *take* anywhere in the south-east, but Hall (1957: 138, C6) has *teck* for *take*. *Unny* ‘only’, i.e. with [ʊ], is not recorded in exactly this form elsewhere.

Two forms of the copula BE are noteworthy. *Ent* for *isn’t* is recorded from west Surrey, whilst north Sussex falls into the zone of *ain’t* like much of south-east England north of the Thames, with *ben’t* in the east of the county and *bain’t* in Warnham (*LAE* map M10). Perhaps the form in the poem is for unstressed *ain’t;* but *en’t* is recorded from Harting. The past tense *wad’n* is found for third-person plural of BE. Most of Sussex is in the was zone for third-person plural (LAE map M23), though BE.past + *not* is not explicitly mapped in LAE. The form in the poem is consistent with this, showing [z] becoming the plosive [d] before [n]. Cf., from Kipling’s story ‘The wish house’ (*Debits and credits*): “Dunno . . . But it come over me, sudden-like – about dat woman from Rye – I’ve slipped the name – Barnsley, wadn’t it?”

As for *puggy* ‘loamy’, *pug* ‘loam’ is in Parish.

TEXT 39

Pam Hughes: 'Jawbation'. The last original work using Sussex dialect? (2004)

Jawbation

My mudder say I'm runagate
Since fader sudding boxed last year
We naun but owings an a'fear
Our spring'll come on leaf too late.

She say 'Youm like they savages'
When I comes home all slummaky.
She wails 'What mun I do with thee?'
As I unbuttons partridges.

The higgler allus calls on Thursday,
Sits tall at table, counts ourn eggs.
He slirrups down his tea to dregs.
'Has packled one come in to lay?'

'She been doddlish, droppin' pinions.'
My mudder scroops her chair and begs
'There's been vast scarcement in the eggs.'
He spets 'This be what I reckons.'

Higgler takes the eggs and leaves.
Cotching hisn two coins in silence
Mudder sobs 'These higgler thieves.'
All the room be full with sadness

Published in *Poetry London* 49 (2004), reprinted by permission of Ralph Taylor.

This poem contains much authentic local vocabulary (*naun, slirrup, packled, doddlish, cotch*), sometimes spelt in a way which owes nothing to the previous literature (*slummaky*), which suggests that the writer did not rely entirely on Parish (1875, C6) as so many others did. *Spet* for *spit* appears authentic (cf. Text 38). <d> in *mother* and *father* is authentic East Sussex and well attested elsewhere.

The grammar is more doubtful. In the verbal system, the 3rd-singular *-s* is unsystematically absent (*mudder say/wails*), but present in non-narrative

1st-singular (*when I comes*); and in BE we find the form *youm (you am)*, and 3rd-singular *be (This be what . . .)* varying with zero (*we naun but owings*) – or is it HAVE that is missing here, as with the auxiliary HAVE in *She been doddlish?*

These features are without parallel in the Sussex literature and are likely to be influenced by knowledge of other non-standard varieties. The author was Devonian by birth and lived some time in Dorset; *youm* is largely confined to Warwickshire, according to *LAE* (map M6). *Hisn* and *ourn* as adjectives rather than pronouns are also unique.

TEXT 40

Ron Saunders in conversation (2006)

'They oosed to run local dances, so I went up there one night. And they got all Canadians billeted round, all up in Ninfield village. So I went to this dance and went in an' was 'avin' a drink or so with some of the sodjers, see, and there was three or four girls – three I think it wus – I s'ppose they got thinkin'. They got in with these sodjers and what 'ave you, an' one of them come up to me, give me a matchbox, the old Swan Vestas match. When I opened it, was a white feather in it. And this sergeant I was talking to, cor! 'e went ver' near willocky. 'E went wild. 'E'd a gone down there and 'ed a bashed the bloody loif out of 'er! 'E didn't agree with it, but anyway 'is mates 'eld 'im off, quietened 'im down. I said "Ah no, forget about it." I said, "You get oosed to that, bloody gels." I joined the 'Ome Guard in the end.'

Ron Saunders, in conversation with David Arscott in 2006, published in *Wunt be druv!* Newbury: Countryside Books (2006), 75. Audio also available on CD *The Sussex Book Club Audio Collection 1* (see Section H below).

Striking for the use of *willocky* 'furious' (in Parish's dictionary), and /u:/ for /ju:/ in *used*. Otherwise the text shares pronunciation and grammar features with general non-standard south-eastern English.

PART THREE

BIBLIOGRAPHY OF WORKS RELEVANT TO SUSSEX DIALECT

CONTENTS

Note on the citation of issues of periodicals

In the bibliography below, journal citations of the form 3, 3 mean 'series 3, volume 3', otherwise expressed '3rd series, 3'; citations of the form 3.3 mean 'volume 3, number 3'. Some journals, like the *Journal of the Folk-Song Society* in its various incarnations, have used hybrid systems with continuous numeration both by volume and by issue.

Section A:

GENERAL WORKS ON ENGLISH DIALECTS

• All the items below contain material on Sussex and adjacent dialects. Those which have a special orientation towards Sussex, or contain much of direct interest about Sussex, or contain an isolable section on Sussex, are repeated in Section C. Some works on the dialects of adjacent counties are catalogued in Section B, and some of those contain material whose interest is not restricted to the county under which they are entered.

Alston, Robin C. (compiler) (1971) *A bibliography of the English language from the invention of printing to the year 1800, vol. IX: English dialects, Scottish dialects, cant and vulgar English.* London: private. [The standard bibliographical resource on the history of the English language as represented in printed material.]

Anderson, Peter M. (1987) *A structural atlas of the English dialects*. London: Croom Helm. [Based on the findings of the Survey of English Dialects, with some orientation towards theoretical issues in the differentiation of dialects.]

Baugner, Ulla (1972) *A study on the use of dialect in Thomas Hardy's novels*. Stockholm: Stockholm Studies in English. [It is of some interest that Angela Thirkell in *Three houses* (Oxford: Oxford University Press, 1931: 92) praises Hardy for the authenticity of his depiction of peasant speech despite its appearing on the printed page to be unbelievable.]

Bonaparte, [Prince] Louis-Lucien (1877) *On the dialects of Monmouthshire, Herefordshire, Worcestershire, Gloucestershire, Berkshire, Oxfordshire, South Warwickshire, South Northamptonshire, Buckinghamshire, Hertfordshire, Middlesex, and Surrey, with a new classification of the English dialects*. London: Trübner, for the English Dialect Society (vol. 17). [Also in *Transactions of the Philological Society* (1875–6), 570-81. Covers most of southern England except the coastal counties.]

Brandl, Alois (1915) *Zur Geographie der altenglischen Dialekte. Berlin:* Akademie der Wissenschaften (Abhandlungen der preussischen Akademie der Wissenschaften, phil.-hist. Klasse 4). [Discusses classes of evidence on the basis of which to draw isoglosses.]

Britten, James, and Robert Holland (1878–86) *A dictionary of English plant-names,* 3 vols. London: Trübner, for the English Dialect Society (vols. 22, 26, 45). [Standard reference-work, if now difficult to obtain.]

Cheshire, Jenny, and Viv Edwards (1984–8) *The Survey of British Dialect Grammar.* Economic and Social Research Council award no. C00 232264. Final report. [A schools-based survey of current English vernacular grammar. Two survey points are in the Brighton area, and other points further north in Sussex are assigned to the London area under the CURDS (University of Newcastle upon Tyne) Functional Regions system. Findings are conveniently available in Milroy and Milroy (1993).]

Edwards, Viv (1990) *A directory of English dialect resources*. Swindon: Economic and Social Research Council. [Contains a perfunctory Sussex bibliography and discography on 81–3, with one authorship error in it.]

Edwards, Viv (1993) The grammar of Southern British English. In James Milroy and Lesley Milroy (eds) *Real English: the grammar of English dialects in the British Isles.* Harlow: Longman, 214–42. [Focuses on London and Reading, but contains much that is valid for modern Sussex too.]

Ekwall, Eilert (1917) *Contributions to the history of Old English dialects.* Lund: Gleerup (Lunds Universitets Årsbok, new series, 12.6). [Deals with breaking of *ea* before *l* followed by a consonant, and with the *i*-mutation of the same.]

Ellis, Alexander J. (1889) *On early English pronunciation, part V: the existing pronunciation of English dialects.* London: Trübner (Early English Text Society, ES 53). [The first *magnum opus* of English dialectology; the phonetic transcriptions, of Ellis's own devising, need careful handling. Ellis's fieldworker was Thomas Hallam.]

Ellis, Alexander J. (1890) *English dialects, their sounds and homes*. London: Kegan Paul, for the English Dialect Society (vol. 60). [Abridged version of the previous item.]

Elmer, Willy (1973) *The terminology of fishing. A survey of English and Welsh inshore fishing: things and words.* Berne: Francke Verlag (Cooper Monographs 19). [Elmer collected information in Littlehampton, Worthing, Newhaven, Eastbourne, Hastings and Rye.]

Elmes, Simon (2005) *Talking for Britain: a journey through the nation's dialects*. London: Penguin. [A beginners' guide.]

Fischer, Andreas, and David Ammann (1991) *Index to dialect maps of Great Britain*. Amsterdam: John Benjamins (Varieties of English Around the World G10).

Forster, Klaus (1980) *A pronouncing dictionary of English place-names.* London: Routledge and Kegan Paul. [Largely a collation from earlier printed sources, including EPNS volumes, covering mainly local (and now obsolete or obsolescent) pronunciations.]

Francis, W. Nelson (1983) *Dialectology: an introduction*. London: Longman. [A good general introduction to the techniques of dialectology and the interpretation of survey results.]

Görlach, Manfred (1999) *English in nineteenth-century English: an introduction*. Cambridge: Cambridge University Press. [Includes some dialect texts. The only anthology of texts from this period compiled to show an overview of the state of the language.]

Grigson, Geoffrey (1955) *The Englishman's flora.* London: Phoenix House. [Reprinted London: Michael Joseph (1959); London: Hart-Davis (1975). Extensive discussion of dialect terms for plants.]

Halliwell, James Orchard (1847) *A dictionary of archaic and provincial words, obsolete phrases, proverbs, and ancient customs, from the fourteenth century.* London: J. Russell Smith. [Second edition (1850); a further private printing of 112 copies, Brixton Hill (1852). Facsimile of second edition (1989).]

Hallquist, Henning (1948) *Studies in Old English fractured* **ea**. Lund: Gleerup (Lund Studies in English 14). [On the dialect distribution of the reflexes of this sound.]

Holloway, William (1839) *A general dictionary of provincialisms, written with a view to rescue from oblivion the fast fading relics of bygone days.* Lewes: Sussex Press/Baxter and Son. [Sometimes said to be of 1838. Skeat (1877) notes its dependence on earlier published glossaries, but says that it "contains much that is new with respect to the counties of Kent, Sussex, and Hampshire". Roper (2007: 184) applauds its appearance of authenticity.]

Hope, R.C. (1882) *A glossary of dialectal place-nomenclature*. London: Simpkin, Marshall. [Second edition (1883), of which Sussex entries are on 124–8. Reprinted Detroit: Gale (1968). Uses an ambiguous and unreliable system for indicating pronunciation.]

Ihalainen, Ossi (1994) The dialects of English since 1776. In R.W. Burchfield, ed., *Cambridge history of the English language*, vol. V. Cambridge: Cambridge University Press, chapter 5. [General survey article.]

Ives, Sumner (1971) A theory of literary dialects. In J.V. Williamson and V.M. Burke, eds, *A various language – perspectives on American dialects*. New York: Holt, Rinehart and Winston, 147–77.

Joyce, Patrick (1991) *Visions of the people: industrial England and the question of class, 1848–1914*. Cambridge: Cambridge University Press. [See esp. chapters 11 and 12 on dialect literature in general.]

Kitson, P.R. (reputedly forthcoming) *Guide to Old English charter boundaries*. Nottingham: English Place-Name Society. [Covers the entire country, but is of great importance in characterizing the dialectally varying vocabulary and grammar of these Anglo-Saxon documents.]

Kolb, Eduard, Beat Glauser, Willi Elmer and Renate Stamm (1979) *Atlas of English sounds*. Bern: Francke. [Phonological atlas deriving from the findings of the Survey of English Dialects.]

Kontic, René (1990/1) *Dialects in East Anglia and the south-east of England*. Basel: Econom Druck, for René Kontic-Guntert. [Based mainly on the vocabulary materials of Kurath and Lowman and the Survey of English Dialects.]

Kristensson, Gillis (2001–2) *A survey of Middle English dialects 1290–1350: the southern counties*. Vol. 1: *Vowels (except diphthongs)*. Vol. 2: *Diphthongs and consonants*. Lund: Lund University Press (Publications of the New Society of Letters at Lund 93 and 94). [Based on name material in the Lay Subsidy Rolls (in Sussex, those of 1327 and 1332).]

Kurath, Hans, and Guy S. Lowman, jr. (1973 for 1970) *The dialectal structure of southern England: phonological evidence*. University (Ala.): University of Alabama Press (Publication of the American Dialect Society 54). [Based on materials collected in 1937–8. There were three sample points in Sussex.]

Lockwood, William B. (1984) *The Oxford book of British bird names*. Oxford: Oxford University Press. [Cf. Knox (1849) in Section B, Swainson (1885).]

Löfvenberg, Matthias T. (1942) *Studies in Middle English local surnames*. Lund: Gleerup. [Discusses evidence of lexical usage in the Sussex Subsidy Rolls (1296, 1327, 1332), and material from three other counties.]

Lowman, Guy S., jr (1937) Sampling survey of the southern counties of England. Collections of the *Linguistic Atlas of the United States*. [Unpublished in this form, so far as is known. Three sample points in Sussex.]

McIntosh, Angus, Michael L. Samuels and Michael Benskin, with the assistance of M. Laing and K. Williamson (1986) *A linguistic atlas of Late Middle English*, vols 1–4. Aberdeen: Aberdeen University Press. [Enormous compendium of written forms from the period c.1350–1460/1, with maps, text profiles and county profiles. 280 linguistic features are analysed countrywide, with a selection of more specifically southern ones also. The best source for the county of Sussex at this period that there is ever likely to be. There is a list of the Sussex texts used in the survey on which it is based in vol. 1, 243–4, and an analysis of 62 selected linguistic features of them in vol. 3, 501–8. For these, see also Part One, Chapter Four, of the present book.]

Maynor, Natalie (1988) Written records of spoken language: how reliable are they? In Alan R. Thomas, ed., *Methods in dialectology. Proceedings of the Sixth International Conference held at the University College of North Wales, 3rd–7th August 1987*. Clevedon: Multilingual Matters, 109–20. [Important methodological article, especially for the evaluation of the literary dialect of a region.]

Milroy, James, and Lesley Milroy (eds) (1993) *Real English: the grammar of English dialects in the British Isles*. Harlow: Longman. [Contains three chapters on educational issues arising from dialect diversity, and a chapter by Viv Edwards (214–42) on the grammar of southern British English dialects.]

Moore, S., S.B. Meech and H. Whitehall (1935) *Middle English dialect characteristics and dialect boundaries*. Ann Arbor: University of Michigan (Essays and Studies in English and Comparative Literature 13, 1–60). [The authors allocate Sussex to 'Kentish'.]

Mugglestone, Lynda (1995) *"Talking proper": the rise of accent as social symbol.* Oxford: Oxford University Press. [Account of the perception of regional and other accents from the eighteenth century onwards.]

Orton, Harold, Stuart F. Sanderson and J.D.A. Widdowson (1978) *The linguistic atlas of England.* London: Croom Helm/Humanities Press. [A mapping of some of the fruits of the Survey of English Dialects (see next item). Referred to as *LAE* throughout this book.]

Orton, Harold, and Martyn Wakelin (1967/8) *The Survey of English Dialects: basic materials. The southern area*, parts 1–3. Leeds: Edward Arnold for the University of Leeds. [The major standard academic source for information on English dialects in England; these volumes include the material from the six reference points in Sussex. Copies of the workbooks for this project are held at the Centre for English Cultural Tradition and Language, University of Sheffield. Referred to as SED throughout this book.]

Orton, Harold, and Nathalia Wright (1974) *A word geography of England.* London: Seminar Press. [An atlas covering lexical variation, based on the Survey of English Dialects (see previous item).]

Page, Norman (1988) *Speech in the English novel* [second edition]. Basingstoke: Macmillan. [Esp. chapter 3 "Speech and dialect: character", 55–96. First edition (1973).]

Paulin, Tom (1990) Introduction. Tom Paulin, ed., *The Faber book of vernacular verse.* London: Faber and Faber, ix-xxii. [The book itself contains no Sussex examples.]

Petyt, Keith M. (1980) *The study of dialect. An introduction to dialectology.* London: André Deutsch. [Note especially chapter 3, 68–100, on traditional English dialectology.]

Ray, John (1674) *A collection of English words, not generally used, with their signification and original* [etc.]. [Three subsequent editions, the first augmented edition being in 1691. Edited for English Dialect Society by Walter Skeat, as their volume 6, in the bicentenary year (1874) of its writing. The first ever dialect dictionary; the second of its two catalogues concerns the southern counties. Ray had at least one informant in Sussex (Peter Courthope); see also the following item.]

Ray, John (1718) *Philosophical letters between the late learned Mr Ray and several of his ingenious correspondents* ['published' (i.e. edited) by W. Derham]. London: W. and J. Innys.

Serjeantson, Mary S. (1922) The dialectal distribution of certain phonological features in Middle English. *English Studies* 4, 93–109, 191–8, 223–33. [Treats breaking before *l* followed by a consonant; the *i*-mutation of *ēa, ȳ* and *y* before a front consonant. Relatively little from Sussex, no evidence existing in local sources for some of these phenomena before the late eleventh century.]

Serjeantson, Mary S. (1927) The development of Old English *ēag/ēah* in Middle English, parts 1 and 2. *Journal of English and Germanic Philology* 26, 198-225 and 350-400. [Uses the Old English words *hēah, lēah, tēag* in place-name evidence in seeking to establish Middle English dialect boundaries.]

Shepherd, Valerie (1990) *Language variety and the art of the everyday*. London: Pinter. [Esp. chapter 2 "The language of men, poets and linguists", 33-72, and chapter 3 "A poetry of their own?", 73–106.]

Skeat, [Rev.] Walter W., and J[ohn] H[oward] Nodal, eds (1877) *A bibliographical list of the works that have been published, or are known to exist in MS., illustrative of the various dialects of English*. London: Trübner (for the English Dialect Society). [An invaluable comprehensive list of early writings in dialect. On pp. 102–3 are listed works in and on Sussex dialect.]

Skeat, [Rev.] Walter W. (1910) The sheep counting score. In Adelaide L.J. Gosset, ed. (1911) *Shepherds of Britain: scenes from shepherd life*. London: Constable, 194-200. [Quotes own letter to W.W. Hunt, 21/06/1907, on 199–200. Curious manner of self-reference make it appear that someone other than Skeat wrote the larger piece. Cf. Ellis (1878), White (1937), Wills (1938).]

Swainson, Charles (1885) *Provincial words and folk lore of British birds*. London: Trübner, for the English Dialect Society (vol. 47) and the Folk-Lore Society. [Cf. Knox (1849) in Section C, Lockwood (1984).]

Toolan, Michael (1992) The significations of representing dialect in writing. *Language and Literature* 1, 29–46. [A general article on the problem of writing spoken dialect, focusing mainly on non-standard South African English.]

Trudgill, Peter (1974) Linguistic change and diffusion: description and explanation in sociolinguistic dialect geography. *Language in Society* 3, 215–46. [On the potential of applying William Labov's methods for investigating social dialects to geographical ones.]

Trudgill, Peter (1988) On the role of dialect contact and interdialect in linguistic change. In Jacek Fisiak, ed., *Historical dialectology: regional and social.* Berlin: Mouton de Gruyter (Trends in Linguistics Studies and Monographs 37), 547–63. [On some odd results of hypercorrection and similar phenomena.]

Trudgill, Peter (1990) *The dialects of England.* Oxford: Blackwell. [General book on regional English, with sparse mentions of Sussex.]

Upton, Clive S., David Parry, and J.D.A. Widdowson (1994) *Survey of English Dialects: the dictionary and grammar.* London: Routledge. [Major resource derived from the findings of the Survey of English Dialects.]

Upton, Clive S., Stuart F. Sanderson, and J.D.A. Widdowson (1987) *Word maps: an atlas of English dialects.* London: Croom Helm. [A selection of mapped findings from the Survey of English Dialects aimed at non-specialists.]

Upton, Clive S., and J.D.A. Widdowson (1999) *Lexical erosion in English regional dialects.* Sheffield: NATCECT (occasional publication 7).

Viereck, Wolfgang (1975) *Lexikalische und grammatische Ergebnisse des Lowman-Survey von Mittel-und Südengland.* 2 vols. Munich: Fink.

Viereck, Wolfgang (1980) The dialect structure of England and Wales: Lowman's evidence. *English World-Wide* 1, 25–44. [Revised version of an article in *Hungarian Studies in English* 12 (1979), 203–31.]

Wade, Stephen (1976) Dialect literature: true and false. *Transactions of the Yorkshire Dialect Society* 14, 30–4. [Some observations on general characteristics of dialect literature.]

Wakelin, Martyn (1972) *English dialects: an introduction.* London: Athlone Press. [Second edition (1977). Some sparse references to Sussex.]

Wright, Joseph (1898–1905) *The English dialect dictionary*, vols 1–6. London: Frowde. [The major standard reference work on dialect vocabulary, representing the raison d'être of the English Dialect Society. Latter part of vol. 6 reprinted separately as *The English dialect grammar*. Oxford: Clarendon (1905).]

Section B:

WORKS ON THE DIALECTS OF COUNTIES ADJACENT TO SUSSEX

The list of works on Hampshire is taken mainly from Richard Coates (1992) *A bibliography of place-names in Hampshire and the Isle of Wight* (second edition). Brighton: Younsmere Press, 41–2, and with extracts from 44–7. It has pretensions to completeness. No attempt has been made to achieve the depth of coverage for Kent and Surrey that has been aimed at for Sussex.

Hampshire

To include material on the Old English dialect of Hampshire would be to include a very substantial amount of Old English literature and charters and related scholarship: a vast undertaking. Readers are referred to the lists of texts in West-Saxon given in Alistair Campbell (1959) *Old English grammar*. Oxford: Clarendon Press, 363–6. A few more recent works are included here.

A number of texts including work on Hampshire are mentioned in the main body of Sections A and C.

Belcher, B. (undated) MS. list of words used in the neighbourhood of Alresford. [Mentioned in *Transactions of the Philological Society* 2 (1845), 109. Now lost.]

Bouchier, J. (1887) [Query on] Hampshire plant-names. *Notes and Queries* 7.3, 387. [Responses on 479 and in 7.4, 19, 175.]

Cope, W.H. (1883) *A glossary of Hampshire words and phrases*. London: Trübner, for the English Dialect Society (vol. 40) [reprinted Vaduz: Kraus (1965)]. [Earlier published works on Hampshire dialect are listed on xiii-xiv. This book subsumes certain other works which are not separately mentioned in this Bibliography.]

Edwards, Heather (1988) *The charters of the early West Saxon kingdom*. Oxford: British Archaeological Reports (British series 198).

Finberg, H.P.R. (1964) *The early charters of Wessex*. Leicester: Leicester University Press.

F.S. See S., F.

Fudge, E.C. (1977) Long and short [æ] in one southern British speaker's English. *Journal of the International Phonetic Association* 7, 55–65. [The speaker analysed is from Southampton.]

Kökeritz, Helge (1924) The Juto-Kentish dialect boundary. *American Speech* 16, 270–7. [Draws attention afresh to some similarities between Kent and south-east Hampshire and the Isle of Wight.]

Lavers, Jack (1988) *The dictionary of the Isle of Wight dialect.* Wimborne: Dovecote Press.

Long, W.H. (1886) *A dictionary of the Isle of Wight dialect and of the provincialisms used in the island.* London. [Reprinted Norwood (Pa.): Norwood Editions (1975).]

Madden, Sir Frederick (undated) MS. glossary of Hampshire words. In the hands of the Philological Society in 1883. [Not known if it was ever published. Not found in any bibliography of the English language.]

Middleton, F.M. (1854) Hampshire provincial words. *Notes and Queries* 1.10, 120, 400–1 [Response on 256. An article with the same title appears in *Living Age* 46 (1855), 738.]

S., F. (1876) Dialect. *Notes and Queries* 5.6, 395. [Short speciment of Wight dialect.]

Skeat, [Rev.] Walter W., and J[ohn] H[oward] Nodal, eds (1877) *A bibliographical list of the works that have been published, or are known to exist in MS., illustrative of the various dialects of English.* London: Trübner/English Dialect Society. [On 52–3 is a list of works on Hampshire dialect.]

Smith, H., and C.R. Smith (1881) *Isle of Wight words*. London: Trübner, for the English Dialect Society (English Dialect Society Original Glossary).

Viereck, Wolfgang (1986) Dialectal speech areas in England: Orton's lexical evidence. In D. Kastovsky and A. Szwedek, with B. Plocińska, eds, *Linguistics across historical and geographical boundaries*. [Festschrift for Professor Jacek Fisiak.] Berlin: Mouton de Gruyter, 725–40. [Notes a major dialect boundary close to the eastern border of Hampshire, amongst much else.]

von Feilitzen, Olof (1976) Notes on the phonology of the names; Latinization, anglicizing and inflection; Lexicographical notes [on names in the Winton Domesday]. In Martin Biddle, ed., *Winchester in the early Middle Ages*. Oxford: Clarendon Press (Winchester studies 1), 222–9.

Wakelin, Martyn (1986) *The southwest of England.* Amsterdam: John Benjamins (Varieties of English Around the World T5). [Includes texts of a variety of origins from "west Hampshire", Hatherden and Burley, 206–13. The first of these, from *Punch* 9 (1845), 264) is also printed in Cope (1883), xii-xiii, but Wakelin does not say so. It is also in Hideo Hirooka (undated [1955]) *Dialects in literature*. Tokyo: Shinozaki-Shorin, 188-91, a collection of texts from all over England with commentary in Japanese. Detailed aspects of west Hampshire dialect are mentioned incidentally throughout the book.]

Weber-Liel, B. (1939) *Die Sprache Winchesters im Spätmittelalter*. Jena: Biedermann (Forschungen zur englischen Philologie 8).

Williams, Michael (1991) Post-vocalic (r) in the urban speech of the Isle of Wight. *Wellington Working Papers in Linguistics* 3, 56–66. [Reports a clearly dying feature.]

Wilson, [Sir] J. (1913) *The dialect of the New Forest in Hampshire (as spoken in the village of Burley)*. Oxford: Philological Society (Publication 4).

Wise, J.R. (1895) *The New Forest. Its history and its scenery* [etc.] [fifth edition]. London: Gibbings. [First edition Smith and Elder (1862). Glossary of local words on 279–88.]

Wood, W. (1940) The Hambledon dialect. Dissertation for the degree of MA, University of Leeds.

Kent

The academic literature on the dialect of Kent deals for the most part with the earlier periods, because of (a) the relative abundance of Kentish texts from the Old and early Middle English periods (especially the ninth century), and (b) the striking characteristics of Old Kentish described in any grammar of Old English.

A number of texts including work on Kent are mentioned in the main body of Sections A and C.

(a) Kentish of the Old English and Middle English periods

No attempt has been made at a complete bibliography of early Kentish, but at a general indication of the issues that scholars have debated about the structure and history of Kentish.

Anderson, John M. (1988) The great Kentish collapse. In Dieter Kastovsky and Gero Bauer, eds, *Luick revisited*. Tübingen: Gunther Narr, 97–107.

Bennett, W.H. (1953) A West Norse-Frisian-Kentish parallel. *International Anthropological and Linguistic Review* 1, 71–80.

Bennett, W.H. (1955) The southern English development of Germanic initial [f, s, þ]. *Language* 31, 367–71. [Reprinted in Roger Lass, ed. (1969) *Approaches to English historical linguistics: an anthology.* New York etc.: Holt, Rinehart and Winston, 349–54. The topic in question is of importance for the early history of all the South Country dialects, but a full bibliography of the discussion is not provided here. See DeCamp (1958), Fisiak (1984), Samuels (1971), Wakelin and Barry (1986).]

Biddulph, Joseph (no date; ?1987) *Early Kentish dialect: an informal portrait: the Middle English of Kent, circa 1300 A.D.* Pontypridd: Languages Information Centre. [Digest of current knowledge.]

Brooks, Nicholas (1984) *The early history of the church at Canterbury.* Leicester: Leicester University Press.

Bryan, W.F. (1915) *Studies in the dialects of the Kentish charters of the Old English period.* Chicago: University of Chicago Press.

Campbell, Alistair (1938) An Old English will. *Journal of English and Germanic Philology* 37, 133–52.

Campbell, Alistair (1959) *Old English grammar*. Oxford: Clarendon Press. [On 8 and 363 are lists of Old Kentish texts and their editions.

Campbell, Alistair, ed. (1973) *Charters of Rochester*. London: Oxford University Press (for the British Academy). [Dialect notes on xxix-xxx.]

DeCamp, David (1958) The genesis of the Old English dialects. *Language* 34, 232-44. [Reprinted in Roger Lass, ed. (1969) *Approaches to English historical linguistics: an anthology*. New York etc.: Holt, Rinehart and Winston, 355–68.]

Dietz, K. (1990) Die südaltenglische Sonorisierung anlautender Spiranten. *Anglia* 108, 292–313.

Evison, Vera (1965) *The fifth-century invasions south of the Thames*. London: Athlone Press.

Fisiak, Jacek (1984) The voicing of initial fricatives in Middle English. *Studia Anglica Posnaniensia* 17, 1–16 plus maps.

Freeman, L.H. (1973) Dialect characteristics of Late Middle English prepositions in two parallel prose works: *Ayenbite of inwyt* and *Book of vices and virtues*. Dissertation for the degree of PhD, University of Oregon.

Heuser, W. (1895) Zum Kent[ischen] Dialect im Mittelenglischen. *Anglia* 17, 72–90.

Holthausen, Friedrich (1917) Die altenglischen Beda-Glossen. *Archiv* 136, 290–2.

Jolliffe, J.E.A. (1933) *Pre-feudal England: the Jutes*. Oxford: Oxford University Press.

Keefer, Sarah Larratt (1991) *Psalm-poem and Psalter-glosses: the Latin and Old English Psalter-text background to "Kentish Psalm 50"*. London: Peter Lang (American University Studies, series 7: Theology and Religion 95).

Kelly, Susan E., ed. (no date; ?1995) *Charters of St Augustine's Abbey, Canterbury and Minster-in-Thanet*. Oxford: Oxford University Press for the British Academy (Anglo-Saxon Charters 4).

Kökeritz, Helge (1924) The Juto-Kentish dialect boundary. *American Speech* 16, 270–7. [Draws attention anew to some similarities between Kent and south-east Hampshire and the Isle of Wight.]

Konrath, M. (1892–3) Zur Laut- und Flexionslehre des Mittelkentischen. *Archiv* 88, 47–66, 157–80; 89, 153–66.

Krapp, G.P. and E. van K. Dobbie, eds, (1942) *The Anglo-Saxon poetic records*, vol. VI. Ithaca: Columbia University Press. [Contains the 'Kentish psalm' and the 'Kentish hymn'.]

Robb, K.A. (1968) Some changes in Kentish OE phonology. *Lingua* 20, 177–86.

Rositzke, H.A. (1937) The speech of Kent before the Norman Conquest. Dissertation for the degree of PhD, Harvard University.

Samuels, Michael L. (1971) Kent and the Low Countries: some linguistic evidence. In Adam J. Aitken, Angus McIntosh and Hermann Pálsson, eds, *Edinburgh studies in English and Scots*. London: Longman, 3–19. [Argues, against De Camp and others, that the distinctive features of Old Kentish arose in the continental homeland of the invaders; and that later influences are at least as likely to be Franconian as Frisian. Argues further that some linguistic featuresnoted in Kent and eastern Sussex are due to influence from Flanders in the middle years of the second millennium. Some Middle English texts from Kent, or possibly from Kent, are listed on 9–13. Footnotes give their publication history, where appropriate.]

Sheppard, J.B., ed. (1877) *Christ Church letters: a volume of medieval letters relating to the affairs of the Priory of Christ Church, Canterbury*. London: Camden Society (new series) 19.

Taxweiler, R. (1906) *Angelsächsische Urkundenbücher von kentischem Lokalcharakter.* Berlin: Mayer and Müller.

Wallenberg, J.K. (1923) *The vocabulary of Dan Michel's* **Ayenbite of inwyt**. Uppsala.

Wallenberg, J.K. (1931) *Kentish place-names: a topographical and etymological study of the place-name material in Kentish charters dated before the Conquest.* Uppsala: AB Lundeqvistka Bokhandeln.

Wallenberg, J.K. (1934) *The place-names of Kent.* Uppsala: Appelbergs Boktryckeri.

Weightman, J. (1905) Vowel-levelling in Early Kentish and the use of the symbol ę in OE charters. *Englische Studien* 35, 337–49.

Williams, Irene F. (1905) *A grammatical investigation of the Old Kentish glosses.* Bonn: Hanstein (Bonner Beiträge zur Anglistik 19, 92–66).

Witney, K.P. (1976) *The Jutish forest: a study of the Weald of Kent from 450 to 1380 A.D.* London: Athlone Press.

Wolff, R. (1893) *Untersuchungen der Laute in den kentischen Urkunden.* Heidelberg.

Zupitza, Julius (1877–8) Kentische Glossen des neunten Jahrhunderts. *Zeitschrift für deutsches Altertum* 21, 1–59; 22, 223–6.

(b) Kentish of later periods

Baker, Dick (1934) *Guide to Tunbridge Wells, wid summat bout de Town Hall writ and prented in de Old Kentish dialect.* Tunbridge Wells: J. Richards. [The only copy of this I have ever traced – the one belonging to Kent Public Libraries – is missing. The section on the Town Hall is almost certainly by James Richards 'Jim Cladpole'.]

Buckingham, C., ed. (1973) *Dick and Sal at Canterbury Fair: an early nineteenth century poem in the Kentish dialect of the period.* Whitstable: Shoestring Press. [See Masters (1821).]

Konrath, M., ed. (1902) *The poems of William of Shoreham.* London: Early English Text Society (Early Series 86).

Lewis, J. (1736) *History and antiquities, as well ecclesiastical as civil, of the Isle of Tenet in Kent* (second edition). London. Reprinted as *Glossary of words used in the Isle of Thanet*; 1736, in Walter Skeat, ed. (1874) Series B: reprinted glossaries, glossary XI. London: Trübner, for the English Dialect Society.

Major, Alan (1981) *A new dictionary of Kent dialect.* Rainham: Meresborough Books.

Major, Alan (2002) *Kentish as she wus spoke: a guide to the Kent dialect.* Seaford: S.B. Publications. [Noticed by George Ward, *Kent Messenger*, 08/02/2002, 50.]

Masters, John White (1821 or before) *Dick and Sal at Canterbury Fair*. Canterbury. [Actually published anonymously. Reprinted in Parish and Shaw (1887), xiii-xxiv.]

Masters, John White (1830) *'Dick and Sal' od J'ack and Joanses Fair' [sic]: a doggerel poem* [third edition]. Dover: Z. Warren.

Nairne, Edward (1790) *Kentish tales in verse and other humorous poems, with notes historical, wittical, critical, wag and pragmatical.* Sandgate. [Second edition (1824).]

North, David J. (1979) Two West Kent dialects: a comparative philological study of the dialects of Hever and Chiddingstone. Dissertation for the degree of MA, University of Leeds.

Parish, [Rev.] William Douglas, and [Rev.] W.F. Shaw (1887) *A dictionary of the Kentish dialect and provincialisms in use in the county of Kent.* London: Trübner, for the English Dialect Society. Also Lewes: Farncombe. [New edition A.P. Major (1981). Includes verse by John White Masters.]

Pegge, Samuel (1735–6) *Alphabet of Kenticisms.* Printed in Walter Skeat, ed. (1876) *Five original provincial glossaries*, glossary III. London: Trübner, for the English Dialect Society (vol. 12), 9–78.

Ravenscroft, T. (1611) *Melismata.* Includes "Kentish wooing song". Reprinted in Walter Skeat, ed. (1896) *Nine specimens of English dialects.* London: Trübner, for the English Dialect Society, 143–7.

Sanders, F.W.T. (1935) *Kentish (Wealden) dialect.* Chatham: the author.

Sanders, F.W.T. (1950) *The dialect of Kent.* Chatham: the author.

Sheppey, John (14th century) Sermons. [New College Oxford MS. 92 contains Sheppey's surviving sermons, which are in Latin but contain a fair amount of English material. See Wenzel (2005).]

Shoreham, William of (14th century) Poems. [In B.L. Add. MS. 17376. See Konrath (1902).]

Wakelin, Martyn, and Michael V. Barry (1986) The voicing of initial fricative consonants in present-day dialectal English. *Leeds Studies in English* (new series) 2, 47–64.

Wenzel, Siegfried, ed. (2005) *Latin sermon collections from later medieval England.* Cambridge: Cambridge University Press. [Chapter 2 deals with the sermons of John Sheppey.]

Surrey

• A number of texts including work on Surrey are mentioned in the main body of Sections A and C.

Leveson Gower, G. (1876) *Surrey provincialisms*. Printed in Walter Skeat, ed., *Original glossaries*, glossary IV. London: Trübner, for the English Dialect Society.

Leveson Gower, G. (1893) *A glossary of Surrey words*. London: Trübner, for the English Dialect Society.

North, David J. (1986) Surrey dialect research. *Surrey Archaeological Collections* 77, 153–62.

Sturt, George (writing as 'George Bourne') (1923) *The wheelwright's shop*. Cambridge: Cambridge University Press. [There is a glossary of smithing terms on 213–24.]

Sundby, Bertil (1950) *The dialect and provenance of the Middle English poem* **The Owl and the Nightingale**. Lund: Gleerup.

Wyld, Henry Cecil (1921) The Surrey dialect in the thirteenth century. *English Studies* 3, 42–5.

Section C:

WORKS ON THE DIALECT OF SUSSEX

CONTENTS

C1: PREVIOUS BIBLIOGRAPHIES

Coates, Richard (1987) *A classified bibliography on Sussex place-names, 1586–1987.* Brighton: Younsmere Press. [Includes many entries on dialect as an aid to the interpretation of place-names. This is supplemented by entries in *Locus focus, newsletter/forum of the Sussex Place-Names Net* (1996–2007).]

Skeat, [Rev.] Walter W., and J[ohn] H[oward] Nodal, eds (1877) *A bibliographical list of the works that have been published, or are known to exist in MS., illustrative of the various dialects of English.* London: Trübner/English Dialect Society. [An invaluable comprehensive list of early writings in dialect. On 102–3 there is a list of works in and on Sussex dialect; James Taylor's *Sussex garland* (1851) is not really relevant.]

C2: GENERAL WORKS ON SUSSEX DIALECT

Arscott, David (2006) *Wunt be druv! A salute to the Sussex dialect.* Newbury: Countryside Books. [Includes chapters on personal and place-names, dialect literature, local vocabulary, folk-song, etc., and extracts from recorded conversations not published elsewhere. Described as a 'celebration'. See also CD1 in Part Four, Section H2.]

Bailey, Bel (1992) Sussex Speak. *Verbatim: the Language Quarterly* 19.4. Reprinted in Erin McKean, ed. (2001) *Verbatim: from the bawdy to the sublime, the best writing on language for word lovers, grammar mavens, and armchair linguists*. San Diego: Harcourt, 49–52.

Barry, Michael V. (1960) Studies in the linguistic geography of Kent, Sussex and Surrey, 2 vols. Dissertation for the degree of Master of Arts, University of Leeds.

Beckett, Arthur (1940) Recording the Sussex dialect. *Sussex County Magazine* 14, 153. [A plea for speakers to be encouraged to make gramophone recordings.]

Brown, Arthur (no date; accessioned 03/1951 by Sussex Archaeological Society) *Lore Sussexiana*, 4 vols. [Handwritten/typed work in the Sussex Archaeological Society library, Barbican House, Lewes (open shelves). Vol. I contains notes on Hastings fishermen's speech, mining terms, milling terms and place-name pronunciations, plus a glossary; all are taken from published works mentioned elsewhere in this bibliography, but accurate sources are not always given.]

C., B.C. [i.e. Bessie C. Curteis] (1874) On dialect. *Monthly Packet* (new series) 17 (98) (February), 171–83. [Some general reflections on dialect, with some Sussex examples. Includes some sensible remarks on dialect, education and the written word, some unhappy etymologies, and some catalogues of curiosities typical of the period.]

Candlin, Lillian (1987) Sussex as she is spoke. In her *Memories of old Sussex*. Newbury: Countryside Books, 49–52. [Previously in a column in *West Sussex Gazette*, date undetermined. The rest of this book contains sporadic information on dialect and folklore, but the author's remarks about Anglo-Saxon should be forgotten.]

Coates, Richard (1983) *The linguistic history of early Sussex: the place-name evidence.* Brighton: University of Sussex Centre for Continuing Education (Occasional Paper 20).

Coates, Richard (1993) Language in the landscape: place-naming and language change. Brighton: University of Sussex (*Cognitive Science Research Paper* 295). [Professorial lecture. Uses Sussex material for much of its exemplification.]

Coates, Richard (2007) Microdialectological investigations in the English south-east. *Locus focus: forum of the Sussex Place-Names Net* 7.1/2, 62–80.

Costello, Miles (1991a) An exploration of the Sussex way with words. *West Sussex Gazette,* 14/02/1991. [This piece set off a correspondence: 21/02 P. Lees; 28/02 M.G. Costello, Nora A. Hillman, G.A. Holleyman, Dr David North; 07/03 L.J. Lemm; 14/03 T. Cawte, Mrs E. Williams, Mary Shelton, E.A. Lees; 04/04 Celia Hammond.]

Daish, W.G. (1956a) The voice of Sussex I, II, and III. *Sussex County Magazine* 30, 8–14, 76–82, 163–8. [Partially derivative. Note Stanley Godman's rejoinder (1956), and his obituary of Daish in *West Sussex Gazette*, 29/08/1963.]

de Putron, [Rev.] Pierre, rector of Rodmell (undated, c.1860) De Putron left notes in a 'journal' about Sussex dialect (ESRO PAR464/7/1/1, entry 345).

Ekwall, Eilert (1951) Comparative place-name study. In *Troisième Congrès international de toponymie et d'anthroponymie*, 133–41. [Material included on the linguistic distinctiveness of the names of the Hastings region.]

Gibbons, Phoebe Earl (1883) English farmers. *Harper's New Monthly Magazine* 66 (395) (April), 651–65. [Reference is to American edition. European edition volume no. is 5. Some brief mention (esp. 664–5) of Sussex dialect expressions, and some notes on vocabulary and pronunciation; comparing, in some places, with Americanisms of the eastern states.]

Godman, Stanley (1956) Letter [on Daish's pieces, *q.v.*] *Sussex County Magazine* 30, 295–6. [This and other pieces may be consulted in a folder of Godman's published work (*A Sussex historical miscellany*) kept at the Sussex Archaeological Society's library at Barbican House, Lewes (open shelves). All may be found in Sussex Pamphlets boxes at Brighton Area Library.]

Griffith, Valerie (1990) The dialect of the Brighton and Hove area. Project for the degree of BA, University of Sheffield. [Held at NATCECT, University of Sheffield. Two audiotapes annexed. A sociolinguistic study with some historical observations.]

Hare, Chris (1995) The language of Sussex. Chapter 2 of *A history of the Sussex people*. Worthing: Southern Heritage, 7-25. [Brief survey of the main writings on dialect, and of some in it, as covered more fully in Part One of the present book.]

Ingram, Walter Feilde (1925) The papers of Mr Ingram of Ades in Chailey (1851-1925), deposited on his death at East Sussex Record Office, include his recollections. [In the MS. is an account of the author's childhood visits to Rottingdean and Ashcombe to 'cure' his Sussex speech (ESRO AMS 5643/1/1, 15–19), and an unpublished story in dialect, 'The story of the darkest night', can be found on p. 244. Whether the story is by Mr Ingram or not is unknown.]

Kaye-Smith, Sheila (1953) *The Weald of Kent and Sussex*. London: Hale. [Part 2, chapter 5, 211–9, has material on dialects, as do 205–10 of the previous chapter. All is apparently taken from M.A. Lower (1854c) and Parish (1875), except a very few personal contributions.]

Kitson, Peter R. (reputedly forthcoming) *Guide to Old English charter boundaries*. Nottingham: English Place-Name Society. [Covers the entire country, but is of great importance in characterizing the dialectally varying vocabulary and grammar of these Anglo-Saxon documents. Sections have been circulating in manuscript for some years, including that for Sussex.]

Lower, Mark Antony. Letters from, to and about Lower, in relation to dialect. Lower Papers, esp. GC/33, CO-L/1, CO-L/2a, CO-L/2b, Sussex Archaeological Society, Barbican House, Lewes. [Lower's other MSS., as opposed to his working papers, are now at East Sussex Record Office, but are calendared at Barbican House.]

Lucas, E.V. (1904) *Highways and byways in Sussex*. London: Macmillan. [Various subsequent editions. Chapter 41 (405–16) is on Sussex dialect. It is largely dependent on Parish (1875). It quotes in full chapter 4 of M.A. Lower's rendering of the *Song of Solomon (q.v.)*. Chapter 42 (417–35) in the second edition also contains dialect material, quoting from M.A. Lower's essay on the South Downs in *Contributions to literature* (1854c). Page-references given here are to the 1928 reprint of the pocket edition of 1923, and may not be accurate for all printings.]

McIntosh, Angus, Michael L. Samuels and Michael Benskin, with the assistance of M. Laing and K. Williamson (1986) *A linguistic atlas of Late Middle English*, vols. I–IV. Aberdeen: Aberdeen University Press. [Enormous compendium of written forms from the period c.1350–1460/1, with maps, text profiles and county profiles. The best source of analysed material for the county of Sussex at this period that there is ever likely to be.]

Marryat, [Capt.] Frederick (1948) Some relics of Sussex dialect. *Sussex County Magazine* 22, 74–5. [Deals with St Leonards.]

McKinley, Richard (1988) *The surnames of Sussex*. Oxford: Leopard's Head Press (English Surnames series volume 5). [Contains material of relevance to Middle English local vocabulary and pronunciation.]

Murdoch, Brian, and J[acqueline] A. Tasioulas, eds (2002) *The apocryphal lives of Adam and Eve.* Exeter: University of Exeter Press (Exeter Medieval English Texts and Studies). [The second Life, *Canticum de creatione* (1375), is claimed, following McIntosh and others (1986), to have been written in Sussex. See Part 2, Text 2.]

North, David J. (1979) Some linguistic and cultural boundaries in south-east England. *Transactions of the Yorkshire Dialect Society* 8–37. [Attempts to trace the westward extent into Sussex and Surrey of some ostensibly Kentish dialect features and artefact types; the supposed coincidence of these boundaries is suggestive but not overwhelming.]

North, David J. (1982b) Aspects of the phonology and agricultural terminology of the rural dialects of Surrey, Kent and Sussex. Dissertation for the degree of PhD, University of Leeds.

North, David J. (1985) Spatial aspects of linguistic change in Surrey, Kent and Sussex. In Wolfgang Viereck, ed., *Focus on: England and Wales*. Amsterdam: John Benjamins (Varieties of English Around the World G4), 79–96.

Orton, Harold and Martyn Wakelin (1967/8) *The Survey of English Dialects: basic materials. The southern area*, parts I–III. Leeds: Arnold/Leeds University Press. [The major standard academic source for information on English dialects in England; these volumes include the material from the six reference-points in Sussex. Copies of the workbooks for this project are held at the Centre for English Cultural Tradition and Language, University of Sheffield.]

Paxton, Margaret (2006) Can you speak Sussex? *Sussex Life* (January), 76–81. [Popular piece featuring an informant for the BBC Voices project (2004–5).]

Payne, Malcolm (1989) The Sussex dialect. *East Grinstead & Weald* 26 (June), 9–11. [Brief survey also mentioning place-names and surnames.]

Pettitt, Joseph (undated) A Sussex dialect. Unpublished brief notes in typescript. [In private hands. Includes apparently original material transcribed in IPA notation. The version I have seen lacks at least one promised section, on 'A Sussex' literature [sic].]

Samuels, Michael L. (1971) Kent and the Low Countries: some linguistic evidence. In Adam J. Aitken, Angus McIntosh and Hermann Pálsson, eds, *Edinburgh studies in English and Scots.* London: Longman, 3–19. [A couple of Middle English Sussex texts showing interesting linguistic features are mentioned specifically on 11–12, and in footnote 52; cf. also 14 on a form in Bullokar's *Booke at large.*]

Sawyer, Frederick E. (1884b) *Sussex dialect and speech. A paper.* Brighton: private. [Text of an address to the Brighton and Sussex Natural History Society, 19/06/1884.]

Sussex County Magazine (1926–1956). This periodical printed much in, on and with relevance to Sussex dialect, and most especially before the death of its founding editor Arthur Beckett in 1943. All the pieces are entered separately in this Bibliography, but they are calendared here to enable easy trawls to be made through the full set of magazines. Even some pieces not indexed here include short passages in dialect spoken by characters in stories. The existing typed indexes to SCM available in most libraries are hopelessly inadequate, and what follows will serve as an improved index for the topic of dialect.

Volume 1 (1926–7), 42–4, 114–7, 164, 192, 490–2, 522–4, 554–6, 560
Volume 2 (1928), 253, 384
Volume 3 (1929), 95–106, 107–12, 162, 742, 885–-6
Volume 4 (1930), 78, 150–1, 166–7, 305–6, 435, 474–7, 563–4, 843–4
Volume 5 (1931), 148, 251–5, 329, 430–1, 431, 500, 516
Volume 6 (1932), 160–4
Volume 7 (1933), 569, 570, 584–7
Volume 8 (1934), 167–8, 230, 674, 714

Volume 9 (1935), 305–7, 387–8, 497, 519–20, 780
Volume 11 (1937), 657
Volume 12 (1938), 216, 280–1, 349, 362, 590
Volume 13 (1939), 14, 167–8, 172, 281, 352–3, 571, 724
Volume 14 (1940), 150, 153, 187, 383–4
Volume 15 (1941), 156–7
Volume 16 (1942), 86-8, 178, 341–5
Volume 17 (1943), 90
Volume 19 (1945), 162–4
Volume 20 (1946), 65
Volume 22 (1948), 74–5
Volume 23 (1949), 48–9, 196–9, 300–1
Volume 24 (1950), 459–60
Volume 28 (1954), 519–22, 606
Volume 29 (1955), 97–9, 204
Volume 30 (1956), 8–14, 76–82, 129, 163–8, 197–8, 295–6, 297

Note also letters by various writers, mainly about the word *lew* 'shelter', in volume 28, 606.

Sussex Life (1965–date). This periodical has published several mainly derivative pieces on dialect, entered separately in the Bibliography but brought together here to enable easy trawls through the full set of periodicals. The main problem is that the volume numbering went awry; 1981 was volume 19 instead of 17; February 1982's issue was volume 20, no. 2 whilst March 1982's was a second volume 18, no. 3. From 1983, no volume numbers were used.

Volume 6 (July 1970), 50
Volume 11 (February 1975), 49
Volume 12 (February 1976), 34
Volume 14 (December 1978), 39
Volume 15 (November 1979), 30–3
Volume 19 [misnumbered] (October 1981), 56–7
Volume [unnumbered] (December 1983), 38–9
Volume [unnumbered] (January 2006), 76–81

Sussex Notes and Queries (1926–1971). This periodical printed several pieces on dialect. All are entered separately in this Bibliography, but they are calendared here to enable easy trawls through the full set of periodicals.

Volume 2 (1929), 156–8
Volume 11 (1947), 180
Volume 12 (1949), 161
Volume 13 (1952), 229–34, 292, 324
Volume 15 (1958), 23–5

This periodical also printed notes on place-names, listed in Coates (1987; see Section C1).

'Sussex Onlooker', pseud. (1973a) Dialect travels far. *West Sussex Gazette*, 10/05/1973.

Wales, Tony (1990) *Sussex customs, curiosities and country lore*. Southampton: Ensign Publications. [90–1 on dialect, 92–3 on ballads and riddles.]

Wales, Tony (2000) *A treasury of Sussex folklore*. Seaford: S.B. Publications. [Incidental dialect occasionally.]

Wright, Simon (1995) Some observations on Sussex dialect. *Hindsight* (Uckfield and District Preservation Society) 1. [Notes possible impact of Sussex dialect on American English.]

C3: WORKS ON LOCAL LITERACY, LEXICOGRAPHY AND OUTSIDE INVESTIGATORS

Allen, Barbara J. (2006) The acquisition and practice of working-class literacy in the nineteenth-century Sussex Weald. Dissertation for the degree of DPhil, University of Sussex. Unpublished. Sussex Theses S6140. [Case-study of the acquisition of literacy in Mayfield, Ticehurst and Withyham; contains material of relevance to the question of locally-coloured writing in general. Useful entry to questions of literacy in the 19th century in general; has large appendix of specimens of not fully standard writing. See also Maidment (2003).]

Godman, Stanley (1961) Napoleon's nephew and the Sussex dialect. *West Sussex Gazette*, 07/12/1961. [About Prince Louis-Lucien Bonaparte's contribution to English dialectology (see M.A. Lower 1860). Godman also delivered a talk on this topic on the BBC Home Service (date unknown, but shortly after the date of publication of this article).]

Howard, Ursula (1993) Writing and literacy in nineteenth-century England, some uses and meanings. Dissertation for the degree of DPhil, University of Sussex. Unpublished. Sussex Theses S3677.

Maidment, Barbara J. (2003) How the Sussex Weald learned to read and write. *University of Sussex Bulletin*, 05/09/2003. [There were also related items in local newspapers. See also Allen (2006), the completed form of the work in progress reported here.]

Maidment, Barbara J. (2003) Nineteenth century working class literacy in the Weald. In Julie Weeds, ed., *The 15th White House Papers – graduate research in Cognitive and Computing Sciences at Sussex* (Cognitive Science Research Papers 552).

Maidment, Barbara J. (2004) To manglen of the syntax up: what a 19th century Sussex diary might reveal about working class literacy. In Kingsley Sage, ed., *The 16th White House Papers – graduate research in Cognitive and Computing Sciences at Sussex* (Cognitive Science Research Papers 564).

Roper, Jonathan (2007) Sussex glossarists and their illustrative quotations. *Sussex Archaeological Collections* 145, 181–194. [Deals with Holloway, Cooper, Parish, Curteis, Hall and Way from an anthropological and methodological perspective.]

Smith, Doreen (1990) Eighteenth-century literacy levels in West Sussex. *Sussex Archaeological Collections* 128, 177–186.

C4: PRONUNCIATION

• This section does not include material specifically on place-names, for which readers are referred to the bibliography of Coates (1987, A) and the regular subsequent bibliographies in *Locus focus, newsletter/forum of the Sussex Place-Names Net* (1996-2007). However, it does cover some aspects of dialect pronunciation as expressed in place-names.

Barraud, F.A. (1922) Sussex pronunciation of place-names. *Notes and Queries* 12.10, 30. [Operates on some incorrect assumptions about place-name elements.]

Biddulph, Joseph (1988) Sussex. In the author's *Supplement* to *The dialect directory*. Pontypridd: Languages Information Centre, 14–16. [Idiosyncratic transcription of an interview conducted by Rev. David Charlton, rector of Cocking, with Gordon Farley, also of Cocking.]

Bishop, J.G. (1899) Etymological anomalies. Chapter 4 of *Articles on miscellaneous subjects: historical and literary*. Brighton: 'Herald' office [not printed for sale]. [Reprinted from the *Brighton Herald* (date not known). Contains remarks on local place-name pronunciations (21–30).]

Bullokar, William (1580) *The booke at large*. London. [On p. 10, Bullokar discusses the Sussex and Kent peculiarity of /d/ for /ð/. Cf. also Samuels (1971: 14). Southern dialectalisms have been noted in his published work, especially *The booke at large*, by E.J. Dobson, *English pronunciation*, 1500–1700, vol. I. Oxford: Oxford University Press, second edition (1968), 93–117, esp. 105–12, and vol. II, 948. Cf. Bror Danielsson and Robin C. Alston, eds, *The works of William Bullokar*, vol. I. Leeds: University of Leeds School of English (1966), x ff., who definitively trace his origins in Sussex. Dobson is able to find little in Bullokar that is undeniably particular to Sussex, though more that is consistent with Sussex. An earlier study of Bullokar by R.E. Zachrisson, *The English pronunciation at Shakespeare's time as taught by William Bullokar*. Lund (1927), can be regarded as superseded, as may certain German dissertations catalogued by Dobson, vol. II, 1031.]

Coates, Richard (1980) A phonological problem in Sussex place-names. *Beiträge zur Namenforschung* (new series) 15, 299–318. [Phonology of stress on final syllables. Cf. Barraud (1922), Leppard (1992b, 1993, etc.).]

Coates, Richard (1981) More on variation between initial [k] and [g] in English. *Notes and Queries* 226, 298–9. [Possible localization of this pronunciation feature to the Hastings area.]

Coates, Richard (1999a) An unusual source of evidence for dialect: the sword inscriptions of William Peachey. *Neophilologus* 83, 617–21. [Peachey was a blacksmith operating at East Dean, West Sussex, in the seventeenth century. See Part Two, Text 7.]

Donne, J. (1949) Sussex pronunciation. [Part of 'A Sussex wayfarer's diary'.] *Sussex County Magazine* 23, 300–1. [On some Sussex place-name pronunciations and some Gipsy words.]

Ellis, Alexander J. (1889) *On early English pronunciation, part V: the existing pronunciation of English dialects*. London: Trübner (Early English Text Society, ES 53). [The first magnum opus of English dialectology; the phonetic transcriptions, of Ellis's own devising, need careful handling. Uses the plosive pronunciation [d] of /ð/ as a criterion for dividing eastern Sussex dialects from western ones (area D9 as opposed to D5, D8).]

Hope, R.C. (1882) *A glossary of dialectal place-nomenclature.* London: Simpkin, Marshall. [Second edition (1883), of which Sussex entries are on 124–8. Reprinted Detroit: Gale (1968). Uses an ambiguous and unreliable system for indicating pronunciation.]

Johnston, G.D. (1947) Eighteenth century pronunciation. *Sussex Notes and Queries* 11, 180. [About names in vicarage documents at Wisborough Green.]

Johnston, G.D. (1958) Eighteenth century (and earlier) pronunciation. *Sussex Notes and Queries* 15, 23–5. [Information derived from Sussex personal names in London registers.]

Leppard, Michael J. (1971) Local pronunciation. *Bulletin of the East Grinstead Society* 7 (May), 6.

Leppard, Michael J. (1992b) Where the stress falls. *Bulletin of the East Grinstead Society* 51 (Autumn), 7–8. [On the position of stress in place-names of the East Grinstead area. Cf. Barraud (1922), Coates (1980); and see next three items and Leppard (1996).]

Leppard, Michael J. (1993a) Final stress: a closer look. *Bulletin of the East Grinstead Society* 52 (Spring), 4–8. [See previous item.]

Leppard, Michael J. (1993b) Final stress: responses and suggestions. *Bulletin of the East Grinstead Society* 53 (Autumn), 9–10. [See previous two items.]

Leppard, Michael J. (1994a) Final stress: further notes. *Bulletin of the East Grinstead Society* 54 (Spring), 10. [See previous three items, and further references there. Judicious comments about the use of dialect as a social counter.]

Leppard, Michael J. (1994b) Local pronunciation of place-names. *Bulletin of the East Grinstead Society* 55 (Autumn), 4. [On the final syllable in *Hoathly*; see also 59 (Autumn 1996), 12; and *East Grinstead Museum Compass* 16 (Spring 2005), 6–7).]

Leppard, Michael J. (1996) Final stress. *Bulletin of the East Grinstead Society* 59 (Autumn), 12. [This thread continued as new documentary evidence came to light; see also *Bulletin* 61 (Spring 1997), 4; 74 (Autumn 2001), 7; 76 (Spring 2002), 20; 83 (Autumn 2004), 16. See also earlier items above.]

Leppard, M.J. (2005) Vernacular pronunciation in the East Grinstead area. *East Grinstead Museum Compass* 17 (Summer), 4–8.

Lodge, K.R. (1984) Peasmarsh, Sussex. Chapter 3 of his *Studies in the phonology of colloquial English*. London: Croom Helm, 64–79. [Text and analytic commentary. One conversation appears above as Part Two, Text 37.]

Lower, Mark Antony (1854b) [Untitled piece about vernacular pronunciation of place-names.] In the "Miscellanea" in his *Contributions to literature*, [etc., see C6 below], 269–71.

Mawer, Allen H., and Frank M. Stenton; with the assistance of J.E.B. Gover (1929/30) *The place-names of Sussex*, two vols. Cambridge: CUP/EPNS vols. 6/7. [The standard source and reference work on Sussex names. The early (i.e. Old and Middle English) dialect is discussed on xxvii-xxix.]

North, David J. (1984) The development of Middle English *ā, ai* and *ī* in Surrey, Kent and Sussex. Leeds Studies in English (new series) 15, 147–64. [Demonstrates the different local realization systems used to maintain the distinction between /a: ~ ai/ and /i:/.]

North, David J. (1988-90) Ordered rules and the diffusion of innovations: a generative approach to the phonological geography of Surrey, Kent and Sussex. *Orbis* 35, 147–61. [Illustrates a topic current in theoretical phonology in the 1960s–80s.]

'[An] old-fashioned man' (1920) *East Sussex place names*. Private (two 'editions', i.e. printings). [A third edition appeared in 1933 from Gillett (Brighton). The author of this small pamphlet has not been identified. He hailed from the Battle area. His grandfather was parson at Bodiam for over 30 years and his mother a native of the place. He was about 70 in 1933 (all this from the introduction to the pamphlet). About local pronunciations of place-names, now mainly defunct. Cf. Also *Sussex County Magazine* 13 (1939), 724.]

Parish, [Rev.] William Douglas (1875) *A dictionary of the Sussex dialect and collection of provincialisms in use in the county of Sussex*. Lewes: Farncombe. [The introduction contains some helpful and some confusing statements about pronunciation. See main entry under Vocabulary, Section C6 below.]

Rubin, Sven (1951) *The phonology of the Middle English dialect of Sussex.* Lund: Gleerup (Lund Studies in English 21). [Major historical study based on place-name spellings in medieval documents. Noticed by R.M. Wilson (1951) *The Year's Work in English Studies* 32, 42–3; reviewed by Archibald A. Hill (1952) *Language* 28.2, 276–8 (who notes that it pays no attention to the phonological structure of the dialect); H. Ch. Matthes (1952–3) *Anglia* 71, 234; and Norman E. Eliason (1954) *Modern Language Notes* 69.2, 135–138.]

Sawyer, Frederick E. (1887) Glossary of Sussex dialectal place-nomenclature. *Sussex Archaeological Collections* 35, 165–72. [Superseded by the standard works; and unreliable.]

Sawyer, Frederick E. (1887–8) Sawyer was the editor (1887–8) of a column in the *Brighton Gazette* called 'Sussex Notes and Queries'. One entry is of phonological interest: VIII (date uncertain), query 3. on dialect rhymes in Shelley.

Turner, J. Clifford, with Elsie Fogerty (no date; 1930s, reprinted 1960) *British Drama League dialect records*. London: British Drama League. [Transcriptions of the BDL's standard passage in IPA notation, by Turner. On p. 18 is the passage as heard in Battle.]

Whittick, Christopher (2000) Sarah Cox, her accent, and 'Cockney'. Paper delivered at the Barber Institute, Birmingham, 02/12/2000. [Sarah Cox is 'Fanny Cornforth', model and mistress of Dante Gabriel Rossetti, born Steyning 1835. Incorporated into Anne Drewery, Julian Moore, and Christopher Whittick (2001) Re-presenting Fanny Cornforth: The makings of an historical identity. *The British Art Journal* 2.3, 3–15.

Wyld, Henry Cecil (1913–14) The treatment of OE *y* in the dialects of the midland and south-eastern counties in ME. *Englische Studien* 47, 1–62. [Covers Sussex, along with much else.]

C5: GRAMMAR

Barry, Michael V. (1972) The morphemic distribution of the definite article in contemporary regional English. In Martyn Wakelin, ed., *Patterns of folk speech in the British Isles*. London: Athlone Press, chapter 8, 164–81. [Discusses the forms of the word the in the Sussex and other south-eastern records of the Survey of English Dialects. It is of interest that Barry does not note the form *t'* before a consonant anywhere outside the north of England; but it occurs separately in works by Fred Wood and Barclay Wills *(qq.v.)*.]

Coates, Richard (1999a) An unusual source of evidence for dialect: the sword inscriptions of William Peachey. *Neophilologus* 83, 617–21. [Draws attention to some long-persisting grammatical features. Peachey was a blacksmith operating at East Dean, West Sussex, in the seventeenth century. See Part Two, Text 7.]

Evans, William (1970) The survival of the second-person singular in the southern counties of England. *Studies by members of the South Central Modern Language Association. South Central Bulletin* 30, 182–6. Reprinted in *Transactions of the Yorkshire Dialect Society* 14 (1976), 17–29.

Kitson, P.H. (reputedly forthcoming) *Guide to Old English charter boundaries.* Nottingham: English Place-Name Society. [Covers the entire country, but is of great importance in characterizing the dialectally varying vocabulary and grammar of these Anglo-Saxon documents.]

Leppard, Michael J. (1970) Some local speech usages. *Bulletin of the East Grinstead Society* 3 (January), unpaginated. [Mainly on the syntax of expressions containing the place-name *Ashdown.*]

Poussa, Patricia (1996) Drifting northward: implicational scales in syntactic levelling. Paper delivered to the Spring meeting of the Linguistics Association of Great Britain, University of Sussex, Brighton, 11–13 April 1996. [Point of departure is the syntactic construction, apparently limited to the traditional dialect of Sussex and the immediately adjacent area, in which normally stranded prepositions are placed after a *wh-* word; e.g. *What for did you do that?*]

C6: VOCABULARY

• This section does not include material specifically on place-names, for which readers are referred to the bibliography of Coates (1987) and the regular subsequent bibliographies in *Locus focus, newsletter/forum of the Sussex Place-Names Net* (1996–2007). However, it does cover some aspects of dialect vocabulary as expressed in place-names.

anonymous (1888) [Article on names for groups of fishermen from different ports.] *Sussex County Herald (???)* (31/12/1888), page not known. [Detached copy only of the article known, laid inside a copy of Parish (1875) in private hands. Earlier in 1888, F.J. Sawyer had entered a query about the origin of the word *chopbacks* 'Hastings fishermen' in his 'Sussex Notes and Queries' column in the *Brighton Gazette* (21/01/1888); this piece provides an answer. There are further notes by B.A. and by A.J. Waterfield on *willick(er)* and *pork-bolter* respectively in *Sussex County Magazine* 8 (1934), 718.]

anonymous (1904) French in Sussex dialect. *St James's Magazine*, 26/09/1904. [On a few words supposedly of French origin used in the Hastings area, e.g. *boco* 'much', *sushy* 'drought-afflicted'. These were known already to Parish (1875); he describes fishermen's speech as 'almost worthy of being called a fourth branch of the dialect'. This article appeared three days after Parish's death.]

anonymous (1927) "Wish" in Sussex. *Word Lore* 2, 48. [As exemplified in field-names of Ripe.]

anonymous [probably Arthur Beckett] (1939) Shoreham 'hufflers'. *Sussex County Magazine* 13, 14. [Word is probably the same as *hoveler* in Parish (1875); see further *Sussex County Magazine* 13, 281 (A. Anderson).]

anonymous (1993) The risk of sounding poundnotish. *[Brighton] Evening Argus* 19/04/1993, 3. [About the potential effect on dialect of the National Curriculum Council's proposals about teaching standard English. Mentions Sussex dialect expressions *furring the heel* 'annoying' and *poundnotish* 'sounding posh' (not noted elsewhere).]

anonymous (1994) Heathland is where the home is for a rare bird. *[Brighton] Evening Argus* 12/11/1994, 7. [Includes supposed local words for the nightjar, some of which (*eve churr, fern owl*) are similar, but not identical, to those given in Hall (1957) (*eve-jar, churn-owl*).]

Appleton, Roger (1990) Some odd words; Sussex dialect in Scotland. *Kipling Journal* 256 (December), 37.

Arnold, F.H. (1887) *Sussex flora*. London: Simpkin; Arundel & Horsham: Mitchell. [New edition (1907). Includes local names for plants.]

Austen, Edmund (1942) Dialect and humour in a Sussex village. *Sussex County Magazine* 16, 341–5. [About Brede. Mainly on picturesque expressions, some idiomatic, some nonce.]

Baring, F.H. (1909) Crundels. *English Historical Review* 24, 300–3. [Reviews the evidence for the word *crundel* (characteristic of place-names near the border of Hampshire and Sussex), and claims it means 'cutting with a shaw' as opposed to 'quarry'.]

Barrett, Robert (1894) How large is the vocabulary of Hodge? *Southward Ho!* 1, 18–19, 111–12. [Vindication of the subtlety of vocabulary of country-dwellers (part 1) and a swipe at the Oxford philologist Max Müller for his belief in the small vocabulary of the same (part 2). Part 1 contains excerpts from a list of some 500 nouns written out by the country boy Daniel White, then aged 10, at Barrett's request. This list was in the hands of the editor of *Southward Ho!* (see footnote on page 18), but its whereabouts are now unknown. This list is Part Two, Text 18.]

Beckett, Arthur (1926) A dissertation on Sussex proverbs and curious sayings. *Sussex County Magazine* 1, 42–4. [Beckett attributes the sayings, as collected, to his gardener Martin Malpass. For Malpass, cf. Beckett (1933) in Section D1.2.]

Beckett, Arthur (1927a) Old woodcraft words. *Sussex County Magazine* 1, 192.

Bell-Irving, E. Margaretta (1903) *Mayfield – the story of an old Wealden village.* London: William Clowes & Son. [Reprinted Lewes: East Sussex County Libraries (1984). Chapter 2 deals with folkways and dialect, mainly vocabulary.]

Birch, Roger, and Roger Cordiner (forthcoming, 2010) [Book on Sussex building stone, no title yet. Includes list of local names for types of building stone.]

Bird, Ruth, ed. (1971) *The journal of Giles Moore*. Lewes: Sussex Record Society, vol. 68. [There is a dialect glossary on xv-xix.]

Bretherton, E. (1927) Fishermen's words. *Sussex County Magazine* 1, 164. [Reprinted in Aylwin Guilmant (1991) *Sussex of one hundred years ago*. Stroud: Alan Sutton, 72.]

Bridger, S. (c.1945) A glossary of Sussex shepherd lore. Unpublished 9-page typescript in East Sussex Record Office (ACC 10024/3); another copy may exist in private hands. [Includes strange entries with a religious slant showing knowledge of Persian mythology.]

Bridger, S. (?1949) 'Shepherds Pottage or Links and relics of a peculiar race.' ii + 87 pp. Unpublished typescript in East Sussex Record Office (ACC 10024/2); another copy may exist in private hands. [Dedicated 'To the Shepherd and his wife in gratitude.' A study, interspersed with original poetry, whose aim, according to the author, is to try 'to preserve some links and relics of a peculiar race in which the Southdown Shepherd and his wife have played such a valuable part'. Includes 'A short dictionary of Sussex lingua'.]

• It is almost certain that the author of these items was the writer of verse anonymized as 'S.B.' elsewhere, and possible but very unlikely that she is also the S. Bridger who was responsible for 'Resting', a religious tract published in Rogate in 1936. The compiler believes she is Salome Bridger, born Alciston (1886), died Tonbridge (1973).

Brierley, G.H. (1942) A packet of old Sussex words. *Sussex County Magazine* 16, 86–8. [Culled from Elizabeth M. Wright's *Rustic speech and folk-lore*. London: Oxford University Press (1913; second ed. 1914); with some comparisons with Devon expressions.]

Brighton Fishing Community Project Team (1996) *Catching stories: voices from Brighton's fishing community.* Brighton: QueenSpark Books (vol. 30). [Glossary of fishing-related terms on 138–40.]

Brown, Arthur (no date; accessioned 03/1951 by Sussex Archaeological Society) Lore Sussexiana, 4 vols. [Handwritten/typed work in the Sussex Archaeological Society library, Barbican House, Lewes (open shelves). Vol. 1 contains notes on Hastings fishermen's speech, mining terms, milling terms and place-name pronunciations, plus a glossary; all are taken from published works mentioned elsewhere in this bibliography, but accurate sources are not always given.]

Brown, Lilian E. (1942) Fish stews and eel spears. *Sussex County Magazine* 16, 178. [On the terms *wheeles* and *pritchers*.]

Butterfield, W. Ruskin (1913) Folk names for fishes and other animals at Hastings. *Hastings and East Sussex Naturalist* 2.2, 83–4. Partially republished by Juliet Millican in *Old folk names used on the Hastings Stade*. Hastings: Old Hastings Bookshop (1982). [Mainly on local words for fish and other marine fauna.]

Butterfield, W. Ruskin (1916) Some Sussex words. *West Sussex Gazette*, 07/09/1916, 2. [A pilot for a column called 'Sussex folk and Sussex ways', a title taken from that of J. Coker Egerton's book (1884). This sporadic column, of some lexical and folkloric interest, was continued on 21/09, 28/09, 05/10, 12/10 and 26/10 (on p. 2 of each issue), after which it vanished. An annotated copy of Butterfield's first piece exists at Hastings Central Library.]

Butterfield, W. Ruskin (1933) The Hastings fishermen. In William Gray, ed., *The book of Hastings. A souvenir of the conference of the National Association of Head Teachers, held at Hastings, June, 1933*. London: Collins, 65–76. Partially republished by Juliet Millican in *Old folk names used on the Hastings Stade*. Hastings: Old Hastings Bookshop (1982). [Information on local surnames and fishing vocabulary. For the latter, see Part Two, Text 27.]

Carr, B.M.H. (1950) Neglected sources for the vocabulary of Kentish and some neighbouring dialects in the eighteenth and nineteenth centuries. *Transactions of the Philological Society* 34–59. [Draws attention to B.L. Add. MS. 39,325 (F), (ff. 46–100), British Library, 'Dialectical expressions, Kent, Surrey, Sussex, etc. Collected by Albert Way', dating from c.1846–56.]

Coates, Richard (1979) OE *steorf* in Sussex place-names. *Beiträge zur Namenforschung* (new series) 14, 320–4. [Use of element meaning 'barren place' in East Sussex place-names.]

Coates, Richard (1985) On the alleged term *wahztrew* in the Pevensey Custumal. *Sussex Archaeological Collections* 123, 271. [On a mistranscription of the word *wargtrew* 'gallows' represented in a medieval place-name.]

Coates, Richard (1988) The term *forrǣpe* in various south-eastern documents. In *Toponymic topics*. Brighton: Younsmere Press, 81–8. [Cf. Ekwall (1944).]

Coates, Richard (1999b) *Twitten* again: an antedating. *Locus focus: forum of the Sussex Place-Names Net* 3.2, 8–9. [Notes a use of this word in the Brighton area older than the earliest in *OED* (second edition), where all the early records are from Brighton and mean 'narrow passage'. Takes up a thread in *Locus focus* 1.3, 2.1 and 2.2; the complete thread about this word in Locus focus is 1.3, Q1.3.4; 2.1, N2.1.3 and R2.1.4; 2.2, R2.2.7; 3.2, N3.2.5; 4.1, N4.1.2; 5.1, R5.1.3; 6.1, 21–2; 7.1/2, N7.1.7 CW (1465), N7.1.8 MJL EG in 1841 census. See also Leppard (2000); Whittick (1998).]

Coates, Richard (2000) An Old English technical term of woodland management in south-east England? *Locus focus: forum of the Sussex Place-Names Net* 4.2, 16–19. [For another, see *Locus focus* 6.1, N6.1.2.]

Coates, Richard (2001) John Dudeney's topographical vocabulary. *Locus focus: forum of the Sussex Place-Names Net* 5.1, 13–18. [Words in use in the mid-South Downs in the mid-nineteenth century.]

Coates, Richard (2003) Word life in a southern county. Richard Jefferies Society Birthday Lecture, Aldbourne, Wiltshire (unpublished).

Coates, Richard (2010a) *A place-name history of Rottingdean and Ovingdean in Sussex (including Woodingdean and Saltdean)*. Nottingham: English Place-Name Society (Regional Series 2). [Contains much on vocabulary of local place-name elements, esp. in the introduction.]

Coates, Richard (2010b) *Trollop*: a Sussex record, an antedating and an etymology. [The crucial early form is from a Burwash will. Published in this book for the first time, as Appendix 2.]

Coleman, [Rev.] William H. (1836) Flora of East Grinstead. MS. [uncatalogued?] in the library, Royal Botanic Gardens, Kew. Edited and published by T.C.G. Rich, East Grinstead: Sussex Botanical Recording Society (1994). [Supplies a note testifying to a local name for *Myrica gale*, page 18 of the published version.]

Cooper, William Durrant (1836) *A glossary of the provincialisms in use in the county of Sussex*. Brighton: W. Fleet. [This work is often said in reference works to date from 1834. The correct date is 1836; see the memoir of Cooper by Henry Campkin in *Sussex Archaeological Collections* 27 (1877), 117–32, esp. p. 121, and L.F. Salzman, History of the Sussex Archaeological Society. *Sussex Archaeological Collections* 85 (1946), 3–76, esp. p. 56. The error seems due to Cooper's own declaration that it was 1834 in the preface to the second edition. Second edition (1853) London: J. Russell Smith. Skeat (1877) judges this edition to be much improved. There is an interesting correspondence about the first, privately circulated, edition in M.A. Lower's papers kept by the Sussex Archaeological Society at Barbican House, Lewes (Lower Papers, CO-L/1 Cooper to John Dudeney (16/07/1836; Dudeney was a close friend of Lower and must have given him this), CO-L/2a Cooper to Lower (25/07/1836)). Lower apparently reviewed Cooper's book in the *Sussex Advertiser* (date not traced, presumably first half of 1836) and made comments there which Cooper took as disparaging his claim to priority. Cooper protests that his material was based on his own collection; he takes Lower as suggesting that he 'borrowed' some of Lower's own collection. A decorous animosity is visible in subsequent correspondence. In the light of this, Lower's remark 'Without wishing to poach upon another man's manor . . . .', whilst offering a few additions to the *Glossary* (1861: 215), is highly interesting. A copy of the second edition of the *Glossary* annotated by J.M. Neale exists in private hands. It is inscribed 'In this copy are to be entered the words picked up by our Sisters [of the Community of St Margaret, East Grinstead], when out nursing'. Another exists with annotations by Amy Sawyer (probably) and Michael Leppard, and another once owned by Mary Willett with notes of uncertain provenance. See Appendix 1 of this book for a previously-unpublished life of Cooper.]

Cooper, William Durrant (1849) Bive and chute lambs. *Notes and Queries* 1.1, 474.

Copper, Bob (1994) *Across Sussex with Belloc. In the footsteps of 'The Four Men'*. Stroud: Alan Sutton. [Cf. Belloc (1914). Some discussion of dialect words, 70–2.]

Costello, Miles (1994) The dialect of Petworth, questionnaire II: the responses. *Petworth Society Magazine* 77, 15–18. [Follow-up to the next item.]

Costello, Miles, and Peter Jerrome (1992) The dialect questionnaire [for a survey of the agricultural vocabulary of Petworth]. *Petworth Society Magazine* 69 (September), 33–7. [A report of the results of the questionnaire circulated with issue 67. Survey and questionnaire deposited in West Sussex Record Office in 1999, Add. MSS. 52259, 52260. See previous item, and Part Two, Text 36 in this book.]

Cross, Fred (1930) [Letter/query on] "Thwartled". *Sussex County Magazine* 4, 435. [= 'cross-ploughed'. Helpful editorial note appended.]

Daish, W.G. (1963) Letter on the origin of the word *twitchell. West Sussex Gazette,* 25/07/1963.

Davies, [Col.] Francis (before 1846) Notebook on Sussex dialect. ESRO MS. ACC 10360. [Davies lived at Danehurst in Fletching. The book has only 38 entries (including one with a glaring accidental error), but an accompanying letter to Davies from the antiquary J.O. Halliwell, 27/01/1846, is endorsed with 11 more in the hand that wrote the book entries. Of far more interest than it appears to merit because it is the very first authenticated work on, as opposed to in, Sussex dialect. See Whittick and Coates, in preparation.]

Davys, M.M. (1973) Childhood words. [Letter to the editor.] *This England* 6 (Summer), 53. [Contains some dialect words consistent with Sussex usage, amongst others. The writer was born in Sussex.]

Duck, Marion (1978) The gooseberry girl. *This England* 11 (Autumn), 26. [Some dialect words and idioms discussed. The writer was brought up in Sussex.]

Dunkin, Edward. Notes on Sussex dialect vocabulary and correspondence involving J.C. Stenning, E.G. Tarrant, G.M. Royce and others (it is not known how Dunkin came by these). Sussex Archaeological Society, Barbican House, Lewes, Dunkin MSS. 5.4. [Dunkin's own major work was the calendar of Sussex marriages compiled for the Sussex Record Society. No fruit of any interest of Dunkin's own in dialect is known.]

Eccles, John, writing as 'Rouser' (2009) White rabbits, Will's mother and willick. *Sussex Express* (17/09/2009).

Egerton, [Rev.] John Coker (1884) *Sussex folk and Sussex ways. Stray studies in the Wealden Formation of human nature.* Lewes: Sussex Advertiser; London: Trübner. [Second edition (1892) London: Chatto and Windus; third edition (1924; edited by Henry Wace, with an introduction by Sheila Kaye-Smith) London: Methuen. The subtitle is omitted in the later editions. The nine pieces originally appeared separately in the Anglican periodical *The Leisure Hour* (1881) and in *The Sussex Advertiser* (1881–2). The third edition also contains the text of a lecture on the history of the parish of Burwash delivered by Egerton in 1871 and 1876 (131–62); and the

John Hogpound letters (167–72; *q.v.*), establishing that W.D. Parish wrote them in c.1870, but not specifying in which local paper they first appeared. Curiously – or modestly – Egerton did not include his own 'Paul Claypuddle' letter, *q.v.*, written in 1878. There are allusions to (mainly Burwash area) dialect, especially vocabulary and sayings, throughout the book. First edition reviewed in e.g. *Notes and Queries* 6.9 (1884), 518; *Pall Mall Gazette* (21/07/1884); *Morning Post* (29/08/1884). See also Roger Wells, ed., *Victorian village. The diaries of the Reverend John Coker Egerton of Burwash, 1857–1888*. Stroud: Alan Sutton (1992).]

Ekwall, Eilert (1944) Old English *forrǣpe. Studia Neophilologica* 16, 33–8. [Of relevance to the term *forrepland* found in various Sussex documents. Cf. Coates (1988).]

Ellis, Alexander J. (1878) The Anglo-Cymric score. *Transactions of the Philological Society,* 316–72. [Versions of the traditional score said to have been used for counting sheep; version F14 was collected in Worthing, but is probably nothing to do with Sussex. Cf. Skeat (1910), White (1937), Wills (1938), and see Texts 28a-b in Part Two.]

Ellis, F.W. (date not known) Letter to the editor of an unknown newspaper, perhaps *The Times,* asking for information about, and discussing, the Sussex words *clappers* 'causeway' and *pimp* 'small bundle of split wood'. *Bavin* 'bundle of spray wood' is contrasted with the latter. [Drawn to the compiler's attention by Nicholas Hills. *Bavin* is recorded since Ray (1674) and is in Samuel Johnson's *A dictionary of the English language* (1755); see also *Linguistic Atlas of England* map L33b.]

Excell, Phyl, and Stanley Excell (1984) Sussex dialect and family history. *Sussex Family Historian* 6.1, 19–20. [On place-name vocabulary and surnames.]

Eyre, Frank (1925) Sussexisms. *Downland Post* (new series) 2.9, 272. [Something on local vocabulary.]

Ferguson, J. DeLancey (1931-2) Sussex words [in four parts]. *Kipling Journal* 17 (April 1931), 27–; 19 (September), 86–; 20 (December), 123–; 21 (March 1932), 28–. [Part 1, *allwhither – eend-on*; part 2, *farabout – spattle*; part 3, *spaulty – usuals*; part 4, *vambrish – yerk.*]

Fowler, J. (1949) [Query about the word] *Tarr* [in place-names]. *Sussex Notes and Queries* 12, 161. [Rejoinder by L.F. in vol. 13 (1952), 228.]

Freeland, Peter (2003) Dialect plant-names: milkmaids, ladies' smocks, old man's nightcap. *East Grinstead Museum Compass* 12 (Autumn), 10–12.

Freeland, Peter (2004) Local birds: variety, names and changing perspectives. *East Grinstead Museum Compass* 14 (Summer), 5–9.

Gaston, T. (1940) Some old Sussex words and phrases. *Sussex County Magazine* 14, 150. ['Surreyite' disputes their attribution to Sussex alone, *Sussex County Magazine* 14 (1940), 187.]

Godman, Stanley (1965) Some additions to Parish's 'Dictionary of Sussex dialect'. *West Sussex Gazette*, 30/09/1965. [Discusses the British Museum (i.e. now British Library) copy of Parish (1875), annotated by J.C. Clough and H.H. Sturmer.]

Greaves, Ralph (1953) Silly Sussex. *The Countryman* 47, 117–8. [Some examples of local expressions.]

Grose, Francis (1787) *A provincial glossary, with a collection of local proverbs and superstitions.* London. [Later printings (1811, 1839). Facsimile reprint (1968) Menston: Scolar Press (English Linguistics 1500–1800). Classic work. Contains 17 words said explicitly to be of Sussex, but almost all beginning with B and C, after which come only *fimble* and *foizon*, said to be shared with Essex, and *leap*, or *lib*, likewise shared. The glossarist's sources, policy or memory clearly faltered as the task progressed alphabetically. There is also a small list of 'best of kind' terms such as *Arundel mullet*.]

Hall, Helena E. (1955) Pedd or ped. *Sussex County Magazine* 29, 97–9. [On word meaning 'chicken box'.]

Hall, Helena E. (1957) *A dictionary of the Sussex dialect and collection of provincialisms in use in the county of Sussex, by the Rev W.D. Parish. Expanded, augmented and illustrated by Helena Hall, together with 'Some Sussex sayings and crafts'*. Chichester: private. [Paperback edition Bexhill: Gardner's (1967). Revised and massively extended edition of Parish (1875), *q.v.* Reviewed editorially in *West Sussex Gazette*, 25/04/1957, 'Does anyone talk Sussex now?' This piece sparked off a correspondence: 23/05 'A Sussex woman' [Miss L.F. Ramsey? – RC] and Sybil Bulstrode; 30/05 Francis Foster, W.J. Dore-Dennis and Robert Reid; 06/06 Stanley Godman, G. Bryant and Lilian E. Brown; 13/06 W.G. Daish, Frank R. James, Mrs E. Bowyer and

Francis Foster (a sceptic about what can properly be called dialect); 20/06 Newall Duke. Copies of Hall's book exist with annotations by Michael Leppard of East Grinstead (owned by Mr Leppard) and by R.H. and P.D. Wood of Ashurst Wood. A copy at West Sussex Record Office bears notes by Miles Costello. Miss Hall's MS. notes are in private hands.]

Harrison, Frederick (1929) 'Sussex dialect', addenda. *Sussex Notes and Queries* 2, 156–8. [An alphabetical list supplementing Parish (1875).]

Heath, Richard (1871) Sussex commons and Sussex sayings. *Golden Hours*. [Further bibliographical details not known. Mentioned in Roger Wells, ed., *Victorian village* [edition of J. Coker Egerton's diaries]. Stroud: Alan Sutton (1993), 119, note 8. Relates to Mayfield, Rotherfield area.]

Holden, Hilda (1994) Letter to the editor, *Sussex Past and Present*, about the Lewes street-name *Bukettwin* and the word *twitten*. Published *Sussex Past and Present* 76 (1995), 7. [Suggests a different account from that proposed by Richard Coates, The lost street-name Bukettwin, Lewes. *Sussex Archaeological Collections* 129 (1991), 252–3. The compiler sticks by his original idea; see *Sussex Past and Present* 77 (1995), 15 (letter).]

Holloway, William (1839) *A general dictionary of provincialisms, written with a view to rescue from oblivion the fast fading relics of bygone days*. Lewes: Sussex Press. [Skeat (1877) notes its dependence on earlier published glossaries, but says that it 'contains much that is new with respect to the counties of Kent, Sussex, and Hampshire'.]

Hopkins, R. Thurston (1930) Some Sussex millers' terms. In *Old watermills and windmills*. London: P. Allan and Co., 200-3. Reprinted in Peter Hemming (1936) *Windmills in Sussex*. London: C.W. Daniel Co., appendix B, 120–1.

Hudson, W.H. (1900) *Nature in downland*. London: Longmans, Green. [New edition Dent (1923). Contains occasional notes of interest about local words or phrases not all in Parish (1875); see 30, 36, 47, 121, 185, 196, 239, 264.]

J[ohnston], G.D. (1952) The Burwash-Etchingham parish boundary. *Sussex Notes and Queries* 13, 229–34. [Contains explanations of dialect words in the notes. Rejoinders by E.R.B. on 292 and by Fred Lester on 324.]

Joiner, C.G. (1929) The derivation of "lydes". *Sussex County Magazine* 3, 504.

Jolliffe, J.E.A. (1935) The Old English term 'snade' *[sic]. Antiquity* 9, 220–2. [On a term (should be Old English *snād*) found in south-eastern place-names.]

Knox, A.E. (1849) *Ornithological rambles in Sussex. With a systematic catalogue of the birds of that county.* London. [Cf. Swainson (1885), Lockwood (1984).]

L., H.A. (1943) Sussex brick-making terms. *Sussex County Magazine* 17, 90. [The author claims that s/he has culled the terms from an issue of *Notes and Queries* of 'many years ago'.]

Leppard, M.J. (1992a) Mount Noddy: Wealden iron or Wealden irony? *Wealden Iron* (second series) 12, 27–8. [On the origin of Straker's view that *noddy* = 'slag'; ascribed to an article by W.H. Hills in the *East Grinstead Observer*, 21/07/1917. See also Leppard (2009).]

Leppard, M.J. (1993c) Noddy. *Bulletin of the East Grinstead Society* 53 (Autumn), 4. [Revises conclusion of Leppard (1992a) to show that the view that *noddy* = 'slag' is traceable ultimately to an anonymous article, actually by J.M. Neale, entitled "The iron-works of Sussex" in *The Penny Post*, August 1854, reprinted on an uncertain date in the *East Grinstead Observer*. This thread continues over subsequent years in the *Bulletin*.]

• Michael J. Leppard of East Grinstead maintains a card-index of vocabulary and local lore from the East Grinstead area, from a variety of published, manuscript and oral sources. This has now been brought into the public domain as follows:

Leppard, M.J. (1999-2008) Dialect vocabulary of the East Grinstead area. *East Grinstead Museum Compass* 1 (1999), 7–12; 2 (Spring 2000), 8–13; 3 (Autumn 2000), 9–13; 4 (Spring 2001), 12-15; 5 (Summer 2001), 6–14; 6 (Autumn 2001), 5–10; 7 (Spring 2002), 7–13; 8 (Summer 2002), 5–11; 9 (Autumn 2002), 7–14; 10 (Spring 2003), 12–15; 12 (Autumn 2003), 13–17; 13 (Spring 2004), 11–15; 14 (Summer 2004), 14-20; 15 (Autumn 2004), 4–9; 16 (Spring 2005), 7 [infra]-8. [Note that each article is accompanied by running addenda to previous instalments. Concluding addenda: 17 (Summer 2005), 8; 18 (Autumn 2005), 9 and 11; 20 (Summer 2006), 9; 27 (Autumn 2008), 6.]

Leppard, M.J. (2001) Twitten. *East Grinstead Museum Compass* 4 (Spring), 10–12. [See also Coates (1999b) and Whittick (1998), and further references there.]

Leppard, M.J. (2005) Some local speech usages. *East Grinstead Museum Compass* 16 (Spring), 5–6.

Leppard, M.J. (2008) See Martin (2007).

Leppard, M.J. (2009) Mount Noddy and Moat Pond. East Grinstead: East Grinstead Society (information leaflet 2). [Summarizes views about whether *noddy* in Mount Noddy is a meaningful word. See also Leppard (1992a).]

Lewis Cohen Urban Studies Centre (no date; before 1992) Twittens and cat creeps. Brighton: Brighton Polytechnic. [Leaflet explaining the terms and showing where these things can be found in Brighton.]

Lister, Sue (1967) Sussex recipes. Project for the degree of BA, University of Leeds, 2 vols. [Contains a glossary.]

Locus focus, forum of the Sussex Place-Names Net, vols 1–7, appeared from 1996-2007 (ed. Richard Coates). [It contains much discussion of local vocabulary as found in place-name elements.]

Löfvenberg, Matthias T. (1942) *Studies in Middle English local surnames.* Lund: Gleerup. [Discusses evidence of lexical usage in the Sussex Subsidy Rolls (1296, 1327, 1332), and material from three other counties.]

Lower, Mark Antony (1854a) On local nomenclature. In his *Contributions to literature, historical, antiquarian, and metrical.* London: John Russell Smith, 1-35. [Reprinted with minor alterations from the second series of the *Retrospective Review*, vol. 1.2 (1853), 350–71. A discussion about vocabulary used for forming place-names (several in Sussex), starting from William Baxter's *Glossarium antiquitatum britannicarum* (1733) and J. Kemble's *Codex diplomaticus aevi saxonici* (1839–48). Sceptical; not bad for its day, but totally superseded.]

Lower, Mark Antony (1854b) [Untitled piece about vernacular pronunciation of place-names.] In the 'Miscellanea' in his *Contributions to literature*, [etc.], as above, 269–71.

Lower, Mark Antony (1861) Old speech and old manners in Sussex. *Sussex Archaeological Collections* 13, 209–36. [Especially 209–18. Noticed in the *Saturday Review* 13 (1862), 599–600. See Part Two, Text 13c.]

Lower, Richard (1862) Glossary [to his own dialect poems, *qq.v.* under 'Tim Cladpole', Section D1.2 below]. In his *Stray leaves from an old tree.* Lewes: Bacon, 187–90.

Markey, Thomas L. (1972) The place-name element *-hurst (-horst). Naamkunde* 4, 26–35. [Claims that this Old English element, frequent in Sussex, relates to slash-and-burn agricultural methods.]

Marshall, Grenville (1978) Well-mannered marrers, sunnuck to yarp about! *Sussex Life* 14 (December), 39. [Some words not in Parish (1875).]

Martin, Ron (2007) What's in a name? *Sussex Industrial Archeology Society Newsletter* 135 (July), 13–14. [On the words *stollage* and *bungaroosh*. Rejoinders on local usage of *stollage* by Michael J. Leppard (2008) Stollage. *SIAS NL* 137 (January), 20; and Martin Snow (2008) Stollage – a rest. *SIAS NL* 138 (April), 21; and by the original author himself on *bungaroosh*, Ron Martin (2008) More on *bungaroosh. SIAS NL* 139 (July), 22.]

Mawer, Allen H., and Frank M. Stenton; with the assistance of J.E.B. Gover (1929/30) *The place-names of Sussex*, two vols. Cambridge: CUP/EPNS vols. 6/7. [The standard source and reference work on Sussex names. The early (i.e. Old and Middle English) dialect is discussed on xxvii-xxix; the discussion is mainly about phonological development, but there are a few vocabulary notes on p. xxix.]

McCann, Timothy J. (1997) Cules: a Sussex variant. *Sussex Archaeological Collections* 135, 311–12. [A variant of the name of the game of ninepins *kayles*, apparently restricted to Sussex, found in 17th-century records.]

Millican, Juliet. See W. Ruskin Butterfield.

Mitchell, Gordon (1948) Some relics of Sussex dialect. *Sussex County Magazine* 22, 74–5. [Culled from Parish (1875) in the main, the rest recycled from secondary writings.]

Moore, Reg (1975) 'Bosky' on 'huckle-my-buff'. *Sussex Life* 11 (February), 49.

Morgan, Quita. See Tony Wales (1992).

Morgan, Roy R. (1992) *Chichester: a documentary history*. Chichester: Phillimore. [On p. 65 is a small selection of spellings taken from tradesmen's accounts of 1533–8 (Dean and Chapter Accounts, WSRO MS. CapI/23/1) which show some regionalisms such as *flowar* for 'floor' and *hapse* for 'hasp'.]

Mortlock, I.N. (1955) Two Sussex words [letter]. *Sussex County Magazine* 29, 204. [*Boffled* and *latchety.*]

Nash, A.E. (1977–8) Perch and acre size in medieval Sussex. *Sussex Archaeological Collections* 116, 59–67. [On the locally-varying application of these terms.]

Nicklin, P.A., and E. Godfrey-Faussett (1935) On the distribution of place-names in Sussex. *Sussex Archaeological Collections* 76, 213–21.

North, David J. (1982a) The importance of local systems in dialectology. *Papers in Folk Life Studies (Leeds Folklore Group)* 2). Mimeograph, 5. [Shows how the same lexical material can be differently structured in different dialects, and how lexical structure can be preserved despite variation in the words used to realize it. Some examples from Sussex and Kent.]

North, David J. (1982b) Aspects of the phonology and agricultural terminology of the rural dialects of Surrey, Kent and Sussex. Dissertation for the degree of PhD, University of Leeds.

North, David J. (1984-5) The one-way plough in south-eastern England. *Folk Life* 23, 49–64. [Much on the terminology concerning ploughing and the turnwrest plough.]

North, David J. (1988) Some notes on the terminology of farm buildings in south-eastern England. *Journal of the Historic Farm Buildings Group* 2, 15–25.

Parish, [Rev.] William Douglas (1875; 1957, etc.) *A dictionary of the Sussex dialect and collection of provincialisms in use in the county of Sussex.* Lewes: Farncombe. [The first edition was reissued unaltered by the English Dialect Society in 1875 for the subscription year 1874. Noticed in the *Saturday Review* 41 (1876), 23–4, and *The Academy* 7 (1875), 291, 376, 402. Reprinted Vaduz: Kraus (1965). Extracts are reprinted in Walter Skeat, *English dialects from the eighth century to the present day*. Cambridge:

Cambridge University Press (1911), 130–2; and piecemeal in innumerable books about Sussex. This is the standard authority on Sussex dialect vocabulary, with the usual shortcomings of its period (discussed in the reviews in *The Academy*). Parish was vicar of Selmeston, and a fair amount of his material relates to that village, but he received collections of spoken material from Bessie Curteis, John Coker Egerton, James Fraser, and some anonymous informants plausibly identified by the detective work of Roper (2007: 186–7, *q.v.*). Butterfield (1916) reports an edition of 1872, and Sawyer (1884b: 2) one of 1873, neither of which I have succeeded in tracing a copy of, and I am extremely sceptical of their existence. (Sawyer is not always a reliable source of information, and I have not seen an earlier edition mentioned anywhere else except by Butterfield. One may have been published privately, but I doubt it.) There was a second 'edition' of later in 1875, mentioned in the *British Museum catalogue of printed books*; it appears to be only a reprinting, to judge by a copy in the library of the University of Sussex. A copy of 1875 at the Sussex Archaeological Society library, Barbican House, Lewes (open shelves), bears many interleaved annotations by James Fraser and friends of Fraser's (apparently including Parish himself). The British Library copy annotated by J.C. Clough and H.H. Sturmer is discussed by Godman (1965). Two other copies are kept at Barbican House, one annotated by J.C. Stenning. One at the University of Sussex bears notes probably by F.W. Bourdillon. A copy at West Sussex Record Office bears notes by Miles Costello. See also Stenning (1907), Harrison (1929). Mr Peter Cox of Horsham owns a lightly-annotated copy once belonging to F.J. Clarke of Haywards Heath. New, much-expanded, edition by Hall (1957), and a further one by Richardson (2001), *qq.v.* Facsimile reprint with an introduction by Lynne Truss (2008) Lewes: Snake River Press. The dictionary entries are 'enlivened' with short recalled or invented dialect passages. See Part Two, Text 15a.]

Parish, [Rev.] William Douglas (1880) To 'ixe'. *Notes and Queries*, 6th series, 1 (24/01/1880), 76.

Parish, [Rev.] William Douglas (1881a) 'Carriage' for baggage. *Notes and Queries*, 6th series, 1 (24/01/1880), 76.

Parish, [Rev.] William Douglas (1881b) Not swimy, but nuddly. *Notes and Queries*, 6th series, 3 (25/06/1881), 513.

Parish, [Rev.] William Douglas (1883) Ballet. *Notes and Queries*, 6th series, 8 (15/12/1883), 468.

Parsons, A.V. (1929) Rustic words and phrases. *Sussex County Magazine* 3, 742. [There are rejoinders by R.J.S. and by E.S[hoosmith]. on 807 and 885–6 respectively.]

Peak, Steve (1985) *Fishermen of Hastings: 200 years of the Hastings fishing community.* St Leonards: News Books. [Appendix 1, 151–2, contains local surnames and nicknames; appendix 2, 152–3, contains some local technical and general vocabulary.]

Pennington, Janet (2007) Roll out the humberton . . . ? *Locus focus, forum of the Sussex Place-Names Net* 7.1/2, 101–2. [On a local 'barrel' word.]

Pile, John (2001) Rithes, rifes and lakes: another view of the toponymy of theWest Sussex coastal plain. *West Sussex History* 67, 16–17. [On the words for 'watercourse' mentioned in the title.]

Image 12: Aldingbourne Rife in wet February 2007
(Robin Webster, reused under a Creative Commons licence)

Pullein, Catherine (1926) Shott or Shutt and Rede or Reed. *Sussex Notes and Queries* 1, 125–6. [On characteristic elements in Sussex minor place-names. See rejoinders on 159, 197–8.]

Radcliffe, John (2002) R[udyard] K[ipling]'s use of Sussex dialect. *Kipling Journal*, 58–9. Available online at www.johnradcliffe.pwp.blueyonder.co.uk /textfiles/KJ301.txt. [About *wildishers* 'inhabitants of the low land around Etchingham'.]

Ramsey, Lilian F. (1923) Quaint Sussex words. *Peacehaven Post* 2.17, 126.

Ramsey, Lilian F. (1930) *The W.W.W.I. [West Wittering Women's Institute] book.* Chichester: Moore and Wingham. [Pages 24–31 on dialect vocabulary; page 44 on field-names.]

Ray, John (1674) *A collection of English words not generally used* [etc.]. [Three subsequent editions, the earliest augmented one dating from 1691. Edited for the English Dialect Society by Walter Skeat, as their volume 6, in the bicentenary year (1874) of its writing. The first ever dialect dictionary; the second of its two catalogues concerns the southern counties. Ray had at least one informant in Sussex; see also the following item.]

Ray, John (1718) *Philosophical letters between the late learned Mr Ray and several of his ingenious correspondents* ['published' (i.e. edited) by W. Derham]. London: W. and J. Innys.

Richardson, Dick (2001) New edition of Parish (1875). Bakewell: Country Books.

Rickman, Thomas 'Clio' (writing as 'The Reflector') (dates not known; c.1805–25) [Titles unknown.] *Brighton Herald.* [Precise publication dates unknown. Contains a 'list of many Sussex provincialisms' which was used by Cooper in preparing his *Glossary* (1836), of which see p. 12. On Rickman, his interest in dialect, and his literary efforts, see Charles Fleet (1878) *Glimpses of our ancestors in Sussex* [spine title *Glimpses of our Sussex ancestors*]. Lewes: Farncombe, 116-8 of the second edition (1882); A. B[eckett]. (1927) 'Clio' Rickman, the 'Citizen of the World'. *Sussex County Magazine* 1, 522-4; and Colin Brent (1993) *Georgian Lewes, 1714–1830: the heyday of a county town.* Lewes: Colin Brent Publications, 121–2, 183.]

Rock, James (jr.) (1862) Old Sussex harvest custom, and peculiarities of speech in use at Hastings. *Sussex Archaeological Collections* 14, 186–90.

'Rouser'. See Eccles, John.

Row, E.F. (1922) Some notes on Sussex words. *Peacehaven Post* 1.9, 253.

S[hoosmith], E. See Parsons (1929).

Salzmann, Louis F. (1901) *The history of the parish of Hailsham, the abbey of Otham and the priory of Michelham*. Lewes: Farncombe. [Glossary on 276–7, though most of the words are legal technical terms rather than local words.]

Sawyer, Frederick E. (1887) Glossary of Sussex dialectal place-nomenclature. *Sussex Archaeological Collections* 35, 165–72. [Superseded by the standard works; and unreliable.]

Sawyer, Frederick E. Sawyer was the editor (1887–8) of a column in the *Brighton Gazette* called 'Sussex Notes and Queries'. A few entries are of dialect interest: VIII (date uncertain), query 3. on dialect rhymes in Shelley; XXV (23/04/1887), query 2. On *dan* 'flag weighted with lead marking the limit of fishing nets at sea', LXIII (21/01/1888), query on *chop-backs* 'fishermen of Hastings'; LXV (06/02/1888), query by E.P. Simmons of Twineham on certain words; the editor refers to *Lewes and East Sussex Church Magazine* 48 and 49 [not traced].

Setford, Stan (1996) Wood-workers' words. *Danehill Parish Historical Society Magazine* 5.6, 19.

Short, Brian, ed. (1997) *The Ashdown Forest dispute, 1876-1882: environmental politics and custom*. Lewes: Sussex Record Society (SRS 80). [The glossary on 52–6 includes some dialect words.]

Silver, Ray (1945) Sussex dialect. *Sussex County Magazine* 19, 162–4. [Discussion of some vocabulary, culled from conversations with Jem Medhurst the elder and the younger, place unknown; with a constructed passage to illustrate the words mentioned. Alludes also to dialect verse-writing by E.F. in *Sussex County Herald*. It has recently been claimed (by Nick Flint, reported in *Sussex Express*) that the poet was Edgar Flint of Lewes.]

Slyfield, G.N. (1958) Letter including some dialect words. *West Sussex Gazette,* 28/08/1958, 6. [Some items are taken from *Sussex County Magazine* 8 (1934), 404; 13 (1939), 650; 15 (1941), 143; 17 (1943), 90).]

Spong, A. Noel (1946) 'Itchells' – a mysterious word. *Sussex County Magazine* 20, 65. [On the expression as *thick as itchells*, said of weeds. [Left unexplained, but see correspondence on p. 156 (especially the letter from Arthur Saunders) and p. 234 (letter from M.S.). These two letters give incompatible solutions, neither implausible. The novelist Bryan Flynn knew the expression *as black as itchul*, which he interpreted (in *The Sussex cuckoo*) as as *black as H--L*. Dunkin MS 5.4 (Dunkin Papers, Sussex Archaeological Society, Barbican House, Lewes) contains a reference to the *East Grinstead Observer*, 15/1/1916, 5, where an interpretation 'as thick as thistles' is offered (cf. also 19/2/1916, said to mean 'icicles'). These look more like attempts to rationalize than to offer a proper etymology.]

Stenning, J.C. (1907) Some local words not mentioned in Parish's Dictionary of the Sussex Dialect. *Sussex Archaeological Collections* 50, 180–1. [Cf. Parish (1875). Includes the only acknowledgement in print, until recent work by M.J. Leppard, of Richard Jefferies's and J.M. Neale's interest in dialect; a word from Neale's story 'Gill's Lap' is mentioned.]

Straker, Ernest (1931) *Wealden iron*. London: G. Bell. [Dialect (especially technical) glossary xii-xiv; sporadic mentions elsewhere, e.g. *noddy* (probably incorrect) on p. 231. Part II is topographical and draws attention to names relevant to past ironworking *passim.* Cf. Leppard (1992a and MS. (in ref. to biography of John Mason Neale in Section F)).]

Sturt, George (writing as 'George Bourne') (1923) *The wheelwright's shop*. Cambridge: Cambridge University Press. [Sturt was a Surrey man who worked in Farnham, but the glossary of his trade given in this book (213–24) is applicable in adjacent parts of Sussex and Hampshire.]

'Surreyite'. See T. Gaston (1940).

Talbot, E[thel] (1937) Letter [about the word *bilbo* 'device for securing the head of a sheep during shearing']. *Sunday Times*, 27/06/1937. [Known to the compiler from a cutting inside the store copy of Parish (1875) in University of Sussex library. The word was also found in Kent by the Survey of English Dialects. See also contributions to *Sussex County Magazine* 12 (1938), 280–1 (Ethel Talbot) and 349, 362 (Maude Robinson).]

Tittler, Robert, ed. (no date; c.1979) *Accounts of the Roberts family of Boarzell, Sussex, c.1568–1582*. Lewes: Sussex Record Society (volume 71). [Glossary on 167-8; should be read in conjunction with the dialectologically more interesting index of subjects and places on 171–6.]

Truss, Lynne (2008) New edition of Parish (1875). Lewes: Snake River Press.

Turner, Edward, of Wiggonholt (1835) List of dialect words sent to Rev. William Turner of Chichester. West Sussex Record Office Add MS. 1729.

Wales, Tony (1979) *A Sussex garland*. London: Godfrey Cave Associates; then Newbury: Countryside Books (1986). [Some dialect vocabulary mentioned, esp. 76–80.]

Wales, Tony (1992) *Sussex ghosts and legends*. Newbury: Countryside Books. [Contains a substantial glossary of local words and phrases. Noticed by Quita Morgan, 'Word has it that today is Bandy-ann-day!' *[Brighton] Evening Argus*, 26/10/1992, 18.]

Wallisch, Roland (1980) Report of a dialectal investigation in Firle, East Sussex. University of Sussex term paper. [MS. only; available from compiler of this bibliography. Deals principally with vocabulary. Cf. Whitfield (1995).]

Warne, Heather (2007) Tar. *Locus focus, forum of the Sussex Place-Names Net* 7.1/2, 81–3. [Use of this element in local place-names.]

Way, Albert. See B.M.H. Carr (1950).

Wells, Roger, ed. (1992) *Victorian village. The diaries of the Reverend John Coker Egerton of Burwash, 1857–1888*. Stroud: Alan Sutton.

Whitaker, F.O. (1935) The popular names of Sussex plants. In 'Sussex nature notes', *Sussex County Magazine* 9, 387–8, 519–20. [Cf. Wolley-Dod (1937). The first piece localizes some names to specific districts of Sussex.]

White, James (1937) Sheep counting. *Sussex County Magazine* 9, 305–7. [Cf. Ellis (1878), Skeat (1910), Wills (1938) and the note to the last item. See Part Two, Texts 28a-b.]

Whitfield, Justine (1995) Vocabulary change in Firle. Dissertation for the degree of BA, University of Sussex. [MS. only; available from compiler of this bibliography. Cf. Wallisch (1980). One of Whitfield's informants, Gilbert West, is profiled by Danny Harding (1996), Where sheep may safely graze? *[Brighton] Evening Argus* (04/04/1996), 21.]

Whittick, Christopher (1998) *Twitten:* is it spreading beyond dialect? *Locus focus: forum of the Sussex Place-Names Net* 2.1, 6–7. [Notes the word in seventeenth-century manuscripts of the Hastings area, far earlier than recorded in *OED* (second edition), and apparently meaning 'parcel of waste ground'. Cf. Coates (1999b), Leppard (2000). The complete sequence of notes on *twitten* in this periodical, by various authors, is as follows: Q1.3.4, N2.1.3, R2.1.4, R2.2.7, N3.2.5, N4.1.2, R5.1.3; 6.1, 21–2; N7.1.7 Whittick on an attestation in 1465, N7.1.8 Leppard on an instance in East Grinstead in the 1841 census.]

Image 13: One of Sussex's distinctive words in a street-name: The Twitten, Ditchling

Whittick, Christopher, and Richard Coates (2007) *Ash-(y)ealer* as an occupational term. *Locus focus, forum of the Sussex Place-Names Net* 7.1/2, 102.

Whittick, Christopher, and Richard Coates (in preparation) An edition of *Sussex vocabulary*, the Davies notebook of about 1845.

Wills, Barclay (1938) Sheep-washing, marking and counting. In his *Shepherds of Sussex (q.v.),* 168–175. [Includes a Sussex sheep-counting score from Slindon, contributed by H. [?possibly should be E.] Walford Lloyd. Cf. Ellis (1878), Skeat (1910), White (1937). For a comparative perspective, see M.V. Barry (1969) Traditional enumeration in north. *Folk-Life* 7, 75–91.]

Wilson, Mary (2002) Cooped up since the Middle Ages. *Sunday Telegraph*, 18 [online 21]/08/2002. [In a piece on New Place Manor, Pulborough, it was said that a mummified hen found 'under the floorboards' was a 'medieval mivern' meant to encourage good spirits. This is doubtless a variant of *midden*. '*Medieval midden* is sometimes used as a descriptive term for a collection of objects used in a ritually protective way' (ex inf. Dr Janet Pennington).]

Wolley-Dod, A.H. (1937) *The flora of Sussex*. Hastings: Saville. [New edition 1970. Sporadic references to vernacular names. Cf. Arnold (1887/1907), Whitaker (1935).]

Young, Arthur (1813) *A general view of the agriculture of the county of Sussex. Drawn up for the consideration of the Board of Agriculture and Internal Improvement*. London: Sherwood, Neely and Jones. [A version of 1793 is also reported in bibliographies. The 1813 version is reprinted Newton Abbot: David and Charles (1970). Includes quite a few provincial semi-technical terms for e.g. diseases of livestock and types of soil.]

The following additional references seen in some of the items mentioned above have not been seen either (a) in their original source, or (b) in their original place of publication.

Individual words:

Boist
Brighton Herald, 20/04/1850. Piece containing the word reprinted *Sussex Family Historian* 10.5 (March 1993), 188.

Canker
The Athenæum, 06/08/1904.

Chopbacks
Sussex Daily News, 15/04/1907, 2. [Awareness of this persists. *Chopback* 'Hastings fisherman' was used as a pseudonym by a blogger in the *Guardian*, 13/03/2009.]

Chopbacks, plarim, queasy
Temple Bar, October 1899, 263 (on *chopbacks*); 264 (on *plarim*); 265 (on *queasy*)

Clutter-headed

Jefferies, Richard (1885) 'The pine wood'. *The Standard* 19076 (03/09/1885), 2.

Dotterell/doted

Scott, [Sir] Sibbald David (1854) 'A booke of orders and rules' of Anthony viscount Montague in 1595. *Sussex Archaeological Collections* 7, 173–212 [212, note 34].

Noddy

East Grinstead Observer, 21/07/1917 (about W.H. Hills' views on this word).

C7: IDIOMS, SAYINGS and other fixed expressions

> • Some of these items duplicate entries in the subsection on vocabulary; where this is so, the entry here may be a reduced version of what appears there.

Austen, Edmund (1938) A bit of Sussex dialect. *Sussex County Magazine* 12, 216. [A trifle.]

Austen, Edmund (1942) Dialect and humour in a Sussex village. *Sussex County Magazine* 16, 341–5. [About Brede. Mainly on picturesque expressions, some idiomatic, some nonce.]

Beckett, Arthur (1926) A dissertation on Sussex proverbs and curious sayings. *Sussex County Magazine* 1, 42–4.

Egerton, [Rev.] John Coker (1884) *Sussex folk and Sussex ways. Stray studies in the Wealden Formation of human nature*. Lewes: *Sussex Advertiser*; London: Trübner. [Second edition (1892) London: Chatto and Windus; third edition (1924; edited by Henry Wace, with an introduction by Sheila Kaye-Smith) London: Methuen. The subtitle is omitted in the later editions. Allusions to (mainly Burwash area) dialect, especially vocabulary and sayings, throughout the book.]

Greaves, Ralph (1953) Silly Sussex. *The Countryman* 47, 117–8. [Some examples of local expressions.]

Heath, Richard (1871) Sussex commons and Sussex sayings. *Golden Hours*. [Further bibliographical details not known. Mentioned in Roger Wells, ed. (1993) *Victorian village* [edition of J. Coker Egerton's diaries]. Stroud: Alan Sutton, 119, note 8. Relates to Mayfield, Rotherfield area.]

Leppard, M.J. (2005) Sayings used in East Grinstead. *East Grinstead Museum Bulletin* 18 (Autumn), 8–9. [Addenda 20 (Summer 2006), 9; 21 (Autumn 2006), 13.]

Parish, [Rev.] William Douglas (1880a) Contrairy as wood's dog. *Notes and Queries* 6th series, 2 (28/08/1880), 166.

Parish, [Rev.] William Douglas (1880b) I only pass the time of day. *Notes and Queries* 6th series, 2 (09/10/1880), 293. [On politeness in address.]

Redman, Glen R. (1976) Sussex phrase and fable. *Sussex Life* 12 (February), 34.

Sawyer, Frederick E. (1884a) Sussex place-rhymes and local proverbs. *Notes and Queries* 6.9, 341–3, 401–3; 6.10, 370.

Simpson, Jacqueline (1973) *The folklore of Sussex*. London: Batsford. [Second edition Stroud: Tempus (2002), reviewed by Terry Gunnell in *Folklore* (December 2004).]

Wales, Tony (1976) *We wunt be druv: songs and stories from Sussex*. London: Galliard/English Folk Dance and Song Society. [Chapter 5 contains local rhymes, sayings and toasts, some with dialect features.]

C8: FOLKLORE

Allen, Andrew (1995) *A dictionary of Sussex folk medicine*. Newbury: Countryside Books. [Contains significant amounts of relevant material, especially local plant-names, but with little information about sources or the location of relevant documents.]

Arscott, David (2006) *Wunt be druv! A salute to the Sussex dialect*. Newbury: Countryside Books. [Includes chapters on personal and place-names, dialect literature, local vocabulary, folk-song, etc., and extracts from recorded conversations not published elsewhere. Described as a 'celebration'.]

Boger, James I.C. (1901) The play acted by the 'Tipteers' at West Wittering, Chichester. *Sussex Archaeological Collections* 44, 178–83. [Cf. Sawyer (1884c), and further references there.]

Burstow, Henry (1911) *Reminiscences of Horsham, being recollections of H.B. the celebrated bellringer and songsinger*. Horsham: Free Christian Church Book Society. [With the assistance of William Albery. Contains details of Burstow's repertoire of local songs and and recitations in dialect, 107-19. New edition by Tony Wales and Tony Green, Norwood, Pa.: Norwood Editions (1975). See also Stanley Godman (1954) Henry Burstow: the Horsham singer and bellringer. *Sussex County Magazine* 28, 519–22.]

Grose, Francis (1787) *A provincial glossary, with a collection of local proverbs and superstitions*. London. [Later printings (1811, 1839). Facsimile reprint Menston: Scolar Press (English Linguistics 1500-1800) (1968). Contains 17 words said explicitly to be of Sussex, but almost all beginning with B and C, after which come only *fimble* and *foizon*, said to be shared with Essex, and *leap*, or *lib*, likewise shared. The glossarist's sources, policy or memory clearly faltered as the task progressed alphabetically. Small list of 'best of kind' terms such as *Arundel mullet*.]

Gutch, Eliza, writing as 'St Swithin' (1880) Local customs. *Notes and Queries* 6.1, 434–5. [The first of two pieces reprinted from daily newspapers (this from the *Daily News*, 26/04/1880) explains the ceremony of *bending-in* performed on Brighton beach at the beginning of the mackerel-fishing season.]

Hall, Helena E. (1957) *A dictionary of the Sussex dialect and collection of provincialisms in use in the county of Sussex, by the Rev W.D. Parish. Expanded, augmented and illustrated by Helena Hall, together with 'Some Sussex sayings and crafts'*. Chichester: private. [Paperback edition Bexhill: Gardner's (1967). Revised and massively extended edition of Parish (1875), *q.v.* Reviewed editorially in *West Sussex Gazette*, 25/04/1957, 'Does anyone talk Sussex now?' This piece sparked off a correspondence: 23/05 'A Sussex woman' [Miss L.F. Ramsey? – RC] and Sybil Bulstrode; 30/05 Francis Foster, W.J. Dore-Dennis and Robert Reid; 06/06 Stanley Godman, G. Bryant and Lilian E. Brown; 13/06 W.G. Daish, Frank R. James, Mrs E. Bowyer and Francis Foster (a sceptic about what can properly be called dialect); 20/06 Newall Duke. Copies of Hall's book exist with annotations by Michael Leppard of East Grinstead (owned by Mr Leppard) and by R.H. and P.D. Wood of Ashurst Wood. Miss Hall's MS. notes are in private hands.]

Latham, Charlotte (1878) Some West Sussex superstitions lingering in 1868. *Folk-Lore Record* 1, 1–67. [What appears to be W.D. Parish's copy is bound in with James Fraser's copy of Parish's *Dictionary* at the Sussex Archaeological Society library, Barbican House, Lewes (open shelves). Note also James Britten, Plant-lore notes to Mrs Latham's 'West Sussex superstitions'. *Folk-Lore Record* 1 (1878), 155–9, though Britten's own comments do not relate specifically to Sussex.]

Lister, Sue (1967) Sussex recipes. Project for the degree of BA, University of Leeds, 2 vols. [Contains a glossary.]

Lovett, Edward (1928) *Folk-lore and legend of the Surrey hills, and of the Sussex downs and forests*. Caterham: Caterham Printing Works. [Reprinted as Publication 8 of the Folklore Society (1991).]

Lower, Mark Antony (1861) Old speech and old manners in Sussex. *Sussex Archaeological Collections* 13, 209–36. [Especially 218–36. Noticed in the *Saturday Review* 13 (1862), 599–600. See Part Two, Text 13c.]

Morgan, Quita. See Tony Wales (1992).

North, David J. (1979) Some linguistic and cultural boundaries in south-east England. *Transactions of the Yorkshire Dialect Society* 8–37. [Attempts to trace the westward extent into Sussex and Surrey of some ostensibly Kentish dialect features and artefact types; the supposed coincidence of these boundaries is suggestive but not overwhelming.]

Paine, M.J. (1967) The fishermen of Newhaven. Project for the degree of BA, University of Leeds. [Ethnographic study. Not seen; relevance for dialect uncertain.]

Parish, [Rev.] William Douglas (1881) Folk-lore of the cuckoo. *Notes and Queries* 6th series, 4 (17/09/1881), 234.

Parish, [Rev.] William Douglas (????) East Sussex superstitions. *Folklore*. [This item was said to be forthcoming each year between 1878–83, but it apparently never materialized and no MS. has been found in Parish's papers in the care of the Sussex Archaeological Society.]

Pearce, Susan M. (1999) Museums of anthropology or museums as anthropology? *Anthropologica* 41.1, 25–33. [Contains interesting example (28-9) of a 'witchcraft' exhibit in Hove Museum, labelled in dialect, and explores the implications.]

Rock, James, jr. (1862) Old Sussex harvest custom, and peculiarities of speech in use at Hastings. *Sussex Archaeological Collections* 14, 186–90.

Ross, Alison (1975) When sossle-wosslers strove to be top of the pops. *The Times*, 24/12/1975, 10. [References to wassailing at South Stoke and Amberley.]

'St Swithin', pseudonym of Eliza Gutch, *q.v.*

Sawyer, Frederick E. (1883a) Christmas customs in Sussex. *Notes and Queries* 6.8, 481–5. [The tipteerers' play is presented on pages 483–4. Cf. Sawyer (1884c), and further references there. The dialect is not very strongly marked.]

Sawyer, Frederick E. (1883b) *Sussex natural history, folk-lore and superstitions. A paper*. Brighton: privately published.

Sawyer, Frederick E. (1883c) Sussex folk-lore and customs connected with the seasons. *Sussex Archaeological Collections* 33, 237–60. [Also published separately.]

Sawyer, Frederick E. (1884a) Sussex place-rhymes and local proverbs. *Notes and Queries* 6.9, 341–3, 401–3; and 6.10, 370.

Sawyer, Frederick E. (1884c) Sussex 'tipteerers'' play. *Folk-Lore Journal* 2.1, 1–8. [The play is the Sussex Christmas mumming play. For full bibliographical discussion, see the entry for 'traditional' in Section D1.2.]

Sharp, R.J. (1931) Sussex mummers or tipteerers. *The Observer*, 04/01/1931. [Reprinted in *Sussex County Magazine* 5 (1931), 148. See also Sawyer (1884c) and further references there.]

Simpson, Jacqueline (1973) *The folklore of Sussex*. London: Batsford. [On 53–6 is a dialect piece, 'The broken peel', told in c.1854 by William Fowington to M.A. Lower and originally printed in Lower's Contributions to literature, [etc.] (1854c), *q.v.*, 161–3; se also Part Two, Text 13a. Simpson's pp. 150–3 deal with place-name rhymes.]

Simpson, Jacqueline (1982) Multi-purpose treacle mines in Sussex and Surrey. *Lore and Language* 3:6A, 61–73. [Of interest here insofar as it deals with the nature of the folkloric allusion(s) in the expression *treacle mine* (not confined to Sussex). See also next item.]

Simpson, Jacqueline (1992/3) A note on *treacle wells. Lore and Language* 11, 95–7. [See previous item.]

Wales, Tony (1976) *We wunt be druv: songs and stories from Sussex.* London: Galliard/English Folk Dance and Song Society. [Chapter 5 contains local rhymes, sayings and toasts, some with dialect features.]

Wales, Tony (1990) *Sussex customs, curiosities and country lore.* Southampton: Ensign Publications. [90-1 on dialect, 92–3 on ballads and riddles.]

Wales, Tony (1992) *Sussex ghosts and legends*. Newbury: Countryside Books. [Contains a substantial glossary of local words and phrases. Noticed by Quita Morgan, 'Word has it that today is Bandy-ann-day!' *[Brighton] Evening Argus,* 26/10/1992, 18.]

Wales, Tony (2000) *A treasury of Sussex folklore*. Seaford: S.B. Publications. [Incidental dialect occasionally.]

C9 : ROMANI (GIPSY) LANGUAGE IN SUSSEX

Donne, J. (1949) Sussex pronunciation. [Part of 'A Sussex wayfarer's diary'.] *Sussex County Magazine* 23, 300–1. [On some Sussex place-name pronunciations and some Gipsy words.]

Evans, A.A. (1933) *On foot in Sussex: a loiterer's notebook.* London: Methuen. [Contains some discussion of the use of Shelta (a partly Irish-based language whose exact history not yet been established) by Sussex travelling people, 98–101.]

Note also the songs sung in Anglo-Romani by the Sussex Gipsy family Willett, Section F.

Section D:

THE DIALECT LITERATURE OF SUSSEX

> 'We may say of Sussex that its native writers have done nothing, or nothing worth doing, for it.' – W.H. Hudson, *Nature in downland*, p. 13.

The following is intended to be a full record of published works written completely in the dialect of Sussex, or where the dialect of certain characters is judged to be the main point of the work; and, as far as possible, also of similar unpublished writings.

No attempt has been made to catalogue systematically the renderings of characters' spoken dialect in books otherwise written in standard English, such as those by Bessie Curteis, Hilaire Belloc, Alice Dudeney, Tickner Edwardes (sometime vicar of Burpham), 'Michael Fairless', Sheila Kaye-Smith, Rhoda Leigh and Barclay Wills; but a number of books and articles containing a significant amount are listed in Section E, and it is hoped that the list tends towards completeness. Nor do I include pieces situated in Sussex, but written in a stagey vernacular maybe best called Mummersex, of which a paradigm example is the poem 'The tramp transfigured (an episode in the life of a corn-flower millionaire)', by Alfred Noyes, who lived at Rottingdean. He may or may not have intended his words to be understood as true local dialect.

There are occasional dialect words in the otherwise standard poetical works of John Turley (see M.J. Leppard, John Turley and his poems. *Bulletin of the East Grinstead Society* 76 (Spring 2002), 16–17) and Wilfrid Scawen Blunt (quoted above at the end of Part A).

I have also not mentioned prose works written in or of Sussex which contain occasional dialectalisms whilst being principally, and intentionally, in standard English (as when the diarist Thomas Turner, mercer and general dealer of East Hoathly, writing of 27/09/1758, describes his experiences in a *travase* 'shoeing-room at a forge'); though I have exceptionally allowed the seventeenth/ eighteenth-century diarists Giles Moore, rector of Horsted Keynes, Timothy Burrell, barrister and farmer of Cuckfield, and Richard Stapley, squire of Hickstead, for the interest of their unforced use of some local (especially outdoor) vocabulary which was evidently completely natural to them. That qualifies them for entry into the 'authentic voices' subsection (D1.1). Some other such sources are recoverable from Andrew Allen's *Dictionary of Sussex folk medicine* (1995).

Contributors to newspapers occasionally intruded dialect speech for certain of their characters. A specimen of the type is the anonymous piece under the pseudonym 'Rambler', entitled 'Farmer Brown: his point of view', in *Sussex County Herald Magazine* (22/01/1927), 1–2. No attempt has been made to track down all ephemera in this category, but the compiler would be pleased to hear of any which readers may discover. Articles elsewhere with dialect dialogue are also catalogued in Section E.

No dialect pieces get into the *Sussex garlands* of James Taylor of Newick (London (1851) or Tony Wales (London: Godfrey Cave Associates (1979)). None occur in the first *Book of Sussex verse* edited by C.F. Cook (Hove: Combridge's (1914, 1920)), unless we accept the very lightly coloured anonymous 'Lines affixed to an old Sussex mill post'; but four appear in his *Another book of Sussex verse* (Hove: Combridge's (1928)), written by Reginald Arkell, Arthur Beckett and G.D. Martineau, and they are catalogued below. Margaret Goldsworthy's collection *The Sussex bedside anthology* (Bognor Regis: The Arundel Press (1950)) contains some Sussex material, but almost nothing of a clearly dialectal character, and the same is true of John Holloway's *The Oxford book of local verses* (Oxford: Oxford University Press (1987)).

The very few works by untutored writers have pride of place in a subsection of their own (D1.1). The word 'authentic' is used to describe their voices, with some diffidence; it is simply meant to suggest that these writers wrote without consciousness that they were writing in dialect – without *choosing* to write in dialect. The prime importance of these is acknowledged, and inclusion of a piece in the rest of the list (D1.2) is no guarantee of an 'authentic' dialect voice, since much was written, as in other counties, by enthusiasts from the leisured classes who were literate in standard English. No doubt some of these efforts are, however, very faithful to the vernacular; the gentry, clerics and professionals, dispersed as they were through the countryside, were often much more closely in touch with the activities of their less favoured neighbours than their modern counterparts are.

However, it is not hard to recognize a school of writing which takes passages or single lexical items in dialect and uses them like talismans in otherwise standard English texts, especially conversations. Authors in this category include Florence Aylward, Arthur Beckett, W. Victor Cook and A. Stanley Cooke. It may very well be that some features in passages invented by non-native speakers are in a sense accurate indicators of Sussex speech, but (1) exaggerated in the frequency of their usage, (2) treated as normal even where obsolescent, or (3), in the case of formal linguistic features such as irregular verb-forms, analogically extended beyond the words which they characterized in the authentic dialect of the time. But several of the pieces simply labelled 'anecdote' below do not carry much conviction. These writers were outsiders, from the perspective of those whom James Richards called 'de old dialecters I used to know', and one mechanism for keeping an appropriate social distance is to magnify what separates you from those you are observing. Such exaggeration may well have the effect of being amusing, which serves the purpose of separation still further. One does not have to search far in the writings of, e.g., Mark Antony Lower, W.H. Hudson or Beckett for evidence of condescension, flippancy or even downright hostility, towards vernacular culture (as they certainly would not have called it).

It has not always proved possible to track down precisely the place and date of original publication of some pieces in unindexed periodicals which were later reprinted in book form (e.g. G.D. Martineau's poems or E.W. Young's prose). It is hoped that a general indication of when and where they first saw daylight will be sufficient to establish the context in which they were written.

NOTE

In the following catalogue, the titles of poems and literary essays are given in "inverted commas", and those of non-literary articles without.

D1.0:
Medieval literary texts

Horobin, Simon (2005) The scribe of Rawlinson Poetry 137 and the copying and circulation of Piers Plowman. *Yearbook of Langland Studies* 19, 3–26. [One Langland MS. is claimed for Sussex.]

Konrath, M., ed. (1902) *The poems of William of Shoreham*. London: Early English Text Society (Early Series 86). [Has been claimed, doubtfully, for Sussex.]

Murdoch, Brian, and J[acqueline] A. Tasioulas, eds (2002) *The apocryphal lives of Adam and Eve*. Exeter: Exeter: University of Exeter Press (Exeter Medieval English Texts and Studies). [The second *Life, Canticum de creatione* (1375), is claimed to have been written in Sussex. See Part Two, Text 2.]

Other, non-literary, medieval texts attributed to Sussex are analysed in:

McIntosh, Angus, Michael L. Samuels and Michael Benskin, with the assistance of M. Laing and K. Williamson (1986) *A linguistic atlas of late Middle English*, vols 1–4. Aberdeen: Aberdeen University Press.

D1.1:
Authentic voices

Andrews, Colin, ed. (1979) *Shepherd of the Downs. The life and songs of Michael Blann of Upper Beeding*. Worthing: Museum and Art Gallery. [Blann's semi-literate writing is dialectally coloured. "Dame Durden" is Part Two, Text 20a.]

Bird, Ruth. See Giles Moore (1655–79).

Blann, Michael. See Andrews (1979).

Bullokar, William, 16th-century grammarian. [Dialectalisms have been attributed to him in his published work by E.J. Dobson (1957, 2nd edn 1967) *English pronunciation, 1500–1700*, vol. I. Oxford: Oxford University Press, 93-117; esp. §374. Cf. Bror Danielsson and Robin C. Alston, eds (1966) *The works of William Bullokar*, vol. I. Leeds: University of Leeds School of English, x ff., who definitively trace his origins in Sussex.]

Burgess, Donald F. See John Burgess (1785-1815).

Burgess, John (1785–1815) Diary [titled *Jernal*] and letters. [Preserved at East Sussex Record Office, MS. AMS 5853/1 and 5853/3. The diary, written at Ditchling, runs from 28/02/1785 to 14/02/1790; the 11 letters were written between 1794 and 1815 from various places in New York State. One was written by John's sons Henry and Thomas (the latter perhaps partly at his father's dictation) and one by Henry alone. Privately published by Leonard Maguire (1982) *The journal and correspondence of John Burgess, 1785–1819*; and republished privately in 1989 with an introduction by Donald F. Burgess as *No continuing city. The diary and letters of John Burgess, a craftsman from Sussex, from 1785–1819*. Title varies slightly between titlepage and cover. Excerpts were published (a) by John Sawyer, Some extracts from the journal and correspondence of Mr John Burgess, of Ditchling, Sussex, 1785–1815. *Sussex Archaeological Collections* 40 (1896), 131–61; and (b) by Walter H. Burgess (unrelated to the author) in *Sussex County Magazine* 12 (1938), 590, as a follow-up to an article by David Maclean, John Burgess of Ditchling and America. *Sussex County Magazine* 11 (1937), 657. See Part Two, Texts 10a-c.]

Burgess, John (1807, 1819) Letters to the writer's cousin William Kensett. [Whereabouts unknown. Typewritten copies were made and Donald F. Burgess published them along with John Burgess's other letters (see previous item) and his will (1815).]

Burgess, Walter H. See John Burgess (1794-1815).

Burrell, Timothy (1683-1714) Journal and account-book. Excerpts published by R.W. Blencowe (1850) Extracts from the journal and account book of Timothy Burrell, Esq., Barrister-at-Law, of Ockenden House, Cuckfield, from the year 1683 to 1714. *Sussex Archaeological Collections* 3, 117–72; Arthur J. Rees (1929) *Old Sussex and her diarists*. London: John Lane The Bodley Head, 91–128; *Sussex Genealogist and Local Historian* 2 (1980), 4, 80. [The Sussex colour of this diary, which was destroyed in a fire in 1903, is quite minimal.]

Carley, Gaius (1963) *The memoirs of Gaius Carley, a Sussex blacksmith.* Privately published. [Written in 1955 and deposited in West Sussex Record Office in 1960. Second edition with notes by Francis W. Steer, Chichester: Moore and Tillyer (for the Marc Fitch Fund). Carley was born in Upper Dicker and worked widely in (mainly West) Sussex. The book is not exactly in dialect but in a colloquial style with regional features including technical terms of smithing. Some of these are reproduced in Part Two, Text 32.]

Copper, James 'Brasser' (1922) Manuscript songbook. [In private hands. A compilation made in 1922 for Mrs D. Corrie of Rottingdean. The published book *The Copper family song book – a living tradition.* Peacehaven: Coppersongs (1995) includes some facsimile material from this manuscript. There are some dialect traces in the lyrics as written. See Part Two, Texts 20b-c.]

Gammon, Vic. See James Nye (c.1860–1888).

Hubble, Bryan. See George White (1829).

Lambert, William, of East Grinstead (1813–????) Unpublished diary in private hands; used as a source for M.J. Leppard's dialect vocabulary articles in *East Grinstead Museum Compass* (1999–2008).

Miles, Sophia [probable author] (1850-62) Diary. Published by Lorna Standing, My old family diary. *Sussex Family Historian* 12 (1997), 214–6. [In private hands. Written by an agricultural labourer's wife from Clayton, later Lindfield. Some genuine local words and pronunciations are discernible through the uneducated spelling; the words are mainly about light labouring duties such as litter-cutting and sowing.]

Moore, Giles (1655–79) Day book. [MS. PAR 384/6/1West Sussex Record Office. Edited for publication by Ruth Bird, *The journal of Giles Moore*. Lewes: Sussex Record Society, vol. 68 (1971). Basically a standard English text using some local vocabulary (Horsted Keynes area). Moore was actually from Suffolk originally. There is a dialect glossary on xv-xix. Excerpts, some inaccurate, were published by R.W. Blencowe, Extracts from the journal and account book of the Reverend Giles Moore. *Sussex Archaeological Collections* 1 (1848), 65–127.]

Nye, James (c.1860-1888) A small account of my travels through the willderness [sic]. MS. B/NYE, Sussex Archaeological Society, Barbican House, Lewes. [Edited by Vic Gammon (c.1981) as *A small account of my travels through the wilderness*. Brighton: QueenSpark (QueenSpark Books 11). The MS. is lightly dialectally coloured and has illiterate spelling and punctuation, which Gammon regrettably normalizes, in some cases normalizing genuine dialect forms too. See Part Two, Text 14a.]

Nye, James (1863-89) Poems and religious discourses. [Nye wrote some 56 poems (in addition to three in the *Small account*) and 7 religious discourses. Five of the poems are appended to Gammon's edition of the previous item, but most remain unpublished and not fully catalogued in the library of the Sussex Archaeological Society. See part Two, Text 14b.]

Rees, Arthur J. See Richard Stapley (1682–1724).

Sawyer, John (1896) See John Burgess (1794–1815).

Standing, Lorna (1997). See Sophia Miles (1850–62).

Stapley, Richard (1682–1724) Diary. [Generally in standard English, but containing in ordinary use a fair number of local words denoting topographical features. Said to be written in 'a clasped interleaved almanack', presently held at East Sussex Record Office, MS. HIC 1166. Excerpts are printed by Edward Turner, Extracts from the diary of Richard Stapley, gent., of Hickstead Place in Twineham, from 1682 to 1724, with a notice of the Stapley family. *Sussex Archaeological Collections* 2 (1849), 102–28; and excerpts from these by Arthur J. Rees, chapter 12 of *Old Sussex and her diarists*.

London: John Lane/The Bodley Head (1929), 155–64. The transcript (by Turner) of the unpublished sections is MS. HIC 1167.]

Swan, William Carter (1909-10) Diary. [Edited by Edmund E. Swan as *Diary of a farm apprentice: William Carter Swan, 1909–10*. Stroud: Alan Sutton (1984). Whereabouts of original unknown; presumably in private hands. Written in standard English with a few regional words and farming technical terms needing footnote glossing. A facsimile page reveals that the editor has occasionally normalized the text. Swan was apprenticed at Dial Post Farm, West Grinstead.]

Turner, Edward (1849). See Richard Stapley (1682–1724).

White, George (1829) Diary. [Written by White aged 11; the text shows some local features. In private hands. Edited by Bryan Hubble as T*he diary of George White of Muddles Green, Chiddingly, Sussex*, 1829. Privately published (2003). Facsimile with transcript and index.]

D1.2:
Literary works, including pastiches by educated writers

The distinction between items in this section and those in section E can be a fine one, and items have been placed in D1.2 where I judge that they are particularly important for the consideration of dialect. For instance, the works of Lilian F. Ramsey might be considered Standard English with the main character speaking in dialect, therefore material for Section E; but the non-dialect material is included to set off the dialect material, which is the main point of the works.

Akehurst, Alfred. See Herbison (1981).

anonymous (date unknown; traditional) Tipteerers' play. Printed in Frederick E. Sawyer (1883a) Christmas customs in Sussex. *Notes and Queries* 6.8, 481–5 (Section C8). [The tipteerers' play is presented on 483–4. See also Frederick E. Sawyer (1884c) Sussex 'tipteerers'' play. *Folk-Lore Journal* 2.1, 1–8 (Section C8); and the rather different version "The mummers' play" forming the first appendix of Parish (1875) (Section C8). A further version of the play appears in Arthur Beckett, *The wonderful Weald, and the quest of the crock of gold.* London: Mills and Boon (1911), 373, and another in Sharp (1931). For all these, see Section C. See also Alex Helm (1981) *The English mummers' play.* Woodbridge: D.S. Brewer/Rowman and Littlefield, for the Folklore Society, 80–3, where a mummers' play from Iping from the Vaughan Williams Collection is printed. There is scarcely a hint of dialect in any of the versions; they are included here for their folkloric importance. The Ashdown Mummers were reviewed in *The Guardian*, 22/12/1997, 2.]

anonymous (date unknown, traditional) "Come, all my jolly boys, . . . " [etc.] A sheep-shearing song. Printed by Charles Fleet (1878) *Glimpses of our ancestors in Sussex*. Lewes: Farncombe, p. 100 of the second edition (1882); C.F. Cook, ed. (1914) *The book of Sussex verse*. Hove: Combridge's; and John Holloway, ed. (1987) *The Oxford book of local verses*. Oxford: Oxford University Press, item 84 (i). [Suggestion of dialect phonology in some of the rhymes, but not fully in dialect.]

anonymous (date unknown) [Published by Mark Antony Lower as] "Lines affixed to an old Sussex mill post", in his *Contributions to literature*, 187; often reprinted, e.g. in C.F. Cook, ed. (1914) *The book of Sussex verse*. Hove: Combridge's, 202); and *Sussex County Magazine* 30 (1956), 76. [Little suggestion of dialect. Printed with a tune by Colin Taylor in *Sussex County Magazine* 4 (1930), 474–7.]

anonymous (writing as 'Tom Cladpole', but despite the name this is not to be associated with the character invented by Richard Lower) (1884) At the Healtheries. See Richard Lower (spine date 1872). [The Healtheries was an exhibition, the International Health Exhibition, held in South Kensington, to which excursion trains were run from Sussex from 29/09/1884, reported in the *Sussex Agricultural Express* at various dates in early October. (It was apparently so called because it followed the Fisheries exhibition, and the popular title was a pun on this.) The piece entered here was not, however, in the *Sussex Agricultural Express*, and its source is unknown.]

anonymous (date unknown) A shepherd's version of Psalm 23. See Kathleen Lee (1971/2; and Section 2, Text 29).

anonymous (1917) The oddities of village life in Sussex, part I: 'The Old'. *Scribble* 1.4, 12-15. [Includes excerpts from pieces published elsewhere (e.g. M.A. Lower) and some novelties; a few local words mentioned also. (The only complete run of this periodical known to me is in West Sussex Record Office. See also Richard W. Standing (1984) Mere *Scribble* [1916–8, 1919]. *West Sussex History* 28, 31–4.)]

anonymous [F.V. Wright] (1953) In the districts. In *A hundred years of the West Sussex Gazette 1853–1953*. Arundel: West Sussex Gazette Office. [In this section is quoted (42) a letter from a reader in light dialect about Mrs Paddick and the Editor.]

Ansell, Harriet E. (1931) A dialect letter. *Sussex County Magazine* 5, 430–1. [Arthur Beckett, the editor of *Sussex County Magazine*, prefaces it with a little glossary.]

Arkell, Reginald (1911?) "The buryin'". [Believed to have been published originally in *Colombine, a fantasy: and other verses.* London: Benn and Cronin; thereafter London: Sidgwick and Jackson (1913). Reprinted in C.F. Cook's second Sussex anthology (1928). Also used as the epigraph to Arkell's book *Old Herbaceous: a story.* London: Michael Joseph (1950), where it is said to be from Arkell's collection *Green fingers again*. London: Herbert Jenkins; but this was published in 1942.]

B., S. (no date) "Downland oxen" and "Cuckmere song". Verses from a handwritten notebook in the care of the Sussex Archaeological Society at Michelham Priory. [The former is a song in dialect, and the latter a rhapsody with very light dialect colour in the vocabulary but otherwise highly conventional. The author has not been definitely identified, but is very likely to be Mrs Salome Bridger of Alciston, see Bridger, S. The first poem can be found as Part Two, Text 34.]

B., S. (c.1950) "Song of the Cuckmere." Bifolium with printed poem; further bibliographical details unknown. East Sussex Record Office MS. (ACC 10024/5). [The poem is the second in the previous entry, but with some differences.]

Beckett, Arthur (1911) *The wonderful Weald, and the quest of the crock of gold.* London: Mills and Boon. [There are invented dialect dialogues on 90–3, 159, 242–3, 251–3 (ascribed to [M.A.] Lower), 273–5, predictably involving ancient rustics. On 377–86 is printed a version of the tipteerers' play; for this, see also entries under anonymous and traditional (in Sections C8 and D1.2).]

Beckett, Arthur (1928a) "Song o' the Sussex men". In C.F. Cook (1928); (in part) in Margaret Goldsworthy (1950), 589–91; and in Patrick Garland (1995), 84.

Beckett, Arthur (1928b) “Revels in Downland”. In C.F. Cook (1928). [Some light dialect colour in the vocabulary.]

Beckett, Arthur (1929) The Sussex parish clerk. *Sussex County Magazine* 3, 95–106. [Contains several anecdotes in dialect, some reprinted from other books, which are mostly cited in the article.]

Beckett, Arthur (1933) *Adventures of a quiet man*. Hove: Combridge’s. [There is a significant amount of dialect speech in chapters 5, 11, 12, 13, 22, 33 and 36, some in the mouth of the character Martin Malpass, the roadmender. Chapter 6 contains discussion of some dialect words, and chapter 19 of local sayings. The chapters first appeared as articles in the *Sussex County Magazine*. But for Malpass, see also Beckett (1926) in Section C6.]

• Beckett, as editor of the *Sussex County Herald*, sometimes published in it verses by himself with a dialect flavour; some are reprinted in *Adventures of a quiet man* (“The Wilmington Giant” (2), “Sailor Willum and Widow Brown” (128–9), “A song of harvest home” (268–9)).

Blackman, Herbert (1868) In this year, Blackman records in his diary a short dialogue between Tom Sutton and Tom Simmons. Printed in *Battle and District Historical Society Transactions* 13 (1962/3), 26–7.

Botting, Winnie [the manner of presentation suggests this is a pseudonym] (1934) “Owd Sussex”. *Sussex County Magazine* 8, 674. [Verse; author said to be 19.]

Bray, A.J. (1933) The champion shrimper: a Hastings story. *Sussex County Magazine* 7, 584–7. [Some reported speech is in (sometimes unconvincing) dialect.]

Bridger, S. (1942) “Call up the Cladpoles, or Sallie Cladpole’s uppishness with an Adversary”. Unpublished 28 pp. typescript in East Sussex Record Office (ACC 10024/1); another copy may exist in private hands. [Dialect poem describing the role of the distaff side of the mythical Sussex family in the county’s struggle against Hitler. Mrs Bridger hailed from Alciston.]

Bridger, S. (?1949) “Shepherds Pottage or Links and relics of a peculiar race.” Unpublished ii + 87 pp. typescript in East Sussex Record Office (ACC 10024/2); another copy may exist in private hands. [Dedicated ‘To the

Shepherd and his wife in gratitude.' A study, interspersed with original poetry, whose aim, according to the author, is to try 'to preserve some links and relics of a peculiar race in which the Southdown Shepherd and his wife have played such a valuable part'. Includes 'A short dictionary of Sussex lingua'.]

- It is almost certain that the author of these items was the writer of verse anonymized as 'S.B.' elsewhere, and possible but very unlikely that she is also the S. Bridger who was responsible for "Resting", a religious tract published in Rogate in 1936. The compiler believes she is Salome Bridger, born Alciston (1886), died Tonbridge (1973).

Brothers, Anthony Chamberlaine (writing as 'Arthur I. Cote, M.A.') (1990) *Alus in Wunnerland*. MS. only. [MS. version of Lewis Carroll's *Alice in Wonderland* with the narrative portions done into Sussex dialect. Commissioned by the Carroll Foundation of Australia for the Carroll anniversary; unpublished. Essay by Richard Coates (in preparation) on this work, to appear in J.A. Lindseth, ed., a book on *Alice in Wonderland* in translation .]

Brown, Frankie (1939) "Middlin' greasy". *Sussex County Magazine* 13, 172. [A versified trifle.]

Butterfield, J. Ruskin (c.1916). Version of the Song of Solomon. [Lost, or existence doubtful. No mention ever seen of it by the compiler outside private correspondence. Not known in Butterfield's papers.]

Cannon, E.M. (1933) The "hollering pot". *Sussex County Magazine* 7, 569. [Quotes the Sussex harvest-home verse.]

'Cladpole, Jim' (pseudonym of James Richards, *q.v.*)

'Cladpole, Tim' (pseudonym of Richard Lower, *q.v.*, and of one impersonator)

'Claypuddle, Paul' (pseudonym of John Coker Egerton, *q.v.*)

Clayton, C.E. A narrative of a shepherd, communicated to E.V. Lucas by Mr Clayton. See E.V. Lucas (1904), 413.

Cook, W. Victor (1929) "Sussex 'wunt be druv'". *Sussex County Magazine* 3, 162. [Reprinted in Goldsworthy (1950), with light respellings.]

• A fuller version of the Sussex saying on which this title is based is that printed by Neville Hilditch, ed. (1950) *In praise of Sussex: an anthology for friends*. London: Frederick Muller, 47:

> You may push and you may shuv
> But I'm hemmed if I'll be druv.

The fullest and most explicit version known to the compiler is:

> And you may pook
> And you may shove,
> But a Sussex pig
> He wunt be druv.

This is quoted in J. Mainwaring Baines (1980) *Sussex pottery*. Brighton: Fisher Publications, 18, where it is also noted that certain nineteenth-century potteries in Sussex produced earthenware flasks in the shape of pigs, with 'Wunt be druv' incised or impressed on the pigs' neck.

How far back beyond that the traditional verse originates is not known. The connection between the motto, pigs, and the county crest is made explicit in an anonymous poem, "The Sussex crest and arms: a Sussex man's reply. 'We wun't be druv.'", published in the *Surrey Gazette* in 1887 and reprinted in C.F. Cook (1928), 230–1.

Note that the motto of the organization called The Men of Sussex is 'Non cogemur', a Latin translation of the motto.

Image 14: A china Sussex pig by Arcadian Pottery, Stoke, with a variant inscription

Copper, Bob (1994) *Across Sussex with Belloc. In the footsteps of 'The Four Men'*. Stroud: Alan Sutton. [Contains a transcript of a conversation with 'Fred' of Fletching (29–33) and of one with 'Goff' from Wisborough Green (70). The last verse of Copper's own poem "A shepherd's prayer" is in dialect (115).]

'Cote, Arthur I., M.A.' (pseudonym of Anthony Chamberlaine Brothers, *q.v.*)

Daish, W.G. (no date) "Selm 23. The Wateringbury version". In both the selections by Kathleen H. Strange noted under James Richards's version of Psalm 23; p. 37 of the 1969 edition (and p. 22 of its reprint) and p. 130 of that of 1978. [Daish was a Sussex man, and this item is included as it is not certain to what degree it is supposed to embody the Kent dialect of Wateringbury. I have heard scepticism about its Kentishness.]

Daish, W.G. (1956b) "De o'd megazine". *Sussex County Magazine* 30, 297. [Verse; addressed to *Sussex County Magazine* on its impending end.]

Daish, W.G. (1957) [Poem on James Richards, written in a letter to Stanley Godman; quoted in full in Godman's obituary of Daish; see Godman (1963) in Section C. Place of original publication, if any, unknown. See Part Two, Text 33.]

Dudeney, V.E. (1940) Heard in a Sussex inn. *Sussex County Magazine* 14, 383–4. [Invented dialogue, not convincing in several features.]

Egerton, [Rev.] John Coker (1857–88) Diaries. [Volumes in East Sussex Record Office, MSS. AMS 5637 and 6193. Contains occasional entries about dialect expressions (e.g. 16/10/1857) and anecdotes in dialect (e.g. 12/01/1878). Partially published by Roger Wells, ed. (1993) *Victorian village. The diaries of the Reverend John Coker Egerton, curate and rector of Burwash, East Sussex, 1857–88*. Stroud: Alan Sutton.]

Egerton, [Rev.] John Coker (writing as 'Paul Claypuddle') (1878) Labelled for Hayward's Heath. *Sussex Agricultural Express* (30/04/1878), 2–3. [The assumed name plays on *Cladpole, q.v.* The author's identity is revealed in his diary (30/04/1878), housed at East Sussex Record Office (see previous entry). The published piece itself may also be found in its original anonymity in the not fully catalogued 'Cladpole' box at the Sussex Archaeological Society library, Barbican House, Lewes.]

Evans, Harry (before 1880) *The Brighton beach loafer. His sentiments, sorrows, sayings and adventures chronicled in six chapters.* Brighton: Beal. [Second edition (1880), third edition (1888). Prose piece whose linguistic features are more those of stereotypical nineteenth-century Cockney than Sussex. Exhibits many deliberate misspellings ('eye dialect') as opposed to true dialect features.]

F., E. (dates unknown) "The downland shepherd". *Sussex County Herald.* [Verses mentioned in *Sussex County Magazine* 19 (1945), 162. Dates of publication not traced. It has recently been claimed, in *Sussex Express*, that E.F. was Edgar Flint of Lewes.]

Garland, George. Touring comedian (1930-60) performing a 'weak version' of rural Sussex dialect as the character Bill Stubbins (letter to the compiler from Miles Costello, 04/08/1991). He spoke "Our tallest story" in the BBC radio Forces Programme "Parish Mag" broadcast from Petworth on 01/08/1940. Miles Costello has notes for a parody used by Garland for National Farmers' Union and Women's Institute functions, and this may be the same material. Fred Streeter *(q.v.)* spoke on the same programme.

Garland, Patrick, ed. (1995) *Angels in the Sussex air. An anthology of Sussex poets.* London: Sinclair-Stevenson.

- The following dialectal or traditional material is included:

Bob Copper, two traditional songs (44–5)
Bob Copper, "A shepherd's prayer" (50)
some dialect words (71)
some notes on fairies (75–6)
extract from Arthur Beckett, "Song o' the Sussex men" (84)
W. Victor Cook, "Sussex won't be druv" (87)
Rudyard Kipling, "A three-part song" (153)
Lilian F. Ramsey, the "Mrs Paddick" story from the *West Sussex Gazette* of 15/02/1945 (191–2)

[Material attributed to an author in this list is also listed or alluded to elsewhere in Section D.]

Geering, Thomas, writing as 'T.G.H.', i.e. 'Thomas Geering of Hailsham' (1884) *Our parish: a medley, by one who has never lived out of it.* Lewes: Sussex Advertiser/ Hailsham: E.H. Baker. [New edition prepared under Geering's own name by Arthur Beckett (1925), entitled *Our Sussex parish.*

London: Methuen. Further reprint, with introduction by Richard Knowles, Bakewell: Country Books (2003). There are occasional slight dialectalisms in the passages of reminiscences about local characters.]

Goldsworthy, Margaret, ed. (1950) *A Sussex bedside anthology*. Bognor Regis: Arundel Press. [Contains several dialect pieces separately mentioned in this Bibliography; see Arthur Beckett, W. Victor Cook, Mark Antony Lower, Alfred Noyes, Frederick F. Wood.]

Hall, Helena E. (1957) *A dictionary of the Sussex dialect and collection of provincialisms in use in the county of Sussex, by the Rev W.D. Parish. Expanded, augmented and illustrated by Helena Hall, together with Some Sussex sayings and crafts*. Chichester: private. [Paperback edition Bexhill: Gardner's (1957). Revised and massively extended edition of Parish (1875), *q.v.* Contains anecdotes in dialect, especially in the section 'Some Sussex sayings and crafts'.]

Harbord, A.M. (1928) "Wildishers" [poem]. *Sussex County Magazine* 2, 253.

Henty, [given name unknown] (date uncertain; 1880s?) The tale of the Jevington organ. [Manuscript (possibly incomplete – end missing?) in private hands, present whereabouts unknown. Jevington's new organ was installed in 1873.]

Herbison, Vida (1979) Rudgwick: 'Where Ol' Nick got 'is gurt bell'. *Sussex Life* 15 (November), 30-3. [On 30–1 is a retelling with regional features of the folk-story about the loss and attempted recovery of Rudgwick bell.]

Herbison, Vida (1981) 'Sparrows is good but bony.' *Sussex Life* 19 [should be 17] (October), 56–7. [Reminiscences of Alfred Akehurst, knife-grinder, as taken down by Herbison; showing some vernacular colouring.]

'Hogpound, John' (pseudonym of W.D. Parish, *q.v.*)

Holmes, Frank (1970s) Letter about the virtue or otherwise of Horsham girls, to *West Sussex County Times*. Reprinted in Tony Wales (2000) *Sussex as she wus spoke*. Seaford: S.B. Publications, 104.Hopkins, R. Thurston (1929) "A windmill chanty". *Kipling's Sussex revisited.* London: Herbert Jenkins, 239–40. [Very slight dialect colouring.]

Hughes, Pam (2004) "Jawbation". *Poetry London* 49 (Autumn), 24, and in privately published anthologies. [Winner of second prize in the Poetry London competition. See Ralph Taylor (2008) Obituary. *The Guardian*, 17/08/2008. Printed in Part Two, Text 39.]

Jackson, E. Hatchett (1894) A page of Sussex dialect. *Southward Ho!* 1, 200–1, 250–1, 288–9, 338–9, 388–9, 432–3. [These amusing stories read well and the dialect is thickly laid on. Much of the text recalls Parish's *Dictionary*, but it would be hard to deny that some contributions were Jackson's own. Jackson was clearly well acquainted with the dialect. The second story is Part Two, Text 17.]

Jenner, J.H. (1935) Two labourers talking. *Sussex County Magazine* 9, 497. [Invented dialogue, appears forced.]

Jones, M. Fletcher (1930) "Dog ca-arts". *Sussex County Magazine* 4, 563–4.

Jones, M. Fletcher (1931) Talks with an old woodman. (1) Bill Spikins, (2) Dr Blackett, (3) Ben Fitt solves the rent problem, (4) Moses 'bests' a witch. *Sussex County Magazine* 5, 329, 431, 500, 516. [The editor of *Sussex County Magazine* calls these pieces 'actual reports of conversations with an old woodman who lives in a West Sussex village'. If this is true, the authentic voice is never fully identified; the 'author' appears to have memorized (and presumably edited) the monologues. Conversation (2) is Part Two, Text 24, in the present work.]

Kaye-Smith, Sheila (1926) The child born at the Plough (a Nativity play) and The shepherd of Lattenden (a Passion play). In *Saints in Sussex*. London: Cassell, 33–82 and 83–136. [Previous limited edition (250) London: Elkin Matthews (1923); but this (not seen) may consist of the poems in *Saints in Sussex* only. Several characters in the plays speak in dialect. See Part Two, Text 23a.]

[Lee, Kathleen] (1971/2) A shepherd's version [of Psalm 23]. *The Countryman* 76.4 (Winter), 135. [Reprinted in the anthologies by Kathleen M. Strange mentioned in the entry for James Richards's *De shepherd psalm*, e.g. p. 131 of the 1987 collection. 'In June 1946 an old shepherd recited this to me <i.e. K. Lee>, surrounded by his flock, on the Downs above Steyning in Sussex.' See Part Two, Text 29.]

Lloyd, E. Walford (1946) *Ol' Jarge: the story of a Sussex countryman.* Lewes: Sussex Express and County Herald. [Earlier versions of the material in this book were printed in the *Hampshire Telegraph and Post* and the *Portsmouth Evening News*. The central character is a farmworker, a sort of male counterpart to Mrs Paddick. Reviewed e.g. *Bognor Pos*t, 01/02/1947, *Hampshire Telegraph and Post*, 07/02/1947, *The Observer*, 08/02/1947. One extract is Part Two, Text 31.]

Lower, Mark Antony (1854c) The South Downs – a sketch. In his *Contributions to literature, historical, antiquarian, and metrical.* London: John Russell Smith, 146–92. [Contains (a) a passage on fairy folklore, 'The broken peel', told to Lower in c.1854 by William Fowington; this passage, partly in dialect, is on 156–63; it is reprinted by Jacqueline Simpson (1973) *The folklore of Sussex.* London: Batsford, 53–6, and see Part Two, Text 13a, of the present work; (b) a passage attributed to an anonymous shepherd, with some dialect colour, 167–71; also (c) the anonymous "Lines affixed to an old Sussex mill post", 187, discovered by Lower and often reprinted elsewhere.]

Lower, Mark Antony (1860) *The Song of Solomon. The dialect of Sussex. From the Authorised English Version*. London: G. Barclay (private (250 copies)). [Dialect notes on iii-iv. Done at the behest of the dialectologist Prince Louis-Lucien Bonaparte in 1859/60. (On Bonaparte's project, see also *The Times* (03/07/1961), 14 'Napoleon's last nephew', and Godman (1961).) Eight letters to Lower from Bonaparte or his secretary about the work are bound with a copy of *The Song of Solomon* in Brighton Area Library (S 223.9, B 47). *The Song of Solomon* is reprinted in Goldsworthy (1950). Chapter 3, verse 11 is reprinted as entry 361 in Eugene A. Nida, ed. (1972) *The book of a thousand tongues* [second edition]. London: United Bible Societies. Chapter 4 is reprinted in Lucas (1904), ch. 41. Note that this piece is often incorrectly ascribed to Richard Lower instead of Mark Antony Lower; most recently by James Milroy and Lesley Milroy, eds., *Real English: the grammar of English dialects in the British Isles* (Harlow: Longmans), 339 – ironically, as it is questionable how 'real' it is. See Part Two, Text 13b.]

Lower, Richard (writing as 'Tim Cladpole') (1830) *Tom Cladpole's jurney to Lunnun, shewing the many difficulties he met with and how he got safe home at last, told by himself and written in pure Sussex doggerel by his Uncle Tim.* Brighton: W. Leppard. [Skeat (1877) names the printer/publisher, but dates the first edition to 1831. Second printing ('the fifth thousand') Hailsham: S. Breads (probably 1844); third ('the seventh thousand') Lewes: Harberd (1849); fourth ('the eighth thousand') Lewes: Farncombe (1860); subsequently Lewes: Farncombe (1870), 'new and improved edition' Lewes: Farncombe (1872); possibly others subsequently, and a further printing, after 1928. There are minor differences of spelling between the various 'editions'. The second printing includes "Tom Cladpole's return". Reprinted also in Lower's *Stray leaves from an old tree, q.v.*, and parts as appendix 14 of Patrick Joyce (1991) *Visions of the people: industrial England and the question of class 1848–1914*. Cambridge: Cambridge University Press. Tony Fairman, in a letter to the Sussex Archaeological Society dated 17/04/1993 (Library, Barbican House, 'Cladpole' box), claims to detect the influence of the Kentish epic *Dick and Sal at Canterbury Fair* by J.W. Masters, published in 1821. Reprinted London: British Library (2010). See Part Two, Text 12a.]

Lower, Richard (writing as 'Tim Cladpole') "Tom Cladpole's return". See previous entry.

Lower, Richard (writing as 'Tim Cladpole') (probably 1844) *Jan Cladpole's trip to 'Merricur, giving an account of the white, black, and yellor folks, wot he met wud in his travels, in search for dollar trees, and how he got rich enough to beg his way home! Written all in rhyme by his father Tim Cladpole.* Hailsham: S. Breads. [Includes "Tim Cladpole's advice; or, No grumblen". Second printing (1860); third printing Lewes: Farncombe (1872); possible further printings (1967). (These are actually reprintings with no more than trivial amendments, but are called new editions.) Reprinted also in Lower's *Stray leaves from an old tree, q.v.* See Part Two, Text 12b.]

Lower, Richard (writing as 'Tim Cladpole') "Tim Cladpole's advice; or, No grumblen". See previous entry.

Lower, Richard (writing as 'Tim Cladpole') (1862) *Stray leaves from an old tree: selections from the scribblings of an octogenarian*. Lewes: G.P. Bacon. [A collection of verse in standard English, with a supplement consisting of a revised version of the *Jurney to Lunnun*, with the *Return* (119–52), and the *Trip to 'Merricur*, with the *Advice* (153–85). These are followed by a running glossary on the two main poems (187–90). The book also includes the essay "A stray leaf concerning old South-Down shepherds" (87–96) with representations of some local speech.]

Lower, Richard (writing as 'Tim Cladpole') (spine date 1872) The library of the Sussex Archaeological Society, Barbican House, Lewes has a bound volume containing the *Jurney to Lunnun* (and the *Return*) and the *Trip to 'Merricur* (and the *Advice*); and at the front is pasted in a newspaper cutting (consisting of a letter and commentary) in dialect, called "At the healtheries", over the name of 'Tom Cladpole', purporting to describe Tom's experiences in London. It is dated by hand "October 1884". (Richard Lower died in 1865.) I have not ascertained from which newspaper it came, nor who really wrote it.]

M., I.P. (1927) Old Tom's views on Labour. *Sussex County Magazine* 1, 490–2. [Author unknown. In (?mock-)interview format, with some eye-dialect. Reprinted in Aylwin Guilmant (1991) *Sussex of one hundred years ago.* Stroud: Alan Sutton, 41–3.]

Martineau, G.D. (1924) *Old Sussex and other poems. (Being the sentiments of a Sussex man expressed in divers surroundings.)* Cambridge: W. Heffer and Sons. [Contains the poems "Tom Jervis. The last of the Sussex shepherds" and "The carrier", in slight dialect. The dialect features of "A Sussex man in Ireland" are no more than conventional rusticisms.]

Martineau, G.D. (1925) *The way of the south wind.* Steyning: The Vine. [Contains the poems "The song of the old crabtree", "The iron waters", "Storm off Rye", "Chanctonbury tales", "The midnight bells" [see Part Two, Text 22] and "Crowborough Fair", all in a slight dialect exhibiting just the most salient local features. Note also "Furrin' parts", which is about, but not in, dialect. "Chanctonbury tales" is reprinted in C.F. Cook (1928). "Chanctonbury tales" appeared first in the *Downland Post* (new series) 1.4 (1924), 97 [cover], and "Furrin' parts" in 2.2 (1925), 55. Reviewed by P.I.B. in *Downland Post* (new series) 2.2 (1925), 57.]

Martineau, G.D. (1927) *A score, a score and ten.* London: Methuen. [Contains the poems "Furrin parts", "Crowborough Fair", "The carrier", "Storm off Rye" and "Tom Jervis (the Sussex shepherd)". See previous two items for other printings of these.]

• The author notes that some of his published verse first appeared in *Roussillon Gazette* (journal of the Royal Sussex Regiment), *Morning Post, Country Life, Downland Post* and other periodicals. The original place of publication of those mentioned has not been checked.

Noyes, Alfred (c.1913) "The silver crook". In his *Collected poems.* London: W. Blackwood. Also reprinted in Margaret Goldsworthy (1950), 99–104. [The shepherd's remarks are in dialect (though the phonological colouring is weak).]

Paddick, Mrs. Character created by Lilian F. Ramsey, *q.v.*

Parish, [Rev.] William Douglas (writing as 'John Hogpound') (c.1870) Account of the wedding of _____ at _____, Sussex, by a labourer of the parish. First published in an unascertained local newspaper, perhaps the *Sussex*

Agricultural Express. [Reprinted as an appendix to Egerton (1924), 167–70, where the identity of John Hogpound is made clear. This in turn is reprinted in Aylwin Guilmant (1991) *Sussex of one hundred years ago*. Stroud: Alan Sutton, 103–4, where it is wrongly ascribed to Egerton. See Part Two, Text 15b.]

Parish, [Rev.] William Douglas (writing as 'John Hogpound') (c.1870) John Hogpound's account of the Shah. First published in an unascertained local newspaper, perhaps the *Sussex Agricultural Express*. [Reprinted as an appendix to Egerton (1924), 170–2; see previous item.]

Parish, [Rev.] William Douglas (1875) *A dictionary of the Sussex dialect and collection of provincialisms in use in the county of Sussex*. Lewes: Farncombe. [The dictionary entries contain numerous brief anecdotes in dialect. Later editions Hall (1957); Richardson (2001); Truss (2008). See Part Two, Text 15a.]

Parsons, A.V. (1933) Takin' a wopses nes'. *Sussex County Magazine* 7, 570.

'Penfold, Mus'', identity unknown (said to be from before 1900) "Mus' Penfold's ABC of Lindfield." [I have not found this poem in print, but it is online at http://www.visitoruk.com/historydetail.php?id=51195&f=Crawley, accessed 11/05/2010.]

Ramsey, Lilian F. (writing as 'A Sussex Woman') Weekly column in the *West Sussex Gazette*, 1936–74; featuring the dialect-speaking character Mrs Paddick. First appeared 06/08/1936 and has been much reprinted by the *Gazette*, most recently from 11/04/1991 onwards. A selection of 18 was printed in a feature in the *Gazette*, 08/01/1998, 6. One such column is printed here in Part Two, Text 30a. [Note the obituary of Miss Ramsey by John Worsley, *West Sussex Gazette*, 21/02/1974, and the letter from him recounting the facts of her life, *West Sussex Gazette*, 14/09/1995.]

Ramsey, Lilian F. (writing as 'A Sussex Woman') (1956) *Mrs. Paddick talks Sussex*. Arundel: West Sussex Gazette. [Selection of 30 stories from *West Sussex Gazette*, see previous item.

Ramsey, Lilian F. (writing as 'Margaret Wyndham') (1947) *Mrs. Paddick*. London: Chapman and Hall. [A selection of *West Sussex Gazette* columns (see above), organized into 18 chapters. One such column is Part Two, Text 30b.]

- Lilian Ramsey's papers are held at West Sussex Record Office, Add MSS. 46195–46244 (1885–1974), but not publicly available till 2013.

‘Rhymeo’, ps., identified as Mark Melford (c.1872) “Dickey Snickle”. A manuscript with this title is referred to in a letter of James Richards to Capt. A.W.F. Fuller dated 18/04/1939 when, according to the letter, it was in Capt. Fuller’s possession. It is now in West Sussex Record Office, Add MSS. 2914. [The Access to Archives copy of the WSRO catalogue entry states: ‘A MS. novel in Sussex dialect, with references to Graffham and Midhurst, and the Midhurst Union Workhouse. The author has been identified by Captain Fuller as Mark Melford (d. 1914). His name does not appear in the *Dictionary of National Biography.* The book is written in a foolscap volume of 182 ff. bound in calf. On the front flyleaf are stuck four cuttings from the *West Sussex Gazette*, 1940, of Sussex dialect articles, and two letters concerning proposed publication of the MS. in the *Sussex County Magazine*, 1937 [which never happened, RC].’]

Richards, James (writing as ‘Jim Cladpole’).

- Note in the entries that follow that several works are described as running to more than one edition. In Richards’s own estimation (letter to Capt. A.W.F. Fuller, 01/04/1939), only *De good news according to Mark* contains substantial revisions in editions subsequent to the first. Barring trivial discrepancies, these ‘editions’ are better called ‘printings’; or would certainly be if Richards had not entirely reset the text for each new printing.

- Seven manuscript letters of Richards, six to Capt. A.W.F. Fuller and one to an unknown person (03–05/1939), which include comment on the genesis and printing history of some of his works, are held by the Sussex Archaeological Society, Barbican House, Lewes (the uncatalogued ‘Cladpole’ box).

Richards, James (writing as ‘Jim Cladpole’) (late 1920s) Some verses in *Local News*, the newsletter of the Tunbridge Wells Labour Party. [I have been unable to trace any of this material. It appears to have gone from the local party archives. See the pieces on Richards’s work in *Methodist Times* (19/12/1935) and *Daily Herald* (15/06/1939).]

Richards, James (writing as ‘Jim Cladpole’) (1927) “Firle Beacon”. [Printed in August. Reprinted (1945); also in full in Godman (1957); and by Miles Costello (1991c). See Part Two, Text 25a.]

Richards, James (writing as 'Jim Cladpole') (no date [1928]) *'Bout me: or my ottybograffy. Writ and prented all by himself.* Tunbridge Wells: private ('very limited', JR). [Second edition (1930) and third edition (1931). Noticed by A[rthur] B[eckett] in *Sussex County Magazine* 2 (1928), 384.]

Richards, James (writing as 'Jim Cladpole') (1930) *Summat 'bout Sussex an sum Sussexers*. Tunbridge Wells: private. [Printed in June. One edition only. See Part Two, Text 25b.]

Richards, James (writing as 'Jim Cladpole') (1934) *De good news according to Mark, put into de Sussex dialect by J.C.* Tunbridge Wells: private (100 copies – 'I be onny printing a hunderd of dese liddle books so ef I dunt sell any at all dere wunt be a gurt lot left over', JR). [The Gospel according to Mark. Second edition (September 1934; 150 copies); third edition (February 1936; 150 copies). With 400 copies printed, this is the least rare of all Jim Cladpole's works. Mark 2.23–28 is reprinted, with some minor alterations, in *Bits from de Old Book, q.v.* The first printing is noticed by B[?].A[?]. in *Sussex County Magazine* 8 (1934), 167–8.]

Richards, James (approx. 1934) A rendering of the Nativity, printed in A.A. Evans, *A saunterer in Sussex*. London: Methuen (1935), chapter 25 "A Sussex mystery play" (233-4 of this). [Note: this is not reprinted in *Bits from de Old Book, q.v.*]

Richards, James (writing as 'Jim Cladpole') (1935a) *De sermons of Amos, a cowman and local preacher from Tekoa.* Tunbridge Wells: private. [The Book of Amos. Printed in January. Second edition March 1936. Excerpts reprinted in *Bits from de Old Book, q.v.* First edition noticed by A.A. E[vans] in *Sussex County Magazine* 9 (1935), 780.]

Richards, James (writing as 'Jim Cladpole'). (1935b) *De Song of Songs, by Solomon.* Tunbridge Wells: private. [Second edition April 1936. Excerpts reprinted in *Bits from de Old Book, q.v.* First edition noticed by A.A. E[vans] in *Sussex County Magazine* 9 (1935), 780. Richards wrote this deliberately without reference to M.A. Lower's version (see the preface "At de wicket gäate"), and without reference to Ruskin Butterfield's, which was apparently unknown to him, *qq.v.*]

Richards, James (writing as 'Jim Cladpole') (1935c) *De lilies of de fills. A liddle sermon in de Sussex dialect by Jim Cladpole.* Tunbridge Wells: private. [Printed in October. Second printing (1936). Prepared for reprinting, coupled with "Firle Beacon", by Miles Costello (1991).]

Richards, James (writing as 'Jim Cladpole') (1935d) *De letter of James.* Tunbridge Wells: private. [The Epistle of James. Printed in September. Second edition May 1936. Excerpts reprinted in *Bits from de Old Book, q.v.* First edition noticed by A.A. E[vans] in *Sussex County Magazine* 9 (1935), 780.]

Richards, James (writing as 'Jim Cladpole') (1936a) *De story of Ruth, a gell from de country* [*couutry* [sic] on title-page]. Tunbridge Wells: private. [The Book of Ruth. Printed in May. Excerpts reprinted in *Bits from de Old Book, q.v.* See Part Two, Text 25c.]

Richards, James (writing as 'Jim Cladpole') (1936b) *A word picter of two sons by Saver of Nazareth. Luke 15: 11–72.* Tunbridge Wells: private. [Parable of the Prodigal Son. Printed in August. Also in *Bits from de Old Book, q.v.*]

Richards, James (writing as 'Jim Cladpole') (1936c) *De love letters of old John.* Tunbridge Wells: private. [The three epistles of John. Printed in August. Excerpts reprinted in *Bits from de Old Book, q.v.*]

Richards, James (writing as 'Jim Cladpole') (1937) *De shepherd psalm.* Tunbridge Wells: private. [Psalm 23. Printed in January. Also printed Tunbridge Wells: Wood Press (1945), according to Godman (1957a) [unverified]; and in *Grail Magazine* (December 1955); *Sussex County Magazine* 30 (March 1956), 129; and Payne (1988a) (*q.v.*). It is further reprinted in two collections: Kathleen H. Strange, ed. (1969) *Psalm 23: several versions collected and put together by K.H. Strange.* Tunbridge Wells: private, 35–6 (republished Edinburgh: St Andrew Press (1970), 20–1); and Kathleen H. Strange and Richard G.E. Sandbach, eds (1978, new edition 1987) *Psalm 23: an anthology*. Edinburgh: Church of Scotland Bookshop (republished Edinburgh: St Andrew Press (1987)), 128 (of the 1987 edition) with a brief biography of Richards on 129. This latter book also contains a version by Daish (*q.v.*) and a third Sussex version by an anonymous shepherd (see Lee (1971/2)). See Part Two, Text 25d.]

Richards, James (writing as 'Jim Cladpole') (1938) *Bits from de Old Book. Being one or more bits from each of de sixtysix books of de Bible. Put into de Sussex tongue by J.C.* Tunbridge Wells: private (120 copies). [Printed in December. The texts sometimes partly duplicate separate printings of the biblical material, and, being reset, differ in small ways from the separate versions. Verses from the Gospel of Mark in this version are Part Two, Text 25e.]

Richards, James (writing as 'Jim Cladpole') (date not ascertained, but c.1938) *Two psalms. Put into de Sussex dialect by J.C.* Tunbridge Wells: private. [A very rare penny pamphlet containing Psalm 112 (see next item) and Psalm 133. A typescript in Brighton Area Library (Sussex pamphlets box 74) and in the library of the Sussex Archaeological Society, Barbican House, Lewes ('Cladpole' box, not fully catalogued), contains Psalm 133.]

Richards, James (writing as 'Jim Cladpole') (1938) *De A.B.C. psalms. Put into de Sussex dialect and in due A.B.C. feshion by J.C.* [Contains the Acrostic Psalms 9, 10, 25, 34, 37, 111, 112, 119, 145. Autograph manuscript notebook at the library of the Sussex Archaeological Society, Barbican House, Lewes ('Cladpole' box). Other typed copies are known to have been made by the good offices of Mrs Wood of Regent's Park, London; present whereabouts not known. Edited for publication by Richard Coates (1992) *De A.B.C. psalms. Put into de Sussex dialect and in due A.B.C. feshion by Jim Cladpole. April 1938.* Brighton: Younsmere Press.]

Richards, James (writing as 'Jim Cladpole') (1939) "De stoolball match. Kent v. Sussex, 14th. June". *Sussex County Magazine* 13, 571. [Richards's last new published work in dialect. The genesis of this poem (presumably written in 1938) is referred to in Richards's letter of 15/04/1939 to Capt. A.W.F. Fuller.]

> • Note that Richards also contributed a piece about the Town Hall in Kent dialect to Dick Baker's *Guide to Tunbridge Wells* (Tunbridge Wells: J. Richards, 1932 or 1934). I have not seen a copy of this.

Tabular chronological summary of Richards's output (bracketed numbers are 'editions' or printings):

before 1928	verses in Newsletter of Tunbridge Wells Labour Party
1927	Firle Beacon (1)
1928	'Bout me (1)
1930 June	Summat 'bout Sussex an sum Sussexers
	'Bout me (2)
1931	'Bout me (3)
1932/4 February	Tunbridge Wells Town Hall (Kent dialec)
1934	Carpenter (not dialect)
	Mark (1)
	Nativity

1934 September	Mark (2)
1935 January	Amos (1)
	Song of Songs (1)
1935 September	James (1)
1935 October	De lilies of de fills (1)
1936 February	Mark (3)
1936 March	Amos (2)
1936 April	Song of Songs (2)
1936	De lilies of de fills (2)
1936 May	Ruth
	James (2)
1936 August	Two sons
	John
1937 January	De shepherd psalm
1937 August	High Brooms (not dialect)
1938 April	De A.B.C. Psalms (unpublished in author's lifetime)
1938 December	Bits from de Old Book
1938?	Two psalms
1939	De stoolball match (written in 1938?)
1945	Firle Beacon (2)
1946	Joseph, the husband of Mary (not dialect)

Sawyer, Amy (1929) The brown pot. *Sussex County Magazine* 3, 107–12. [Also in Sawyer (1934), 1–14.]

Sawyer, Amy (1931) The black tea party: a one act play. *Sussex County Magazine* 5, 251–5. [Also in Sawyer (1934), 33–50. See Part Two, Text 26.]

Sawyer, Amy (1934) *Sussex village plays and others*. Hove: Combridge's. [A significant number of the plays are totally or almost totally in dialect (for help with which the author thanks Fred Wood *(q.v.)* and George Davey), and others contain dialect-speaking characters. The author makes a clear distinction between Sussex and Cockney characters, but the depth of the Sussex vernacular is variable. Some characters speak a somewhat general non-standard dialect. All the plays were written for performance by the Ditchling Village Players. *The weeping willow* was performed in Chichester by The Chichester Players on 6 November 1997.]

In dialect:
The brown pot
The s'tif'icate
The token
The black tea party

The weeping willow
At the sign of the bow-legged blackbird
Mrs. Puttock and the ocean

With some dialect-speaking characters:
Miss Dove
King Alfred
A quiet day in Arcadia
Old Marthy
Granny's wireless
The wind from Fairyland

Sellens, Robert (1950s) Untitled poem about West Hoathly church spire. *East Grinstead Observer*, date uncertain. [Reprinted *East Grinstead Museum Compass* 5 (2001), 5.] Also "Turnin' up rough", *EGM Compass* 8 (Summer 2002), 4; see Text 38.)

Thorpe, Stewart M. (no date) "The Wilmington Giant." Publisher unknown. [Poem in convincing dialect published on a folded card. Bound copy (differing title on front board) held by the Sussex Archaeological Society Library, Barbican House, Lewes. Nothing whatever known about its author or its origin.]

traditional; published by F.E. Sawyer (1884c) Sussex 'tipteerers'' play. *Folk-Lore Journal* 2.1, 1–8. [The play is the Sussex Christmas mumming play, called "The seven champions of Christendom" (though note that it has never been restricted to Sussex). This version is from Steyning, with bits from versions from Sompting and Brighton, cf. Sawyer (1883a); and cf. 'The mummers' play' forming the first appendix of Parish (1875), not localized, but implied by Hall (1957) to have been the version of Selmeston and other places. Sawyer's version is reprinted by Frank Rinder in 'Fragments of Sussex folk lore VIII', *Southward Ho!* 2 (1895), 3–9, esp. 6–9. The West Wittering version is printed by Boger (1901, see Section C8). A further version of the play, from Compton, appears in Arthur Beckett (1911) *The wonderful Weald, and the quest of the crock of gold.* London: Mills and Boon, 377-86, and there is extended relevant material in his *Adventures of a quiet man*. Hove: Combridge's (1933), chapter 37. The Compton play is reprinted in Geoff Doel and Fran Doel (1992) *Mumming, howling and hoodening: midwinter rituals in Sussex, Kent and Surrey.* Rainham: Meresborough Books (1992), 48–55. Another version is in Sharp (1931); this is from East Preston, padded out with bits from the Iping version. For this latter, see also Alex Helm (1981) *The English mummers' play*. Woodbridge:

D.S. Brewer/Rowman and Littlefield, for the Folklore Society, 80–3, where the mummers' play from Iping from the Vaughan Williams Collection at Cecil Sharp House, London, is printed. A Ditchling version, taken down by T. Standing, was collected by Isobel Horn and published in 1921 as *King George and the Turkish knight.* Ditchling: St. Dominic's Press. There is scarcely a hint of dialect in any of the versions; they are included mainly for their folkloric importance. For more comment, see Lillian Candlin (1987) The Sussex tipteerers. In her *Memories of old Sussex*. Newbury: Countryside Books, 36–40.]

Wills, Barclay (1938) *Shepherds of Sussex*. London: Skeffington and son. [Includes the poem "By the way", largely in dialect (246–7), and the chapter "An old shepherd's opinion" (242–5); there are other snippets of dialect *passim*, esp. 185–207, 239–41. Wills's area was the west-central Downs. For the anecdote on p. 198, see Part Two, Text 21.]

Wills, Barclay (1989) *The downland shepherds* [ed. by Shaun Payne and Richard Pailthorpe; illustrated by Gordon Beningfield; extracts from books published in Wills's lifetime]. Gloucester: Alan Sutton. [Includes a section on sheep-counting (58–9; cf. Ellis (1889)); a shepherding glossary on 165–70; and the poem "I be 'bout done" on 159–60. There is scattered dialect in Wills's *Shepherds of Sussex* (see previous entry), *Bypaths in downland* (London: Methuen, 1927) and *Downland treasure* (London: Methuen, 1929). In the first of these, Wills uses *t'* for the definite article (*t'sheep*), giving his dialogues a Yorkshire appearance, but this usage is also found in the work of Fred Wood from Ditchling.]

Winckler, Doris M. (1956) Letter to the editor [in dialect]. *Sussex County Magazine* 30, 197–8. [Response to Daish (1956a), Section C2. Nothing else by this writer is known.]

Wood, Frederick F. (1925) *Round about Sussex Downs*. London: Duckworth. [Chapter XIV is entitled "Old sayings, and dialect".]

Wood, Frederick F. (1928) *Sport and nature in Sussex Downs*. London: Duckworth. [35-6 and Chapter X "Tales of old Sussex folk" (110–6) contain representations of dialect speech. There are smaller instances scattered elsewhere in the book. The story of "The wandering apothecary" (112–4) is reprinted in Margaret Goldsworthy (1950), 336–7.]

'Wyndham, Margaret' (pseudonym of Lilian F. Ramsey, *q.v.*)

Young, Ernest W. (no date [1936]) *The pageant of East Grinstead High Street and Reminiscences of Old George*. East Grinstead: Cullen's. [The six *Reminiscences* and the associated *Epilogue* appeared in the *East Grinstead Observer* in 1928 and 1929 respectively (see biography of Young in Leppard 2000; Section F). The dialect colour of these playlets/conversations is thin and marked with the conventional features of written uneducated speech, but for the most part the dialect is not even conventional Sussex.]

Section D1.3:
REJECTS

The following books are entered in the Bibliography to Joseph Wright's *English dialect dictionary* as being of relevance to Sussex. Others mentioned by Wright are entered in the appropriate place in the Bibliography.

Crommelin, Maria Henrietta de la Cherois (writing as 'May Crommelin') (1890) *Midge*. London: Trischler. [The small amount of non-standard English used in direct speech does not suggest Sussex, and nothing in the book localizes it to Sussex.]

Gordon, James (1897) *The village and the doctor*. London: Methuen. [Eight stories, set in West Sussex. Dialogue contains non-standard features, of which the few that definitely suggest Sussex dialect are not consistently applied and are sometimes wrong. But it is found convincing by an anonymous writer in *Scribble* 1.4 (1917).]

These items should perhaps also be tabulated in Section E.

Section D2:
REGIONAL TRACES IN LOCAL DOCUMENTS

No systematic work has been done on Sussex regionalisms in otherwise standard English documents from the late Middle Ages onwards. It is not possible, of course, to list every document which contains some linguistic trace of Sussex, but an account can be given of the types of document which might fruitfully be studied. The following subsections D2a-2e indicate material on which such work might build. Attention is drawn especially to the publications of the Sussex Record Society, which include early registers, wills, court documents, stewards' accounts and custom-books, and so on. Smaller documents have been published or excerpted in *Sussex Archaeological Collections* and the now-defunct *Sussex Notes and Queries*.

It should be remembered that standardized spelling did not become a serious issue even among intellectuals till the eighteenth century. The capricious spellings of local churchwardens and yeomen found in early documents are not necessarily evidence of dialect, and require careful interpretation. For instance, the West Tarring church accounts (Pressey 1931–41) mention the *pore vockes* (1563), which surely represents local pronunciation, as do *charche house* and *plonnke* 'plank' (1564) and *hoscloth* (1574). But whilst *myelmas* (1568) may be a genuine archaic survival or regionalism (cf. *myhell slattar* (1571) 'Michael Slatter'), to be set against *mykelmas* in the following entry, it is quite possible that it represents *myclmas*, as found in 1564, and may be a true error or a mistranscription.

Other variants of the word CHURCH, e.g. *chirche, cherch(e), cheurche, chearch, church(e), chyrche,* are probably of no significance, with all these vowel combinations probably representing the still-current pronunciation. The ornate *leygke* of mutton noted in 1562, and the *whale* 'wall' of 1559, probably tell us nothing (unless that the /w~ʍ/ distinction was under threat), and neither does the *mendedyng of tthe chyresys getteyes* 'mending of the church gates' (1597), in a passage where the writer seems addicted to duplication of letters and letter-sequences.

Section D2a: INVENTORIES, ACCOUNT-BOOKS and comparable documents

An unusual surviving document is the parish inventory and accounts of Cowfold from the end of the fifteenth century, mentioned in the Introduction (Otter 1849; see Part Two, Text 4). A very few other sets of early accounts of this type have been published. They are often of some linguistic interest, especially as sources of regional vocabulary. Attention is drawn especially to the extensive accounts of West Tarring from the late sixteenth century onwards published by Pressey (1931–41).

Probate inventories are also an occasional source of local vocabulary, since their golden age (c.1520–1750) spanned a period when local usage was not yet totally moribund, and since their contents, lists of common household objects, were unusually resistant to replacement by equivalent legal terminology. Drawing them up was entrusted to two neighbours of good standing, who might be fully literate but employ a local accent, so that there might be indications of local pronunciation in their spelling too. In later decades, workhouse and estate agents' inventories also contain regionalisms. Few of any of these later sorts of document have been published, and the dialectologist may still have a good deal to learn from them and from those which remain unread in archives, especially county record offices. The list below comprises only published (including excerpted) documents, and is not intended to be exhaustive.

anonymous (1928) A Warnham farmer's goods. *Sussex Notes and Queries* 2, 86–7. [Of George Worsfold.]

anonymous [probably Arundell Esdaile] (1941) Live and dead stock at Alciston manor, 1536. *Sussex Notes and Queries* 9, 129–31.

Dale, Joseph (1853) Extracts from churchwardens' accounts and other matters belonging to the parish of Bolney contained in a manuscript book of the time of Henry VIII. *Sussex Archaeological Collections* 6, 244–52.

Ellis, [Sir] Henry (1861) Inventories of goods, &c., in the manor of Cheseworth, Sedgwick, and other parks [etc.] *Sussex Archaeological Collections* 13, 118–31. [Contains some indications of a disyllabic pronunciation of words like *four, ore*, well attested later. See Part Two, Text 8a.]

Godman, Percy S. (1908) Two Sussex inventories. *Sussex Archaeological Collections* 51, 115–122. [Those of James Stilwell (1677) and Elizabeth Capron (1747); the latter from Ambersham.]

Hall, Helena (1940) An inventory of 1804. *Sussex Notes and Queries* 8, 40–2. [A Lindfield workhouse document.]

Hall, Maurice (1985) *Bosham and its Berkeley barons: a medieval manor 1483–1919.* Privately published. [Includes inventories of Robert Trimlet (1612) and Thomas Pannell (1644), on 137–42, 169–71).]

Hughes, Annabelle F. (1994) Horsham probate inventories. *West Sussex History* 53, 29–32. [Includes transcriptions of one from the seventeenth and one from the eighteenth century.]

Hughes, Annabelle F. (2007) *Sussex clergy inventories, 1660–1750.* Lewes: Sussex Record Society (SRS vol. 91).

Kean, Graham, and Tony Ketteman (1995) *Sussex downland portraits. Life in Patcham, Preston, Hangleton and West Blatchington as seen through probate and other records, 1650–1750.* Privately published. [Includes over a dozen complete inventories, and a glossary (203–6).]

Kenyon, G.H. (1954-6) Three Kirdford inventories. *Sussex Notes and Queries* 14, 3–10, 43–6, 145–57.

Kenyon, G.H. (1955) Kirdford inventories, 1611 to 1776. *Sussex Archaeological Collections* 93, 78–156. [See Part Two, Text 8b.]

Kenyon, G.H. (1960, 1961) Petworth town and trades, 1610–1760, parts II and III. *Sussex Archaeological Collections* 98, 71–117, and 99, 102–35 (appendices to parts II and III). [Includes (abstracts of) inventories, mostly in modernized spelling, however.]

McCann, Timothy J., comp. (1981) *West Sussex probate inventories, 1521–1834: a catalogue.* Chichester: West Sussex County Council. [Four-microfiche set.]

Otter, W. Bruere (1849) Churchwardens' accounts of the parish of Cowfold in the time of king Edward IV. *Sussex Archaeological Collections* 2, 316–25. [See Part Two, Text 4.]

P[eckham], W.D. (1957) A Chichester inventory of 1653. *Sussex Notes and Queries* 14, 243–5. [Of Thomas Teeling.]

Perry, [Capt.] John L. (1939) Hay's Farm, Beckley: some notes from an inventory of 1825. *Sussex County Magazine* 13, 352–3.

Pressey, W.J. (1931-41) The churchwardens' accounts of West Tarring, 1579–1631. *Sussex Notes and Queries* 3–8, in numerous separate parts.

Salzman, Louis F. (1911) Early churchwardens' accounts, Arlington. *Sussex Archaeological Collections* 54, 85–112. [These fifteenth-century accounts are in Latin, but contain a good number of interesting English words evidently too hard for the clerk to translate.]

Standing, Richard W. (1980) Probate inventories: East Preston and Kingston. *West Sussex History* 17, 1–5.

Steer, Francis W. (1956) A Sussex mansion in the eighteenth century. *Sussex Archaeological Collections* 94, 13–34. [Includes several inventories from Sheffield Park.]

Steer, Francis W. (1967) A Cowdray inventory of 1682. *Sussex Archaeological Collections* 105, 84–102. [Glossary on page 102.]

Storey, Harry (1939) An inventory of 1615. *Sussex Notes and Queries* 7, 201–4. [Of John Fuller, Waldron.]

Whitley, H. Michell (1902) The churchwardens' accounts of St Andrew's and St Michael's, Lewes, from 1522 to 1601. *Sussex Archaeological Collections* 45, 40–61.

Whitley, H. Michell (1912) Inventory of the goods and chattels of William Shelley of Michelgrove. *Sussex Archaeological Collections* 55, 284–298. [A sixteenth-century document in TNA, catalogue ref. E 199/43/32.]

Williams, I.L. (1992) A first look at Midhurst inventories. *West Sussex History* 49, 29–31.

• In addition to those in the county record offices, there are early Sussex inventories in The National Archives (in addition to any mentioned above); their catalogue references are E 199/43/22, E 199/43/23, E 199/43/31 (all sixteenth century), PROB 32/31/306 and PROB 32/67/96 (both seventeenth century), and PROB 32/46/86 (1702).

• A linguistically very interesting bill for repairs to Chichester cathedral weathercock, dating from 1638, was published by C.E. Welch in *Sussex Notes and Queries* 15 (1961), 273–4. [See Part Two, Text 6.]

Section D2b: WILLS

Early wills, where written in English, occasionally show local linguistic features, sometimes mysteriously. For instance, Tudor wills of the far west of the county (Westbourne) – not to mention Tudor account-books from the far east – sporadically have such spellings as *wyker* for 'vicar', and the significance of this is unknown. No systematic dialectological work has been done on them, so far as I know. (For the phenomenon itself, see now Poussa (1995).) Rock (1862: 188-9) noted the inverse phenomenon of /v/ for /w/ at Hastings, a feature which at the time of his writing was stereotypically associated with Folkestone. Any such work is not likely to be very productive because wills, unlike inventories, were normally drawn up by writers fully literate in the standard language.

Several volumes of Sussex wills have been published by the Sussex Record Society, Lewes, by R. Garraway Rice and W.H. Godfrey (vols. 41–43, 45 (1935, 1937, 1938, 1940)). Calendars are available of others, which will lead researchers to the relevant originals. Those proved in the consistory court of the diocese of Chichester between 1482 and 1800 have been calendared by the British Record Society as volume 49 of their Index Library (1915), and those in the Dean of Chichester's peculiar court between 1577 and 1800 by the same society (1940). The archdeaconry of Lewes calendars appear as volume 24 of the Index Library (1901). The British Record Society issued an earlier calendar of Sussex wills dating from 1541 to 1652 (1895). Mark Antony Lower published an article entitled 'On some wills of inhabitants of Herstmonceux and neighbouring parishes' in *Sussex Archaeological Collections* 4 (1851), 203–8, containing extracts.

Section D2c: MONUMENTAL INSCRIPTIONS

No systematic work has yet been done on monumental inscriptions as a source of information about dialect, though certain ones are very well known as showing local – or at least non-standard – features. These include the ones commemorating Sir Nicholas Pelham (St Michael's, Lewes (1559)), John Parson (West Tarring (1683)), Alice Woolldridge (Poling (1740)), Richard Turner (Lindfield (1768)), Thomas Tipper (Newhaven (1785)), Sarah Strevens (Edburton (1792)) and Wilfrid Scawen Blunt (Newbuildings Place, Southwater (1922)); these may be found collected in Arscott (1997).

Turner's was the only one displaying dialect features known to Helena Hall (1957: 171), but I have come across others. Inscriptions in the churchyards of Wadhurst and Bishopstone, for example, contain instances of the spelling *daftar* for *daughter*; the graveslab of Rev. Thomas Scriven (Poling (1722)) features the dialect grammatical form 'near 15 year', whilst the same slab says his son at death was 'aged above 3 Years'. It is extremely unlikely that any gravemarkers in Sussex made after about 1820 show any features of non-standard English at all except the self-conscious one of Blunt which is also quoted above at the end of Chapter 5 in Part One.

A start to a research project might be made by considering the extensive transcripts made by E.H.W. Dunkin, E. Sayers and others, and kept in binders entitled 'Sussex monumental inscriptions' at the East and West Sussex Record Offices and on open shelves in the library of ths Sussex Archaeological Society, Barbican House, Lewes. These volumes observe, very usefully, the convention of reproducing in full all inscriptions dating from before 1700, which is the period when unconscious dialect usage is most likely to occur, emanating either from the drafter's or the stonecutter's vernacular.

Note occasional regionalisms in the epitaphs recorded in:

Arscott, David (1997) *Dead and buried in Sussex*. Seaford: S.B. Publications; new edition (2007), Lewes: Pomegranate Press.

Section D2d: PARISH REGISTERS

Early parish registers, where written in English as opposed to Latin, may show some local features, but they have not been the subject of systematic study. We may note, for instance, that the Hove registers for 1632 and subsequent years give evidence for a regional pronunciation of the word *daughter* in such spellings as *Dafhter, dather, dafter*; on the other hand *datar* presumably represents something like the standard pronunciation.

Many of the oldest survivors were written up by the parish priest himself, and are thus relatively unlikely to show many dialect forms, all priests of the established church being university-educated (or at least that was the episcopal aspiration) since around 1800, and very many before then. Some Sussex registers are excerpted by R. Blencowe in *Sussex Archaeological Collections* 4 (1851), 243–90, but the English is largely modernized, unfortunately for our purposes. A number of registers have been published by the Sussex Record Society (mainly in the 1910s) and by private individuals with a similar interest; these are listed below, but with no guarantee of any importance for dialect study.

Crawfurd, R.P., ed. (1917) *The parish register of East Grinstead, Sussex, 1558–1661*. Lewes: Sussex Record Society (vol. 24).

Godman, P.S., ed. (1916) *The parish register of Cowfold, Sussex, 1558–1812.* Lewes: Sussex Record Society (vol. 22).

Huth, E., ed. (1912) *The parish registers of Bolney, Sussex, 1541–1812.* Lewes: Sussex Record Society (vol. 15).

Loder, G.W.E., ed. (1913) *The parish registers of Ardingly, Sussex, 1558–1812*. Lewes: Sussex Record Society (vol. 17).

Penfold, E.W.D., ed. (1913) *The first book of the parish registers of Angmering, Sussex, 1562–1687*. Lewes: Sussex Record Society (vol. 18).

Renshaw, W.C., ed. (1911) *The parish registers of Cuckfield, Sussex, 1598–1699*. Lewes: Sussex Record Society (vol. 13).

Rice, R. Garraway, ed. (1915) *The parish register of Horsham in the county of Sussex, 1541–1635*. Lewes: Sussex Record Society (vol. 21).

Salmon, Ernest F., ed. (1912) *The parish registers of Hove and Preston, 1538–1812*. London: Mitchell Hughes (by subscription).

Salzman, Louis F., ed. (1924) *The parish register of Glynde, Sussex, 1558–1812*. Lewes: Sussex Record Society (vol. 30).

Wilkie, C.H., ed. (1900) *Second parish register book, 1656–1812, St. Andrew's Church (Edburton)*. Brighton: Bishop. [Limited edition of 30 copies.]

Other Sussex registers are indexed in the following:

Palgrave-Moore, P.T.R., ed. (1980) *National index of parish registers, vol. 4: South East England : Kent, Surrey and Sussex*. London: Society of Genealogists.

Tallis, J.A., comp. (1974) *Original parish registers in record offices and libraries*. Cambridge: Cambridge Group for the History of Population and Social Structure/ Matlock: Local Population Studies. [Note also subsequent supplements.]

Section D2e: DEPOSITIONS TO QUARTER SESSIONS

A further potential source may be the personal depositions to quarter sessions; but again, no linguistic work has been done on these, to the compiler's knowledge. They are usually written on paper in English, and may be found among the sessions rolls. In 1954, the authorities in East Sussex issued *A descriptive report on the quarter sessions, other official and ecclesiastical records in the custody of the county councils of East and West Sussex, with a guide to the development and historical interest of the archives* (Lewes: East Sussex County Council), which provides a starting point for anyone motivated to do the groundwork. Sussex quarter sessions orders from 1642–7 have been published by the Sussex Record Society (volume 54), under the editorship of B.C. Redwood (Lewes, no date [?1955]).

Section E:
BOOKS AND SHORTER WORKS IN STANDARD ENGLISH WITH A SIGNIFICANT AMOUNT OF DIRECT SPEECH IN DIALECT OR WITH DIALECT WORDS USED AND EXPLAINED

The distinction between items in this section and those in section D1.2 is a fine one, and items have been placed in D1.2 where I judge that they are particularly important for the consideration of dialect.

anonymous (1954a) "The snaring of 'The Albatross'". *The Worthing Parade Number Two*. Worthing: Aldridge Bros (Worthing Art Development Scheme), 81–90. [Dialect used in the speech of some characters.]

anonymous (1954b) "Caught". *The Worthing Parade Number Two.* Worthing: Aldridge Bros (Worthing Art Development Scheme), 91–7. [Dialect used in the speech of some characters.]

Aylward, Florence (1930) The warmin' pan: a true story. *Sussex County Magazine* 4, 843–4.

Aylward, Florence (1939) Malachi once more. *Sussex County Magazine* 13, 167–8. [Anecdote, revolving around terms *bastards* 'antirrhinums' and *sky pilots* 'rain harbingers', possibly idiosyncratic.]

Barber, Margaret Fairless (writing as 'Michael Fairless') (1903) *The roadmender.* London: Duckworth. [New edition (1926). Note the biographical sketch by W. Scott Palmer (M.E. Dowson) and A.M. Haggard, *Michael Fairless. Her life and writings*. London: Duckworth, 1913. A dialect-coloured extract is printed to accompany Beryl Netherclift (1978) The Road-mender's country. *This England* 11 (Spring), 16–21.]

Beckett, Arthur (1911) *The wonderful Weald, and the quest of the crock of gold.* London: Mills and Boon. [There are invented dialect dialogues on 90–3, 159, 242–3, 251–3 (ascribed to [M.A.] Lower), 273–5, predictably involving ancient rustics. On 377–86 is printed a version of the tipteerers' play; see entries under anonymous and traditional (in Sections C8 and D1.2).]

Belloc, Hilaire (1914) *The four men: a farrago*. London: Nelson. [Cf. also Copper (1994). A small amount of dialect speech and song appears, though the colour is slight, conventional, and sometimes not Sussex but nearer Mummerset.]

Blackmore, Richard D. (1875) *Alice Lorraine: a tale of the South Downs.* London: Sampson Low. [Set in Sussex, but there is little dialect in evidence.]

Blackmore, Richard D. (1886) *Springhaven*. London: Sampson Low. [Said by the National Union Catalog to have been published first in *Harper's Magazine* between April 1886 and April 1887. Set in Sussex, but the snippets of dialogue are not convincing: e.g. 'Do 'e think of things as consarneth your homer life' (184).]

• Both of these books by Blackmore are mentioned in the bibliography of the *English dialect dictionary*, but carry a mark from its compiler Joseph Wright expressing doubt about the authenticity of the dialect; correctly, I believe.

Blaker, Nathaniel P. (1906) *Reminiscences of Nathaniel Paine Blaker.* Privately published. Republished as *Sussex in bygone days: reminiscences of Nathaniel Paine Blaker.* Hove: Combridge's (1919). [Small recollected or invented passages in the dialect of Steyning, p. 98. Reprinted in part in Aylwin Guilmant (1991) *Sussex of one hundred years ago*. Stroud: Alan Sutton, 67.]

'Bogarde, Dirk' (pseudonym of Dirk van den Bogaerde, *q.v.*)

Budd, Mavis (1966) *Dust to dust.* London: Dent. [A certain amount of direct speech in plausible dialect (Stedham district), and mention of some regional words used by the author.]

Budd, Mavis (1968) *A prospect of love*. London: Dent. [Of possible relevance, but not seen by the compiler.]

Budd, Mavis (1970) *Fit for a duchess.* London: Dent. [A small amount of direct speech in plausible dialect (Stedham district).]

Copper, Bob (1971) *A song for every season: a hundred years of a Sussex farming family.* London: Heinemann. [Principally a biography of Jim Copper of Rottingdean. Some of Jim Copper's (otherwise unpublished) reminiscences are printed in it; some of these show light dialect colouring. Some of the songs printed as an appendix show occasional dialectalisms, especially in the vocabulary. The main text of this and Bob Copper's other books show dialect features in reported conversations. New edition (1996).]

Copper, Bob (1973) *Songs and southern breezes: country folk and country ways.* London: Heinemann. [See note to previous entry. Details Bob Copper's activity as a folk-song collector for the BBC in the early 1950s, with songs and anecdotes from Sussex and Hampshire.]

Copper, Bob (1976) *Early to rise: a Sussex boyhood.* London: Heinemann. [Further printing: Javelin (1988). See note to last entry but one. Autobiography of Bob Copper. Two extracts appear as Part Two, Texts 35a-b.]

Copper, Bob (1994) *Across Sussex with Belloc. In the footsteps of 'The four men'.* Stroud: Alan Sutton. [Short conversations reported, e.g. 29–33, 70.]

Copper, Bob (1997) *Bob Copper's Sussex.* Seaford: S.B. Publications. [Some dialect words and other features in reported conversations and in the author's own verse.]

- Bob Copper's papers are deposited at the library of the University of Sussex.

Copper, Jim (1953) Work on a Sussex Farm year 1900. [Unpublished manuscript. Partly incorporated into Bob Copper (1971). Contains quite a few dialect words in unaffected usage.]

Copper family (1995) *The Copper family song book – a living tradition.* Peacehaven: Coppersongs. [Bob Copper's contribution to the introduction, reprinted from Copper (1971), contains snatches of remembered or reinvented dialect speech.]

Curteis, Bessie C. (1876) *In the Marsh.* London: Society for Promoting Christian Knowledge. [Novel set in the Rye area.]

Davies, A.J. (1901) *Athirt the Downs: a tale of church folk.* London: Skeffington and son. [Contains some dialogue in dialect, esp. Part I, chapters 5 and 8; part II, chapters 4 and 6; part III, chapters 1 and 5. Although this contains some genuine Sussex words (sometimes glossed in footnotes), the orthography and the implied phonology suggests Dorset (the book's epigraph is from William Barnes). Tom Peacey the shepherd 'spoke in such a broad dialect as few people who are in the habit of reading books would have understood'.]

Donne, J. (1949) [Part of 'A Sussex wayfarer's diary'.] *Sussex County Magazine* 23, 49. [Includes anecdote.]

Dudeney, Alice (writing as Mrs H[enry] E. Dudeney). Between 1897 and 1937, Mrs Dudeney wrote numerous short stories and novels with a Sussex setting, and many of these contain small amounts of conversation in passable dialect; for instance *Robin Brilliant* (London: Hodder and Stoughton (1902)), *The story of Susan* (London: Heinemann (1903)), *Gossips Green* (London: Collins (1905)) and *The treasure field* (London: Collins (1932)).

Edwardes, E. Tickner (1910) *Lift-luck on southern roads*. London: Methuen. [A little dialect in the Sussex chapters (23 and 24).]

Edwardes, E. Tickner (1911) *Neighbourhood. A year's life in and about an English village.* London: Methuen. [About 'Windlecombe', i.e. Burpham, where Edwardes was rector. Some renderings of dialect conversation on 242–6, 294–9 and elsewhere.]

'Fairless, Michael' (pseudonym of Margaret Fairless Barber, *q.v.*)

Flatt, C.P. (1949) Old Garge - an echo from 1905. *Sussex County Magazine* 23, 196–9. [Anecdote.]

'Gaffer', pseud. (1950) Squire Gratwick's 'orses. *Sussex County Magazine* 24, 459–60. [Anecdote. Author not identified.]

'Halsham, John' (pseudonym of G. Forrester Scott, *q.v.*)

Hewlett, Joseph Thomas James (1841) *The parish clerk, a novel, by the author of 'Peter Priggins'* [i.e. Hewlett], ed. by Theodore Hook, esq., 3 vols. London: Henry Colburn.

Jefferies, Richard. His works are catalogued and put into context by George Miller and Hugoe Matthews, eds (1993) *Richard Jefferies: a bibliographical study*. Aldershot: Scolar Press.

Jefferies, Richard (1878) *The gamekeeper at home*. London: Smith, Elder and co. [Essays originally published in *Pall Mall Gazette* anonymously, as was the first edition of the book. It contains numerous dialect words, but it is unclear how many, if any, are intended to represent Sussex. Some are consistent with other reports about Sussex vocabulary. Written before Jefferies's move to Brighton in 1882; but he had made some brief visits to Sussex in childhood and later.]

Jefferies, Richard (1883) "Clematis Lane". Originally published in *The Standard* 18457 (12/09/1883), 2, and reprinted in Jefferies' *The life of the fields*. London: Chatto and Windus (1884), reprinted (1908), 67–74 of this reprinting (esp. 69, 71, 72 for dialect vocabulary).

Jefferies, Richard (1885) "The pine wood". Originally published in *The Standard* 19076 (03/09/1885), 2, and reprinted in Jefferies' *The open air*. London: Chatto and Windus (1885), reprinted London: Lutterworth Press (1948), 91–101 of this reprinting (esp. 98–9 for dialect vocabulary).

Jefferies, Richard (1886) "The country-side: Sussex". Originally published in two parts in the *Manchester Guardian* 12489 (24/08/1886), 8, and 12495 (31/08/1886), 6, and reprinted in Jefferies' *Field and hedgerow*. London: Longmans, Green (1889). This combined item was reprinted London: Lutterworth Press (1948), 98–115 of this reprinting. [Contains some dialect vocabulary and local expressions throughout.]

- Jefferies' use of dialect in general was discussed by Richard Coates (2003) 'Word life in a southern county'. Jefferies Birthday Lecture to the Richard Jefferies Society, Aldbourne, Wiltshire (unpublished).

Jennings, Louis J. (1877) *Field paths and green lanes; being country walks chiefly in Surrey and Sussex*. London: Murray [fourth edition (1884), etc.]. [Some of the place-name pronunciations given foreshadow those in 'An old-fashioned man''s pamphlet (1920).]

Kaye-Smith, Sheila. Numerous novels by Kaye-Smith feature representations of the dialect speech of the extreme east of Sussex and Romney Marsh, including at least the following:

Kaye-Smith, Sheila (1908) *The tramping Methodist*. London: Cassell.

Kaye-Smith, Sheila (1909) *Starbrace*. London: Cassell.

Kaye-Smith, Sheila (1910) *Spell land: the story of a Sussex farm*. London: G. Bell and son; thereafter Cassell.

Kaye-Smith, Sheila (1916) *Sussex gorse: the story of a fight*. London: Nisbet. [Contains interesting exemplification of the pressures to abandon dialect, 136, 170-1.]

Kaye-Smith, Sheila (1917) *The challenge to Sirius*. London: Cassell.

Kaye-Smith, Sheila (1918) *Little England*. London: Cassell.

Kaye-Smith, Sheila (1919) *Tamarisk Town*. London: Cassell. [A small amount of direct speech in dialect.]

Kaye-Smith, Sheila (1920) *Green apple harvest*. London: Cassell. [A small amount of direct speech in dialect. See Part Two, Text 23b.]

Kaye-Smith, Sheila (1921) *Joanna Godden*. London: Cassell.

Kaye-Smith, Sheila (1926) *Three ways home*. London: Cassell.

Kaye-Smith, Sheila (1930) *Shepherds in sackcloth*. London: Cassell.

Kaye-Smith, Sheila (1931) *The history of Susan Spray, the female preacher*. London: Cassell.

Kaye-Smith, Sheila (1933) *The ploughman's progress*. London: Cassell and New York: Harper & Brothers. [Published in North America as *Gipsy waggon. The story of a ploughman's progress.*]

• Kaye-Smith's use of dialect is briefly discussed by R. Thurston Hopkins (1925) *Sheila Kaye-Smith and the Weald Country*. London: Cecil Palmer, 19–21. This book also contains excerpts from the novels, some featuring conversation in dialect.

• Kaye-Smith's papers are preserved at the University of Texas.

Kipling, J. Rudyard (1905) “A three-part song”, in ‘Dymchurch Flit’, in his *Puck of Pook's Hill*. London: Macmillan.

• Kipling exploited an enormous range of vernacular voices, and his attempts at Sussex dialect are no mean achievement, even where not fully consistent. Craig Raine describes his use of another dialect as ‘an evocation rather than a phonetically pedantic transcription’ (Introduction, *A choice of Kipling's prose* (London: Faber and Faber (1987), 4) – that is fair enough comment on the Sussex pieces too. Some dialect may also be found scattered in *Puck of Pook's Hill* (London: Macmillan (1905)) and *Rewards and fairies* (London: Macmillan (1910)).

Kipling, J. Rudyard (1914) “Friendly Brook”. With the poem “The land”, also in his *A diversity of creatures*. London: Macmillan (1917).

Kipling, J. Rudyard (1924) “The wish house”. *Maclean's Magazine*, 19/10/1924. Reprinted in his *Debits and credits*. London: Macmillan (1926).

Leigh, Rhoda (1932) *Past and passing: tales from remote Sussex*. London: Heath Cranton. [Contains a fair amount of dialogue involving dialect-speaking characters; not always fully convincing as to pronunciation (“naw” for *no*, “oop” for *up*).]

MacDermott, K.H. (1922) *Sussex church music in the past.* Chichester: Moore and Wingham. [Sparse dialect material on 3–4, 11, 16, 32, 39, 40, 80, including inscriptions in church books.]

Martineau, G.D. (1941) “Rarbuts”. *Sussex County Magazine* 15, 156–7. [Anecdote with dialogue in dialect.]

Murray, D.L. (1936) *Regency*. London: Hodder and Stoughton. [Murray's use of dialect does not get beyond the stereotypical, mixing Dickensian Cockneyisms with Sussexisms culled from standard texts such as Parish's *Dictionary*. Murray wrote other novels localized in Brighton; this one is cited as representative.]

Neale, John Mason (1855a) “The oak of Luxford's Lane”. Chapter 4 of *Lent legends. Stories for children from Church history.* London: Masters. [Third edition (1884); another, Society for Promoting Christian Knowledge (no date [1928]). [The story includes sparse North Sussex dialect features.]

Neale, John Mason (1855b) "Gill's Lap". In *The Penny Post.* [Occasional North Sussex dialect features. Reprinted separately London: Parker (1858) and subsequently. Summarized in Old-fashioned tales, no. 5. *Sussex County Magazine* 6 (1932), 160–4.]

• Michael J. Leppard notes that 'other material is to be found incidentally in [Neale's] letters, verse, articles and sermons'. See also Neale's usages recorded in Leppard's series of articles on dialect in *East Grinstead Museum Compass* (1999–2008).

Netherclift, Beryl (1935) *No road runs by. A collection of country sketches.* Cambridge: W. Heffer and sons. [Rare item. Copy formerly in Lewes Library, Albion St. Some of these stories were first printed in the *Christian Science Monitor* and *Mid Sussex Times* (dates unknown). Dialect of central Sussex (Ardingly) area is represented in some stories, especially "Mus' Willums", "On the Downs", "Discovery of a friend" and "Summer", and occasionally in others. The author recognizes true Sussex as something distinct from incomers' vernacular, e.g. 84. Has (e.g. 26) the *t'* for the definite article recorded also from a little to the south(-east) by Fred Wood and Barclay Wills, *qq.v.*; but there are other features that appear to be really northern (26, 29).]

Netherclift, Beryl (1939) *Greensleeves*. London: Heath Cranton. [Contains somewhat less dialect than the previous item.]

O'Reilly, Eleanor Grace (otherwise Mrs R. O'Reilly) (1880) *Sussex stories*, 3 vols. London: Strahan. [These stories contain some dialect in the dialogue, but it is thin and generalized (as might be expected from the reference to the "queer Sussex way of speaking" in the story "Miss Olive's boys", vol. II).]

O'Reilly, Eleanor Grace (otherwise Mrs R. O'Reilly) (1884) *Meg's mistake and other Sussex stories.* London: Hodder and Stoughton. [This appears to be a new single-volume edition of the preceding item.]

Parsons, M. (1942) [Letter about dead horses hung on trees.] *Sussex County Magazine* 16, 178. [Anecdote.]

Ridley, Ursula (1971) *The story of a forest village: West Hoathly.* West Hoathly: Friends of Priest House. [A small amount of the anecdote contains representations of dialect speech.]

Rudkin, Mabel Spencer (1927) The philosophy of Henry Banister: a Sussex gardener. *Sussex County Magazine* 1, 554–6, 560.

Scott, G. Forrester (writing as 'John Halsham') (1898) *Idlehurst*. London: Smith and Elder. [Second edition (1908).]

Scott, G. Forrester (writing as 'John Halsham') (1907) *Lonewood Corner: a countryman's horizons*. London: Smith and Elder. [Chapters 19 and 21 contain some direct and indirect speech in dialect from the character Jethro Tully.]

Scott, G. Forrester (writing as 'John Halsham') (1918) *Old standards: south country sketches*. London: Murray.

van den Bogaerde, Dirk (writing as 'Dirk Bogarde') (1977) *A postillion struck by lightning*. London: Chatto and Windus. [Bogarde lived for part of the year during much of his childhood at Lullington, and some of his dialogue is locally coloured.]

van den Bogaerde, Dirk (writing as 'Dirk Bogarde') (1992) *Great Meadow*. London: Chatto and Windus. [As previous item. Bogarde read extracts on BBC Radio 4 in 1993.]

Wells, Herbert George (1898) *The invisible man*. London: Harper. [The opening chapters include some rather half-hearted representations of the speech of West Sussex.]

Wiggin, Kate Douglas (afterwards Riggs) (1902) *The diary of a goose girl*. London: Gay and Bird; Boston (Mass.) and New York: Houghton, Mifflin. [Includes some localisms, but unconvincing as Sussex of c.1900 (*bryke up, nowble*).]

Willard, Barbara (1970-81) The *Mantlemass* novels. Harmondsworth: Kestrel Books. [These novels are briefly reviewed by Belinda Copson (1999) Barbara Willard, 1909-1994. *Folly Magazine* 27 (July); also online at www.collectingbooksandmagazines.com/history.html, accessed 29 March 2010.]

Wilson, G. Herbert (1930a) London (as seen by Mas Jarge Pilbeam, of Puddingcake Farm in the county of Sussex). *Sussex County Magazine* 4, 78.

Wilson, G. Herbert (1930b) Mas Jarge Pilbeam pays his rent. *Sussex County Magazine* 4, 166–7.

Wilson, G. Herbert (1930c) The "jumpshort". *Sussex County Magazine* 4, 305–6.

Woodward, Marcus (1938) *The mistress of Stantons Farm*. London: Heath Cranton. [Second edition 1939. Reprinted Bakewell: Country Books (2004). Some dialect, ostensibly of the East Chiltington area where not taken from Parish's *Dictionary* (1875), as most is.]

Note that:

Gibbons, Stella (1932) *Cold Comfort Farm*. London: Longmans.

is set in Sussex, and the dialogue contains some conventional Sussex features and some unusual words which are parodies of authentic dialect.

Section F: BIOGRAPHICAL WORKS ON PERSONALITIES OF SIGNIFICANCE FOR SUSSEX DIALECT

This list does not pretend to be exhaustive. See also Part Four, Section G4: Reminiscences of Sussex singers.

John Burgess

Burgess, Donald F. (1989) *No continuing city. The diary and letters of John Burgess, a craftsman from Sussex, from 1785–1819*. [Title varies slightly between titlepage and cover.] Redhill: private, ix-xxii.

Maclean, David (1937) John Burgess of Ditchling and America. *Sussex County Magazine* 11, 657.

William Durrant Cooper

Campkin, Henry (1877) *Two Sussex archaeologists* [i.e. Cooper and M.A. Lower]. Privately printed. Reprinted from *Sussex Archaeological Collections* 27, 116–51 [on Cooper, see 117–32].

Coates, Richard (1996) A brief biography of William Durrant Cooper (1812–75). Prepared for the 150th anniversary of the Sussex Archaeological Society, remaining unpublished at the time. [Published for the first time as Appendix 1 to this book.]

Farrant, John H. (2004) Cooper, William Durrant (1812–1875). *Oxford Dictionary of National Biography*. Oxford: Oxford University Press. [Online at www.oxforddnb.com/view/article/6236.]

Stephen, Leslie, and S. Lee, eds, (1885–1900) *Dictionary of national biography*. Oxford: Oxford University Press, vol. IV, 1079–80.

W.G. Daish

Godman, Stanley (1956) Letter [on Daish's pieces, *q.v.*] *Sussex County Magazine* 30, 295–6. [This and the next two pieces may be consulted in a folder of Godman's published work (*A Sussex historical miscellany*) kept at the Sussex Archaeological Society's library at Barbican House, Lewes (open shelves). All may be found in Sussex Pamphlets boxes at Brighton Area Library.]

Godman, Stanley (1963) Mr W.G. Daish's acute ear for the Sussex dialect. *West Sussex Gazette*, 29/08/1963, page no. not known. [Obituary of W.G. Daish.]

John Dudeney

Blencowe, R.W. (1849) South-Down shepherds. *Sussex Archaeological Collections* 2, 247–56, especially 253–6, quoted verbatim from an autograph MS. of Dudeney's, once in the care of the Sussex Archaeological Society and now in East Sussex Record Office among the MSS. Acc 3785. [It is further reproduced by Charles Fleet (1878) *Glimpses of our ancestors in Sussex*. Lewes: Farncombe, 92–4 of the second edition (1882), and is partly quoted by W.H. Hudson, *Nature in Downland*. London: Longmans, Green (1900), 126–7 of the 1923 edition (London: Dent); and that extract in turn by Gosset (1911; see Skeat (1910), Section A).]

Philcox, Richard (1995) John Dudeney, 1782-1852. Brief biography prepared for the 150th anniversary of the Sussex Archaeological Society, unpublished MS.

• The basic facts of Dudeney's life are mentioned in many places. He is often presented as the archetypal Sussex man of his period.

‘John Halsham’

Holland, Michael (1924) The Sussex countryman. *Downland Post* (new series) 1.6, 172. [Amongst other things, commends writers such as Rudyard Kipling and ‘John Halsham’ for their accuracy in conveying local idiom.]

William Hersee

Tibble, Ronald (1989) William Hersee, 1786–1854. *West Sussex History* 42 (January), 11–15.

Sheila Kaye-Smith

Bristow-Smith, Michael, comp. (2000) *A chronology of the life and works of Sheila Kaye-Smith, 1887–1956.* St Leonards on Sea: Sheila Kaye-Smith Society.

Doyle, Paul A. (1972-5) Sheila Kaye-Smith: an annotated bibliography of writings about her. *English Literature in Transition 1880–1920* 15 (1972), 189–198; 16 (1973), 152 f.; 17 (1974), 45 f.; 18 (1975), 62.

Lane, Michael (1996) *On the trail of writers in Sussex.* Seaford: S.B. Publications. [One of the eight principal literary tours concerns Kaye-Smith.]

Malone, Andrew E. (1924) Sheila Kaye-Smith: a novelist of the farm. *Living Age* 323 (November), 388.

Malone, Andrew E. (1926) The novelist of Sussex: Sheila Kaye-Smith. *Fortnightly Review* (2 August) 120, 199–209.

Smith, Peter D. (2004) Smith, (Emily) Sheila Kaye- (1887–1956). *Oxford Dictionary of National Biography*. Oxford: Oxford University Press. [Online at www.oxforddnb.com/view/article/51136.]

Villard, Léonie. (1926) Sheila Kaye-Smith et les ‘romans de Sussex’. *Revue anglo-américaine* 3 (August), 494–504.

Walker, Dorothea (1980) *Sheila Kaye-Smith*. Boston: Twayne Publishers. [There is a bibliography on 163–6.]

Rudyard Kipling (only in relation to his use of dialect)

Holland, Michael (1924) The Sussex countryman. *Downland Post* (new series) 1.6, 172. [Amongst other things, commends writers such as Rudyard Kipling and 'John Halsham' for their accuracy in conveying local idiom.]

Radcliffe, John (2002) R[udyard] K[ipling]'s use of Sussex dialect. *Kipling Journal* [Online], 58–9. [About *wildishers* 'inhabitants of the low land around Etchingham'.]

Mark Antony Lower

Campkin, Henry (1877) *Two Sussex archaeologists* [i.e. Lower and W. Durrant Cooper]. Privately circulated. Reprinted from *Sussex Archaeological Collections* 27 (1877), 116–51 [on Lower, see 132–51].

Farrant, John H. (2004) Lower, Mark Antony (1813–1876). *Oxford Dictionary of National Biography*. Oxford: Oxford University Press. [Online at www.oxforddnb.com/view/article/17090.]

Stephen, Leslie, and S. Lee, eds (1885–1900) *Dictionary of national biography.* Oxford: Oxford University Press, vol. 12, 202–3.

Richard W. Lower

Boase, G. C. (2004) Lower, Richard (1782–1865), rev. Megan A. Stephan. *Oxford Dictionary of National Biography*. Oxford: Oxford University Press. [Online at www.oxforddnb.com/view/article/17092.]

Evans, A.A. (1933) A village dominie. Chapter 14 of *On foot in Sussex: a loiterer's notebook*. London: Methuen, 182–8.

Evans, A.A. (1935) *A saunterer in Sussex*. London: Methuen, 69–70.

Stephen, Leslie and S. Lee, eds (1885–1900) *Dictionary of national biography*. Oxford: Oxford University Press, vol. 12, 204.

John Mason Neale

Leppard, M.J. (MS.) John Mason Neale and Sussex lore. [Draws attention to Neale's writings involving dialect, totally overlooked in modern times, and other aspects of his interest in dialect. Subsumed into Leppard's series of articles in *East Grinstead Museum Compass* (1999–2008).]

William Douglas Parish

Short biography in the new edition of his *Dictionary* by Helena Hall (1957), xi.

Ellman, John Boys (1912) Chapter 52 of *Recollections of a Sussex parson*. London: Skeffington and sons, 239–42. [Also 209, especially.]

Lucas, Perceval (2004) Parish, William Douglas (1833–1904), rev. John D. Haigh. *Oxford Dictionary of National Biography*. Oxford: Oxford University Press. [Online at www.oxforddnb.com/view/article/3538.]

Wright, John (1983) The season when men went scuggy-hunting. *Sussex Life* [unnumbered] (December), 38–9. [On Parish's life and work.]

Lilian F. Ramsey

Obituaries in *West Sussex Gazette*, 14/02/1974, and the *Chichester Observer*, 22/02/1974; the piece in *West Sussex Gazette*, 04/04/1991 "Mrs. Paddick makes a welcome return"; and the letter from John Worsley in *West Sussex Gazette*, 18/09/1995 (page nos not known).

James Richards

anonymous ['Our own correspondent'] (1935) Rendering the Bible in Sussex dialect. *Methodist Times*, 19/12/1935, 1–2. [On the work of James Richards. His pseudonym 'Jim Cladpole' is never mentioned.]

anonymous (1939) [On the work of James Richards.] *Daily Herald*, 15/06/1939, page no. not known.

Coates, Richard, ed. (1992) *De A.B.C. Psalms. Put into de Sussex dialect and in due A.B.C. feshion by Jim Cladpole. April 1938*. Brighton: Younsmere Press. [The afterword (39–43) contains a commentary on James Richards' life and work.]

Costello, Miles (1991b) James Richards – the greatest of our Sussex dialect authors. *West Sussex Gazette*, 30/05/1991, page no. not known.

Eccles, John (1999) Stary arv moi loif. Cladpole's autobiography in yokel-speak. *Sussex Express*, 26/11/1999, 13 L. [On James Richards.]

Godman, Stanley (1957a) The work of James Richards. Sussex dialect poet, preacher and 'translator'. *West Sussex Gazette*, 01/08/1957, page no. not known. [See further the afterword of Coates (1992).]

Page, André (1970) I loike to remember how dey said it! *Sussex Life* 6 (July), 50. [On the life of James Richards.]

Payne, Malcolm (1988a) James Richards, the Tunbridge Wells poet, photographer and preacher. *Tunbridge Wells and Weald Magazine* (August), page no. not known. [Shares some text with the next item. Contains factual errors.]

Payne, Malcolm (1988b) The mystery of Jim Cladpole. *Country Magazine* 179 (02/09/1988), 28–9. [Shares some text with the previous item. There never really was any long-standing mystery about the identity of 'Jim Cladpole'; it was public knowledge by 1928, before he began his biblical work in dialect (see *Sussex County Magazine* 2 (1928), 384).]

'Sussex Onlooker', pseud. (1973a) Dialect travels far. *West Sussex Gazette*, 10/05/1973, page no. not known.

'Sussex Onlooker', pseud. (1973b) Jim Cladpole – poet. *West Sussex Gazette*, 24/05/1973, page no. not known.

• Newspaper articles (and similar) on his life and work exist as follows: *Methodist Times* (19/12/1935), the *Daily Herald* (15/06/1939), *West Sussex Gazette* (01/08/1957, 24/05/1973 and 30/05/1991), *Sussex Life* 6 (July 1970), *Sussex Express* (26/11/1999), and the two pieces by Payne (1988a,b).

• There is an autobiographical piece in dialect by Richards (*'Bout me*), and also a piece by him in standard English entitled 'Bell Banks: reminiscences of old Hailsham' in a local newspaper, perhaps *Sussex Advertiser* (20/09/1927). It looks as though it may have been the last of a series.

Amy Sawyer

A brief biography develops piecemeal in *East Grinstead Museum Compass* 2 (1999), 3; 3 (2000), 3; 4 (2000), 9; 5 (2001), 3; 15 (2004), 3.

Ernest William Young

M.J. Leppard (2000) East Grinstead's historians (5): E.W. Young. *Bulletin of the East Grinstead Society* 71, 6.

There are brief biographies of numerous Sussex folk-singers in Part Four, Section G4, including:

Stubbs, Ken (1970) *The life of a man*. London: English Folk Dance and Song Society, 92–4.

More generally on dialect users, see:

Daish, W.G. (1956a) The voice of Sussex I, II, and III. *Sussex County Magazine* 30, 8–14, 76–82, 163–8. [This discusses the work of W.D. Parish and M.A. Lower, amongst other topics.]

PART FOUR

DISCOGRAPHY OF RECORDED MATERIAL WITH SUSSEX VOICES

CONTENTS

• It has been decided to restrict Part Four to works in existence, available or published on gramophone record or audiotape, reflecting the compiler's view that the tradition of singing in dialect which they represent reached the end of the line in the 1960s. The cut-off date is arbitrarily fixed at 1962, the year of 'Pop' Maynard's death. The tradition continued only insofar as practitioners of dialect and folksong active before that remained active after it. So only the works of speakers and singers active before that date are included, but any of their work recorded after that date using older technologies is included. Rare exceptions are made for especially important material.

• The explosion in digital media, especially since about 2001–2, has meant that many of the works mentioned are now available on CD or through web-sites. Since the latter may not be durable, no systematic attempt has been made to catalogue them in this book; a book seems an inappropriate place for them. However, some of the more important CDs and web-sites for Sussex dialect – those which are judged to stand a chance of lasting – are listed in a final brief section (H1 and H2).

Abbreviations

BBC = British Broadcasting Company/Corporation
BLNSA = British Library National Sound Archive
CECTAL = Centre for English Cultural Tradition and Language, University of Sheffield, now called NATCECT, National Centre for English Cultural Tradition
JEFDSS = *Journal of the English Folk Dance and Song Society*
JFSS = *Journal of the Folk-Song Society*

The BL National Sound Archive (until 1983 the British Institute of Recorded Sound) is situated at 29 Exhibition Road, London SW7 2AS. It has a free listening service is available by appointment and its library is open, without an appointment at advertised times. It offers an information and archival service. It has had since 1986 a separate Department of Language and Dialect, and its premises are host to the Oral History Society.

The Centre for English Cultural Tradition and Language, now the National Centre for English Cultural Tradition, is at the University of Sheffield, Sheffield S10 2TN.

The English Folk Dance and Song Society (continuing and absorbing the Folk-Song Society) is situated at Cecil Sharp House, 2 Regents Park Road, London NW1.

Elixir Publications of Horsham have produced commercially available audiocassettes of Sussex dialect stories interspersed with music. Their address is Elixir Publications, Glistar Studios, PO Box 110, Horsham RH12 1ZS.

Other possible items of local interest are catalogued in Lali Weerasinghe (1989) *Directory of recorded sound resources in the United Kingdom*. London: British Library, entries 338–44.

G1: Speech

anonymous (11/10/1954) Village cricket, etc. [Wisborough Green.] BLNSA AL(Eng)1. 22734.

anonymous (11/11/1958) Rye lifeboat disaster - local people. BLNSA FA. LP25911.

anonymous (male, aged 78) (/06/1959) Life on the land. [Firle.] BLNSA AL(Eng)1. LP 26428.[18] [The Survey of English Dialects recording, in fact by Harry Burgess.]

anonymous (male, aged 60) (/06/1959) Early days. [Fletching.] BLNSA AL(Eng)1. LP 26428. [The Survey of English Dialects recording, in fact by a Mr Bellingham.]

Atkinson, Oliver (1980) Rural life in East Sussex, 1885–1945. University of Sussex Library, audiocassettes R5294-300, R7972–8, with transcript. [Reminiscences recorded by C.P. Ravilious. Regional colour is light; speaker is very old, probably with reasonable education, some dysphasia. Transcripts available.]

BBC Home Service (1950/1951, date uncertain) The life of James Copper.

BBC Radio 2 (20/05/1992) County tales 4: Sussex. [Contains a fair number of traditional-Sussex voices, including Bob Copper; others not identified.]

BBC Radio 2 (21/12/1994) Sussex material was broadcast on this date. [Further details unknown.]

BBC archive (1998) Leslie Luff of Milland: interview. Shelfmark C900/16412. Available online at www.bl.uk/learning/langlit/sounds/text-only/england/milland/ and http://sounds.bl.uk/View.aspx?item=021M-C0900X16412X-0200V0.xml. [Some linguistic notes appended.]

BBC archive (1999) Aubrey Charman of Southwater: interview. Shelfmark C900/16004. Available online at http://sounds.bl.uk/View.aspx?item=021M-C0900X16004X-1000V0.xml. [Some linguistic notes appended.]

[18] In fact BLNSA holds the SED recordings for all six Sussex locations.

BBC archive (1999) Bert Deacon of Ringmer: interview. Shelfmark C900/07554. Available online at http://sounds.bl.uk/View.aspx?item=021M-C0900X07554X-1900V0.xml. [Some linguistic notes appended.]

Blackman, R[ichard] (12/04/1950) A story. [Arundel.] BLNSA AL(Eng)1. 14870.

Brighton area, various voices (1990). Audiotapes submitted with Valerie Griffith (1990) The dialect of the Brighton and Hove area. Project for the degree of BA, University of Sheffield. Deposited at CECTAL/NATCECT, University of Sheffield.

British Drama League (date unknown; 1936 or after) Recordings of regional dialects. These are deposited at CECTAL/NATCECT, University of Sheffield. The collection includes an EP (BDL LYN 675) recorded by Mr R.W. White of Battle, reading the BDL's standard passage, two further passages entitled "Old Mother Cornford" and "The fire brigade", and a song from Kipling's *Puck of Pook's Hill.*

Brothers, Anthony Chamberlaine (*c.*1991) Recording of Mark Antony Lower's and James Richards's versions of the *Song of Solomon*, Richard Lower's *Tom Cladpole's journey to Lunnun* and Jan Cladpole's *trip to 'Merricur,* and his own *Alus in Wunnerland* and other material. [Available privately.]

Charman, Aubrey. See BBC archive.

Clarke, F.C. (1987a) Bungalow Town, 1940–1950: reminiscences of West Sussex life in the 1940s. [Talk given for BBC Radio Sussex. University of Sussex Library, audiocassette R7043. Relatively light accent features. The place referred to is the one between Lancing and Shoreham-by-Sea.]

Clarke, F.C. (1987b) George Ford, poacher: reminiscences of West Sussex life in the 1940s. [Talk given for BBC Radio Sussex. University of Sussex Library, audiocassette R7042. Relatively light accent features.]

Copper, Jim (1951) Talk about old Rottingdean. Given to the compiler by Bob Copper; public status unknown. [Also includes songs by Jim, Bob and Ron Copper listed below in F2.]

Copper, Bob (1957) Talk about Christmas supper customs. BBC 25616. EFDSS 999.

Deacon, Bert. See BBC archive.

Farley, Gordon (no date) Recording transcribed by Biddulph (1988, Part Three, Section C4), *q.v.* In the possession of Miles Costello.

Garland, George. Touring comedian (1930–60) performing a 'weak version' of rural Sussex dialect as the character Bill Stubbins. He spoke "Our tallest story" in the BBC radio Forces Programme "Parish Mag" broadcast from Petworth on 01/08/1940. Miles Costello has notes for a parody used by Garland for National Farmers' Union and Women's Institute functions, and this may be the same material. Fred Streeter (*q.v.*) spoke on the same programme.

Glaysher, Shirley. See Wales (1994a,b).

Holden, Eric W. (1986) Recording of Richard Lower's ('Tim Cladpole"s) *Tom Cladpole's jurney to Lunnun*, held on audiotape (uncatalogued) in the library of the Sussex Archaeological Society, Barbican House, Lewes, and elsewhere privately.

Knight, Harry (01/12/1952) Description of life and work on a farm by a folk singer. BLNSA MN(Eng)70. 18715&6.

Lindfield, Bill. See Wales (1994a,b).

Littlehampton Museum (1983–4) The museum holds about 50 tapes of oral history interviews with local people about life in the town from 1905 onwards. Not systematically checked for dialect/accent features.

Luff, Leslie. See BBC archive.

Martin, E. Le Breton (25/11/1927) Martin arranged for a broadcast on BBC radio of a Sussex dialect talk, said (bizarrely) in the details to be 'the most famous of all the county dialects of England'. No further information about it has come to light.

North, David J. (1979) Recordings made c. 14/11/1979 in connection with his follow-up survey to the Survey of English Dialects in Sussex, Kent and Surrey. [Private archive with speakers from Bolney, Funtington, Robertsbridge and Turners Hill.]

Oliver, L. (1980) Rushlake Green, East Sussex, during and after the First World War. University of Sussex Library audiocassettes R5301, R7979. [Reminiscences recorded by C.P. Ravilious. Speaker old, quality of audiotape fairly good. Some marked traditional accent features audible. Transcript available.]

Plumb, P. (16/04/1961) Legend of Devil's Dyke. BLNSA AL(Eng)1. LP 26611.

Sargent, Gilbert. Recordings made by Dave Arthur (c.1980) for the BBC radio series "Folk with tales". (Cf. Arthur (1989) in Section G4: Reminiscences (below).)

Streeter, Fred. The Pulborough dialect, or at least its accent, became nationally known in the 1960s and 70s through the radio broadcasts (esp. "Thought for the day", BBC Radio 4) of the (by then) nonagenarian gardener Fred Streeter. At least some probably survive in BBC archives. See also Garland, George.

Stubbs, Ken (1963). Stubbs's audiotaped reminiscences of George 'Pop' Maynard are kept at the Museum of English Rural Life, University of Reading.

Survey of English Dialects. The audiotapes of basic data are stored at the School of English, University of Leeds (with copies at CECTAL/NATCECT, University of Sheffield). They also exist in digital form and can be accessed at sounds.bl.uk/Browse.aspx?category=Accents-and-dialects&collection=Survey-of-English-dialects. [The material is filed at "Sussex". Each speaker is interviewed for about five minutes.]

Tait, David (early 1990s). Mr Tait has supplied the compiler with taped recordings of R. Herridge (Lancing), Vera Hodsoll (Jevington), Mr Povey, C. Wells (Brighton), Bert Winborne (Hurstpierpoint), and 'a downland shepherd' (Worthing Museum). The status of these recordings is not clear; this entry is simply to alert readers to their existence.

van den Bogaerde, Dirk (writing as 'Dirk Bogarde') (date uncertain, 1993) *Great Meadow*. [Bogarde read extracts from his book (Chatto and Windus (1992)) on BBC Radio4. These presumably survive in the BBC Sound Archive. At least one character (Lally) has a Sussex accent.]

Wales, Tony, ed. (1994a) *Smugglers, saints and sinners*. Cassette audiotape. Elixir ETW 1. [Includes stories in Sussex dialect narrated by Shirley Glaysher and Bill Lindfield.]

Wales, Tony, ed. (1994b) *Dragons, devils and demons*. Cassette audiotape. Elixir ETW 2. [Includes stories in Sussex dialect narrated by Shirley Glaysher and Bill Lindfield.]

- A promotional video about the genesis of the two previous items also exists, likewise published by Elixir (1994). It may have been used in an excerpted form on a Meridian regional commercial TV programme in 1994.

West Sussex Record Office, Chichester, holds an audiotaped archive interviews (catalogue reference OH) with elderly residents of West Sussex about life in their younger days. [This archive has not been systematically checked for regional speech, but at least some tapes feature standard speakers and speakers with the accents of other regions.]

White, R.W. See British Drama League.

G2: Songs

WARNINGS:

> 'Dialect, not unnaturally, is richer in everyday speech than in folk-song singing. Folk-song words mostly come to peasant singers as it were 'from without'. They are handed down orally from past ages, or on ballad sheets, and are often full of phrases that singers repeat parrot-like without grasping their meaning.' — Percy Grainger, *Journal of the Folk-Song Society* 3.12 (1908), 160

> '. . . it seems clear that while ordinary people spoke in their local dialect, they did not sing in it.' — Dick Leith (1983) *A social history of English*. London: Routledge, 39 (writing of all times from the sixteenth century onwards)

Numeration

In the following discography, BBC numbers are of recordings in the BBC's sound archive not (so far as the compiler knows) commercially available unless additional information given in the relevant entry says otherwise. EFDSS numbers refer to the sound archive of the English Folk Dance and Song Society. Caedmon/ Topic numbers are of recordings marketed on these labels in the United States and Britain respectively. Kennedy numbers are references to songs in Peter Kennedy, ed. (1975) *Folksongs of Britain and Ireland*. London: Cassell. Some of these songs are available on cassette from Kennedy's label Folk Trax (see also the separate entry for this in the alphabetical list). This series of recorded music on cassette (later also videocassette) ran 1975–2007.

Compilations

There is some inconsistency in the way the contents of compilation albums is presented. Some important albums are listed in their proper alphabetical place in the list of singers (e.g. *Rolling in the dew* between Richardson and Saunders), and the main entry for some songs is there, with the singers on them placed also in the alphabetical list and cross-referred to the title. For some singers contributing to compilations, the main entry for the song is under the singer's name, with the album mentioned in the entry for the individual songs. Some compilations appear in the list without the contents being analysed.

The Coppers

This discography was compiled independently of the one dealing with the work of the Copper family accompanying the following article:

Blackman, Bob (2001) The Copper family. *Sing Out!* 45.2 (May).

Blackman's work has been amplified by Tony Rees with the assistance of Garry Gillard, and published online at www.thecopperfamily.com/books-recordings/recordings/discog.html (state of February 2009; accessed 2009–2010). The Blackman-Rees-Gillard discography is authoritative and has been used to check what appears below. They give their own acknowledgements of assistance. In the present discography, there may be some inadvertent duplication in cases where the singers on individual tracks are uncertain.

Not all the Coppers' songs appearing in 'Various artists' compilations have been entered here; those omitted are believed to be re-releases. The family continues to record, but this discography does not include any items released on CD since the first Coppers CD in 1995 unless the material is previously unreleased, nor anything recorded in any medium since the death of Bob Copper in 2004.

The Coppers' central role in Sussex folk music, over a very long period, will be readily apparent.

Disclaimer

With the exception of the Coppers' work, the discography is likely be incomplete, and readers with more detailed knowledge are encouraged to contact the compiler about omissions and errors. An entry in this list is not a guarantee that the song is commercially available. There are minor inconsistencies of presentation between the entries, and some expected details are omitted in others, as dictated by what evidence was available to the compiler. What follows is considered to give a reliable impression of the later sung dialect, or at least accent, of Sussex.

Adams, Ned 'Wintry' [Hastings Old Town] (1954) "The bold *Princess Royal*." Caedmon TC 1162/Topic 12T194. *Folksongs of Britain*, vol. VI.

Adams: also on *Rolling in the dew*.

Ainger, Alf [West Sussex] (1969) Three songs in the Rod and Danny Stradling Collection.

Attrill, George [Fittleworth] (1954) "The nightingales sing." BBC 22737. Kennedy 185.

Attrill, George (1954) "Epsom races." BBC 22737. Kennedy 318.

Attrill, George (1954) "Oxford city." BBC 22738. Kennedy 329.

Attrill, George (1954) "John Barleycorn's a hero bold." BBC 22738. Kennedy 277.

Attrill, George (1954) "The nutting maid." BBC 22739. Kennedy 186.

Attrill, George (1954) "The spotted cow." BBC 22739. Kennedy 142.

Attrill, George (date unknown) "The nightingale." EFDSS FTA 102 .

Attrill, George (date unknown) "All jolly fellows that follow the plough." EFDSS FTA 102 .

Attrill: also on Folk Trax FSB 025, 029, *Rolling in the dew.*

Baxter, Ern(est) 'Rabbidy' (date unknown) "Will the weaver." On *Sussex harvest.* Topic 12T258. Also Magic Buddha WMS 8083 (1995).

Belton, George [Arundel] (1967) "Green brooms." EDFSS LP 1008.

Belton, George (1967) "Jim, the carter lad." EDFSS LP 1008.

Belton, George (1967) "All jolly fellows." EDFSS LP 1008.

Belton, George (1967) "I have drunk one"; also known as "The Sussex toast". EDFSS LP 1008.

Belton, George (date unknown) "Dark-eyed sailor." EFDSS FTA 102 .

Belton, George (date unknown) "My old man"; also known as "Our goodman". EFDSS FTA 102 .

Belton: also on *Brave ploughboy.*

Blackman, George [Wisborough Green] (1954) "I bought myself a cock." BBC 22735. Caedmon TC 1225/Topic 12T198. Kennedy 297.

Blackman, George: also on *Rolling in the dew.*

Blackman, Richard [Arundel] (1954) "The herring song." BBC 22736. Kennedy 296.

Blackman, Richard: also on *Rolling in the dew* and *When sheepshearing's done.*

Blake, Bob [Horsham] (date unknown) "The grey hawk." EFDSS FTA 102.

Blake, Bob (1975) "When sheepshearing's done." *When sheepshearing's done*. Topic 12T254.

Blake, Bob (date???)"The basket of eggs." *Sussex harvest*. Topic 12T258. Also Magic Buddha WMS 8083 (1995).

Blake, Bob (date???) "The bonny labouring boy." *Sussex harvest*. Topic 12T258. Also Magic Buddha WMS 8083 (1995).

Blake: also on *Brave ploughboy* and *When sheepshearing's done*.

The brave ploughboy (1975). XTRA1150. [Live recording from the Lewes Arms, Mount Place, Lewes (May 1974), produced by Karl Dallas; insert included.] Contains: Cyril Phillips, "Sussex molecatcher"; Bob Lewis, "Lost door key", "Ale, ale, glorious ale"; Bob Blake, "Courting with a light", "Old John Braddlem"; Coppers, "Young bretheren"; George Belton, "Carter lad"; George Spicer, "Triplets", "Down in the fields where the buttercups all grow"; Coppers, "Brisk young ploughboy"; George Belton, "All jolly fellows that follow the plough"; Bob Blake, "Basket of eggs"; Bob Lewis, "Lost sheep", "John Barleycorn"; Cyril Phillips, "Lakes of Coolfin"; George Spicer, "Barley mow"; George Belton, "Sussex toast".

Burton, George: on *Rolling in the dew*.

Collins, Shirley [Hastings] (1953) Contributions to *A jug of punch*. HMV CLP 1327, XLP 50003. Includes: "Higher Germanie", "The horse named Bill".

Collins, Shirley (1954) "Rolling in the dew." Recorded by Peter Kennedy. Kennedy 189.

Collins: recordings referred to by Wales (1976: 20, Part Three, Section C7).

Cook, Lily [North Chailey] (1954) "Her serving man." BBC 22735. Kennedy 161.

Cook, Lily (1954) "The ploughboy." BBC 22736. Kennedy 140. Also on Folk Trax FSB 015.

Cook: also on *Rolling in the dew*.

- *The Coppers: Bob Copper*

Copper, Bob [Rottingdean] (1951) "Brisk young ploughboy." BBC 16064. EFDSS 239.

Copper, Bob (1951) "Sweet primroses." BBC 17987. EFDSS 309. [Also BBC 17990. EFDSS 312.]

Copper, Bob (1951) "The month of May." BBC 16067. Kennedy 255. EFDSS 242.

Copper, Bob (1951) "Two brethren." BBC 16061, EFDSS 236.

Copper, Bob (1951) "Thousands or more." BBC 17989. EFDSS 311.

Copper, Bob (1952) "The false bride." BBC 17990. Also Caedmon TC 1142 /Topic 12T157 *Folk songs of Britain*, vol. I. Kennedy 152. EFDSS 312. [The same as "Week before Easter".]

Copper, Bob (1952) "The sweet primeroses." Caedmon TC 1142/Topic 12T157 *Folk songs of Britain*, vol. I.

Copper, Bob (1952) "No John no." Caedmon TC 1142/Topic 12T157 *Folk songs of Britain*, vol. I.

Copper, Bob (1955) "Brisk and lively lad." BBC 21545. EFDSS 824.

Copper, Bob (1955) "Swet Lemeney." BBC 21545. EFDSS 824.

Copper, Bob (1955) "Haying cock." BBC 21545. EFDSS 824.

Copper, Bob (1955) "Spotted cow." BBC 21546. EFDSS 825.

Copper, Bob (1955) "Sheep shearing song." BBC 21546. EFDSS 825.

Copper, Bob (1955) "Bold dragoon." BBC 21547. EFDSS 826.

Copper, Bob (1955) "Hares in the plantation." BBC 21547. EFDSS 826.

Copper, Bob (1955) "White cockade." BBC 21547. EFDSS 826.

Copper, Bob (1955) "The spotted cow." BBC 21546. Kennedy 142. EFDSS 825.

Copper, Bob (1955) "The sheepshearing song"; also known as "The black ram". BBC 21546. Kennedy 267. EFDSS 825. Also on Folk Trax FSB 025.

Copper, Bob (1955) "I keep my dogs." BBC 21547. Kennedy 249. EFDSS 826.

Copper, Bob (1955) "Jovial tradesmen." Caedmon TC 1144/Topic 12T159, *Folk songs of Britain*, vol. III.

Copper, Bob (1956) "The e-choin' horn." Recorded by Peter Kennedy. Kennedy 246. Also on Folk Trax FSB 023. [See Part Two, Text 20c.]

Copper, Bob (1957) "Babes in the wood." BBC 25616. EFDSS 999.

Copper, Bob (1977) *Sweet rose in June*. Topic 12TS 328. [Contents of this compilation are stated to be "countryside songs from the South .... from outside the Copper family's repertoire".]

Copper, Bob (1996) "Rags and old iron." On *Froots* #6, free CD issued with *Folk Roots* (January/February 1996).

Copper, Bob: also on *When the may is all in bloom*.

Copper, Bob, and John Copper jr. [Rottingdean] (1965) "The wedding song." On *Folksound of Britain*, HMV CLP 1910.

Copper, Bob, and John Copper, jr. (1974) "Brisk young ploughboy." On *The brave ploughboy*.

Copper, Bob, John Copper jr., Jill Copper, and Jon Dudley (1987) *Will's Barn*. EFDSS LP VWML 002. [Contains seven live songs.]

Copper, Bob, John Copper jr., and Lynne Copper [Rottingdean] (1974) "Two young brethren." On *The brave ploughboy*.

Copper, Bob, and Ron Copper [Rottingdean] (1953) "Twankydillo"; also known as "The blacksmith's song". *A jug of punch*. HMV CLP 1327, XLP 50003. [For the tune see *Sussex County Magazine* 4 (1930), 150–1; words as printed there not in dialect.]

Copper, Bob, and Ron Copper (1953) "When the old dun cow caught fire." *A jug of punch.* HMV CLP 1327, XLP 50003.

Copper, Bob, and Ron Copper (1953) "A pinch of salt." HMV CLP 1362, XLP 50004.

Copper, Bob, and Ron Copper (1953) "Claudy Banks." HMV CLP 1362, XLP 50004.

Copper, Bob, and Ron Copper (1953) "Twelve days of Christmas." *Folksong today: songs and ballads of England and Scotland collected by Peter Kennedy.* HMV DLP 1143. Also on Caedmon TC 1224/Topic 12T197, *Folksongs of Britain*, vol. IX.

Copper, Bob, and Ron Copper (1953) "Thousands or more." Recorded by Peter Kennedy. Kennedy 284. Also on Folk Trax FSB 025.

Copper, Bob, and Ron Copper (1953) "Old daddy fox." Recorded by Peter Kennedy. Kennedy 301.

Copper, Bob, and Ron Copper (1955) "A lawyer bold." Recorded by Peter Kennedy. BBC 21544. EFDSS 823.

Copper, Bob, and Ron Copper (1955) "Shepherd's song." Recorded by Peter Kennedy. BBC 21544. EFDSS 823.

Copper, Bob, and Ron Copper (1955) "The machiner's song." (Also known as "The threshing machine.") EFDSS 1002. Kennedy 231. Also on Folk Trax FSB 021.

Copper, Bob, and Ron Copper (1955) "The innocent hare." EFDSS LP 1002. Kennedy 251. Also on Folk Trax FSB 023.

Copper, Bob, and Ron Copper (1955) "Two brethren." EFDSS LP 1002.

Copper, Bob, and Ron Copper (1955) "By the green grove." EFDSS LP 1002.

Copper, Bob, and Ron Copper (1955) "Shepherd of the downs." EFDSS LP 1002.

Copper, Bob, and Ron Copper (1955) “The ploughshare.” EFDSS LP 1002.

Copper, Bob, and Ron Copper (1955) “Sportsmen arouse.” EFDSS LP 1002.

Copper, Bob, and Ron Copper (1955) “Hard times of old England.” EFDSS LP 1002.

Copper, Bob, and Ron Copper (1955) “Spring glee.” EFDSS LP 1002.

Copper, Bob, and Ron Copper (1955) “The (honest) labourer.” EFDSS LP 1002. Kennedy 253.

Copper, Bob, and Ron Copper (1955) “ (O) Good ale.” EFDSS LP 1002. Kennedy 273. Also on Folk Trax FSB 025.

Copper, Bob, and Ron Copper (1955) “Spencer the rover.” EFDSS LP 1002 (1963). Kennedy 331. Also on Folk Trax FSB 029.

Copper, Bob, and Ron Copper (1955) “Sweep, chim-nie sweep.” Caedmon TC 1144/Topic 12T159, *Folk songs of Britain*, vol. III. Kennedy 240.

Copper, Bob, and Ron Copper (1955) “The merry haymakers.” Caedmon TC 1144/Topic 12T159, *Folk songs of Britain*, vol. III. Kennedy 255. Also on Folk Trax FSB 023.

Copper, Bob, and Ron Copper (1955) “When Jones’s ale was new.” Caedmon TC 1144/Topic 12T159 *Folk songs of Britain*, vol. III. Kennedy 287. [Possibly only on the Caedmon issue.] Also on Folk Trax FSB 025.

Copper, Bob, and Ron Copper (1955) “Dame Durden.” Caedmon TC 1142/Topic 12T157, *Folk songs of Britain*, vol. I. Also EFDSS LP 1002 (1963). Kennedy 293.

Copper, Bob, and Ron Copper (1955) “My father had an acre of land.” Caedmon TC 1145/Topic 12T160 *Folk songs of Britain*, vol. IV. Kennedy 300. Also on Folk Trax FSB 027.

Copper, Bob, and Ron Copper (1955) “The hungry fox” and “Claudy Banks”. EFDSS JL1 (RLP 718–9). [78 rpm recording.]

Copper, Bob, and Ron Copper (1963) *Traditional songs from Rottingdean.* EFDSS LP 1002; limited release, EFDSS members only. Reissued in 1964 on cassette by Folk Legacy as *English shepherd and farming songs sung by Bob and Ron Copper*, FSB 019. [All recordings by Peter Kennedy. A date of 1962, implicitly for the original issue, is given by Miller (1976), but this cannot be right. *The Guinness encyclopedia of popular music* says '1960s'. The sleeve-notes are identical with Bob Copper (1955) Traditional songs from Rottingdean, Sussex. *Folkus* 1.1.]

Copper, Bob, and Ron Copper (1975) *The two brethren. Country songs the season round.* Folk Trax FSA 081. [All recordings by Peter Kennedy (1962). Also catalogued as *The banks of Claudy*.]

Contains:

"Claudy Banks", "Old dun cow", "Lark in the morning", "Hungry fox", "Babes in the wood", "Cupid's garden", "Irish captain", "Spring glee", "The seasons", "Shepherd of the downs", "Week before Easter", "By the green grove", "Two brethren", "The labourer", "Dame Durden", "Acre of land", "No John no", "Sweet primroses".

Copper, Bob, and Ron Copper (date uncertain) "Warlike seamen." On Caedmon TC 1162/Topic 12T194, *Folk songs of Britain*, vol. VI.

Copper, Bob, Ron Copper and Jim Copper [Rottingdean] (1975) *Twankydillo. Two generations of country singers*. Folk Trax FSA 082. [All recordings by Peter Kennedy (1962).]

Contains:

"Twankydillo", "Threshing machine", "Jones' ale", "Sportsmen arouse", "Sweep chimney sweep", "Hard times of old England", "Month of May", "Spencer the rover", "Thousands or more", "Shepherds arise", "The Irish girl", "Bold General Wolfe", "You seamen bold", "Bold fisherman", "The spotted cow", "Old farmer of Hampshire", "Sweet Lemonay", "Christmas presents".

Copper, Bob, Ron Copper, John Copper and Jill Copper [Rottingdean] (1971) *A song for every season.* Recorded by Bill Leader. Leader LEAB 4046–9. [4 LP records with 16-page booklet. A selection from the four was released as a single LP, Leader LED 2067.]

Contains:

1: "Dame Durden", "By the green grove", "Spencer the rover", "Charming Molly", "Sweep chimney sweep", "Rose of Allendale",

"Pleasant month of May", "When spring comes on", "Spotted cow", "Wop she ad it-io", "A week before Easter", "Brisk and lively lad".

2: "Sheep shearing song", "Adieu sweet lovely Nancy", "Claudy Banks", "Sweet Lemeney", "Corduroy", "Come all bold Britons", "No John no", "The shepherd's song", "Thousands or more", "Shepherd of the downs", "As I walked out".

3: "Seaman bold", "When Adam was first created", "A lawyer bold", "Gentlemen of high renown", "My love is gone", "Battle of Alma", "Warlike seamen", "Brisk and lively lad", "Sportsmen arouse", "Admiral Benbow", "Wind across the moor", "O good ale".

4: "Shepherds arise", "Softly the night", "Christmas songs", "Babes in the wood", "The dying soldier", "Brisk young ploughboy", "Heigh ho sing ivy", "Jolly good song", "Two young brethren", "The ploughshare", "Come write me down".

- *Copper, Jim (1882–1954)*

Copper, Jim [Rottingdean] (1951) "No sir." (Also known as "O no John".) BBC 16063. Kennedy 138. EFDSS 238.

Copper, Jim (1951) "Charming Molly." BBC 16063. EFDSS 238.

Copper, Jim (1951) "Farmer of Cheshire." BBC 17988. EFDSS 310.

Copper, Jim (1951) "Thousands or more." BBC 17989. Kennedy 284. EFDSS 311.

Copper, Jim (1951) "Bold forester." BBC 17989. EFDSS 311.

Copper, Jim (1951) "The labourer." BBC 16064. Kennedy 253. EFDSS 239.

Copper, Jim (1951) "The seasons." BBC 16065. EFDSS 240.

Copper, Jim (1951) "The threshing song." BBC 16067. Also Columbia KL 206, AKL 4943, *The world library of primitive music: England.* Kennedy 231. EFDSS 242. (Song by Frank Bond (1906/7), originally "The chiners song". Also known as "The threshing machine.")

Copper, Jim (1951) “When Jones’s ale was new.” (Also known as “Joan’s ale”.) BBC 16067. Kennedy 287. EFDSS 242.

Copper, Jim (1951) “The spotted cow.” Recorded by Peter Kennedy. Kennedy 142.

Copper, Jim (1951) “The lark in the morning.” Recorded by Peter Kennedy. Kennedy 140.

Copper, Jim (1951) “The week before Easter.” Recorded by Peter Kennedy. Kennedy 152. [The same as “The false bride”.]

Copper, Jim (1951) “Dame Durden.” Recorded by Peter Kennedy. Kennedy 293.

Copper, Jim (1951) “What’s the life of a man?” Recorded by Peter Kennedy. Kennedy 264.

Copper, Jim (1951) “Benbow.” BBC 17987. EFDSS 309.

Copper, Jim (1951) “Old daddy fox. “ Recorded by Peter Kennedy. Kennedy 301.

Copper, Jim (1951) “Thousands or more.” Recorded by Peter Kennedy. Also BBC 17989. Kennedy 284. EFDSS 311.

Copper, Jim (1951) “Twankydillo”; also known as “The blacksmith’s song”. Recorded by Peter Kennedy. Kennedy 286. Also on Folk Trax FSB 025.

Copper, Jim, and Bob Copper [Rottingdean] (1951) “Brisk and bonny lad”; also known as “The contented country lad.” BBC 16062. Also on Columbia KL 206, AKL 4943, *The world library of primitive music: England.* Kennedy 244. EFDSS 237.

Copper, Jim, and Bob Copper (1951) “Charming Molly.” BBC 16062.

Copper, Jim, and Bob Copper (1951) “When Spring comes in.” BBC 16062. EFDSS 237.

Copper, Jim, and Bob Copper (1951) “Sweep chimney sweep.” BBC 16063. EFDSS 237. [Version said to be by Ron and Bob on Folk Trax FSB 021.]

Copper, Jim, and Bob Copper (1951) "The wedding song." BBC 16065. EFDSS 240.

Copper, Jim, and Bob Copper (1951) "The ploughshare." BBC 16065.

Copper, Jim, and Bob Copper (1951) "Come write me down." BBC 16065.

Copper, Jim, and Bob Copper (1951) "Spencer the rover." BBC 16066. EFDSS 241.

Copper, Jim, and Bob Copper (1951) "Shepherd of the downs." BBC 16066. EFDSS 241.

Copper, Jim, and Bob Copper (1951) "Babes in the wood." BBC 16067. EFDSS 242.

Copper, Jim, and Bob Copper (1951) "Pleasant month of May." BBC 16067.

Copper, Jim, and Bob Copper (1951) "Brisk young ploughboy." BBC 16063. EFDSS 238. Also on BBC 16064.

Copper, Jim, and Bob Copper (1951) "No John no." BBC 16063.

Copper, Jim, and Bob Copper (1951) "Adieu sweet lovely Nancy." BBC 16060. EFDSS 235. [See Part Two, Text 20b.]

Copper, Jim, and Bob Copper (1951) "Claudy Banks." BBC 16060. EFDSS 235.

Copper, Jim, and Bob Copper (1951) "Two brethren " (two versions?). BBC 16061, EFDSS 236.

Copper, Jim, and Bob Copper (1952) "[My father had an] acre of land." BBC 17989. Kennedy 300. EFDSS 311.

Copper, Jim, and Bob Copper (1952) "Thousands or more." BBC 17989.

Copper, Jim, and Bob Copper (1952) "My love has gone [fragment]." BBC 17989.

Copper, Jim, and Bob Copper (1952) "Sing ivy." BBC 17989.

Copper, Jim, and Bob Copper (1952) "Heigh ho." BBC 17989.

Copper, Jim, and Bob Copper (1952) "Old daddy fox." (Also known as "Hungry fox.") BBC 17990. Kennedy 301. EFDSS 312.

Copper, Jim, and Bob Copper (1952) "A week before Easter." BBC 17990.

Copper, Jim, John Copper, Bob Copper and Ron Copper [Rottingdean] (1952) "Come write me down the powers." Recorded by Seamus Ennis. BBC 17986. Kennedy 126. EFDSS 308.

Copper, Jim, John Copper, Bob Copper and Ron Copper (1952) "The Irish captain (Warlike seamen)." BBC 17986. EFDSS 308. Recorded by Seamus Ennis. Released for the first time on the Copper family's LP *Coppersongs (q.v.)*.

Copper, Jim, John Copper, Bob Copper and Ron Copper (1952) "The wedding song." Recorded by Seamus Ennis. BBC 17986. EFDSS 308.

Copper, Jim, John Copper, Bob Copper and Ron Copper (1952) "General Wolfe." Recorded by Seamus Ennis. BBC 17987. EFDSS 309.

Copper, John, Jim Copper, Bob Copper and Ron Copper (1952) "Banks of the sweet primroses." Recorded by Seamus Ennis. BBC 17987. On *The electric muse*. Island/Transatlantic Folk 1001. [Said by Hugh Miller (1976) to be at that time not deposited at EFDSS library, though the note in Lloyd (1954: 151, G3) suggests otherwise.]

Copper, John jr. [Rottingdean] (1957) "Brisk and bonny lad." BBC 26349. EFDSS 2005.

Copper, John jr. (1957) "Heigh ho." BBC 26349. EFDSS 2005.

Copper, John jr. (1957) "Hungry fox." BBC 26349. EFDSS 2005.

Copper, John jr. (1957) "Sing ivy." BBC 26349. EFDSS 2005.

Copper, John jr.: also on *When the may is all in bloom*.

Copper, Ron [Rottingdean] (1955) "The hard times of old England." EFDSS LP 1004. Kennedy 224.

Copper, Ron, and Bob Copper [Rottingdean] (1955) "Joan's ale." BBC 21543. EFDSS 822.

Copper, Ron, and Bob Copper (1955) "When Adam was first created." BBC 21543. EFDSS 822.

Copper, Ron, and Bob Copper (1955) "Cupid's garden." BBC 21543. EFDSS 822.

Copper, Ron, and Bob Copper (1955) "The lark in the morning." EFDSS LP 1002. Kennedy 140.

Copper, Ron, and Bob Copper (1955) "Shepherds arise." BBC 21544. EFDSS 823. Caedmon TC 1224/ Topic 12T197, *Folksongs of Britain*, vol. IX.

Copper family [Rottingdean] (1987) [Contribution to] *Will's Barn*. EFDSS LP VWML 002. [7 songs sung live. Other well-known non-Sussex singers are featured.]

Image 15: The Coppers

Copper family (1987/8) *Coppersongs.* EFDSS LP VWML004. [Compilation album of 13 songs.]

Contains:

"Claudy Banks", "Cupid's garden", "Seasons or ploughshare", "Two young brethren", "Sweep chimney sweep" (Kennedy 240), "Warlike seamen (The Irish captain)", "Brisk young ploughboy", "Bold fisherman", "The battle of Alma", "Come write me down" (Kennedy 126), "Adieu sweet lovely Nancy", "Sportsmen arise", "Thousands or more" (Kennedy 284).

Copper family (1998) "By the green groves." On *Rich at the roots: Folk Alliance showcase complilation,* vol. 2. [No other details.]

Copper family (no date) *Come all you old Britons. Songs and talk about music and traditions*. Recorded and edited 1963–83 by Peter Kennedy. Folk Trax Cassettes FTX-238.

Contains:

"The hard times of old England", "The shepherd and his bride", "The sheepshearing song" ("The black ram"), "Adieu, sweet lovely Nancy", "Admiral Benbow", "The mummer's song" ("The dying British soldier"), "Lord Thomas and fair Eleanor", "Softly the night" ("Shepherd's carol"), "The turn of the year", "The lawyer bold", "The brisk and lively (Gloucester) lad", "Come all you bold Britons", "Wop-she-ad-it-i-o", "The white cockade", "The suit of cord-e-roy", "The heights of Alma"; interspersed with talk by Bob Copper.

Copper family (no date) *Adam and Eve*. Folk Trax Cassettes FTX-239.

Contains:

"Bold princess royal", "Rose of Allendale", "Charming Molly", "While the gamekeeper lies sleeping", "Bold Reynard", "Bold General Wolfe, "Bold dragoon", "Mary on the wild moor", "Game-cock", "Ship in distress", "Codfish", "What's the life of a man?", "When Adam was first created", "Pull the string", "Lemeney", "My love in June", "No, John", "Spotted cow", "Drowned lover", "Cupid's garden", "Highwayman outwitted", "False bride", "Spring glee".

Copper family (no date) *Shepherds of the Downs*. Folk Trax Video Cassette V12. [Contents not ascertained.]

County singers from Hampshire and Sussex (no date) *Songs and southern breezes*. Topic 12T 317. [Accompanies Bob Copper's book of the same title (1973, G4).]

Dore, Bill: on *When the may is all in bloom*.

Doughty, Johnny [Brighton] (1977) *Round Rye Bay for more. Traditional songs from the Sussex coast*. Topic 12TS 324. [Recorded by Mike Yates in 1976 (some with Camilla Saunders).]

> Contains:
> "Herrings' heads", "The wreck of the *Northfleet*", "When I was single", "The Golden Vanity", "The saucy sailor", "Baltimore", "While going round the Cape/Round Rye Bay for more", "Spanish ladies", "The sailor's alphabet", "The mermaid", "Marry me", "I'm going to be mother today", "Barbara Allen", "My boy Billy", "Dick Turpin/Let her go back", "Rye Harbour girl", "The streets of Port Arthur".

Figg, Gabriel [West Chiltington] (1952) "What's the life of a man?" Recorded by Peter Kennedy. Kennedy 264.

Figg, Gabriel (1953) "Wild rover." Recorded by Peter Kennedy. Kennedy 288.

Figg, Gabriel (1953) "Twankydillo"; also known as "The blacksmith's song". Recorded by Peter Kennedy. Also recorded by Joy Hyman (1964/5) BBC 29821. Kennedy 286.

Figg, Gabriel (1958) "The barley mow." Recorded by P. Kennedy. Also recorded by Joy Hyman (1964/5) BBC 29821. Kennedy 265.

Figg, Gabriel (1958) "My father had an acre of land"; also known as "Holloman's ivy". Recorded by Peter Kennedy. Also recorded by Joy Hyman (1964/5) BBC 29821. Kennedy 300.

Figg, Gabriel (1958) "Epsom races." Recorded by Peter Kennedy. Kennedy 318.

Figg: also on Folk Trax FSB 025.]

Folk Trax compilations believed to contain Sussex material recorded by Peter Kennedy (whose label this was), as indicated:

Folk Trax FSB 015: Gladys Stone
Folk Trax FSB 017: Chris Willett
Folk Trax FSB 025: George Attrill, Gabriel Figg
Folk Trax FSB 029: George Attrill
Folk Trax FSB 031: Tom Willett

Four Sussex singers (1961) Collector JEB7 (7" EP). Recorded by Mervyn Plunkett. Contains: George Spicer "I wish there was no prisons"; 'Pop' Maynard "Polly on the shore"; Jean Hopkins "The sprig of thyme"; Jim Wilson "Barbara Allen".

Fuller, Mark, and Luther Hills [East Dean] (1952) "The innocent hare." BBC 18714. Kennedy 251.

Fuller, Mark, and Luther Hills (1952) "The brisk and bonny lass." BBC 18714. Kennedy 251.

Fuller, Mark, and Luther Hills (1952) "Dame Durden." BBC 18714. Kennedy 293.

Fuller, Mark, and Luther Hills (1952) "Rosin, the beau." Kennedy 281. [Also Folk Trax FSB 023, 027.]

Fuller, Wally [Laughton] (1952) "Bring in the punch ladle." Recorded by Peter Kennedy. Kennedy 268.

Fuller, Wally (1952) "The game of cards." BBC 18719. Kennedy 175.

Fuller, Wally (1952) "Bold poachers." BBC 18719. Kennedy 354.

Gillette, Noah [Hastings]: on *Rolling in the dew.*

Hall, Gordon [Pease Pottage]: on *When the may is all in bloom.*

Haynes, Mary Ann (date unknown) "The female drummer." On *Sussex harvest.* Also Magic Buddha WMS 8083 (1995).

Haynes, Mary Ann (date unknown) "Poor Leonard." On *Sussex harvest.* Also Magic Buddha WMS 8083 (1995).

Haynes, Mary Ann (date unknown) "The old miser." On *Sussex harvest.* Also Magic Buddha WMS 8083 (1995).

Haynes, Mary Ann (date unknown) "Riding down to Portsmouth." On *Sussex harvest.* Also Magic Buddha WMS 8083 (1995).

Haynes, Mary Ann (date unknown) "Long a-growing." On *Sussex harvest.* Also Magic Buddha WMS 8083 (1995).

Haynes, Mary Ann (date unknown) "The ball of yarn." On *Sussex harvest.* Also Magic Buddha WMS 8083 (1995).

Haynes, Mary Ann (date unknown) "At the atchin tan." On *Songs of the open road*, Topic 12T253 (1975). [Gipsy song sung in Anglo-Romani.]

Haynes, Mary Ann (date unknown) "All through mi rakli." On *Songs of the open road*, Topic 12T253 (1975). [Gipsy song sung in Anglo-Romani.]

Holman, Harry [Copthorne] "Life of a man." On *When sheepshearing's done.*

Hopkins, Jean: on *Four Sussex singers.*

Johnson, Leslie [Fittleworth] (1954) "The cook's choice." BBC 22762. Kennedy 129.

Johnson, Leslie (1954) "Rolling in the dew." BBC 22762. Kennedy 189. [Also on Folk Trax FSB 017.]

Johnson: also on *Rolling in the dew.*

Just another Saturday night (1960) Songs recorded by Brian Matthews in 1959–60. Released as a 2-CD set, MTCD309–10 with a 40-page booklet.

Knight, Harry [Laughton] (1952) "The herring song." BBC 17715. Kennedy 296.

Lewis, Bob: on *The brave ploughboy.*

• *Image 16*
George 'Pop' Maynard (1872–1962) [NB another George Maynard from the same area was apparently recorded by Ken Stubbs. No further details known.]

Maynard, George [Copthorne] (1953) "Three jolly brewers." BBC 16067. Kennedy 287.

Maynard, George (1955) "Three scamping rogues." BBC 23093. Kennedy 307.

Maynard, George (1955) "Bold William Taylor." BBC 23093. Kennedy 254.

Maynard, George (1955) "The little gipsy girl." Recorded by Peter Kennedy and M. Plunkett. Kennedy 346.

Maynard, George (1955) "Shooting Goschen's cock-ups." Recorded by Peter Kennedy and M. Plunkett. Kennedy 354. Also, as "Shooting Goshen's cocks up", recorded by Paul Carter and Ken Stubbs (1962).

Maynard, George (1956) "Ground for the floor." BBC 23092. Kennedy 250.

Maynard, George (1956) "Lansdown Fair." BBC 23092. Also Caedmon TC 1225/ Topic 12T198, *Folk songs of Britain*, vol. X. Kennedy 308.

Maynard, George (1956) "Three jolly brewers." BBC 23092. Kennedy 287.

Maynard, George (1956) "The Aylesbury girl." BBC 23092. Kennedy 176.

Maynard, George (1956) "Young Willie." BBC 23092. Kennedy 324.

Maynard, George (1956) "Rolling in the dew." BBC 23093. Kennedy 189.

[There may be some misdating in Kennedy of the Maynard recordings.]

Maynard, [George] 'Pop' (1976) *Ye subjects of England*. Topic 12T286. [Recorded by Peter Kennedy (1956).]

Contains:

"Polly on the shore", "The sweet nightingale" ("The birds in the spring"), "Locks and bolts", "Down by the seaside", "Jack the jolly tar-o", "The seeds of love", "Shooting Goschen's cocks up", "William Taylor", "Rolling in the dew", "A sailor in the North Country", "The banks of Claudy", "Three sons of rogues", "The weaver'sdaughter", "A wager, a wager", "The sun being set".

Maynard: also on Folk Trax FSA 60-076, FSB 015, 023, 027, 031, and *Four Sussex singers*.

Maynard also recorded 25 songs for Brian Matthews in 1959-60. These are released on *Down the Cherry Tree*, a 2-CD set, MTCD401–2.

Newman, George 'Tom': on *When the may is all in bloom*.

Palmer, Freda: on *When the may is all in bloom*.

Phillips, Cyril (date unknown) "Farmer Giles." EFDSS FTA 102.

Phillips: also on *The brave ploughboy*.

Potter, Charlie, and Marjorie Potter. See Tony Wales below.

Powell, Ethel (date unknown) "Green broom." EFDSS FTA 102.

Powell, Ethel (date unknown) "Saucy sailor boy." EFDSS FTA 102.

Richardson, Arthur [Burwash], also known as 'Buttercup Joe'. Said to have recorded four Sussex songs in the 1930s (and possibly earlier); see brief on-line biography by Michael Oakley (*Enthusiasm* 27, at www.mustrad.org/enthuse.htm). See *Sussex County Magazine* 8 (1934), 230, where the first verse of "The flies be on the turmits" is printed, and the allusion to this in the 'Mrs Paddick' column, *West Sussex Gazette*, 25/10/1945.

Rolling in the dew. Folksongs from Sussex (1985) Folk Trax FTX-427. Recorded by Bob Copper (1954), ed. Peter Kennedy (1985).

Features: Ned Adams [Hastings], George Attrill [Fittleworth], George Blackman [Wisborough Green], Richard Blackman [Arundel], George Burton [Southwater], Lily Cook [North Chailey], Noah Gillette [Hastings], Leslie Johnson [Fittleworth], Bill Sebbage [Fittleworth], Fred Smale [Hassocks], Gladys Stone [Fittleworth] and Jim Swain [Angmering].

Saunders, Mrs (date unknown) "Oxford City." On EFDSS FTA 102 .

Sebbage, Bill [Fittleworth] (1954) "Green bushes." BBC 22740. Kennedy 156.

Sebbage: also on *Rolling in the dew.*

Smale, Fred [Hassocks]: on *Rolling in the dew.*

Smith, Wisdom: on *When the may is all in bloom.*

Songs and music of the Sussex Weald (date unknown) Folktapes FTB102. Recorded by Tony Wales. [Contents not ascertained, apart from some concertina tracks by Scan Tester.]

Songs of Sussex (1995) Magic Buddha WMS 8083. [A re-recording of *Sussex harvest*, Topic 12T258, and *Ye subjects of England*, Topic 12T286; copyright status unclear.]

- *George Spicer (1906–????) [Spicer was born in Kent; he lived in Copthorne, Sussex from 1940, aged 34.]*

Spicer, George 'Spike' [Copthorne] (1956) "The long and wishing eye." BBC 23093. Kennedy 197.

Spicer, George 'Spike' (1956) "The Folkestone murder." BBC 23093. Kennedy 320.

Spicer, George 'Spike' (1956) "Blackberry Fold." BBC 23093. Kennedy 314.

Spicer, George 'Spike' (1956) "The cunning cobbler." BBC 23093. Also *Folk songs of Britain*, vol. II, Caedmon TC 1143/ Topic 12T158. Kennedy 134.

Spicer, George 'Spike' (1956) "The barley mow." BBC 23093. Also *Folk songs of Britain*, vol. X, Caedmon TC 1225/ Topic 12T198. Kennedy 265.

Spicer, George 'Spike'(1970) Two songs in the Rod and Danny Stradling Collection.

Spicer, George 'Spike' (date uncertain) "The threshing machine." [Said to be on *Sussex harvest*, Topic 12T258 – but is not.]

Spicer, George 'Spike' (date uncertain) "The lilywhite hand." [Said to be on *Sussex harvest*, Topic 12T258 – but is not.]

Spicer, George 'Spike' (1974) *Blackberry Fold*. Topic 12T235.
Contains: "Cut away Mike", "The oyster girl", "The faithful sailor boy", "Three jolly boys", "The Irish hop-pole puller", "The cunning cobbler", "The Folkestone murder", "The German clockmender", "Henry my son", "Coming home late", "I wish there was no prisons", "Searching for young lambs", "The old militia drum".

Spicer: also on *Four Sussex singers*, Folk Trax FSB 013, 019, 029, *The brave ploughboy*, and *When sheepshearing's done*.

Stone, Gladys [Fittleworth] (1954) "Deep in love." BBC 22740. Kennedy 149.

Stone: also on Folk Trax FSB 015 and *Rolling in the dew*.

Stradling, Rod, and Danny Stradling (1967–71) Material collected in Sussex [indexed individually here] and elsewhere. [When last heard of, the collection was in audiotape and DAT format in Gloucestershire.]

Sussex harvest (1975) Topic 12T258.
Features Ern(est) 'Rabbidy' Baxter, Bob Blake, Mary Ann Haynes and Harry Upton. [Individual songs are listed under these singers' names.]

Swain, [Harold] 'Jim' [Angmering] (1954) "Jim, the carter lad." BBC 22763. Kennedy 228.

Swain, [Harold] 'Jim' (1964) "William Riley." BBC 22763. Kennedy 353.

Swain: also on *Rolling in the dew*.

Tester, 'Scan' (1971) Seven tunes, two songs and interview, in the Rod and Danny Stradling Collection.

• *Image 17.*
George Townshend (pictured at the age of 84). His name is also spelt 'Townsend'.

Townshend, George [Lewes] (1956) "Wild rover." Recorded by Peter Kennedy. Kennedy 288.

Townshend, George (1956) "Glittering dewdrops." Recorded by Peter Kennedy. Kennedy 246.

Townshend, George (date unknown) "When the spring comes in." EFDSS FTA 102 .

Townshend, George (date unknown) "The echoing horn." EFDSS FTA 102 .

• Townshend recorded 25 songs for Brian Matthews in 1960–1, and these are released on *Come, hand to me the glass* (MTCD304, with a 24-page booklet).

Upton, Harry [Balcombe] (date unknown) "The wreck of the *Northfleet*." On *Sussex harvest*. Also Magic Buddha WMS 8083 (1995).

Upton, Harry (date unknown) "Canadee-I-O." On *Sussex harvest*. Also Magic Buddha WMS 8083 (1995).

Upton, Harry (date unknown) "The freckless [sic] young girl." On *Sussex harvest.* Also Magic Buddha WMS 8083 (1995).

Upton, Harry (date unknown) "Poison in a glass of wine." On *Sussex harvest.* Also Magic Buddha WMS 8083 (1995).

• *Tony Wales*

The late Tony Wales had a large collection of non-commercial recordings of traditional Sussex singers, including George Attrill, George Belton, Bob Blake, Gordon Hall, [George] 'Pop' Maynard, Charlie and Marjorie Potter and George Townshend. See *Songs and music of the Sussex Weald*. Wales himself recorded the first LP devoted to Sussex folk songs, *Sussex folk songs and ballads* (Folkways FG 3515, New York, 1957). He also organized the first Horsham folk festival (1961); recordings made at the festival were broadcast on BBC radio, and others were released commercially. Note that Wales was a revival performer, but he stated that the songs on the Folkways album are 'sung not, I admit, in the traditional style' of Sussex.

When the may is all in bloom (1995) Veteran Tapes VT 131 CD. South East Arts.
Features at least the following artists: Bob Copper "The trees they do grow high", "George Collins"; John Copper "Shift up a little bit farther", "The clothes horse"; Gordon Hall [Pease Pottage]. [Mentioned *[Brighton] Evening Argus*, 16/06/1995, 6.]

When sheepshearing's done. Countryside songs from southern England (1975) Topic 12T254 .
Contains: Freda Palmer "The fox and the grey goose", "The wandering girl", "The Warwickshire RHA", "Oxford City", "As I was a'walking", "Up in the North", "The bailiff's daughter of Islington", "William and Mary", "Maria Marten"; George 'Tom' Newman "All for the grog", "Sing ovy and sing ivy"; Bill Whiting "The broken-down gentleman", "I'm going to the woods"; Wisdom Smith "The Galloway man"; Bob Blake "When sheepshearing's done", "The grey hawk"; Harry Holman "The life of a man", "Toast"; George Spicer "The thrashing machine", "The lily white hand"; Bill Dore "Jolly Jarge".

Whiting, Bill: on *When sheepshearing's done.*

Willett family: Tom, Chris and Ben (no date) *The roving journeymen.* Topic 12T 84. [Gipsy singers.]
Contains: "Lord Bateman", "The blacksmith courted me", "The little ball of yarn", "Died for love", "The rambling sailor", "Riding down to Portsmouth", "As I was going to Salisbury", "The roving journeyman", "While the gamekeepers lie sleeping", "The old miser", "The game of cards". [Note also Folk Trax FSB 017 (Chris Willett), 031 (Tom Willett).]

Wilson, Jean: on *Four Sussex singers.*

G3: Published Sussex songs and literature about them

• What appears below may be somewhat misleading, as a Sussex song is not necessarily a song in Sussex dialect, and vice versa. The standard collections of Sussex songs are given, however, and readers interested in pursuing the folkloric as opposed to the dialectal path are referred to the bibliography of Vic Gammon's doctoral dissertation (1985). On the history of collecting in Sussex, see Gammon (1980).

Andrews, Colin, ed. (1979) *Shepherd of the Downs. The life and songs of Michael Blann of Upper Beeding*. Worthing: Museum and Art Gallery. [Published version of the collection of song-lyrics in Blann's notebook (1901), now in Worthing Museum. Blann's unpractised writing is dialectally coloured. "Dame Durden" is Part Two, Text 20a.]

Barrett, W.A. (no date [after 1900]) *English folk songs*. London: Novello. [Sussex songs mainly from the Shoreham area.]

Bellamy, Peter (1970) The Copper family of Sussex. *Sing Out!* 20.1 (February/March), 2–9. [Interviews with Bob and John Copper, plus a transcription of "Sportsmen arouse".]

Blackman, Bob (2001) The Copper family. *Sing Out!* 45.2 (May). [The discography in Blackman's work has been amplified by Tony Rees with the assistance of Garry Gillard, and published online at www.thecopperfamily.com/books-recordings/recordings/discog.html (state of February 2009; accessed 2009–2010).]

Broadwood, [Rev.] John (1843) *Old English songs, as now sung by the peasantry of the Weald of Surrey and Sussex*. London: Balls and Co. [16 songs from Sussex and Surrey.]

Broadwood, [Rev.] John, and Lucy E. Broadwood (1889 or 1890) *Sussex songs* [arranged by H. F. Birch-Reynardson]. (*Popular songs of Sussex.*) London: Stanley, Lucas and Weber / Leonard and Co.

Broadwood, Lucy E. (1902) Songs from Sussex and Surrey. *Journal of the Folk-Song Society* 1.4, 139–225. [Songs from Henry Burstow, Horsham, and others in the Sussex/Surrey border area (cf. Nicholson and others (1908)).]

Broadwood, Lucy E. (1908) *English traditional songs and carols.* London: Boosey. [Contains some from Sussex, including those of Henry Burstow.]

Broadwood, Lucy E. (1911) [Two healths from Cuckfield.] *Journal of the Folk-Song Society* 4.15, 136–9. [The same issue of *Journal of the Folk-Song Society* contains Broadwood's transcription of a Henry Burstow song (136).]

Broadwood, Lucy E. (1918) "Rosemary Lane". *Journal of the Folk-Song Society* 6.21, 2–3. [A Henry Burstow song collected in 1893.)

Broadwood, Lucy E. and J.A. Fuller-Maitland (1893) *English county songs.* London: Cramer.

Butterworth, George S.K. (1912) *Folk songs from Sussex.* London: Augener. [Songs collected by Butterworth and Francis Jekyll. Reprinted Boca Raton (Fla.): Masters Music (1992).]

Butterworth, George S.K. (1913) Songs collected from Sussex. *Journal of the Folk-Song Society* 4.17, 279–324.

Butterworth, George S.K. (1974) *Folk songs from Sussex and other songs.* London: Galliard/English Folk Dance and Song Society. [Further edition or printing London: Stainer and Bell (no date), with an introduction by Peter Pirie.]

Carey, Clive (1912) *Ten English folk songs.* London: Curwen. [Eight are from Surrey/Sussex.]

Cook, C.F., ed. (1914) *The book of Sussex verse.* Hove: Combridge's. [Includes eight Sussex traditional songs.]

Cook, C.F., ed. (1928) *Another book of Sussex verse.* Hove: Combridge's. [Includes a few traditional songs.]

Copper, Bob (1955) Traditional songs from Rottingdean, Sussex. *Folkus* 1.1. [Reprinted as the notes accompanying the English Folk Dance and Song Society LP *English shepherd and farming songs* (EFDSS LP 1002).]

Copper, Bob (1961) Five songs from Hampshire and one from Sussex. *Journal of the English Folk Dance and Song Society* 9.2, 72–80. [The Sussex song is "The herring", by Richard Blackman of Arundel, recorded October 1954, BBC RPL 22736.]

Copper, Bob (1971) *A song for every season: a hundred years of a Sussex farming family.* London: Heinemann. [Principally a biography of Jim Copper, the author's father. Some of the songs printed as an appendix show occasional dialectalisms, especially in the vocabulary. The Copper family as a group of musicians have kept alive numerous Sussex songs and a traditional singing style (but cf. the discussion in Lloyd (1954)), and they are generally regarded as an outstanding example of the 'uncorrupted' English folk music tradition. The main text of this and Bob Copper's other books show dialect features in reported conversations; and they are of the greatest interest about village life in Sussex (Rottingdean) in the first part of the twentieth century. New edition (1996).]

Copper, Bob (1973) *Songs and southern breezes: country folk and country ways*. London: Heinemann. [See note to previous entry. Details Bob Copper's activity as a folk-song collector for the BBC in the early 1950s, with songs and anecdotes from Sussex and Hampshire.]

Copper, Bob (1976) *Early to rise: a Sussex boyhood.* London: Heinemann. [Further printing London etc.: Javelin (1988). See note to last entry but one. Autobiography of Bob Copper.]

Copper, James, and Robert [i.e. Bob] Copper (c.1950, exact date not known) *The BBC songbook.* [Mentioned in Miller (1976) and known to Bellamy (1970). This is a manuscript book, a version of the one of 1936 referred to in the notes to the next item, purged of non-traditional songs; it was requested by Francis Collinson of the BBC in 1950. A radio programme based on Jim Copper's life was broadcast on the Home Service in 1952.]

Copper family (1995) *The Copper family song book – a living tradition.* Peacehaven: Coppersongs. [A compilation was made by James 'Brasser' Copper made in 1922 for Mrs D. Corrie of Rottingdean (see previous item). The published book includes some facsimile material from this manuscript. The bulk of the book is essentially a published version of a second manuscript book written out by Jim Copper, 'Brasser''s son, in 1936. The 1936 book was exhibited at The Grange, Rottingdean, in 1996. The published book is designed to look like it the 1950 'BBC' version (see notes to previous entry).

Some songs reproduce those printed in Copper (1971, 1976). Some are attributed to other local singers.]

Dallas, Karl (1975) The Coppers' lot. *Melody Maker*, 31/05/1975). [Based on the writings of Bob Copper (*q.v.*) and on Lloyd (1954).]

Dawney, Michael, ed. (1977) *The ploughboy's glory*. London: English Folk Dance and Song Society. [Includes many Sussex songs collected by George Butterworth but not previously published: "All round my hat", "The American king", "The bold fisherman", "The banks of green willow", "Green bushes", "Jack went up to London city", "Ploughboy's glory", "Our captain calls", "The rambling sailor", "The servant man", "Thomas Hegan and Sally Blair", "Young Collins". The names of the singers supplying them are given.]

English Dance and Song. See *Journal of the English Folk (Dance and) Song Society.*

Frampton, George (2007) " . . . and they calls I Buttercup Joe": Albert Richardson, the singing sexton of Burwash, 1905–76. *Folk Music Journal* 9.2. [Article refers to a further piece on Richardson in *Musical Traditions* (2001).]

Gammon, Vic (1980) Folk song collecting in Sussex and Surrey, 1814–1943. *History Workshop Journal* 10, 61–89.

Gammon, Vic (1985) Popular music in rural society: Sussex 1815–1914. Dissertation for the degree of DPhil, University of Sussex (Sussex theses S2355; BLL D67899/86). [Includes extensive bibliography and discography. There are copies in the libraries of the Sussex Archaeological Society, Barbican House, Lewes (open shelves) and the University of Sussex (Audio-Visual counter).]

Gammon, Vic (1987) "Hail happy morn": two Sussex church band carols in old harmony. *English Dance and Song* 49.3, 11–13. [Two carols from before the time of the demise of church bands.]

Gardiner, George (1905-9) Manuscripts in the Vaughan Williams Memorial Library, Cecil Sharp House, London. Apart from songs published elsewhere, these include a Sussex variant of "Deep in love" (Kennedy 149) and of "The smoothing iron" (Kennedy 205).

Gilchrist, Annie (1915) "The Folkestone murder." *Journal of the Folk-Song Society* 5.19, 138.

Gilchrist, Annie (1919) A note on the "lavender" and some other cries. *Journal of the Folk-Song Society* 6.22, 73–7. [Includes two lavender cries from Brighton.]

Gill, W.H. (1917) *Songs of the Sussex folk*. London: Curwen.

Godman, Stanley G. (1957b) Horn Fair. *Journal of the English Folk Dance and Song Society* 8, 105–8. [About the song featured at Ebernoe Horn Fair. Includes the version by Jimmie Booker (Warnham, 1950). Cf. Also *Journal of the English Folk Dance and Song Society* 7 (1956), 253, and the song collected by Ralph Vaughan Williams in *Journal of the Folk-Song Society* 2.8 (1906).]

Journal of the Folk-Song Society. In addition to the articles indexed by author, the *Journal* contains Sussex songs scattered in more general collections. No attempt has been made to index these in this bibliography. An index to the songs published in the *Journal* (not organized by county of collection) was published in 1951. [The *Journal* in its first five years (1899–1904) contained far more songs collected in Sussex and the bordering counties than from anywhere else in England. As time progressed, it contained ever less material organized on a county basis; it came to be realized that this was an inappropriate way to catalogue such widely-known material. A glance at the songs collected by Broadwood, Butterworth, Vaughan Williams and others in Sussex will reveal that they are often common to many other counties. The dialect researcher's interest will be in the songs as performed for collection rather than on the songs themselves, and s/he will be disappointed by the sparseness of the dialect features noted by the collectors. Note that this journal merged into the *Journal of the English Folk Dance and Song Society* (1932–64). The *Bulletin* of the same society appeared from 1936 as *English Dance and Song*. The combined journal became *Folk Music Journal* as from 1965.]

Keel, Frederick (1918) Songs from Surrey, Kent and Sussex. *Journal of the Folk-Song Society* 6.21.

Kennedy, Peter (1975) *Folksongs of Britain and Ireland*. London: Cassell. [Contains many songs taken down in Sussex, and provides the standard numerical reference system used in the list of recordings in the previous section.]

Lee, Kate (1899) Experiences of a folk-song collector. *Journal of the Folk-Song Society* 1.1, 7–12. [Songs collected from William (incorrectly for James sr. 'Brasser') Copper and Thomas Copper, Rottingdean, 13-25. Partially reprinted in the booklet accompanying the set of records *A song for every season* (Leader LEAB404).]

Lloyd, A.L. (1954) The singing style of the Copper family. *Journal of the English Folk Dance and Song Society* 7, 145–51. [Discusses whether the Coppers' harmonic (i.e. non-monodic) style may genuinely be regarded as traditional. Partially reprinted in the booklet accompanying the set of records *A song for every season* (Leader LEAB406-9). Contains Francis Collinson's transcriptions of three songs recorded by Seamus Ennis in 1952.]

McCarthy(-Fox), Sam (1982) Pop Maynard – Lord of the Ring. Journal untraced. The content may be related to the same author's articles: Marble players and teams from Tinsley Green, online at mm.bglances.com/1-06-07-01%20Tinsley%20Green%20Players.htm, and Unusual pub games: marbles, online at pubhistorysociety.co.uk/html/marbles.html. [The original title alludes to Maynard's prowess at marbles into old age.]

Merrick, W. Percy (1901) [No title.] *Journal of the Folk-Song Society* 1.3, 64–138. [Songs collected principally from Henry Hills (Lodsworth and Petworth).]

Merrick, W. Percy (1903) Sussex songs. *Journal of the Folk-Song Society* 1.5, 268–76. [More songs from Henry Hills (see previous entry).]

Merrick, W. Percy (?1912) *Folk songs from Sussex*, with pianoforte accompaniments by R. Vaughan Williams and Albert Robins. London: Novello (Folk-Songs of England 5). [15 songs. Last book in the Folk-Songs of England series, ed. Cecil Sharp.]

Miller, Hugh (1976) Interview with Bob Copper. *Traditional Music* 3, 30–7. [Interview took place 1975. The same issue also contains an index to the Coppers' songbooks (manuscript and printed), a review of four of their record(-set)s, and a discography and bibliography of the Copper family (38–43), to which the present work is indebted.]

Myer, Michael Grosvenor (1989) An unpublished Copper family song: extracts from a correspondence. *Folk Music Journal* 5.5, 623.

Nicholson, S., and others (1908) Songs from the southern counties of England [etc.]. *Journal of the Folk-Song Society* 3.10, 53–4. [Songs from Henry Burstow of Horsham (cf. Broadwood (1902)).]

Palmer, Roy, ed. (1987) *Folksongs collected by Ralph Vaughan Williams.* London: Dent. [20 songs from Sussex. Wales (1976: 17) says that Vaughan Williams collected 138 songs in the county.]

Richardson, Arthur. A verse of "The flies be on the turmits", as performed in the 1930s by Arthur Richardson of Burwash, is printed in *Sussex County Magazine* 8 (1934), 230, where it is implied that Richardson was on the point of recording it. [This seems to be alluded to in Mrs Paddick's column, *West Sussex Gazette*, 25/10/1945.]

Sawyer, Frank J., nephew of Frederick Sawyer *(q.v.).* Frank Sawyer is known to have been interested in folk-song, and was due to deliver a paper at Hove on 'Folk-songs from Sussex villages' the day after his death on 29/04/1908. [Nothing by Frank Sawyer is known to have appeared in print under his own name, but he advised Frederick Sawyer in musicological aspects of the latter's work on folk customs.]

Sharp, Cecil J., ed., based on the collection of W. Percy Merrick (1912) *Folk songs of England, vol. V: folk songs from Sussex.* London: Novello. [See Merrick (1901, 1903). This book is sometimes catalogued under Merrick's name.]

Smith, Vic (1976) Interview with Scan Tester. *Traditional Music* 4, 4–10. [Light dialect colour in the musician's reminiscences.]

Stubbs, Ken (1963) The life and songs of George Maynard. *Journal of the English Folk Dance and Song Society* 9.4, 180–96. [Stubbs's audiotaped reminiscences of George 'Pop' Maynard are kept at the Museum of English Rural Life, University of Reading.]

Stubbs, Ken (1970) *The life of a man*. London: English Folk Dance and Song Society Publications. [Contains songs collected in Sussex and the Surrey border area by Roger Nicholls from George Townshend, George ('Pop') Maynard, Jim ('Brick') Harber, George ('Spike') Spicer, George Maynard (*not 'Pop'*), Fanny Pronger, Harry Upton, Ursula Ridley, Elizabeth Smith, Walter ('Pop') Weller, Henry Steele, Bill ('Corn') Botting, Jim Wilson, Harry Holman, Jack Arnoll, Ern(est) ('Rabbidy') Baxter, Louey Saunders and Noah Willett.]

Vaughan Williams, Ralph (1906) Songs collected from Sussex. *Journal of the Folk-Song Society* 2.8, 184–209. [Various singers represented.]

Vaughan Williams, Ralph, and A.L. Lloyd (1959) *The Penguin book of English folk-song. Selections from the* Journal of the Folk-Song Society *and* Journal of the English Folk Dance and Song Society. London: Penguin. [Includes songs collected between 1899 and 1907 from Henry Burstow of Horsham (18, 34, 84: "The basket of eggs", "The devil and the ploughman", "The ploughman"), the Verralls of Horsham (38, 88, 93, 95: "Fare thee well, my dearest dear", "Robin Hood and the pedlar", "A sailor in the north country", "Salisbury Plain"), Ted Baines of Lower Beeding (13: "All things are quite silent"), Mr Harwood of Watersfield (96: "The ship in distress"), Henry Hills of Lodsworth (94, 100: "A sailor's life", "The whale-catchers"), Mrs Ford of Blackham (71: "Mother, mother, make my bed"), Mr Coomber of Blackham (40: "The gentleman soldier").]

Wales, Tony (1976) *We wunt be druv: songs and stories from Sussex.* London: Galliard/English Folk Dance and Song Society. [Includes 12 songs from Sussex, showing light dialect features in some cases.]

Wales, Tony (1985) *Ballads, bands and bellringers: singers, musicians and story-tellers in old Sussex.* Horsham: Field and Furrow. [Includes 3 songs from Sussex.]

G4: Reminiscences of Sussex singers

Arthur, Dave, ed. (1989) *A Sussex life: the memories of Gilbert Sargent* [of Catsfield], *countryman.* London: Barrie and Jenkins. [Cf. Sargent in Section F: Speech.]

Burstow, Henry (1911) *Reminiscences of Horsham, being recollections of H.B. the celebrated bellringer and songsinger.* Horsham: Free Christian Church Book Society. [With the assistance of William Albery. Contains details of his repertoire of local songs and and recitations in dialect, 107–19. New edition by Tony Wales and Tony Green, Norwood, Pa.: Norwood Editions (1975). See also Stanley Godman (1954) Henry Burstow: the Horsham singer and bellringer. *Sussex County Magazine* 28, 519–22.]

Copper, Bob (1973) *Songs and southern breezes: country folk and country ways.* London: Heinemann. [Recounts Bob Copper's activity as a folk-song collector for the BBC in Sussex and Hampshire in the early 1950s. See also Copper's works listed in Section F3.]

Hall, Reg, ed. (1990) *"I never played to many posh dances."* Rochford: Musical Traditions. [Biography of Scan Tester, concertina player, violinist, etc., of Horsted Keynes.]

Oakley, Michael (2001) Arthur Richardson, 1905–76, a brief biography. [Also known as 'Buttercup Joe'.] *Musical Traditions: Enthusiasm 27*, at www.mustrad.org/enthuse.htm.

Smith, Vic (1976) Interview with Scan Tester. *Traditional Music* 4, 4–10. [Interview took place 1971. Light regional colour in the musician's reminiscences.]

Smith, Vic (1987) Johnny Doughty, an interview with Vic Smith. *Musical Traditions* 7, 22–29.

Stubbs, Ken (1963) The life and songs of George Maynard. *Journal of the English Folk Dance and Song Society* 9.4, 180–96. [Stubbs's audiotaped reminiscences of George 'Pop' Maynard are kept at the Museum of English Rural Life, University of Reading.]

Wales, Tony (1965) George Attrill of Sussex [obituary]. *English Dance and Song* 27, 46–47.

H: ONLINE AND OTHER DIGITAL MATERIAL

This is a very small catalogue of digital resources intended to supplement the main bibliography, or to make finding some of the key material easier. No pretension to completeness is, or can be, made.

H1: Material on the Web

Online books or articles:

Parish, W.D. (1875) *A dictionary of the Sussex dialect:*

Facsimile of original edition: www.archive.org/stream/dictionaryofsuss00pariuoft#page/n1/mode/2up

transcribed: www.sussexhistory.co.uk/sussex-dialect/sussex-dialect%20-%200205.htm

Skeat, Walter W. (1911) *English dialects from the eighth century to the present day:* **www.gutenberg.org/ebooks/15755**

Audio – speech:

Native speaker: Aubrey Charman (Southwater): http://sounds.bl.uk/View.aspx?item=021M-C0900X16004X-1000V0.xml

Native speaker: Bert Deacon (Ringmer): http://sounds.bl.uk/View.aspx?item=021M-C0900X07554X-1900V0.xml

Native speaker: Leslie Luff (Milland): www.bl.uk/learning/langlit/sounds/text-only/england/milland/ (with some commentary) and www.fairhall.id.au/resources/sussex/dialect.htm (with some commentary)

Survey of English Dialects material: sounds.bl.uk/Browse.aspx?category=Accents-and-dialects&collection=Survey-of-English-dialects

Audio – songs:

Copper family website www.thecopperfamily.com/index.html

Folk-song indices can be found at:
British Library National Sound Archive (sounds.bl.uk)
Complete Topic Records discography (www.mustrad.org.uk/discos/discog.htm)
Folk Trax online catalogue (www.folktrax.com/aa_catalogue.php)

All sites mentioned above were successfully accessed 25–30 January 2010 or 29 March 2010.

H2: Material on digital media

Native speakers recorded by David Arscott in preparation for his book *Wunt be druv!* (Sussex Book Club Audio Collection 1). Also *The Glory of the Garden* (Sussex Book Club Audio Collection 3), featuring Bert Winborne. See: www.room152.lewesonline.com/index4.php

Topic Records have produced an excellent series of 20 CDs edited by Reg Hall (1998) called *The voice of the people* (TDSC 651–670), which includes the work of a number of the traditional Sussex singers mentioned above scattered throughout.

Veteran Records, *When the wind blows: an anthology of traditional music from coastal England* (VTC5CD).

A small number of other CDs are mentioned incidentally in Section G2.

APPENDICES

Appendix 1

A brief biography of William Durrant Cooper (1812–75) (written in 1996 for a planned volume to celebrate 150 years of the Sussex Archaeological Society)

A founder member of the Sussex Archaeological Society, Cooper was a man of early and fulfilled promise. After being articled to his father, he qualified as a solicitor at the age of twenty, specializing in conveyancing, which necessarily brought him into daily contact with the classes of ancient document that fascinated him. In the longer run, he also engaged in parliamentary agency.

But he was not to spend long as a straightforward legal professional. He first got a fair breeze in his literary sails by contributing before the age of fifteen to a magazine produced by a group of pupils at Lewes Grammar School. On this basis, he developed a second career as a serious writer from a prodigiously young age. Overwhelmingly, but by no means exclusively, his writings concerned Sussex; yet from 1837 he conducted his historical and literary passion from his address in Bloomsbury, supported by an income derived from positions as solicitor to the Reform Club, and, at the height of a somewhat desultory legal career, also to the vestry of St Pancras, Euston Road.

More useful to him in a literary capacity were the near-sinecures arranged for him by the Duke of Norfolk as steward to the court leet of the borough of Lewes (whose meetings regularly brought him back to Sussex) and auditor to Skelton Castle, North Riding of Yorkshire; for these positions let him loose among whole archives of uncatalogued and unpublished documents of great historical interest. This fact played to what was perhaps his strongest suit: as a collector, arranger, annotator and editor of material.

As we shall see, much of his vast output can be attributed to his relentless practice of this related bunch of skills, which led to his being elected a Fellow of the Society of Antiquaries in 1841 and to his serving the Society both by writing and by administration for many years. It is easy to imagine the frustration of the last three years of the life of a man having these talents, his capabilities impaired by paralysis until his death in 1875.

His first published solo literary work was an offshoot from his activity as an assistant to Horsfield, a retina-torturing *Parliamentary history of the county of Sussex* published as appendix III to his mentor's *History and antiquities of*

Sussex. As a liberal reformer in a county rejoicing in some of the rottenest of pre-1832 boroughs, he no doubt produced this with relish. He wrote extensively on the local history of the county (especially the east, Hastings, Rye and Winchelsea, no doubt with personal interest due to his own family's roots in Icklesham). In addition, he edited many historical documents and literary texts for publication.

He was an assiduous family historian (especially of Lewknor, Oxenbridge, Poynings and Bruce (Braose)) and compiler of lists of persons (e.g. the followers of Jack Cade, foreign protestants, Sussex men at Agincourt and beneficiaries of Crown presentations to local livings). Whilst his interests were centred on Sussex, they were by no means confined by narrow local patriotism, as he wrote on matters concerning other southern counties, and especially London, in a range of antiquarian journals and series, such as the *Archaeologia*, the texts of the Camden Society and those of the Shakespeare Society.

My own dealings with Cooper across the decades have to do with his interest in the local speech and the place-names of Sussex. From the 1810s, there had begun to appear a burgeoning number of dialect dictionaries; and by the age of 24, in 1836, he felt himself sufficiently equipped to have *A glossary of provincialisms in use in the county of Sussex* printed privately by the office of the *Brighton Herald*, in whose columns the entries may first have seen the light of day. This was for circulation amongst friends, amongst whom commentators number Mark Antony Lower. Lower wrote a notice about Cooper's booklet in a local newspaper, and Cooper evidently interpreted Lower as believing that Cooper had filched some of Lower's own collection of words and phrases. Some rather stiff correspondence passed between them, preserved in Lower's papers at Barbican House.

The *Glossary* in fact suffered mainly from its philologically unsound speculations about the history of particular words. Cooper laid aside his dialectological work after that until a revised edition of the *Glossary* came out in 1853 from the house of John Russell Smith; this was declared rather tartly by Skeat, the leading philologist of the time, to be 'much improved'. The minor spat over the *Glossary* did not prevent a good deal of collaboration in the longer term between Cooper and Lower; in the 1860s they worked jointly on papers about Seaford and about Sussex castles, among other things, and Lower is known to be indebted to Cooper for some material in his *Sussex worthies* of 1865. Another early work of Cooper's dealing with questions of language was a published lecture on 'The Sussex poets', which, however, concerns writers in the standard form of English rather than dialect.

Dialect and style did not represent the limit of Cooper's linguistic interests. Volume 7 of the *Collections* included his paper 'On the retention of British and Saxon names in Sussex', i.e. place-names, which now rests in richly-deserved oblivion. One has a certain sympathy with an author endeavouring to break ground in an area which has, as yet, no established methodology and therefore no restraint on theorizing. But, perhaps strangely, Cooper appears to have had no idea that old manuscripts might hold clues to the history of names, as they did to that of families or events; and the more strangely because he shared the view of the time that older phases of languages could be elucidated by dialect, and therefore had some notion of historical depth in linguistic evidence. But there is no use in complaining if a man is not ahead of his time.

Other work which might loosely be called ethnographical, as opposed to purely historical, included a further paper privately printed in 1842 expounding 'Reasons for a new edition of the Nursery Rhymes'.

As noted above, perhaps Cooper's greatest gifts were those of collecting, arranging, annotating and editing material. We have already noted his work as a glossarist. These talents, along with his generous temperament, made him ideally suited to he the editor of the *Collections*, which he did without stipend from 1859 until he left the office in 1865 with a handsome gift from the Society. Even whilst serving as Hon. Editor, Cooper was active as an independent researcher, including on average a couple of major papers of his own in the *Collections* (not to mention those elsewhere) each year – roughly the same rate as he achieved before and after his stewardship of that post.

He was a man of generous intelligence, who put his knowledge and time freely at the disposal of others. To this, we can call as witnesses his amplifications for publication of the work which was not his own in volumes 9 and 17 of the *Collections*; his editorial footnotes in the *Collections*, a fair collection unto themselves, as the index to the first twenty-five volumes testifies; and his legendary willingness to help anyone prepared to take a serious and scholarly attitude to history with their labours. But he did not suffer airheads or braggarts gladly. This characteristic was all of a piece with his willingness to make enemies of the parish clergy at the time when the deplorable state of the parish registers was a hot topic, just prior to the introduction of general registration in 1837, and with his unwillingness to tone down his open espousal of liberalism in the interests of his legal practice.

Cooper was wedded to his muse and never to a wife. Campkin's notice of his life tells us that his affection towards his sister (whose name I have not discovered) and his mother Lucy was of a 'most devoted and self-sacrificing' character. We should remember with gratitude those who sustained him whilst he pursued the not inconsiderable amount of his historical work which remains of use even today, e.g. his history of Winchelsea and his catalogues and genealogies.

Articles originally intended for the same volume on other relevant people were later written up in the new Oxford dictionary of national biography *by John H. Farrant (see Section F above).*

Appendix 2

Trollop: *a Sussex record, an antedating and an etymology*

The earliest records of *trollop* 'slattern; prostitute' given in *OED* are of the early seventeenth century. In his will, dated 22 December 1542, Thomas Denet of Burwash, East Sussex, bequeathed to his son a mare called *trouleppe*. Lower (1850: 114-5) prints *Donet*; this is corrected by Rice (1935). Lower adds (ingenuously?) in a footnote that whatever *trouleppe* might be, it gives rise to the common Sussex horse-name *Tulip*. I submit that this is an earlier record of the word, though applied as a name; and that its very use as a name for a female animal suggests its still earlier use as a disparaging term for a woman. Both *OED* and Schulz (1975: 69) appear to imply that the sense 'unkempt woman' is the earliest, but I find no obvious warrant for this in following up the first two mentions, of 1615 and 1621; these, significantly, apply to hounds – though as a lexical word here, not a name (1615) – and to a maypole-dancing partner who was a parson's wife (1621).

Both printed and online editions of *OED* suggest a connection between *trollop* and the (in most of its senses intransitive) verb *troll*, I:1, variously 'sing . . . in a casual fashion', 'fish, with rod & line and dead bait or with spoon bait . . . drawn along behind boat', 'cause (bottle) to circulate at table &c.'. There is a further transitive sense (I:2), 'roll about', which could have body-part terms as direct object; of which more later. No specific explanation is given by *OED* for the morphology of *trollop*, and no hint about which sense is the one supposed to underlie it. A sense 'go hunting aimlessly' is also on record for *troll* from the fifteenth century, and appears to have been imported from France to yield a verb homonymous with the one just mentioned. Mills (1989: 241) believes this French loan to be the source of *trollop* but there is nothing to support this.

The editor of the seventh *Concise OED* (1982) prefers a morphologically and phonologically obscure connection with the apparently sixteenth-century German borrowing *trull* 'prostitute' without explicitly noting the historical obscurity of that word, which is covered merely by 'perh.'. Such a connection is also favoured by *Webster's* (third edn). The *ODEE* (1966) offers an array of supposedly possible relatives, including *trull*; the *Concise ODEE* (1986) concedes that *trollop* is of unknown origin, but invites the reader to compare *trull* without specifying the tools for performing the comparison. German *Trulle* means 'slattern' or 'fat woman'; its older form is *Trolle*, and Kluge (1963: *s.v.*) suggests a connection with the Scandinavian *troll* 'monster'. Lexer notes a

Middle High German *trülle* 'kebsweib, hure' ['concubine, whore'], whose umlauted vowel is problematic if we suppose it to be connected with *trollop*; this form is still harder to square with the English word.

Notwithstanding any continental connections, the spelling of 1542 suggests a native etymology for (or perhaps novel reinterpretation of) this obscure word: *troll-hip*, with Kentish <e> for OE <y> in *hip*; Burwash is just five miles from the Kentish border. It may feature *troll* in the transitive sense of 'roll (about)' (*OED*, sense I:2, used of the head in the earliest mention, c.1425; and see also with local relevance *trull*, 'roll along' in a transitive sense, in Parish (1875: *s.v.*).

Hip may be taken either as literal or as metonymic and/or euphemistic for 'lower part of the trunk' or 'buttocks' (cf. *hype* glossing *clunis* 'buttock' in Ælfric's 10th-century glossary; Zupitza 1880: 299). A trollop was a 'roller-about of the hips', on which I do not need to put a more specific gloss, though more than one might be imagined. A very close parallel is afforded by *wag-tail* in the sense of 'slattern' (1592). As for the phonological form of the word: Middle English unstressed /i/ is almost never represented by later <o> (though this is attested occasionally in *gossip* from the 15th–17th centuries). The modern phonology of *trollop* may rather be due to the association of the word, once its structure had become obscure through the loss of /h/ in the post-tonic syllable, with the rhyming phonological pattern offered by *collop, dollop, jollop, lollop, scallop* and *wallop*; most of these are 'expressive' in some sense, and only the learned borrowing *polyp* violates this formula.

The alternative would be to allow that an original *-op* could be represented by *-ep* or the like. This is never found in such frequently recorded words as *bishop, hyssop* and *wallop* (and the later *gallop*), and just once each in *scallop* (16th) and *collop* (15th). Such a proposal also, crucially, still leaves the morphology of *trollop* unexplained.

The present proposal gains in credibility because the compound-noun structure [bare-stem verb + noun-as-nounphrase-object] is known from the late Middle Ages, regularly denotes a person, and is frequently applied to a person in recognition of negative characteristics. Note the nouns recorded in 1601 or earlier *pick-pocket, kill-courtesy, lack-land, toss-pot, spend-thrift, tell-tale,* all known to Shakespeare in either this precise form or a perfect analogue. It is of interest that two of these randomly selected six are first recorded in the sixteenth century as quasi-proper names (*toss-pot, lack-land*), to which one can immediately add Shakespeare's character-names *Tearsheet* and *Pick-bone*, the anonymous *Marprelate* and Richard Greene's *Shake-scene*; the structure seems to have been thought particularly suitable for use in uncomplimentary by-names. Marchand (1969: 380–2) notes that '[p]ersonal [agent] substantives [of the type *pickpocket*] have at all times had a pejorative tinge' and that proper names with this structure appear earlier than corresponding common nouns of the *trail-*

bastoun type in Old French. Many such by-names survive as surnames, most under suspicion of identifying a characteristic that marks the bearer out as odd or different, e.g. *Waghorn, Catchpenny, Scattergood, Dou(b)tfire, Drinkwater*.

Several early records suggest that *trollop* could have a morphological alternant in *-s* in the singular (e.g. that in Richard Brathwait's *Natures Embassie* (1621), alluded to above). This might be accounted for by a duality of hips, but such a formation would be unparalleled till *sawbones* in the nineteenth century. Rather, the *-s* cannot be explained separately from the formation seen in the semantically similar nouns *mops, trape(s)* and perhaps *minx*. This seems to have been especially characteristic of expressions deriving from or from expressions used as names, e.g. *jackanapes, mollyblobs*. It was presumably used in pet address-forms ending in a consonant, much as even today we find in various circles *Babs* for *Barbara*, *Debs* for *Deborah*, *Bets-y* for *Elizabeth*, *Pats-y* for *Patrick* or *Patricia* and *Wills* for *William*, and, with other types of base, *Fats, Bugs-y*.

Perhaps it should be said that the surname *Trollope* derives from a lost Northumberland place-name (Mawer 1920: 200–1), and has nothing to do with the word under discussion.

References

Concise ODEE = T.F. Hoad, ed. (1966) *Concise Oxford dictionary of English etymology*. Oxford: Clarendon Press.

Concise OED = J.B. Sykes, ed. (1982) *Concise Oxford dictionary of current English*, 7th ed. Oxford: Clarendon Press.

Kluge, Friedrich, ed. (1963) *Etymologisches deutsches Wörterbuch der deutschen Sprache*, 19th edn by Walther Mitzka. Berlin: Walther de Gruyter.

Lexer, Matthias, ed. (1969) *Mittelhochdeutsches Taschenwörterbuch*, 33rd "edn". Stuttgart: Hirzel.

Lower, M[ark] A[ntony] (1850) Notes on wills proved at the consistory courts of Lewes and Chichester, *Sussex Archaeological Collections* 3, 108–16.

Marchand, Hans (1969) *The categories and types of Present-Day English word-formation*, 2nd edn. Munich: Beck.

Mawer, Allen H. (1920) *The place-names of Northumberland and Durham*. Cambridge: Cambridge University Press.

Mills, Jane (1992) *Womanwords: a dictionary of words about women,* 2nd edn. New York: The Free Press.

ODEE = C.T. Onions, with G.W.S. Friedrichsen and Robert Burchfield, eds (1966) *Oxford dictionary of English etymology*. Oxford: Clarendon Press.

OED = J. Sinclair and E.S.B. Weiner, eds (1991) *Oxford English dictionary*, 2nd edn. Oxford: Oxford University Press. [Revised second edn available online at dictionary.oed.com, accessed 23/01/2010.]

Parish, William Douglas (1875) *A dictionary of the Sussex dialect*. Lewes: Farncombe.

Rice, R[obert] Garraway, ed. by Walter H. Godfrey (1935) *Transcripts of Sussex wills as far as they relate to ecclesiological and parochial subjects, up to the year 1560*, vol. I. Lewes: Sussex Record Society (vol. 41).

Schulz, Muriel (1975) The semantic derogation of women. In Barrie Thorne and Nancy Henley, eds, *Language and sex: difference and dominance*. Rowley, Mass.: Newbury House, 64–75.

Webster's = Philip B. Gove and others, eds (1966 etc.) *Webster's third new international dictionary of the English language*. Chicago: Encyclopaedia Britannica.

Zupitza, Julius, ed. (1880) *Aelfrics grammatik und glossar: text und varianten*. Berlin: Weidmann.